DRAWINGS BY:

Lynn Lucas Jones

Theresia Travers Boland

Cindy Pendleton

PHOTOGRAPHS BY:

James T. Long

Ralph C. Smith III

Peter J. Christensen

ALSO BY JO IPPOLITO CHRISTENSEN

The Needlepoint Scraps Book

Needlepoint: The Third Dimension

Teach Yourself Needlepoint

Trapunto

WITH SONIE ASHNER:

Appliqué and Reverse Appliqué

Cross Stitchery

Bargello Stitchery

Needlepoint Simplified

The Needlepoint Book

REVISED EDITION

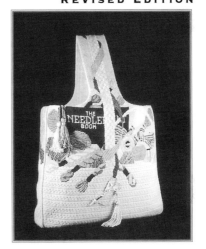

JO IPPOLITO
CHRISTENSEN

A Fireside Book published by Simon & Schuster

FIRESIDE
Rockefeller Center
1230 Avenue of the Americas
New York, NY 10020

For information to reproduce this book
or portions thereof, address Simon & Schuster Inc.,
Permissions Department,
1230 Avenue of the Americas,
New York, NY 10020.

This Revised Fireside Edition 1999

FIRESIDE and colophon are registered trademarks of Simon & Schuster Inc.

Design concept by Theresia Travers Boland

Manufactured in the United States of America

20   19   18   17   16   15

Library of Congress Cataloging-in-Publication Data

Christensen, Jo Ippolito.
    The needlepoint book/by Jo Ippolito Christensen.—Rev. ed.
        p.   cm.
    "A Fireside book."
    Includes bibliographical references and index.
    1. Canvas embroidery.   I. Title.
TT778.C3C478   1999
746.44'2—dc21   99-33812
                                                           CIP

ISBN-13: 978-0-684-83230-2
ISBN-10:   0-684-83230-5

On the front cover (clockwise, from top left):

Art Nouveau Frame—stitched by Barbara Budlow; designed by Aunna Elmore; yarns and stitches selected by Barbara Budlow. [Smith]

Blue Bachelor Buttons—designed and stitched by Lani Silver. [Smith]

Child's Director's Chair—stitched by Dorothy D. Benson; designed by Bonnie Drain; yarns and stitches selected by Dee Benson. [P. Christensen]

Illusions, Bargello Pillow—designed and stitched by Lois Caron. [Smith]

Hydrangea Flowers—designed and stitched by Sally Ann Licocci. [P. Christensen]

Joy, Beaded Purse—designed and stitched by Margery Williams. [Smith]

On the title page: *Photo 1—Needlepointer's Tote Bag:* stitched by Pat Fifield-Saenz, Bernice Abernathy, Sara Galligan, Patricia Glynn, Virginia O'Brien, Pat Wagner, Patricia Miles Barken, Kristin Thomas, Elaine Maffie, Vicky DeAngelis, Mary Brandon, Elsie May Cary, Beth Kuzman, Joanne Lanning, Babs Miley, Marjorie Shelton, Nancy Wiener, Marian Barry, Barbara Bovee, Israela Harkham, Nancy Hewitt, Barbara Roemer, Sally Sulek, Pam Vose, Dee Benson, Mary Lou Gilbert, Beverly Little, Carole Mayo, Sue Schaar and Virginia Vasiliou; designed by Jane Nichols; yarns and stitches selected by Bernice Abernathy, Pat Fifield-Saenz, and Pat Wagner. [Smith]

THIS BOOK IS DEDICATED TO:

Lynne Lumsden,

first editor of *The Needlepoint Book,*

for her vision.

THE HUSBAND'S COMPLAINT

I've heard of wives too musical—too talkative—too quiet

Of scolding and of gaming wives and those too fond of riot;

But yet of all the errors I know, which to the women fall;

For ever doing fancy work, I think exceeds them all.

The other day when I went home no dinner was for me,

I asked my wife the reason; she answered, "One, two, three."

I told her I was hungry and stamped upon the floor.

She never even looked at me, but murmured "One green more."

If any lady comes to tea, her bag is first surveyed,

And if the pattern pleases her, a copy there is made.

She stares too at the gentlemen, and when I ask her why,

'Tis, "Oh my love, the pattern of his waistcoat struck my eye."

Ah? The misery of a working wife, with fancy work run wild;

And hands that never do aught else for husband or for child;

Our clothes are rent, our bills unpaid; my house is in disorder;

And all because my lady wife has taken to embroider.

—M. T. Morrall, *A History of Needlemaking*, 1852

*i-1 Canvassing Cuties!
Life-size soft sculpture
[designed and stitched
by Elaine Warner].*

CONTENTS

*A*n appreciation of handmade needlework was instilled in me during my childhood. My mother spent what seemed to me an endless number of hours creating beautiful things. Not everything she created became a family heirloom. Some pieces were used, abused, and later discarded. But those that remain are cherished because they are beautiful examples of her creativity and profound skill. The pleasure for her was in the creating. The pleasure for me is in the beauty and the memories.

The beauty of needlepoint has been a frequent topic of conversation between Jo Christensen and me during a friendship that spans thirty-five years. We met when she was a student and I was a faculty member in the Textiles and Clothing Department at the University of Maryland, College Park. Our shared philosophy of learning and our many common interests, including the needle arts, brought us together. Lasting friendships of this type are cherished rewards from my many years as a university professor.

Many years ago I accepted Jo's invitation to write the foreword for the original version of *The Needlepoint Book.* At that time, I viewed it as a valuable comprehensive reference book designed to inspire creativity and hone the skills of people interested in creating beautiful needlepoint projects. Twenty-two years later, when this popular reference book was in the process of being revised, Jo again invited me to write the foreword. As I reviewed the artwork for the revised manuscript in preparation for my task, I was excited and overwhelmed by the degree to which needlepoint has moved from "stitchery" to "art." The number of varieties of canvas and yarn types has exploded. Hard-and-fast stitchery rules have softened, unusual textures are being combined, and designs are often contemporary. But even if the dominant rule of today seems to be "please the eye," the importance of "execute with skill" remains.

Although Jo has added new design dimensions to this revised edition of *The Needlepoint Book,* she also has preserved the basic instructions and tips that were so successful in the first edition. As in the past, the book has an abundance of simple illustrations, step-by-step instructions, and charts. Throughout, you will find suggested procedures to follow to ensure the professional appearance of your completed project. In addition, you'll find valuable, up-to-date information about new products and techniques. And, in true Jo Christensen style, you'll be prepared and challenged to step beyond the traditional; to make choices of your own in design, materials, and workmanship; and to create truly unique and functional pieces of artwork.

The Needlepoint Book is a resource to guide, inspire, and encourage you to create at the level you choose, from the simplest to the most elaborate of patterns and projects. Having tasted my own joy of creating in the textiles and clothing field, and knowing how much I treasure my mother's beautiful needlework, I feel certain your needlepoint adventures will be rewarding.

Eleanor F. Young, Ph.D.
Associate Professor *Emerita*
Textiles and Clothing Specialist
University of Maryland, College Park

or centuries needlepoint, also called canvas embroidery, was worked in one stitch—the Tent Stitch—in wool on canvas. The women of many countries did this traditional version of needlepoint in addition to the distinctive ethnic embroideries of their societies. As the earth has grown smaller in the last quarter of the twentieth century, the lines between these ethnic embroideries have blurred. The yarns, threads, and embellishments of these beautiful art forms are being mixed with different needlework techniques to some degree or another and are being done on needlepoint canvas! Some of them are amazingly simple, yet elegant; others are so complex that advanced skills must be developed in order to execute them. Unfortunately, it is far beyond the scope of this book to give detailed instructions on all of these forms of needlework. I have tried, at least, to introduce you to the predominant methods of this new needlepoint.

This book is directed to *you*, the student of needlepoint—both in the classroom and out. Nearly fourteen hundred illustrations are included to help you over the rough spots. Procedures that are considered difficult—or at best hazy—are clarified in this book. Techniques such as blocking, framing, and appliqué are explained in many steps. **Nothing** is left to your imagination.

Chapter 1 gives you a variety of information on equipment, fibers, yarns, and canvas. The equipment needed for needlepoint is neither complicated nor horribly costly. However, the choice of a wrong marker, for example, can ruin your work, so having the **right** equipment is all-important. A thorough discussion of all the things you will need is given in Chapter 1. Your options in selection of equipment are listed; even though I have told you what I think, the choice is still yours.

The different **kinds** of needlepoint are discussed. Again, you decide what appeals to you. Choices crop up again in the selection of canvases and yarns. A section on canvas, fibers, and yarns will help you decide.

Chapters 2 and 3 tell you how to get started and help you progress toward more difficult undertakings.

Over 370 stitches are explained with both photographs and drawings. A guide to the drawings leads off the section. If a stitch is worked in steps, the steps are clearly indicated on the drawings. Numbers tell you just where to begin and where to go next. Often there are two, three, or four different drawings of one stitch to make it crystal clear. Some suggestions on how and where to use the stitches are included.

Common errors in working the basic stitches are pointed out in the text. Hints on how to avoid or overcome these errors are given. Suggestions are sometimes made for more than one approach to working a stitch.

If you really feel that designing your own work is what you want to do, Part 2 is for you! Often, getting an idea is the hardest part for some people. Others think that actually drawing the design is hardest. Still others have trouble with the color choice.

The basic art principles will help you in making your own design. Both right and wrong choices are well illustrated in drawings. A discussion of the color wheel aids you in color choices. Helpful hints are given on adapting designs from other sources. Try your hand at your own design—you might surprise yourself.

Nothing is more important than proper finishing. Mediocre stitching can be overlooked if the finishing is perfect. And even flawless stitches won't be noticed if one is preoccupied with poor finishing. But **nothing** can beat the winning combination of error-free stitching and exquisite finishing. This book can help you achieve both. Please do not lose sight of the idea that this is FUN. *If striving for perfection makes it work, just have fun!*

Your needlepoint can be both useful and decorative. The color plates and a long list give you ideas on what to do with needlepoint—besides the obvious pictures and pillows.

Jump in with both feet. Try making an heirloom. Let the many color photographs inspire you to make beautiful and admired works of art. I hope you will come to love needlepoint as I do!

Jo Christensen
Alexandria, Virginia

A WORD OF THANKS

hese few words of thanks seem inadequate for the many, many hours that dozens of people have donated to put this book together. The first time around, this book was a very big undertaking; the revision was almost as much of an assembly job. I could not have done it alone. I am eternally grateful!

There are a few people whom I nominate for sainthood! Ralph C. Smith III is at the top of my list. He was not only my able photographer but my guy Friday! Supposedly only Robinson Crusoe got everything done by Friday, but I did too! Ralph was there every step of the way and every minute of the day. He rolled up his sleeves and cheerfully did whatever needed doing! He took wonderfully clear pictures—hundreds and hundreds of photos—both black-and-white and color; he cropped them; and he organized them. He ran errands; typed; proofread text, charts (he nearly went dotty!), and drawings; and he, too, lost sleep when the crunch times came. He kept track of legal releases and drawings for every project—five pieces of paper per project! Do the math; that is *lots* of trees! He made what seemed like hundreds of phone calls, tracking down this name or that address so that every form could be completely and accurately filled out. The list is endless! "Thank you very much, Ralph!" is hardly adequate for all he did! What a jewel!

Lynn Lucas Jones did not have computer technology when she did the original drawings, so she did them all by hand! We'd all be lost without them. Lynn was the mother of the bride and could not work on this revision, so Theresia Travers Boland took over. She gave her all to the revision! She burned the midnight oil with the rest of us! Talented Terry produced equally clear diagrams to tell you how to do the stitches—and on the computer! Not only did Terry do the drawings, but she pitched in and proofread, typed, and just did whatever needed doing. She was, like Ralph, ever willing and cheerful, especially when I was sure no publisher's deadline would ever be met!

Cindy Pendleton illustrated the design and color chapters. Some drawings by Lynn and Cindy were reprinted from *Teach Yourself Needlepoint* and *Needlepoint: The Third Dimension,* both by Jo Ippolito Christensen, published by Prentice-Hall.

Bernice Abernathy, Pat Wagner, and Pat Fifield-Saenz are angels! Not only did they help me plan The Needlepoint Contest, but their shop participated by submitting the largest number of entries of any registering shop. Every time I had a question, they provided the answer—and in record time! Anything I needed—Bernice and her staff made it happen. They made crises go away—not once or twice, but many times. I don't know how they did it; maybe they have divine help!

Leslie Green diligently turned my hen scratching into a legible manuscript! In spite of a full-time load as a college student, she was a member of our night owl club. She patiently inserted dots on charts and edits to the manuscript; she dependably delivered the computer its requisite cursing when it crashed and burned, losing her latest creations. I am indebted to Leslie for this and more.

Photos are an essential element of this book. My son, Peter J. Christensen, took some of the color photos. (He's the one whose diapers his father was changing when I wrote *The Needlepoint Book* in 1974 and 1975!) When Peter went back to college, Ralph masterfully assumed his responsibilities. Some of the photographs that were taken by Richard Moats, Paul Hagerty, Tom Novak, and Carolyn McVadon have been reprinted from the other two books mentioned above. Without their wonderful photography, stitching from this book would be guesswork on your part.

Elza Daniel performed magic when she took my picture for the back of the book. She managed to pull the rabbit out of the hat in reponse to my request that she make me look twenty pounds thinner and twenty years younger!

Eleanor Young was my college textiles professor, too many years ago. She wrote the foreword to *The Needlepoint Book* when it first came out, and twenty-two years later, she did it again! Another thing she did *again* was teach me textiles—hour after hour! This time it was over weekly lunches and I did not have any tests! It was much more fun the second time around. She diligently proofread the new sections on fibers and yarns. She painstakingly prepared the fiber properties chart in Figure 1-8.

The many beautiful and imaginative projects that appear in this book were graciously lent to me to photograph by many, many generous people. See the captions that accompany the photos of their artistry to read their names.

These people and their needlepoint came to me by several sources. The first was The Needlepoint Contest. Creative Christine Day had the idea to have a worldwide contest! Her adroit sister, Sarah Albertus, jumped in with lots of fertile ideas.

Jackie Beaty and I spent many hours on the phone (New Mexico to Virginia) planning and sorting every detail of the contest and the book. She provided moral support when I felt overwhelmed by the details. She even made a trip to the East Coast to help me! She organized, typed, and made phone calls by the dozen too. Jackie is a pro at giving this kind of assistance, you see, because she filled the same role four times before! Twenty-odd years ago, when *The Needlepoint Book* was in the making the first time around, we at least lived in the same town—Anchorage, Alaska. But for the three books after that—and now this revision—we've done it on the phone. She has also stitched projects for the books. (In the process, she developed the popular Beaty and Diagonal Beaty Stitches.) We planned those and many others on the phone. We both sat with our color samples of embroidery floss and yarn in our laps, books, magazines, and paper and pencil with the phones tucked between ears and shoulders. Somehow we succeeded. Jackie also proofread each time. Thank you very much, Jackie!

Sharon Snyder and Gail Bloom could get jobs delivering pizza if they did it as quickly as they did research and provided me with answers to questions! They were particularly helpful with providing diagrams of new stitches or new information for old stitches. Sharon has her finger on the pulse of needlepoint trends worldwide. She is a veritable walking needlepoint news source. No new stitch, technique, tip, designer, teacher, or gadget goes unnoticed by Sharon! She generously shares her exciting finds with me and others. Sharon is also a vigorous supporter of one of my favorite needlepoint organizations, the American Needlepoint Guild. She and Gail are very active in their local chapters and regularly lend their expertise to the national seminar, held yearly.

Always ready with answers was Jay Patterson, who has forgotten more about fibers and yarns than I ever knew. Ever willing to share and to test hypotheses, he became a relied-upon source of accurate information.

Once Christine, Sarah, and Jackie got the ball rolling on the contest, inventive Jan Gavin, Deb Lucketta, and Sally Hemmes helped me plan the event. Of course, Simon & Schuster had guidelines to follow. Unfortunately, the copyright laws contributed lots of fine print and complication to the project.

Barb Winer contributed a lot of good thoughts to this process too. In addition, once the plan was set, she very efficiently typed, proofread, reproduced, and distributed all the paperwork to shops and the media. Barb was on top of every detail. She also kept me on track! Bud Stolker then used his vast knowledge of computers to put the contest information on my own Web page on the Internet! He also upgraded my computer and my secretary's computer so they could handle this job.

Hundreds of slides of beautiful needlepoint works were submitted to The Needlepoint Contest by industrious, insightful needlepoint shop owners and managers from shops in several countries. They and wholesale business owners were immensely supportive, as were their staffs. They filled out legal forms and dealt with shipping, insurance, and packing problems for the contest entrants. When entrants placed as finalists, they helped gather the stitch diagrams you can see in the Appendix. I am very grateful for the cooperation of these shop owners and their staffs in taking care of the chores and ironing out the legal difficulties in this undertaking.

The following shop owners or managers were particularly helpful: Eleanor C. Bajobe, Jinice Beacon, Maria W. Chaikin, Paddie Engleman, Lois Eynor, Peggi Haegman, Nandra Hotchkiss, Marjorie Hudgins, Davie Hyman, Bernice Janofsky, Sue Jennings, Sandy Kohrino, Angel Krumray, Nancy Laux, Carolyn Lewis, Shellie Lubowitz, Sallie Luedtke, Lori McGrath, Ginger McTeague, Kitty Moeller, Joan Pickett, Monica Pratt, Jill Rigoli, Harriet N. Segal, Martha Shevett, Mrs. Francis Voris, Joyce Wiest, and Machiko Yamanaka.

Besides readying needlepoint pieces for the contest, many shop owners also helped with the photography and removed glass from framed pictures so they could be photographed. Others allowed us to rearrange furniture and pictures in their homes or stores. Ralph's helpers were Barbara Budlow, Judy and Jerry Greer, Ed Holland, and Cassie Prescott. Pat and Jogina Picariello kindly opened their warm home so that Ralph and I could photograph a number of entries from Martha Shevett's shop— Jogina's needlepoint included, of course. Shop owner Sue Jennings also wore more than one hat; she faithfully sent entries to the contest, proofread, gave valued advice, and lent supplies and equipment from her shop for photographing.

Many other shop owners and managers, far too numerous to mention, contributed lots of precious works of art. Without these shop owners and managers, the variety of the projects in the color plates would not have been possible. Thank you all!

A panel of multidisciplined judges narrowed the slides of the countless entries to a list of semifinalists. These needlepoint projects were hung in The Needlepoint Exhibit sponsored by the Gaithersburg Council for the Arts, Gaithersburg, Maryland. Literally hundreds of people visited the museum and admired this display of exquisite artistry. Many thanks to the Gaithersburg Council for the Arts for sponsoring The Needlepoint Exhibit. The very capable executive director, Elizabeth Lay, and her expert staff hung the lovely works of fiber art at the Kentland Mansions, a historic museum in Gaithersburg. They also hosted a lovely reception in honor of the exhibit's opening. Thank you very much!

While the pieces were on display, they were photographed. Every needlepoint piece was of superb quality! Narrowing the field was difficult for another panel of judges who reviewed this batch of slides and was reluctantly forced to select pieces solely on how well they photographed. Just like people, some works of needlepoint are more photogenic than others—especially when the style of photography had to be kept uniform.

Unfortunately, a majority of the contest entries were on a Christmas theme or other duplicated ideas, such as cottages with lovely flower gardens and ladies in the Art Deco style. So in order to have a wider variety of subject matter and techniques, I accepted offers of needlepoint pieces from other sources.

In addition to those mentioned above, Carolyn Bohling and Jackie Henderson also tirelessly typed and typed and typed! Even though they proofread and proofread, and in spite of the excellence of the whole typing team, there was still more proofreading to be done. The human mind is a funny thing; you can read typing on a page and think the printed word says something it doesn't! The following people also goodheartedly proofread text, charts, and drawings: Ira Branson, Sue Jennings, Andi McKinsey, Beth Robertson, Phyllis and Ralph C. Smith, Jr., and Marie Wiser.

Another panel of judges forced me to narrow the field yet again, reluctantly. These pieces became my children! I didn't want to part with any of them; I wanted to put way too many in the book! If I had won, this would be a coffee table book of color plates—maybe next time. Of course, the editorial staff of Simon & Schuster, in their infinite wisdom, made the final selections for the book based on publishing and marketing considerations that have nothing to do with the quality of the stitching.

Ever wonder what goes on in hotel rooms? Well, here's a new one: Eve Ingraham taught me Brazilian Embroidery at midnight in a hotel room in Tucson, Arizona! What a ball of fire!

Ann Strite-Kurz gave me a crash course by phone and fax on Diaper Patterns. What a wealth of knowledge she has on this little-understood subject. Needlework framer Jane Morgan Henry readily gave me hints on museum conservation techniques. Elsa Parrish taught me the tip about stitching with the threads of old jeans. Many kind, but unfortunately unnamed, people generously shared with me their expertise on a variety of subjects. I appreciate the hard-earned knowledge all these people so freely gave me.

Marlene Hobeck kindly stopped everything to finish the tote bag overnight! Thanks!

B. J. Travers marked photos for cropping and labeled them for the publisher. Carrie Fitch spent hours matching drawings, photos, and text. Susan San Agustin happily ran errands for me.

A word of thanks goes also to the following people who graciously gave me permission to reprint:

1. Chottie Alderson—detached canvas technique.

2. Doris Drake—reproduction of her alphabet from *Doris Drake Needlework Designs*.

3. Famous Artists School, Westport, Connecticut—value scale.

4. Ed Sibbett, Jr.—designs from *Stained Glass Pattern Book* (New York: Dover Publications, Inc.).

5. Phyllis G. Tortora and Robert S. Merkel, definitions of textile terms, *Fairchilds Dictionary of Textiles* (New York: Fairchild Publications, a division of ABC Media, Inc.).

6. Elsa Williams—French Knot.

7. Erica Wilson—the Rose Leaf Stitch from *Erica Wilson's Embroidery Book* (New York: Scribner's).

8. Jane D. Zimmerman—Arrowhead Fly, Crossed Mosaic, Dotted Scotch, Horizontal Old Florentine, Irregular Byzantine, Irregular Continental, Irregular Jacquard, Long-Arm Smyrna, Padded Brick, and Raised Cross, from the *Encyclopedia of 375 Needlepoint Stitch Variations*.

Now you can see that writing the words of this book is the least of the job. I hope you appreciate our hard work, for it is the combined efforts of all of us that bring you this revised edition of *The Needlepoint Book*.

Photo 2—Candle Tunic: In spite of all this help, I'm still burning my candle at both ends [designed and stitched by the author].

GETTING STARTED

Photo 3—Shop Till You Drop and I Shall Wear Purple: *stitched by Sharon Snyder; designed by and yarns and stitches selected by Deborah Wilson. [Smith]*

Photo 4—Akiko (close-up): *stitched by Amy H. Bunger; designed by Marjorie Hunter; yarns and stitches selected by Amy H. Bunger. [Smith]*

*N*eedlepoint can be compared to creating a painting—only you do it with yarn instead of paint. Needlepoint is also known as canvas embroidery, canvas work, and tapestry. It is fun and relaxing to do. You can express your personality and create attractive accessories for your home, family, and friends. There are several ways you can get into needlepoint.

CHOOSING YOUR PROJECT

PREWORKED PIECES

Many people enjoy filling in the background of a ready-center piece. This is a piece that has the center, or design, already stitched by a skilled artisan. This kind of needlepoint can be very relaxing and satisfying. However, if you believe the artisan has already done the best part in preworked pieces, perhaps you should consider other types of needlepoint. You may buy a stamped design, a hand-painted design, or a charted design. As you will see, there are differences and similarities between these types of needlework. It is up to you to decide which you prefer.

STAMPED DESIGNS

A stamped design is pressed onto a piece of blank canvas by machine or by a hand press. When the straight lines of the design line up with the threads—or the mesh—on the canvas, the registration is good. Hand-stamped lines are usually straight, but they cost more than machine-stamped pieces. Sometimes such patterns do not line up. Colors sometimes overlap or leave blank spaces. All these things mean that you must compensate for the errors. However, once you have had some experience in needlepoint, these things might not bother you.

HAND-PAINTED DESIGNS

The hand-painted designs cost much more, as you might imagine. In a stitch-painted canvas, the design is painted by an artist who does needlepoint, so each intersection of canvas threads is painted exactly the way the artist intended it to be stitched. There are no decisions for you to make. This is an easier project for the beginner to tackle than a stamped design.

Many hand-painted designs are just painted on the canvas by an artist who does not follow the canvas threads. These are usually more expensive than stamped designs but not quite so expensive as the more carefully stitch-painted designs. They are not necessarily more difficult to stitch, but they could be.

In between these two (both in cost and amount of handwork) lies the hand-painted canvas that is partially stitch-painted. Only details are stitch-painted—for example, faces, fences, and lettering. These are the kinds of decisions that are critical to the overall design. It helps the beginner to have those details worked out by the artist.

The cost of hand-painted designs is also driven by the skill of the artist. Proper color choice is **critical** to the success of a design. (See Chapter 5.) Often, but not always, artists who **understand** color command higher prices. Design is also important, but it seems to be easier for artists to master than color.

If the stamped design is accurate enough so that you can figure out what you need to do, then you are doing basically the same kind of needlepoint involved in a hand-painted design. There is, then, only the cost difference between them.

DESIGNS ON CHARTS

If you are good at counting, you might wish to try a design on a chart (page 107). This chart looks like graph paper on which the design has been shown with symbols. To work this type of design, you count the symbols a few at a time and then work those stitches on your canvas—count and stitch, count and stitch, and so on. This is the best way to achieve accuracy and detail. The tunic on page xix, among others, was stitched this way.

PREFINISHED ARTICLES

Also available is the prefinished article. These needlepoint canvases have already been made into completed items. For those of you whose weakness is finishing or for those who are not in an area in which professional finishing is available, this is quite a boon. Professional finishing is also very expensive.

Among the many prefinished items are pillows, purses, wallets, tennis racket covers, golf club covers, and tote bags. Some of these have zippers that allow removal of the canvas for working.

The big drawback is that you must be very careful in your choice of stitches. Blocking is difficult at best. When you work with prefinished pieces, be sure to choose a stitch that does not distort the canvas. (See page 109.) Even if you work on a frame, canvas distortion is still an issue to be considered. Humidity can—and will—get to the canvas and soften the sizing. Stitches that distort the canvas will then do so, no matter how carefully worked.

KITS

All of the above types of needlepoint come in kits. Some kits are more complete than others. For example, a pillow kit might contain the canvas, yarn, and instructions only. Or it might include the pillow backing, the cording, and the zipper, as well as the canvas, yarn, and instructions. Read the fine print so that you will know what you are buying.

Quality varies. Check to see that the finishing aids are of good quality. You do not want to put a cheap-looking frame on the exquisite needlepoint picture you have just created. Flimsy fabric for a pillow backing will lower the value of your work—and it will soon wear out.

Sometimes kits come with just enough yarn to do the Half Cross Stitch. (See page 179.) Unless you follow their directions to the letter, you will run out of yarn. Many kits are available (at a higher cost than the ones mentioned above) that provide sufficient yarn to work Basketweave or Continental Stitches. (See pages 180 and 177.) With these you will have enough yarn to work **almost** any stitch you choose. Should you run out of yarn, all you need to do is write the company, sending a snip of the color you need. You will usually receive a prompt reply.

Kits can save you money—or cost you money. If you have a large cache of scrap yarn, you might be able to create the project with a painted or stamped canvas for less money. However, if you have to buy all your yarn, it might be cheaper to buy a kit.

YOUR OWN DESIGNS

Of course, you can always create your own designs. (We will talk more about this in Part 2.) Blank canvas may be purchased so you can apply your own or an adapted design. This book is written to help you do this, as well as the other types of needlepoint.

Whichever form of needlepoint you choose, I hope you will enjoy doing it as much as I do. Perhaps I can entice you to try more than one type.

After you have had fun making your needlepoint, it will serve many purposes. The following list suggests some uses:

address book cover	coat hanger cover	golf club cover	notebook cover	suspenders
barrette	collar and cuffs	guitar strap	note cards	swinging door plate
beanbag	compass case	hat	paperweight	(under acrylic)
bed headboard	computer keyboard	hatband	party invitations	tabletop wastebasket
bellpull	cover	headband	passport folder	tape recorder cover
belt	cornice boards	ice bucket	patch pocket	teapot cozy
bicycle seat cover	cosmetics case	jacket	pen or pencil case	tennis racket cover
blender cover	credit card case	jewelry	phone book cover	tie
bookends	cummerbund	jewelry box cover	piano bench cushion	tissue box cover
box top	desk set	key chain	picture	toaster cover
brick doorstop	dice	lamp base	picture frame	toilet seat cover
bridge score pad cover	director's chair cover	laptop computer cover	pillow	tote bag
bridge tallies	dog or cat collar	letterbox	pincushion	toys
brooch	dog snow boots	lighter case	portfolio	traveling jewelry case
button cover	dog sweater	light switch plate	purse	traveling sewing kit
calculator cover	dolls	luggage rack	purse strap	tray (under glass)
card table cover	drapery tieback	luggage tag	rug	trivet
chair cover	electronic game cover	mirror frame	sandals	typewriter cover
checkbook cover	eyeglass case	mobile phone cover	scissors case	upholstered furniture
child's grow-chart	fireplace screen	musical instrument case	scrapbook cover	vest
Christmas card	flowerpot cover	nameplate	screen divider	wallet
Christmas tree	fly swatter cover	name tag	shoe buckles	wastebasket cover
ornament	footstool	napkin ring	shoes	watchband
Christmas tree skirt	game board (chess,	necklace	shutters	yardstick cover
coasters	backgammon)	needlebook	slippers	yoke of garment

And the list is not complete—believe it or not! Come up with your own ideas. **Cover anything!**

SUPPLIES

CANVAS

The canvas that is made specially for needlepoint is loosely woven, with holes in it for the yarn to go through. It is made quite stiff with sizing (starch). Just how much sizing varies from manufacturer to manufacturer. Handle needlepoint canvas carefully. Once the sizing is cracked, humidity, in all but the *driest* of climates, will seep in, relaxing the canvas, sometimes to the point of sagging.

Canvas should be stored flat or rolled. My mother taught me to value the ounce of prevention over the pound of cure. Standing the roll on end will eventually crack the sizing; storing it on its side prevents the crumples that break sizing. Should the canvas get folds in it, the pound of cure is a light steaming without touching the iron to the canvas. Let it dry flat.

Buy only the best-quality canvas. If the very foundation of your needlepoint is weak, your handwork will not last. Reject any piece of canvas with flaws; these will weaken the canvas. Any reputable shop owner will gladly make accommodations for you.

Canvas is made from several different fibers. (See page 11 for a discussion of fiber properties.) The most popular, by far, is cotton. Some linen and polyester canvases are also available. Gauze comes in silk and polyester versions. Canvas usually comes in either white, tan, or ecru. Congress Cloth comes in a range of lovely colors.

Needlepoint canvas is essentially starched gauze. Its components are called canvas threads—or, sometimes, mesh. There are basically two kinds of woven patterns for canvas: Penelope and Mono.

PENELOPE CANVAS

Penelope Canvas is woven with pairs of threads. (See Figure 1-1.) You must learn to see each pair as one. You might be a bit dizzy at first, but it becomes much easier after a while. Note that one pair of threads is woven more closely together than the pair running perpendicular to it. It is this closely woven pair that is always parallel to the selvages. The selvages are the lengthwise finished edges of all fabrics, including canvas. They do not ravel. The canvas should be held vertically because, on all woven fabrics, the vertical threads are stronger.

Penelope canvas is quite strong. It should always be used for items that will receive heavy wear, such as rugs, chairs, footstools, and upholstered furniture. However, it may be used for other things as well.

1-1 Penelope canvas (junction of canvas threads circled).

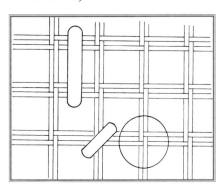

MONO CANVASES

Mono canvas is so called because one thread is the basic stitching unit. It is made from a variety of materials. There are two types of single-thread canvas: Mono and Interlock.

Mono Canvas. Mono canvas (see Figure 1-2) is woven with a single thread. You need to use a frame when stitching on this canvas. It is somewhat unstable because the junctions of the threads are not secured by anything but sizing.

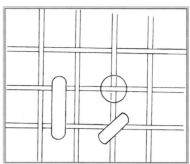

1-2 Mono canvas (junction of canvas threads circled).

Once the sizing has been cracked, the threads slip and slide where they intersect. This is a positive attribute when the finished piece is a chair seat. The canvas will give instead of breaking when it is stressed. On the other hand, the sliding junctions mean that certain stitches may not be worked on Mono canvas.

Sometimes renumbering the stitch diagram will enable a stitch to be worked on Mono canvas. The Basketweave Stitch (page 180) keeps this canvas in line. There are special instructions for working Basketweave on Mono canvas. (See page 181.)

If you do not stitch on a frame, it is a chore to work with sliding threads. Your stitches will not be as neat and even as they would be if you used a frame. However, try it and decide for yourself.

Congress Cloth. This canvas is really a fabric with an even weave that is open enough for stitchers to do needlepoint. It normally comes in sizes smaller than needlepoint canvas. There is a narrow range where the sizes overlap.

The amount of sizing varies from one manufacturer to another. Congress Cloth comes in lots of pretty colors. This allows us to incorporate the background color into our designs. Unfortunately, these pretty colors are not usually colorfast. (See page 95.) When water hits a noncolorfast surface in spots, wetting some of it and leaving other parts dry, a water spot or watermark forms. If the wet parts of the canvas are allowed to dry, these marks become permanent. So, if your canvas does get wet, the *very best* solution is to wet the rest of it and let it air-dry. When you do Pulled Thread on Congress Cloth (page 383), remember to test it for colorfastness first.

Interlock Mono Canvas. (See Figure 1-3.) This canvas secures the junctions of canvas threads with the addition of a tiny thread wrapped around the canvas threads. This thread allows us to lift the restrictions on certain stitches for Mono canvas. Interlock canvas is wonderful for cutting the canvas into irregular shapes, as in Plate 23, because it does not ravel easily. I have been told that the threads on Interlock Mono canvas break, but neither my students nor I have ever had this experience.

1-3 Interlock Mono canvas.

Silk Gauze. Silk gauze is constructed in the interlocked manner. It is very fine and soft, with little or no sizing. A frame is very helpful in working on this fine material.

Plastic Canvas. This type of canvas has no canvas threads, so the term mesh is more appropriate for it. (Mesh is also the correct term for canvas thread, but it is not commonly so called. See page 11.) Plastic canvas

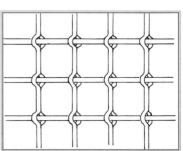

1-4, left: Plastic canvas.

1-5, right: Variety of canvases. Left to right, top row: Mono 10, 12, 13, 14, 16, 18, 22; Congress cloth 24. Middle row: Penelope 6.5, 7.5, 10, 12, 14, 16. Bottom row: Interlock Mono: 3.5, 5, 10, 12, 13, 14, 18.

comes in rectangular sheets, squares, circles, triangles, etc. (Figure 1-4.) It is a bit stiff to work on, but it is nice because it has no raw edges to conceal or ravel. It makes fine wall hangings (Plate 50) and three-dimensional items such as tissue box covers. It can be cut to almost any size you need. Plastic canvas comes in limited sizes—most of them large; therefore, a lot of detail is not possible.

CANVAS THREAD COUNT AND STITCH SIZE

Canvas and some fabrics are called *even weave.* This means that the number of threads per inch horizontally is roughly the same as it is vertically, creating a nearly square hole. Congress Cloth usually varies more than needlepoint canvas. For the most part the evenness that is created is close enough for our purposes.

Following either "Penelope" or "Mono" on the canvas label is a number. This number tells how many threads there are per linear inch. (It is not always accurate over a large area.) (See page 107.)

Canvases are usually available in many sizes. (See Figure 1-5.) This varies with the manufacturers.

Penelope 10/20 is the most widely used Penelope canvas. The "10" refers to pairs of threads and the "20" to single threads. Both numbers are used to help distinguish it from Mono canvas. It is very versatile. Many stitches can be worked on it with a minimum of thickening and thinning of wool yarn. Also, it can be stitched on every thread, rather than on the pairs, making twenty stitches per inch instead of ten.

Penelope 7/14 or 8/16 is best for working Cross Stitches with a minimum of thickening and thinning of wool yarn.

Mono comes in many sizes also. Mono 18 is very popular for working fine designs. The "18" indicates that there are eighteen single canvas threads per linear inch.

Mono 22 is used in the execution of intricate designs. Mono 14 gives the best yarn coverage for working Bargello and Straight Stitches with wool.

Congress Cloth comes in sizes 22 to 28.

Silk gauze is a tiny-count canvas that you stitch with one to three plies of embroidery floss. It comes in sizes 24 and up.

What is available at any given time depends on an age-old economic principle: supply and demand. So inquire at your favorite needlework shop for the currently available canvas sizes.

The sizes of needlepoint stitches have been defined by three terms: Petit Point, Gros Point, and Quickpoint. **Petit Point** is worked on canvas sizes 16 and up. (See page 8.) **Gros Point** refers to those stitches worked on eight to fourteen threads per inch. **Quickpoint** is needlepoint worked on rug canvas, three and a half to seven threads per inch. The more stitches per square inch, the more detail is achieved.

Canvas is sold in varying widths. You may purchase canvas by the yard or in fractions of yards (⅛, ¼, ⅓, ⅜, ½, etc.). Many shops will sell canvas by the inch or square inch.

WASTE CANVAS

Beware of waste canvas (Figure 1-6). It is designed for stitching counted Cross Stitches onto fabric. When it is wet it **dissolves.** To block needlepoint, the properly finished product is dampened. If you have worked your needlepoint on waste canvas, it will disintegrate when blocked! It is very tempting to buy waste canvas. It is half the price of good needlepoint canvas, but it is actually much lighter in weight and much weaker. **Do not use waste canvas for needlepoint!**

Keep in mind that all supplies (canvas and yarns in particular) are better for some uses than others; they all have pros and cons. No one is better than the other. The chart in Figure 1-7 points out some of these advantages and disadvantages.

FIBER AND YARNS

Manufacturers and distributors of yarns package and label a wide variety of yarns especially for needlepointers. Commonly used yarns include cotton embroidery floss, silk, wool (Persian, crewel, and tapestry), rayon embroidery floss, pearl cotton, metals, and a whole host of synthetic yarns.

This section will tell you about fibers and yarns and how they are made. Later you will learn how to observe, in a systematic fashion, and answer *for yourself* such questions as: How will it stitch up? How easy will it be to handle? Do I need any special stitch techniques?

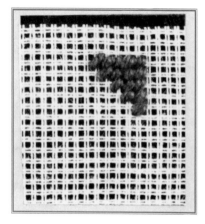
1-6 Waste canvas.

PROPERTIES OF CANVAS

Penelope Canvas

Pros	Cons
• Splits readily into finer canvas for stitching details. • Accommodates all stitches without restrictions. • Strong. • Frame not required.	• Flat threads, harder to cover. • Harder for beginners to grasp the concept of one pair of threads per Tent Stitch, the basic stitch (page 177). • Does not come in many sizes.

Mono Canvas

Pros	Cons
• Round thread covers better. • Soft; good for Pulled Thread techniques (page 54). • Basketweave (page 180) has even more give than on other canvases. • Best for appliqué.	• Stitch tensions cause it to distort more easily. • *Must* stitch on a frame. • Harder for beginners to learn on without a frame (page 24).

Interlock Mono Canvas

Pros	Cons
• Helps maintain even stitch tension, which is invaluable for beginners. • Finishing is easier because it does not ravel easily. • Cuts easily without raveling. • No frame needed.	• Harsher than other kinds of needlepoint canvas. • Must stitch with shorter yarn than other kinds of needlepoint canvas because harshness shreds yarn. • When distorted, harder to block. • Not as strong as Penelope or Mono.

Plastic Canvas

Pros	Cons
• Easier to see. • Does not distort easily under stitch tensions. • Washable and does not need blocking. • Assembles readily into freestanding three-dimensional items. • Cuts easily without raveling. • No frame needed.	• Limited sizes, especially in finer mesh. • Not dry-cleanable. • Not flexible. • Comes in sheets of limited sizes.

1-7 Properties of canvas.

HOW YARNS ARE MADE

First, let us define a few terms so we all are talking about the same thing. These definitions are from *Fairchild's Dictionary of Textiles,* seventh edition, 1996. This is the basic reference used at the Fashion Institute of Technology in New York City and other professional schools, colleges, and universities; by manufacturers of fibers, yarns, and fabrics; and by many others in the textiles industry.

Fiber—the basic component of strands of yarn, such as cotton, wool, silk, polyester, etc.

Filament fiber—a fiber of very long length. It is the equivalent of a strand of spun fibers. Silk and man-made fibers are filaments unless they have been cut.

Filament yarn—a yarn made from strands that consist of single filaments.

Mesh—the threads that make up an open, gauzelike, or netlike fabric, as in needlepoint canvas.

Pearl—a loosely twisted yarn. Its twist is so distinct that it resembles a rope or cord. Its smaller cousin is Buttonhole Twist, used primarily in sewing machines.

Ply—two or more strands or filaments twisted together in the opposite direction from the twists of each of the strands.

Spun yarn—a yarn made from strands or plies that are made from staple fibers.

Staple fiber—short lengths of fibers that must be twisted or spun into a strand.

Staple yarn—a yarn made from strands (or plies) that are made from staple fibers.

Strand—the basic indivisible unit of a yarn. Made from staple fibers or filaments that are twisted together with a one-direction twist. Two strands are twisted together to form a ply. "Strand" is sometimes mistakenly used to refer to what is technically called a ply and/or yarn.

Thread—a thin, tightly twisted yarn, used mainly for sewing; generally of the size that will pass through the eye of a sewing machine needle. Also used to define the components of woven fabrics. *Used in this book to apply to the elements that make needlepoint canvas.*

Yarn—any number of twisted filaments or plies. *Used in this book to describe the material with which we stitch.*

FIBER CONTENT OF YARNS

Fibers can be divided into two main groups: natural and man-made. The natural fibers are further subdivided into those from plants (cellulose) and those from animals (protein). Animal fibers come from three sources: silk (from the cocoon of the silk worm), hair (from pelts), and fleece (hair growth sheared, combed, or shed from the living animal). Man-made fibers are made from all sorts of chemicals and vary greatly. Both natural and man-made fibers have inherent attributes, known as properties. (See Figure 1-8.)

Natural fibers occur in nature in short, medium, or long lengths, called **staple fibers.** Silk is the only exception; a perfect cocoon produces a very long continuous **filament**. Damaged cocoons produce filaments that are broken into pieces of varying lengths. Natural fibers are normally used as they come in nature, but sometimes they are cut into shorter pieces to create variety in the appearance of finished products. The longer the fiber, the higher the price.

Man-made fibers begin as a liquid mixture of laboratory chemicals, except for rayon, acetate, and triacetate. These transition fibers begin as cotton and wood pulp

PROPERTIES OF FIBERS	Spun (Staple) Yarn	Filament Yarn	High Shine	Low Luster	Very Soft	Coarse, Generally	Flexible	Stiff, Couch Only	High Abrasion Resistance	Frays and/or Pills Easily	Strong	Weak	Wide Color Range Possible	Overdyes Possible/Absorbent	Washable if Colorfast	Withstands Ironing and Steaming	Resistant to Sunlight	Resistant to Mildew and Rot	Resistant to Insects	Dry-cleanable
NATURAL FIBERS																				
Cellulose																				
Cotton	•						•						•	•	•	•			•	•
Linen (flax)	•						•			•			•	•	•	•			•	•
Jute	•					•		•		•		•							•	•
Ramie	•						•		•	•	•		•	•	•	•			•	•
Hemp	•						•				•		•	•	•	•	•		•	•
Protein																				
Silk	•	•			•		•						•	•	•	•		•	•	•
Wool (shorn fleece)	•						•			•		•	•	•	•	•		•		•
Hair: Camel family (hand-combed or hand-collected as the animal sheds it) Alpaca, camel, juanaco, haurizo, llama, misti, vicuña	•				•	•	•			•			•			•		•		•
Hair: Goat family Mohair, also called angora goat or angora wool (shorn fleece), cashmere (hand-combed from fleece)	•						•		•	•								•		•
Fur: Beaver, mink, seal, chinchilla, fox, muskrat, nutria, raccoon (all from pelts), and angora rabbit (from shearing)	•				•		•			•		•						•		•

1-8 Properties of fibers.

and wind up as essentially liquid cotton and liquid wood pulp. In this liquid form, dyes, fire retardants, insect repellents, and other additives can be, but are not always, added to change the fiber's properties. The liquid is poured through a device that looks sort of like a shower head. The liquid comes out in streams, and the streams harden into filaments. The shape of the holes dictates the shape of the filaments. This shape is usually visible only under a microscope. These long filaments may be made into yarns as is or cut into shorter lengths.

PROPERTIES OF FIBERS	Spun (Staple) Yarn	Filament Yarn	High Shine	Low Luster	Very Soft	Coarse, Generally	Flexible	Stiff, Couch Only	High Abrasion Resistance	Frays and/or Pills Easily	Strong	Weak	Wide Color Range Possible	Overdyes Possible/Absorbent	Washable if Colorfast	Withstands Ironing and Steaming	Resistant to Sunlight	Resistant to Mildew and Rot	Resistant to Insects	Dry-cleanable
TRANSITION FIBERS																				
Regenerated Cellulose																				
Acetate (made from chemically altered cellulose)	•	•	•	•									•	•		•	•		•	•
Rayon (made from cotton and wood pulp)	•	•	•	•	•		•				•		•	•	•	•	•			•
Triacetate (made from chemically altered cellulose)	•	•	•	•	•								•	•		•	•	•	•	•
Regenerated Protein																				
Chinon (made from milk)	•	•			•		•						•	•		•	•	•	•	•
MAN-MADE FIBERS																				
Acrylic	•	•	•	•	•		•			•			•			•	•	•	•	•
Aramid	•	•	•	•			•		•				•			•	•		•	•
Modacrylic	•	•	•	•	•		•			•	•		•			•		•	•	•
Novoloid	•	•														•	•	•	•	
Nylon	•	•	•	•			•		•	•			•			•		•	•	•
Olefin	•	•	•	•					•		•					•		•	•	
Polyester	•	•	•	•			•		•	•			•			•				•
Rubber		•			•		•				•			•				•	•	
Saran	•	•	•	•				•	•		•					•		•	•	
Spandex		•		•			•						•	•		•		•	•	•
Vinal		•	•	•			•			•		•	•		•	•	•	•	•	

1-8 (con't.)

Some fibers are naturally shinier than others. Rayon is very shiny, for example, while linen is not. The shape of the filament can reduce or increase shine; the simpler the shape, the shinier the filament. The texture of the fiber affects shine as well. Some fibers are naturally irregular, like wool; man-made fibers have texture added by the manufacturer. This texture makes the color look more interesting and makes the final product feel more interesting. It also reduces the amount of light that is reflected and, thus, produces a less shiny fiber, as well as texture. The length of the fiber is a contributing factor to the luster of a yarn. Shorter fibers are not so lustrous as longer fibers. More uniform fibers are shinier. Therefore, synthetic filament fibers are the shiniest.

Blends are literally that—a combination of fibers. The resulting yarn will have the properties of both (or all) fibers. We have to estimate how one fiber's strength overcomes the other's weakness. The most familiar blend to us all is perhaps a polyester/cotton blended fabric. Cotton is a cool fiber to wear; polyester needs no ironing. A fabric of 65% polyester and 35% cotton will need less ironing than one that is 65% cotton and 35% polyester. The fabric that requires less ironing will not be as cool to wear, and the fabric that needs to be ironed will be cooler to wear. Similar conclusions can be made about yarns and their properties.

Yarn Construction. Simple yarns are made by combining fibers into strands. The strands may be combined in three main ways: twisting, braiding, and crocheting a chain or chainette.

Staple fibers are spun or twisted into strands, which are the basic, indivisible units of a spun yarn. Many labels on yarn and/or brochures from manufacturers will tell you whether a silk or synthetic yarn is composed of spun or filament strands. But you can easily find out for yourself by untwisting a yarn. A strand will untwist into many fibers.

Filaments may be used as is or be twisted into a yarn. When used as is, the resulting yarn is called a **monofilament strand;** when two or more filaments are used together the result is a **multifilament yarn.**

1-9 Yarn construction.

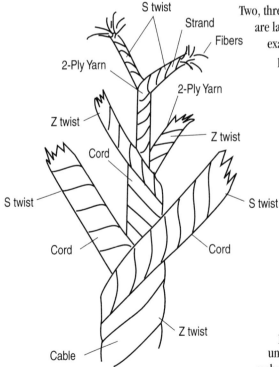

Two, three, four, or more strands are twisted into ply yarns and are labeled by the number of plies that are combined—for example: "2-ply," "3-ply," "4-ply," etc. When two or more ply yarns are combined, the result is called a cord; two or more cords make a cable; two or more cables make a rope, and so on. (See Figure 1-9.)

There is some confusion about embroidery floss. Some refer to it as a 6-ply yarn; others, as a 6-strand yarn. In the strictest sense of the word, a strand is the smallest indivisible component of a yarn that will stand on its own. A ply is two or more strands twisted together. If you untwist a piece of embroidery floss, you will get six units that stand alone easily. If you study each of these units carefully, you will see that each is composed of two strands that are twisted together. However, when you untwist these two strands, they are so weak that they do not stand alone. When two strands are combined to make a ply, two S-twist strands (see page 100) are twisted together in a Z-twist. This process untwists the S-twist somewhat. Accordingly, it follows that embroidery floss is a 6-ply yarn. Sometimes the whole thing is incorrectly called a strand! Confusing, isn't it?

Yarn construction techniques also affect shine. When man cuts a natural staple fiber or a synthetic filament into shorter lengths and spins it into the yarn, the luster is thereby reduced. The more a yarn is twisted, the more firm, fine, and strong it becomes. Loosely twisted yarns with a lot of nap (fuzz) have a duller appearance. Very tightly twisted yarns become bumpy or pebbly, like crepe yarns.

Nap also produces a variation in shine and, seemingly, in color. Consistently stitching with the nap going in the same direction will produce a more even texture and color within a stitched area. (See page 31 for more on nap.)

Twist also affects absorbency, yarn diameter, elasticity, smoothness, abrasion resistance, and a yarn's ability to shed soil. Notice how stripping and laying yarns as you stitch changes some yarn properties created by twist. See the chart in Figure 1-10 to understand these relationships. See pages 32 and 40 for a discussion of stripping and laying.

Complex or novelty yarns are made by a variety of methods. For example, slub yarns have intermittent areas of fatter spots along the yarn; bouclé yarns have loops or curls that project from a core yarn; and chenille yarns have a fuzzy, caterpillar-like appearance. (See Figure 1-11.) Some yarns are a combination of different construction methods. Almost all kinds of yarn can be used on some kind or size of canvas to create special effects. Be aware that yarns of uneven diameter will present problems in going through the holes of the canvas. Test the performance of any of these yarns on a scrap of canvas. With an open mind, you might find what you see quite interesting.

Nonwoven products such as synthetic suede, vinyl, and holograms are cut into very long, very thin strips and made into yarns for stitching. Ribbons come in woven and nonwoven varieties and can also be used for stitching. Wonderful special effects can be created with these products.

Dyes can be of several types, such as acid, reactive, cationic, etc. We will probably never know which was used on our yarns. All fibers can be dyed in big kettles. Synthetic fibers can also be dyed while they are in the liquid form; this is called solution dyeing. Color can be applied by several methods in the yarn stage, usually vat dyeing by the skein (bundle of yarn) or in bulk, but yarns can also be printed! Variegated embroidery floss is printed with different shades of the same color.

Solution dyeing produces colorfast colors, but it is not economically feasible to produce yarns in requisite large quantities in a wide range of colors. In addition, solution dyeing makes flat, boring colors with no depth because light cannot bounce off microscopic irregularities as it does on natural fibers. This play of light creates depth of color and subtle variations that make it rich and interesting. Whether synthetic filament fibers can be vat-dyed depends on the absorbency of the fiber. Those that are not absorbent will not absorb dyes. Most synthetics are not very absorbent.

In spite of improving technology, colors of dye are not exactly the same from one batch to the next. Humidity, which varies from day to day, affects dyes. Making colors is not an exact science. Some manufacturers claim that their yarns come in matched dye lots and others do not. Whether or not they do, you should still buy all the yarn

RELATIONSHIP OF YARN PROPERTIES AND YARN CONSTRUCTION		
Low Luster	**High Luster**	**High Shine**
naturally dull fiber	naturally lustrous fiber	naturally shiny fiber
loose twist		tight twist
short staple fibers	long staple fibers	filament fibers
lots of nap		little or no nap
lots of texture		little or no texture
Soft		**Hard**
loose twist		tight twist
short staple fibers		filament fibers
more nap		little or no nap
more texture		little or no texture
Weak		**Strong**
naturally weak fiber		naturally strong fiber
loose twist		tight twist
short staple fibers		long staple fibers
		filament fibers
Loosely Twisted		**Tightly Twisted**
soft		hard
more absorbent		less absorbent
soils more easily		sheds soil
fatter yarn		thinner yarn
less elastic		more elastic
more delicate		more abrasion resistant
more texture		little or no texture
more nap		little or no nap
Delicate		**Abrasion Resistant**
naturally weak fiber		naturally strong fiber
loose twist		tight twist
more texture		little or no texture
more nap		little or no nap
short staple fibers		filament fibers

you will need for your project at the same time. There may still be slight differences from skein to skein.

Dyes change the properties of fibers. The most common example is silk. Silk is a washable fiber, yet many dyes used on silk and other fibers run or bleed in water. So a washable fiber is not washable unless you do not mind the color running! Normally, running dyes would produce disastrous results, but think of the wonderful possibilities when stitching an abstract design or a field of flowers or a stand of trees where the running of colors could be used deliberately to create an impressionistic effect in your stitching. My father, an artist, always called these events happy accidents.

Finishes are usually applied to fabrics, rather than yarns, to enhance the positive properties of fibers and yarns and downplay or compensate for the negative properties. Their use on yarns is not widespread, if they are used at all. Some property-changing chemicals can be added in the solution stage of the manufacture of synthetic fibers, such as a fire retardant. (See page 12.)

Finishes can change properties of fibers a great deal. They are widely used in the manufacturing of fabrics. They can make washable fibers "dry clean only" fabrics. For example, rayon is a washable fiber, but it has little body. A fabric finish can give a rayon fabric body. This finish may be water soluble, thus making a washable rayon shirt a "dry clean only" item. **Keep in mind that the chart of fiber properties in Figure 1-8 is more applicable to yarns than it is to fabrics.**

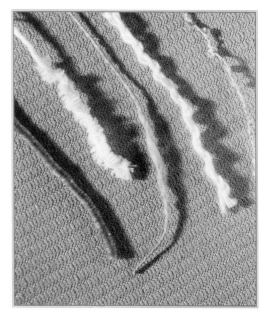

1-11 Novelty yarns. Left to right: two chenille yarns, one slub yarn, two bouclé yarns.

NEEDLEPOINT YARNS: NATURAL FIBERS

Yarns commonly used in needlepoint projects are pictured in Figure 1-12. The labels of many yarns are clearly marked with fiber content and number of plies. Some labels tell you the recommended canvas and needle sizes. You may come across some yarns with no useful information on the label. This section of the book will help you to figure out what you have and how to use it.

The basic yarns for needlepoint come in the familiar natural fibers: cotton, wool, and silk. They are produced in a wide variety of construction techniques. This discussion is limited to the most common yarns.

COTTON

Cotton is manufactured with probably the widest variety of yarn construction techniques of all the fibers. Cotton is the most common and, thus, the most inexpensive. It takes dyes very well and can be produced in a wide range of colors.

Embroidery floss consists of six or more tightly twisted plies that are loosely twisted together. The plies can be easily separated or stripped. (See page 32.) This cotton yarn comes in hundreds of beautiful colors that are made in magnificent color families. This is by far the most popular yarn for stitching size 18 or smaller canvas.

Pearl (*perle,* in French) is a loosely twisted, soft, lustrous yarn that is a mainstay for small canvases. (Sewing and other embroidery threads are tightly twisted.) It comes in sizes 3 (the fattest), 5, 8, and 12 (the skinniest), and is a wonderful choice for Pulled Thread (Plates 8, 38, and 48) and Open Work (Plates 4, 34, and others).

1-12a, left: Yarns used in needlepoint. Left to right: silk floss, multi-plied cotton yarn with medium twist; tightly twisted 3-ply cotton yarn; tightly twisted, hard 2-ply yarn; pearl cotton, size 12; pearl cotton, size 8; pearl cotton, size 5; wool crewel yarn; wool, 3-ply Persian yarn; 4-ply wool tapestry yarn; loosely twisted 3-ply mohair yarn; wide overdyed silk ribbon; medium-width silk ribbon; very narrow silk ribbon; 12-ply silk floss; filament silk. Bottom center: 6-ply cotton embroidery floss.

1-12b, right: Miscellaneous metallic yarns.

Cotton is also produced in several other kinds of yarns. Matte cotton is a soft, loosely twisted yarn with a dull or matte finish. It comes in many colors, although not as many as embroidery floss. There are also cable yarns, crepe yarns (very tightly twisted), and others.

WOOL

The manufacturers of wool needlepoint yarn make their yarn strong. Wool yarn has long fibers that give protection against the rough canvas. Wool needlepoint yarn is also mothproofed.

Crewel yarn is a 2-ply, fine, loosely twisted yarn that comes in a wide range of colors. Crewel yarn is ideal for stitching on most sizes of canvas. It can be readily thickened by adding additional plies.

Persian yarn is a loosely twisted, 3-ply yarn. The colors are magnificent! They do not come in matched dye lots. Persian yarn is not smooth in appearance and it does not work up as smoothly as tapestry yarn. However, when you have to thicken or thin, it is a blessing. Persian yarn is sold in prepackaged skeins (bundles) and by the strand (by the strictest definition, by the yarn—not the strand), ounce, or pound. Quality varies tremendously.

Tapestry yarn is a smooth, tightly twisted, 4-ply yarn. It is sold in skeins of varying sizes, often in matched dye lots. Some tapestry wool comes in a tremendous range of colors and well-blended families of colors that are very good for Bargello and shading. Because tapestry yarn is a smooth yarn, it makes a smooth stitch; I like the looks of a piece stitched with it. However, tapestry yarn does not separate readily; it is not meant to be stripped. The difference between tapestry yarn and Persian yarn is that tapestry yarn can be used on 10- to 12-count canvas, whereas Persian yarn can be split and used on very fine canvases or thickened and used on larger size canvases.

Rug yarn is a fat, loosely twisted yarn used for Quickpoint on large canvas. You may also combine several plies of Persian yarn to cover the canvas. Be sure to keep the plies smooth; do not allow them to twist. See the discussion on laying yarns on page 41.

SILK

Silk yarns are made from spun fibers and filaments. The spun yarns are less lustrous than the filament yarns. The filaments can be made into twisted yarns, as can the staple fibers. The filament yarns are shinier than the staple fiber yarns. Long stitches show off the luster of filament silk beautifully. Silk is also blended with wool for interesting effects. Silk is more expensive than other fibers.

Silk comes in **embroidery floss,** just as cotton and rayon do. It is a multiple-ply yarn that can be easily separated or stripped. (See page 32.) The silk yarn is available in a great many gorgeous colors. If you are looking for maximum sheen, be sure to choose a filament embroidery floss. Silk gives a touch of elegance that no fiber can match. However, a good-quality cotton floss can be an excellent substitute.

Pearl is made from silk staple fibers and from filaments as well. Silk is also made into a chenille yarn, sewing thread, Buttonhole Twist, ribbon, and others.

Ribbons make lovely decorative stitches and special effects that cannot be created with other types of yarns. They come in silk, as well as in rayon and polyester. A wide range of colors is possible and some are overdyed in lovely colors, especially those used for flowers and leaves. Ribbons come in several widths for use on different size canvases and to achieve different and beautiful effects (Plates 3, 4, 6, 8, and 47). Be sure to use a chenille needle with ribbon. Some of the ribbon stitches, like Ribbon Loop Stitch, need its sharp point to pierce the ribbon.

Silk yarns can be shiny or dull, or somewhere in between. Choose the one that serves your purpose best. Remember that some dyes for silk are not colorfast. Test your yarn. Some silk yarns are colorfast; read the fine print on the label.

NEEDLEPOINT YARNS: MAN-MADE FIBERS

RAYON

Rayon, like silk, comes in spun and filament yarns. As is characteristic, spun yarns are less lustrous than filament yarns. It is possible to make the filaments and the staple fibers into various twisted yarns. Use the filament yarn for long stitches to take advantage of the maximum shine of the fiber.

Rayon is available in **embroidery floss, pearl, ribbon,** and others.

METALLICS

Metallic yarn is a novelty yarn that gives a spark where needed. (See Plates 14, 21, 36, 54, and many others.) These fun yarns are either synthetic or real metals, like gold, silver, copper, and bronze. Real metals require very special handling that is beyond the scope of this book. As you can imagine, they are quite pricey! The synthetics are much more diverse and much easier to work with. They are made into yarns with a variety of yarn construction techniques, such as embroidery floss, chainettes, and threads. The **hologram yarn** (see page 101) gives amazing depth to your stitching!

OTHER NOVELTY YARNS

Unusual novelty yarns may be used in needlepoint—but only with **caution.** (See Figure 1-13.) Never use them on pieces that will receive any wear; usually only pictures fit this category. This is because the novelty yarns are not strong enough and can fray easily. Exciting effects can be achieved with these interesting yarns and with your imagination!

Polyester ribbons are available and make interestingly textured flowers and leaves. They come in varying widths, starting at ⅟₁₆" and going to 3½" or 4".

Angora and **mohair** can give a special spot extra fluff (Plates 5 and 38). **Patent leather** and **suede** yarns are fun to use for stitching shoes and other leather objects. **Nylon tubing** can create translucent effects (see "Hydrangea Flowers," front cover). Only your imagination can stop you.

Try these novelty yarns and the many others available! Have fun! But listen to my mother: "Too much of a good thing is bad!"

ACRYLIC YARNS

Acrylic yarns are a fine choice for plastic canvas projects. The wonderful dimensional stability of the plastic canvas is not affected too badly if the yarn's elasticity causes uneven tension in your stitches. Don't throw caution to the wind, however; you still need to watch stitch tension. Acrylic yarns are washable and inexpensive, just like the canvas. They are an ideal solution for quick projects.

Acrylic yarns should not be used for heirloom needlepoint, although some kits do include them. They pill (see page 95) and become ugly soon, and they do not block well. Stitch tensions are tedious to get even. Synthetic yarns have memory. After being

1-13 Novelty yarns used in needlepoint (left to right): heavily napped yarn, rayon braid, synthetic suede, novelty ribbon, rayon embroidery floss, novelty yarn, nylon tubing, novelty yarn, bouclé yarn. A chenille yarn is at the bottom center.

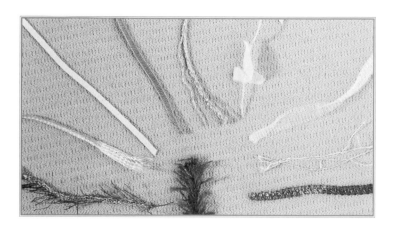

wet they go back to their original position. This is what makes garments knitted with them machine-washable and machine-dryable. This also means that any needlepoint worked with them will always be out of shape because the blocking will not hold without rabbit-skin glue (page 118). Acrylic yarns come in various weights and sizes.

Rug yarn and **craft yarn** (made especially for plastic canvas) are great choices for stitching on plastic canvas. They are thick enough to cover a couple of the most popular canvas sizes.

Knitting worsted is too springy and elastic to achieve even stitches. This yarn, too, pills and does not block well.

Accent your needlepoint with unusual yarns. You are limited only by your imagination.

FABRIC STRIPS

When you are seeking a special look or just want to do something different, stitch with fabric! When I say the possibilities are endless, it's really true! Not only are there zillions of fabrics out there, but you have a few options on how to use the fabrics.

Stitch with their threads or with strips of the fabric. If you want to ravel the threads and stitch with them, they work just like stitching yarns. Using the raveled threads of old jeans will give an area that just-right-blue-jean color that is so elusive in needlepoint yarns. These threads are not as strong as the fabric that they came from. Be especially mindful of this when using threads from denim, which we think of as being indestructible. Remember that you are stitching with a novelty yarn and take the appropriate care (page 19).

Fabric strips can produce a variety of looks. Tear the fabric into strips that will work for your canvas or cut them with a rotary cutter or scissors. A strip that is too wide for your canvas will crumple in the canvas holes and add texture. Do this with a textured fabric and you will get even more texture. If the edges of the fabric ravel easily, the rough edges can be just the extra oomph that your design needs.

Experiment. There is no telling how far you can go with this idea!

HOW MUCH TO BUY

How much yarn do you need? This question baffles beginners. It's not really such a mystery. Ideally, you should work a square inch of the stitch you want to use, on the canvas you choose, with the same brand and color of yarn you will use. Keep track of the amount of yarn used. Then figure out how many square inches there are in your design. Multiply the amount of yarn used by the number of square inches. This gives you roughly the amount of yarn you will need. The figure will vary with the length of yarn you use, the stitches you choose, and how much you rip!

This method is not always convenient. A competent shop owner can usually estimate quite accurately. Most—but not all—of the stitches in this book can be worked with the same amount of yarn needed for the Continental or Basketweave Stitches. Choose your colors in daylight, if at all possible.

EMBELLISHMENTS

Embellishments are things you sew on to enhance your design. Buttons are quite varied and very decorative. (See Plates 4, 11, 36, and 54.) Of the thousands of kinds of beads, surely there is room for one on your needlepoint pieces, as in Plates 12, 18, 31, 47, 53, and 54. Some needlepoint can be primarily beading, as in "Joy, Beaded Purse" (front cover).

Charms add delightful interest. (See Plates 3, 36, and 37.) Miniatures are also useful in dressing up your stitchery. (See Plates 11, 13, and 29.) In Plates 32 and 38, the needlepoint serves as a frame for the miniature dioramas.

Gemstones—real or fake—can be attached with one or more rows of the Buttonhole Stitch (page 347), worked in a circle around the gem or found object. See Plates 13, 26, 35, and 36 for examples. Found objects from nature are often just the touch you need, as in Plates 15, 16, 33, and 50. Old jewelry can be recycled. (See Plates 12 and 36.)

Lace can add delicacy, elegance (Plate 18), and accent. The appliqué of fabric and fake or real leather offers a change of texture, as in Plate 54.

EQUIPMENT

Not much equipment is needed to do needlepoint. Besides the yarn, canvas, and needles, you will need those items shown in Figure 1-14.

NEEDLES

A special needle is used for needlepoint. It is a blunt-tip **tapestry needle.** Choose the correct needle for the size canvas you use. A needle should not distort the canvas; it should drop through the hole easily.

1-14 Equipment needed for needlepoint: masking tape, ruler, waterproof marker, embroidery scissors, crochet hook, needles, tweezers, and thimble. Optional equipment includes laying tool (Fig. 1-17) and a frame (Fig. 1-18).

A beginner can start with a bigger needle (for example, an 18 needle with Penelope 10 canvas) and later switch to a smaller one when the task of threading the needle has been conquered.

Always keep needles dry. Once the plating wears off your needle, throw it away! The black stuff that rubs off can permanently stain your stitchery. That would make you *very* unhappy, I'm sure.

A **chenille needle** is a tapestry needle with a sharp point. It comes in many of the same sizes as tapestry needles. It is used when stitching with ribbons or other yarns that need a sharp point to pierce them.

Beading needles are long and *very* thin with a *very* tiny eye. They come in sizes that match the sizes of the beads. They are used, obviously, for sewing on beads.

Milliner's needles are long and the same diameter for the entire length of the needle. They are needed for Brazilian embroidery stitches, such as the Drizzle Stitch and the Cast-on Stitch (pages 370–371).

Figure 1-15 gives you a guide to which size needle to use on which size canvas. The photo in Figure 1-16 shows different size needles. Buy needles in packages of six or one at a time.

SCISSORS

You will want three pairs of **scissors.** One pair should be small with fine points; embroidery or nail scissors do nicely. Use these to cut soft yarns. Keep one old pair of large scissors just to cut canvas, because the canvas dulls them quickly. Keep another pair of old embroidery scissors to cut metal and synthetic yarns; they also dull scissors rapidly. Next, make a needlepoint scissors case for your embroidery scissors like the one in Plate 43, and they will be portable!

LAYING TOOLS

When laying yarns (see page 40), you will need something to help you keep the plies of a multi-plied yarn lying flat and smooth (not twisted) against the canvas. It is usually a long, narrow, pointed tool. There are many kinds. (See Figure 1-17.) Some are about 4" long and have a handle that fits in the palm of your hand. The idea here is to prevent a cramp in your hand. The sharp point helps you lay the plies of the yarn more easily side by side.

There are other laying tools on the market. There is a type of laying tool that fits around your index finger; a long needle sticks out from the tip of your finger about an inch. True, it solves the problem of a cramp in your hand from holding a laying tool. But use it with caution. Don't scratch an itchy eye while forgetting that it is on your finger.

Other items can serve as laying tools, such as a large tapestry needle, a knitting needle, a sail needle (a triangular needle with three flat sides

RELATIONSHIPS OF CANVAS SIZES TO NEEDLE SIZES	
Canvas sizes	**Needle sizes**
3–5	13
7–8	14–16
10	18–20
12–14	20
16–20	22
22–24	24–26
26–28	26–28

1-15 Relationships of canvas sizes to needle sizes.

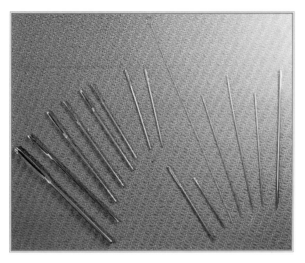

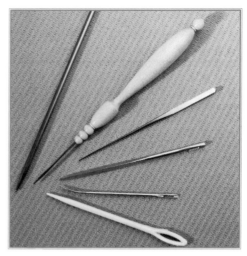

1-16, left: Needles. Top row: Blunt-tip tapestry needles. Left to right: sizes 13, 16, 18, 20, 22, 24, 26, 28. Bottom row: Chenille needle, size 24; quilter's needle, size 10 (for beading); large-eye beading needle; beading needle, size 13; milliner's needle, size 3; milliner's needle, size 9; milliner's needle, size 8 (a different brand from the other two milliner's needles).

1-17, right: Laying tools. Left to right: knitting needle, two commercial laying tools, two sail needles, plastic yarn needle.

and a sharp point), an upholstery needle, a collar stay, or a bodkin (a flat needle used to guide elastic through a casing).

My favorite is the sail needle. The shaft of the needle is round at the eye and at the tip, but the middle is triangular! Those flat sides give me a little help in straightening out the plies. I had the sharp point on mine dulled *slightly.* I found I was donating blood on a regular basis to my needlepoint. If you do get blood on your work, keep in mind that your own saliva will get your blood out. (Neat trick, huh?) Cold water works too, but saliva may do less damage (if any) to nonwashable fibers and unstable dyes.

FRAMES

And then there is the Great Frame Debate. There are many staunch advocates of frame use. There are many who think frames are more trouble than they are worth. A frame is a gadget, usually wooden, that is made to hold your canvas taut across two or four bars. (See Figure 1-18.) These bars are adjustable to any size canvas. Some styles roll up the excess canvas on two opposite sides, leaving a relatively small area that is still large enough for you to work. If you like to create texture in your stitching, I do not recommend a roller or scroll frame, because the textured stitches will be crushed. A four-sided frame is made from stretcher strips that are purchased in pairs of various lengths. You assemble them. Stitcher's stretcher bars are narrower than artist's and therefore lighter in weight. You'll need a larger canvas margin to accommodate the artist's stretcher strips, but they can be used.

Some small frames can be held in your nondominant hand while your dominant hand does all the stitching. I think this is slow and inefficient. If you have a frame holder—a third hand, so to speak—you can stitch with your dominant hand below the canvas and the other one above the canvas. If you are using a laying tool you *must* have something to support the frame.

There are many types of frame holders or stands. Some models stand on the floor, a table, or your lap; others you sit on. You may also secure your frame so that one corner of it sits on the edge of a table and the rest hangs over it. This can be done with a C-clamp (from the hardware store) or a five-pound weight. The weight can be a book, a brick (covered), a beanbag filled with lead shot, or anything else heavy.

I really like being able to get to the back of my canvas without having to undo a clamp, frame holders, wing nuts, or whatever. Some frame holders will simply flip to the back—my favorite kind. I like to use a frame weight when attending classes. It is easily moved to access the back of the canvas and is compact to carry. When you stitch on canvas, it sometimes stretches slightly. I like a frame that makes it easy to retighten the canvas as you work. It is essential to keep a taut surface while you stitch; otherwise, you defeat the purpose of using the frame in the first place.

1-18 Frames. Top of the pile to the bottom: Scroll frame, stitcher's stretcher bars (narrow), and artist's stretcher bars (wide).

Just as for everything else, there are advantages and disadvantages to using a frame. The main advantage in using a frame is that your finished canvas is not badly out of shape, if at all. (Some stitches distort the canvas and others do not.) Also, long, less-stable stitches are placed properly with much better tension. There is no doubt that many yarns and fibers we stitch with do not tolerate blocking with water. In this case, you *must* use a frame. I believe that all needlepoint canvas should be blocked, wet or dry, whether or not it is out of shape. This process resets the starch (sizing) and helps protect the canvas threads from humidity. More important, it evens out the stitch tension, making more uniform stitches. Even misshapen pieces can be blocked to size without a lot of trouble.

As for the disadvantages of using a frame, you are forced to stab, rather than stitch with continuous motion. (See page 38.) Continuous motion (sewing), in my opinion, creates a smooth, even tension in your stitches. Rhythm develops as you stitch and you pick up speed. Much of this rhythm is lost in stabbing. In addition, some stitches, primarily Basketweave, have a smoother backing when stitched in continuous motion. (See page 181.)

Your needlepoint is less portable when on a frame. As this family's chief errand runner, I spend a lot of idle fifteen- or twenty-minute periods here and there. My needlepoint bag is always ready to go. You would be surprised at what I—and you, too—can create while waiting for doctors, dentists, kids at baseball games, music lessons, and swim practice, etc. I do try to save background, Bargello, or a large area to fill in with one stitch for this time. This allows fewer chances for mistakes due to reduced concentration.

I'm glad to have a frame, but sometimes it hampers my style. You might like it—many of my friends and students do too. I always use a frame for fibers that cannot be wet-blocked, for stitches that are long and unstable, and for Mono canvas. Go to your local shop and ask to see the frames. They might even have a display model set up so that you can try it out.

The wrong frame holder makes my back hurt. (My mother told me once I hit forty I'd start to fall apart. How right she was!) I never liked working on a frame because of that—until I found a frame holder that works. Keep trying until you find one that works. I eventually did; you will too. I now like stitching on a frame.

OTHER ITEMS

Besides scissors, you will need a pair of **tweezers** for ripping. (See page 44.) A **ruler,** a **waterproof marker,** and masking or freezer **tape** are needed to ready your canvas for stitching. (See page 27.)

In looking for a marker, shop wisely. Choose only a marker whose manufacturer guarantees that it is *waterproof*—not water resistant. Read the fine print! Some manufacturers state in the fine print that their marker is not permanent on fabrics that are highly sized. In essence, that is what needlepoint canvas is.

After you have a marker that is guaranteed, *test it yourself.* Do not trust the manufacturer. Even those markers advertised as waterproof might still run on canvas. To test a marker, write on a piece of the canvas—the same brand as the one you will use. Run it under cold water. Blot with a white tissue or a paper towel. If the color runs, you cannot use that marker on that piece of canvas, so keep it and try again with another marker. The best color to choose is a light blue or medium gray. Most brands of yarns, including pastels and whites, will cover the blue or gray line. Do not use black.

A needle book or holder will keep your needles handy. There are several styles available commercially, or you can make one.

Unfortunately, not all of us have young eyes. That does not have to stop us from stitching! There are wonderful magnifiers and lamps on the market, and even greater combination magnifiers and lamps! Some magnifiers clip onto your glasses; some *are* glasses. Others clip onto a frame; others sit on a table or the floor. There's even a type that hangs around your neck. Good light is essential. Lamps come in a similar variety of styles, as do magnifier-and-light combinations.

If at all possible, try before you buy. Leaning toward a light can cause back strain—ouch!

Now that you have gathered all these things together, you need to have a needlepoint bag to put them in. There are many styles available; most will accommodate your frame too.

Now your needlepoint bag is ready to go! The next chapter will tell you how to get started. Get ready to have fun!

Two

BASIC PROCEDURES

W onderful needlepoint projects do not just happen. It takes a little learning, a little planning, and a little practice. It is possible to create lovely things with a minimum of easy preparations and precautions and to have a good time too!

PREPARING THE CANVAS

Different canvases need different techniques. Woven canvases, as a group, are treated the same. Plastic canvas handling techniques are different.

WOVEN CANVASES

There are several simple steps you must take before you begin to stitch. First, measure carefully. (For complete information on measuring, see Chapter 7, "Blocking and Finishing.") Next, cut the canvas—between the canvas threads and in a straight line.

Mark your margin with a waterproof marker. How wide your margin is depends on what kind of project you are working on.

Canvas ravels quite easily. Bind the edges with masking or freezer tape. (See Figure 2-1.) Rub the handle of the scissors over the tape on both sides of the canvas to make it stick firmly. Even if you are concerned about museum preservation techniques, you should still bind your canvas with masking tape; it's so easy. Just cut it away when you are finished. This means you will need to cut a margin of canvas just ½" bigger all the way around to make up for this loss. At first you may think that because the canvas is so stiff it cannot possibly ravel. However, the canvas will soon lose its stiffness, and then the damage begins. Even when you're working on a frame, those edges can snag your clothes and yarn.

With such a large, stiff piece of canvas, you may wonder how you are going to get to the center to stitch. **Do not crumple the canvas.** You may put it on a frame or you may roll up one side as shown in Figure 2-2. If you want to roll it, pin at both ends. Then roll the opposite side, leaving a 3" or 4" strip down the middle. Pin it in place. Large safety pins are good for this. When rolling a canvas that has already been worked in textured stitches, you run the risk of crushing them. Be careful. A better option is to mount your canvas on a frame. (See page 24.)

If you are using a roller or scroll frame, attach your canvas to the twill tape on the roller bars by sewing (Figure 2-3a). Put the edge of the canvas *under* the tape. Arrange the frame so that the wing nuts will be on top. If you put them on the bottom, they snag your clothes as you work. Caution must be taken in using a scroll frame in three-dimensional needlepoint.

2-1 Bind canvas with masking tape.

2-2, above left: Roll canvas for easy access to working areas.

2-3a, above right: Sew needlepoint canvas to the twill tape on a scroll frame.

2-3b, below: Work a Double Leviathan Stitch to park your needles, especially when working on a frame. Parking the needle in your design distorts the canvas.

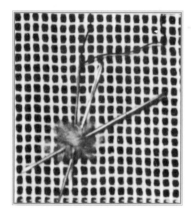

Rolling the canvas will crush any three-dimensional work done. Ergonomic wing-nut tighteners make it easier to loosen and tighten the wing nuts.

When using stretcher bars, use a staple gun or thumbtacks to attach your canvas to the frame (Figure 2-4).

PLASTIC CANVAS

Working with plastic canvas is different. It does not give you the same problems. For example, it does not ravel; it does not wrinkle; and the larger sizes do not distort easily with various stitch tensions.

Plastic canvas does have one problem that seems the same, but the solution is peculiar to it alone. Cutting all canvas produces sharp edges that can snag your yarn and your clothes. The rough edges produced in cutting plastic canvas often show and are most undesirable. Figure 2-5 shows how to prepare the edge of plastic so as to produce a neat finished edge. Use whatever cutting tool helps you to get a good edge. Among those that work are a utility knife, an artist's knife, small scissors, a diagonal craft cutter (looks like scissors with wire-cutter-type ends), or a rotary cutter.

When laying out the pattern pieces, look for broken mesh. Quality seems to vary sometimes. One broken mesh can ruin a design, for it will not hold a stitch. Search the uncut canvas for defects and avoid them when cutting out your pattern pieces.

Covering the canvas is easier with rug yarn and craft yarns made especially for plastic canvas. They do, however, come in fewer colors than many needlepoint yarns. The very useful families of colors, in particular, are missing. Ribbon does especially well on plastic canvas.

The chart in Figure 2-6 gives you a rough guide to matching yarn sizes to canvas sizes. Manufacturers vary in the diameter of yarns; for example,

2-4 Tack or staple canvas to stretcher bars. A piece of felt stapled to the stretcher bars holds needles conveniently.

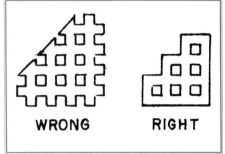

WRONG   RIGHT

2-5 How to cut plastic canvas properly.

knitting worsted. Some brands of knitting worsted will cover where others will not on the same size canvas. Test for yourself to be sure.

As with other kinds of canvas, you can leave some areas open for another dimension. Experiment and see what you like.

The sturdiness of plastic canvas allows it to support heavier embellishments whose weight would bend many other kinds of

RELATIONSHIPS OF COMMON SIZES OF PLASTIC CANVAS TO STITCHES AND YARNS FOR PLASTIC CANVAS

Canvas size	5		7		10		14	
Stitch type	straight	diagonal	straight	diagonal	straight	diagonal	straight	diagonal
craft yarn			•	•				
embroidery floss							•	•
fabric strips	•	•	•	•	•	•	•	•
knitting worsted				•		•		
pearl cotton 3						•	•	•
pearl cotton 5								•
Persian yarn				•	•	•		
ribbon ⅛"			•	•	•	•		
ribbon ¼"	•	•	•					
rug yarn		•		•				
sport yarn						•	•	
tapestry yarn					•	•	•	•

Yarn Type (minimum of thickening and thinning of yarn)

2-6 Relationships of common sizes of plastic canvas to stitches and yarns for plastic canvas.

canvas. Using embellishments such as silk flowers, buttons, and others adds interest and texture to your needlepoint. (See page 22.)

HANDLING THE YARN

Needlepoint canvas is quite rough. It is hard on yarn. For this reason, needlepoint is worked with a strand of yarn about 18" long. Lengths vary with the type of yarn. Novelty yarns might have to be quite short.

To help you resist the temptation to use a longer piece of yarn, you might want to cut your yarn to standardized lengths just before you use it. Because yarn comes packaged several ways, there are many techniques to cut it to size. Note: If you are planning a twisted cord for finishing, you will need some uncut yarn (page 125). Also, Open Stitches need a longer yarn. (See page 37.) Some kinds of fibers can withstand the harsh canvas better than others and thus may be cut longer. The 18" length is a good guide, but experiment yourself. (See page 103.)

Persian yarn, which is sold by the ounce, usually comes in about 66" lengths. Cut them in thirds. You may want to knot your yarn for storage, as shown in Figure 2-7. This keeps it tangle-free yet easy to untie when you want a strand of yarn. Loop the colors for your current project around the plastic holder from a six-pack of sodas or

2-7a-d Knotting yarn for storage.

a

b

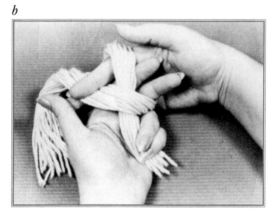

c

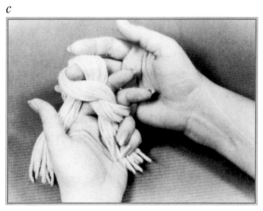

d

beer (Figure 2-8a). If your range of colors is very close, this will help to keep them sorted. One strand is easy to get (Figure 2-8b). Finer yarns can be stored on a piece of cardboard or poster board along with color numbers, as shown in Figure 2-9. There are many yarn-storage gadgets available commercially.

Some Persian and tapestry yarns come in a twisted skein. Untwist the skein. The yarn will be in one big circle. Cut it once. Then cut the yarn into halves or thirds to make whatever length yarn you need. Knot each section.

Tapestry yarn sometimes comes in a skein like the one shown in Figure 2-10. Leave the paper wrapper on and cut the loops at one end of the skein. To get one strand, pull it out from the other end.

Some yarns come in skeins that do not lend themselves to the above methods. Many books come 9" high. Wind the yarn all the way around the book and cut the resulting circle of yarn once. You now have a quick way to measure and cut lots of pieces of yarn into 18" lengths (very roughly). To vary the length, choose another size book or a box.

2-8a, left: Yarn for current project, looped on plastic holder for soda or beer.

2-8b, right: It's easy to remove one strand for use.

2-9 Yarn for current project looped on poster board and marked with color number.

NAP

Yarns made with staple fibers have **nap** or direction; some have more than others. When staple yarns are made, the staple fibers are aligned and then twisted together. The short ends stick out, as in braided hair, creating nap. The tighter the twist, the less nap. Hold a strand of yarn up with one hand; run the other hand down the strand. Then turn the strand upside down and feel it again with the same hand. The yarn will feel smoother one way than the other. The smooth way is the way the yarn should be used in stitching. (See Figure 2-11.) Using the yarn with the nap all going the same way will produce neater needlepoint stitches. The sample of the Medieval Mosaic Stitch was stitched

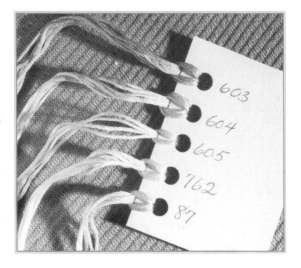

2-10, left: Some skeins of yarn may be precut into the desired length. Measure before you cut.

2-11, right: Threading the needle with the nap of the yarn.

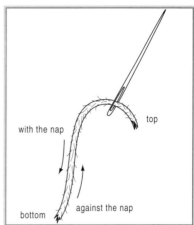

with the nap

top

against the nap

bottom

against the nap. (See page 172.) Note how uneven the stitches are. The Wild Goose Chase Stitch (page 152) was stitched with the nap. It is smoother.

STRIPPING

PERSIAN YARN

Stripping Persian yarn restores it to its original state. Shipping yarn to retailers crushes the yarn considerably. A plumper yarn covers the canvas better. Stripping merely means separating the three plies of Persian yarn and putting them back together again (Figure 2-12a). Tapestry yarn is not stripped.

If you closely examine an absorbent-fiber staple yarn that has been cut for twenty-four hours or more, you will notice that the yarn has relaxed more at one end than at the other. This end is called the Blooming End (Figure 2-12c). The staple ends that stick out absorb humidity and swell. The cut end at the bottom of the yarn has more staple ends that stick out than the cut end at the top. Thus, the yarn will spread more at the bottom, creating the Blooming End.

Usually it is the Blooming End that is knotted. However, before you thread the needle, you need to strip all stranded yarns. Hold the end opposite the Blooming End between the fingers of one hand and run two fingers between the three plies.

Stripping gives you a double-check on the nap. Once in a while it's hard to see which end is blooming. If you're holding the end opposite the Blooming End, the strand should strip easily. If it does not, turn the strand of yarn upside down and try it again.

After you've stripped the yarn, run your hand down the strand two or three times. This *stroking* of the yarn will get the extra fuzzies off. Stroke until they're gone.

EMBROIDERY FLOSS

It is easier to strip floss by holding the end that comes off the skein and pulling one ply at a time straight up (Figure 2-12b). Then put them back together again.

OTHER YARNS

More tightly twisted yarns will need to be untwisted before stripping. Some should not be untwisted for stripping; it will ruin the yarn. Experiment, develop your own systems, and trust your own judgment.

THICKENING AND THINNING OF YARNS

Unfortunately, we cannot thread our needles and just stitch if we want to cover the canvas. One strand of yarn does not always cover the canvas. The thickness of yarn varies with the type of yarn, fiber, brand, and even color. For example, the white 3-ply wool yarn of Brand X is decidedly fatter than the black 3-ply wool yarn of Brand X. It seems that some fibers do not absorb different colored dyes consistently, thus producing thicker or thinner yarns with different colors. Wool seems to be worse about this than other fibers. Simple observation will tell you. Always double-check for yourself.

Other factors that affect coverage are the size and brand of canvas and the stitch used. With so many variables, it is impossible to tell in advance just exactly how much yarn you need to work a given area of one particular stitch.

Experiment with thickening and thinning yarn. Use embroidery floss, Persian yarn, or other stranded yarn that can be stripped and, thus, thinned. Experiment for yourself. When you cut your yarn, as described on page 30, store each bundle separately. Each strand will then be exactly the same length. This makes it easier to thicken and thin.

To thicken, separate a 3-ply Persian yarn into three pieces. Then simply add one or two of these plies to a 3-ply strand. The addition of one ply creates a 4-ply strand; two plies, a 5-ply strand. If you need a 6-ply strand, put two 3-ply strands together. Too thick? Just remove one or two plies as you need to.

In order to find out how thick a strand must be to work a certain stitch, you need to experiment. Work on a piece of canvas exactly like that of your project; use the same brand and *color* of yarn to work the stitch you want. Experiment until the desired effect has been produced (Figure 2-13).

2-12a, left: Stripping Persian yarn.

2-12b, center: Stripping embroidery floss.

2-12c, right: Absorbent staple fibers might have a Blooming End (left).

2-13, left: Stitches on the left show yarn so thin it does not cover the canvas; stitches on the right were worked with thickened yarn and cover properly.

2-14a, center: The three plies of Persian yarn are not all the same size. Think of the three sizes as a fat, a medium, and a skinny.

2-14b, right: One skinny and one fat equal two mediums.

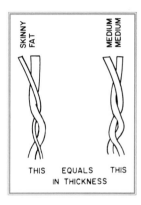

Sometimes adding one ply makes the yarn too thick and subtracting one makes the yarn too thin, causing the canvas to show slightly. This **grin-through** of canvas can be reduced by painting the canvas. Another trick for covering the canvas is to add French Knots (page 356) or a Backstitch (page 334).

When stitching Diagonal Stitches on Mono 14 with Persian yarn, only two plies are needed. You may have noticed that sometimes these two plies cover the canvas and sometimes they don't. This can be corrected if you watch carefully which ply you remove.

Take a *good* look at a length of Persian yarn. Sometimes there is a fat, a medium, and a skinny ply. Now, we've always laid one of the three aside and used the odd one with the odd one from another strand later. This way, we get three 2-ply yarns from two 3-ply yarns. If we always take the medium away when we separate (or thin) the yarn, we will always have yarns of reasonably equal thickness (Figure 2-14). So one fat and one skinny make the same thickness as two mediums, and each strand will cover as well as the one before it.

Hint: If you are having trouble telling which is which, put a little tension on the yarn. Sometimes it helps. If you still cannot tell them apart, it won't make that much difference which one you choose. This situation does not arise often.

THREADING THE NEEDLE

Threading the needle is regarded by many of my students as the most difficult part of learning needlepoint! It really does not matter how you get the needle threaded so long as you do not in any way damage or fray the yarn.

The needle-threading techniques in Figure 2-15 show how to thread a needle with wool or acrylic yarn because they are probably the hardest. The same techniques should work with all yarns.

The paper method (Figure 2-15a and b) is quite a reliable technique. However, if you, like me, cannot keep up with the little piece of paper, perfect another method.

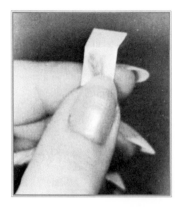 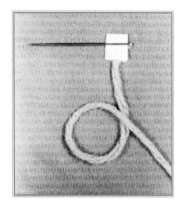 

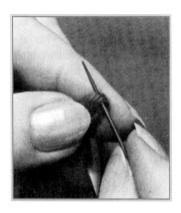 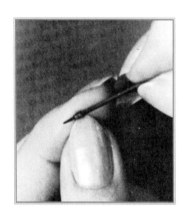 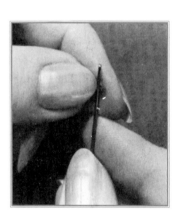

My favorite method is shown in Figure 2-15c. Give the yarn tip an extra twist, making it more tightly twisted. If you are right-handed, place this tip of yarn between the thumbnail and index finger of your left hand. Let only a tiny bit of yarn stick out. Holding the needle in your right hand, push the needle between your fingers. And presto! It works—most of the time. Figure 2-15d, e, and f show yet another method for threading the needle. It works, too—most of the time.

If all else fails, try one of those metal needle threaders for yarn. Of course, you can always invent your own method. Let's face it—if you cannot thread the needle, you cannot continue with needlepoint!

STITCHING IN GENERAL

BEGINNING AND ENDING YARNS

"**Never** knot the yarn in needlepoint" used to be the rule, but the wide variety of yarns available changes this. We still want to avoid knots that stay on the wrong side of stitched areas. If you plan to cover the canvas with your stitches, catch the tail as you begin to stitch each new yarn (Figure 2-16). When taking your first stitch, leave about an inch or so of yarn on the wrong side of the canvas. Hold on to this tail so that it will not slip through. Carefully take several more stitches, making sure that you cover the tail with each successive stitch. This buries and anchors the tail securely.

2-15a–b, top left and center: Threading the needle—the paper method.

2-15c, top right: Threading the needle—my favorite method.

2-15d–f, bottom left to right: Threading the needle—the loop method.

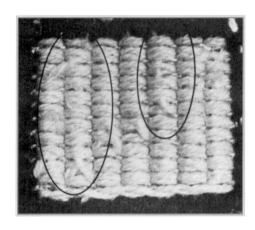

2-16, top left: When stitching in continuous motion, you may catch the yarn tail on the wrong side of the canvas with the needle and continue catching the tail until it is completely buried.

2-17, top right: When ending a resilient yarn, you may run the needle under the worked areas. Clip the loose ends closely (after burying them) to produce a neat back. Long ends look messy, can get caught up in other stitches, and produce lumps on the right side of the canvas.

2-18, below: Bargello Tuck.

To end your yarn, weave the needle in and out of the wrong side of the stitches you have just worked—*if* you are stitching with a yarn that is resilient enough to absorb the extra bulk that the tail adds. Clip the yarn close to the back, leaving none sticking out (Figure 2-17). To begin the next yarn, bury the tail in these stitches you have just worked. There are some exceptions, which are cited below.

The **over-under weaving method** to bury the tail is not always secure enough for long, loose stitches and for stitches that have a lot of stress on them (like Spider Webs and the Binding Stitch). Take a **Bargello Tuck** or two in these cases (Figure 2-18). It is simply a Backstitch taken after you've woven the tail in but before you bring the needle to the right side of the canvas.

A **Waste Knot** is really easier than trying to catch as catch can. This is especially true if you are working on a frame with a very slippery yarn (such as rayon) that won't hold a buried tail or if you're working with a nonresilient yarn that will not absorb the extra bulk of weaving the yarn over and under already worked stitches.

First, knot the yarn (see Figure 2-19). Next, put the needle *down* into the canvas from the *right* side, leaving the knot on the *right* side. Bring the needle up to the right side of the canvas about an inch from the knot. Place this re-entry point so that your first few stitches will catch this tail (Figure 2-20). When you come to the knot sticking up on top of your canvas in your stitching, tug on it a little and then clip it off and throw it away. After you pull and cut, the rest will pop to the back side of the canvas. Note that if you begin the next yarn with a Waste Knot, you will be stitching over two tails. Taking a few Running Stitches (Figure 2-21) between the Waste Knot and your first stitch is particularly helpful for working stitches that have little or no backing. For Open Stitches, you may also take a tiny **Pin Stitch** just before making your first stitch. To do this, simply take a Straight Stitch over one canvas thread—not at the junction of the canvas threads. When ending this yarn, merely bring the needle up on the right side of the canvas an inch

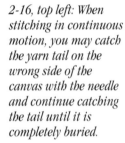

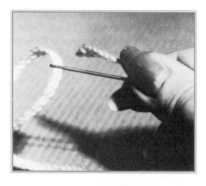

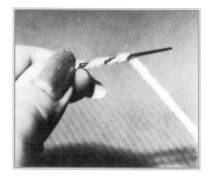

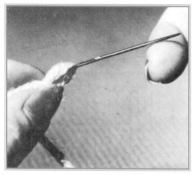

2-19a, top left: To make a good, easy knot quickly, place the end of the yarn over the eye of the needle.

2-19b, top right: Wrap the yarn around the needle three times.

2-19c, bottom left: Pull the wrapped yarn over the eye of the needle and down the yarn.

2-19d And presto! There's a knot!

or two from your last stitch. Place it in the path of the next few stitches. If you start the next yarn with a Waste Knot, you will be stitching over two yarns in the same space.

An **Away Knot** is started like a Waste Knot, but it is not quite the same. When the row of stitching is not long or big enough for a Waste Knot, you may place the Away Knot in the margins, going into the canvas the same as the Waste Knot. Use an Away Knot when working open stitches. Come up where your next stitch needs to be. There may be 4" to 6" of yarn between the knot and the first stitch. This is okay. Be careful not to run this long piece of yarn under an area of canvas that is to be left open.

When you have finished stitching, you may clip the knot and run the tail under any finished stitches if that yarn is resilient enough to absorb the thickness of the tail. If you are not working with a resilient fiber, the extra bulk of the tail will pull the stitches on the front side of the canvas. This pull will make them appear more tightly stitched because light is reflected differently. You also have the option of leaving the knot in place if it will be secured by the finishing process of your needlepoint.

Generally, it is best to end each yarn in the same area that it covers. Try not to bury the tail of your current yarn in a neighboring area. Stagger your starts and stops. If you do not, the tails will leave lumps. Never start or end all yarns in the same area. As a general rule, do not begin each yarn piece at the beginning of every row if you can help it, unless you are using an Away Knot that will stay in the margin permanently.

In working two or more areas of the same color, do not carry your yarn on the back more than 1½" or so. When you do carry it 1½", weave the yarn in and out of the

2-20a, top left: To use the Waste Knot, place the knot an inch or so from your starting point, in the path of your next stitches.

2-20b, top right: Stitch toward the knot, catching the yarn under the canvas as you go.

2-21, bottom: Running Stitch.

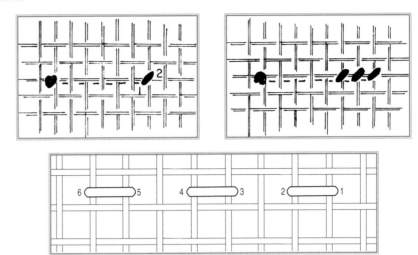

stitches already there. However, avoid carrying a dark yarn across a light-colored area; it will show through on the right side. For the same reason, you should not bury a dark-colored tail on the wrong side of a light-colored area.

STITCH TENSION

The tension of your needlepoint stitches should be even, not too tight or too loose (Figure 2-22a). Each stitch should look like the rest and should hug the canvas snugly. If your tension is too tight, the canvas will ripple (Figure 2-22b) and/or the yarn can be stretched. This must not happen. Do not confuse this ripple with the distortion of a canvas that is out of shape because the stitch pulls the canvas out of square. In this case the canvas still lies relatively flat.

You may find that long stitches require slightly more tension than shorter ones (see Mosaic and Scotch Stitches, pages 210 and 220). A too-loose tension will look sloppy (Figure 2-22c).

CONTINUOUS MOTION VS. STABBING

Continuous motion, shown in Figure 2-23, is like sewing—putting the needle into the canvas and bringing it out all in the same motion. **Stabbing** (Figure 2-24) is putting the needle into the canvas with the dominant hand—the right hand, for example—pulling it out onto the wrong side with the right hand, inserting it into the canvas from the wrong side with the right hand, and pulling the needle through with the right hand on the right side of the canvas. This way your right hand is over and under and over and under the canvas. This may be done with or without a frame.

The other method of stabbing is used only with a frame supported by a frame holder or stand. This is the preferred method of stitching on a frame. The dominant hand is always held on the wrong side of the canvas and the other hand is held on the right side. The two hands now work together in stitching.

2-22a, top left: Correct tension.

2-22b, top right: Too-tight tension.

2-22c, bottom: Too-loose tension.

When working without a frame, I believe that continuous motion produces a stitch with the most even tension. Rhythm is developed. This method is definitely faster than stabbing. But speed is not usually what this is all about!

If you are working with a frame, the whole idea is for it to hold the canvas tautly. You then cannot use continuous motion; you must stab. You do have a choice of whether or not to use a frame holder or stand. If you are laying yarns (page 40), you must use a frame holder because you will need both hands to stitch. I personally like using the frame stand, even if I am not laying yarns, but I think you should choose the method that suits you best.

YARN TWIST

After you have threaded your needle, fold the yarn nearly in half (Figure 2-25). Slide the needle down the yarn as you stitch. This prevents the eye of the needle from wearing a thin spot at the end of the yarn where the needle's eye was. Alternately, you

2-23, left: Continuous motion stitching.

2-24a–b, middle and right: Stabbing.

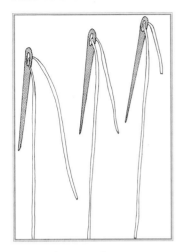

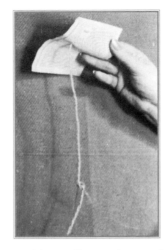

2-25, left: Generally, move the needle along the yarn as you use it.

2-26a, center: When the yarn becomes tightly twisted during stiching, turn the canvas upside down.

2-26b, right: Let the needle dangle until the yarn straightens out. Better yet, try giving the needle a half turn every few stitches to keep the yarn from getting this badly twisted.

can put the eye of the needle an inch or two from the end and cut off the spot where the needle wore the yarn thin.

As you work, your yarn may tend to untwist or twist too much. (See the information on S- and Z-twists on page 100.) If you can get in the habit of giving the needle a quarter or a half turn or so, in the correct direction, after every stitch, this can be prevented. Otherwise, simply let go of the needle and let it dangle. It will spin the yarn back into place (Figure 2-26). If you do not do this often it will show up in your stitching as sloppy work.

LAYING

When you are stitching with many plies that have been stripped (page 32), keeping the original twist of the yarn is not enough to get an even-looking stitch. Each of the plies of the yarn needs to be laid neatly side by side. The photos in Figure 2-27 show how to do this.

To keep your neatly laid yarns straight, you will probably want to work on a frame (page 24). Since laying yarns is a two-handed job in itself, a frame holder (see page 39) will help immensely. Other information about laying can be found on page 23.

DIRECTION OF WORK

Try to stitch with the needle going down in a full hole and up in an empty hole. This will help eliminate snagging and splitting the yarn in rows already worked. The numbering of stitches in this book has been arranged so that this will be done wherever possible. You do not always have a choice. In that case, try not to snag the yarn of stitches you have already worked.

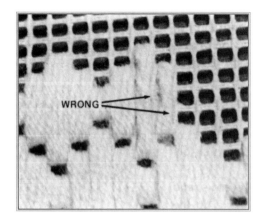

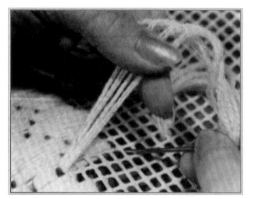

2-27a, top left: This sample was stitched with eight plies of Persian yarn. The stitches labeled wrong are lumpy. This is caused by the plies of the yarn being twisted during stitching. A stitching technique called laying solves this problem.

2-27b, top right: If the plies of the yarn are carefully laid side by side when you make each stitch, the yarn will lie between the canvas threads smoothly. Use a laying tool to help you. (See page 23.) Use the fine point of your laying tool to get the yarn straight just before it goes into the hole to the back of the canvas.

2-27c, middle left: When needlepointing on a large scale as in the sample, you might find that using your fingers instead of a laying tool is easier.

2-27d, middle right: When using finer yarn, this step is not possible to do with your fingers. A laying tool of some sort is really necessary, then.

2-27e, bottom: Notice how much smoother the last stitch looks when compared with the others stitches that were not carefully laid.

BACKING

Backing, or how the yarn covers the back of the canvas, is very important. How well a needlepoint piece wears depends on how good the backing is. This is critical for upholstered pieces.

Some stitches produce an excellent backing, such as Basketweave (Figure 2-28a); some, a good backing, such as Continental (Figure 2-28b); some, like the Half Cross, make a poor backing (Figure 2-28c); and others provide almost no backing at all (Figure 2-28d)—for example, the Six-Trip Herringbone, Needlelace, Needleweaving, and the Waffle Stitch.

In addition, the backing dictates how a stitch looks on the front (Figure 2-29). The more neatly and completely the yarn wraps around canvas threads, the neater the stitch looks on the front.

COVERING THE CANVAS

If the name of your game is "cover the canvas," and if you have finished a stitch and it does not quite cover—do not panic. There are lots of ways to salvage the stitch without ripping.

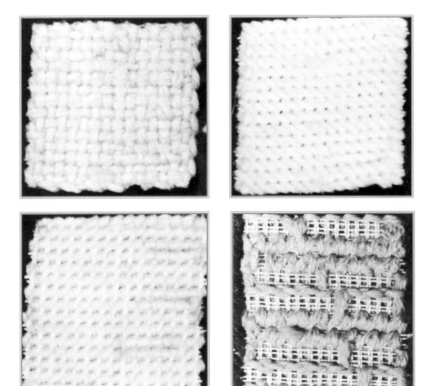

2-28a, top left:
Excellent backing.

2-28b, top right:
Good backing.

2-28c, bottom left:
Poor backing.

2-28d, bottom right:
Almost no backing.

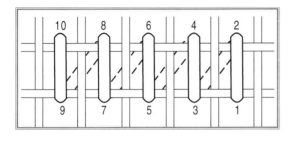

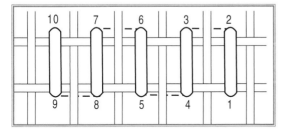

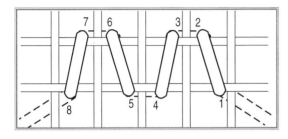

2-29a, top left: Good backing results in even stitches on the front.

2-29b, middle left: Poor backing is made by this stitching sequence.

2-29c, bottom left: When stitched according to the sequence in Fig. 2-29b, the stitches will lie crooked on the front of the canvas.

2-29d, top right: Good backing makes nice, even stitches on the front. Bottom row: Poor appearance on the front is caused by poor backing.

Before you start to stitch you should check to be sure you have the optimum yarn thickness for that stitch, the brand and color of yarn, and the size of canvas.

If you have done this and canvas still shows, then fill in areas of blank canvas with French Knots, Tramé (Figure 2-30), Backstitch (Figure 2-31), or Frame Stitch (Figure 2-32). Once in a while you can get away with sticking in an extra stitch. For example, see the Diagonal Beaty Stitch, on page 194. However, do not let this throw your pattern off. Often, beads or pearls may be sewn on to help cover the canvas. (See Periwinkle Stitch, page 305.)

Remember, as long as you achieve the effect you want, it is **not** wrong. Just have fun and add your own special touches!

COMPENSATING STITCHES

When you are working on a decorative stitch, you are faced with the problem of having to fill in areas that are too small for a whole motif of the stitch. The places are filled in with what are known as **compensating stitches.**

To establish your stitch in an irregularly shaped area, work one row across the widest part. Stitch as much as you can of the motif. It is a lot easier to go back and fill the

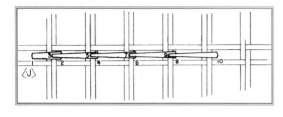

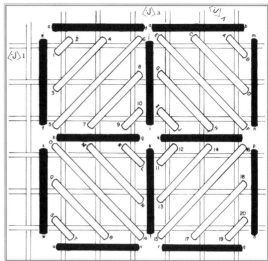

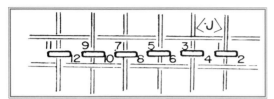

2-30, top: Tramé.

2-31, bottom: Backstitch.

2-32, right: Frame Stitch around the Scotch Stitch.

small areas with as much of the stitch as possible. (See Figure 2-33.) Doing them as you go is a little harder, but once you get the hang of the stitch you may make the compensating stitches as you go.

Once in a great while you will come across a stitch that will not allow you to put these stitches in later. (See Split Bargello, page 170.) Then the compensating stitches must be worked first or as you go.

STITCHING A DESIGN

When stitching a piece with a design, it is usually best to work the design first. Then work the background in one direction: top to bottom or upper right corner to lower left corner, or left to right, or whatever direction your background stitch follows. Do not start in one corner, stop, and then pick up in another. Your stitch pattern might not meet where the two areas come together.

2-33 Compensating stitches on the Hungarian Stitch.

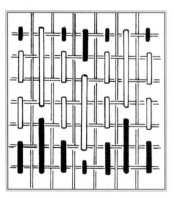

After the stitching is done, and before blocking, check for errors. Do this holding your piece up to the light. Any missed, uneven, or thin stitches will immediately become obvious.

Be sure all ends are secure and clipped close to the surface. If they are not, lumps will show through on the right side.

RIPPING AND MENDING

Sad as it may be, we all have to do a little reverse stitching every now and then. Learning how to do this quickly and properly will help make it less traumatic.

Never reuse yarn. The canvas is much too rough on the yarn to allow a smooth stitch the second time around. Sometimes ripping only a few stitches will cause problems. (See Nobuko Stitch, page 194.)

Carefully cut the wrong stitches on the right side of the canvas with your embroidery scissors (Figure 2-34a). **Be careful not to cut the canvas.** Turn the canvas over and pull out the wrong stitches with tweezers (Figure 2-34b). I do not recommend using a seam ripper to rip needlepoint. It is too easy to become carried away and rip more than you wanted to (canvas included). Ask me how I know!

You will have to unstitch a few good stitches in order to have enough yarn to work the end in. A fine crochet hook is handy for this.

In case you do cut the canvas, it is not difficult to remedy. Cut another piece of canvas that is a little larger than your cut (Figure 2-35a). Place it underneath the cut. Match the canvas threads perfectly. Baste it in place with sewing thread. Simply work your stitch through both layers of canvas, treating the two as if they were one (Figure 2-35b).

If you are doing Open Stitches, this method of mending the canvas does not work because it will show. But you can still salvage the piece! Since open work is usually done on Mono canvas or Penelope, we're not talking about Interlock canvas. (If you are doing open work on Interlock canvas, repair will be very difficult at best. This is because of the additional thread that is woven into Interlock canvas to stabilize the junctions of the canvas threads.) Rip out the rest of the cut canvas thread. Pull out one canvas thread from the width (or length, as necessary) of the canvas. There should be a thread long enough in the margin of bare canvas you left around your design area. (See page 120.) When you remove this thread, notice that it is wavy. This crimp is caused by the over and under weaving of the canvas threads that crossed this one in the finished piece of canvas. Thread a tapestry needle with this canvas thread and reweave the new canvas thread in place of the broken thread. Take care to line up the over-under crimp in the thread with the perpendicular threads (Figure 2-36). If you have stitching on this cut canvas thread, you may have to rip a little, but this is a problem that can be repaired with time and patience. Chin up! Once you have done this mending you will know why reweavers charge so much to repair tears in clothing!

2-34a, left: To rip, cut the wrong stitches on the right side of the canvas. Be careful not to cut the canvas.

2-34b, right: With tweezers, pull out the incorrect stitches from the wrong side of the canvas.

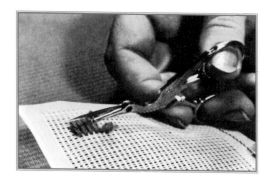

2-35a, left: To mend cut or broken canvas threads, cut a patch slightly bigger than the hole.

2-35b, right: Hold the patch in place on the wrong side of the canvas as you work the needlepoint stitches through both pieces of canvas as if they were one piece. The photo shows the wrong side of the mended area.

PIECING CANVAS

Once in a while we all miscalculate and find we need more canvas to finish a certain project. The canvas can be pieced, but I do not like to do so unless absolutely necessary. Two pieces of canvas put together can never be as strong or as seamless looking as one piece.

There are several methods for joining two pieces of canvas. However, I have found only one that I think is both reasonably invisible and sufficiently strong.

Place two pieces of canvas right sides together and stitch a seam, either by hand or on a sewing machine, as in making a seam in fabric. Match the canvas threads perfectly. Basting them in place first will help. On Penelope canvas, using silk sewing thread, Backstitch between the two canvas threads (Figure 2-37a). When you turn the canvas to the right side, one thread will be on one side of the seam and the other thread on the other side of the seam (Figure 2-37b). Finger-press the seam open and baste it in place with sewing thread. Work your needlepoint stitch through both thicknesses as if they were one (Figures 2-37b and c).

On Mono canvas, take a Backstitch between the canvas threads. Follow the same procedure as described above. The only difference is that on Penelope canvas one Tent Stitch will bridge the seam and on Mono canvas there will be a Tent Stitch on either side of the seam. This makes a weaker seam than the one on Penelope canvas because only the silk sewing thread is holding the two pieces together. Placing a needlepoint stitch (like Slanted Gobelin) across the seam will make it stronger.

2-36 Reweaving a broken canvas thread.

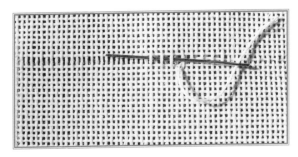

It is ***very*** difficult to get two pieces to line up so perfectly that they look like one piece. A change of color or stitch on the seam helps. A natural break in the design also may contribute to a seamless look.

Emphasizing the fact that there are two pieces of canvas can be an option with the correct design. Use the Fagoting technique to make a decorative, but not strong, seam. Prepare the edge by using the Two-Step

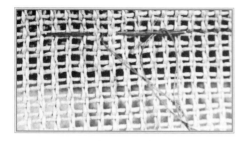

2-37a, top left: To piece canvas, place the right sides of the canvas together. Backstitch between the canvas threads with a needle and strong sewing thread ½" or so from the edge on the wrong side of the canvas.

2-37b, top right: There will be one canvas thread on one side of the seam and one canvas thread on the other side of the seam. See the arrows on the photograph, which shows the right side of the canvas.

2-37c, bottom: Pull the masking tape away as you stitch, but not all at once or the canvas will ravel. The wrong side of the canvas is shown.

Edge Finishing method on page 129 or the Hemstitching approach on page 379. Then join the two pieces of canvas with a decorative stitch. The traditional Fagoting Stitch is shown on page 378. You may also place a Looped Turkey Work Stitch on one edge and then lace the two pieces of canvas together as you stitch the Turkey Work on the second piece of canvas. (See Figure 2-38 and the directions for Looped Turkey Work, page 359.)

MAKING A SAMPLER

Making a sampler is the best way to learn your stitches. You may use Penelope 10 canvas with wool yarn. Both are versatile and allow you to do the largest number of stitches with a minimum of thickening and thinning of wool yarn. Smaller canvas may be used with other yarns. Six-ply embroidery floss works well on Mono 14.

There are many styles of samplers. See Plates 16, 25, 30, 37, 44, 45, and 50 for examples.

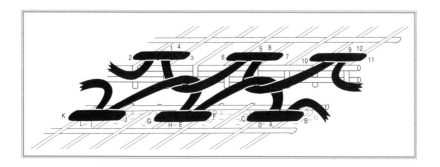

2-38 Piecing canvas with Looped Turkey Work.

To get the feel of the stitch and to have a large enough sample to see the stitch's pattern completely, I recommend that you work an average of four square inches (a square of about 2" x 2"). Sometimes there will be stitches that will not require an area that large, and others will need an even larger area to show off the stitch's pattern. Some will need a long, thin area as opposed to a square one. This sampler will be a useful reference in the future.

Place these stitch areas on your canvas at random, as in Plate 45, or plan their placement, as in Plates 25 and 30. Or place each stitch next to the preceding one, leaving a three-canvas-thread border, or divider, of 2 x 2 Slanted Gobelin. Simply work each stitch until you believe you understand its construction and have enough to be able to see the pattern.

Enlarge and reduce a stitch to make it many sizes. Study relationships between stitches. The Box Stitches are a good place to start (see Chapter 10). Do you see how a Cashmere Stitch is merely a long Mosaic? Study Giant Scotch to see how to make it bigger. Diamond Leviathan is merely a Triple Leviathan turned diagonally. Other stitches have similar relationships.

Next rotate your stitches 45° or 90° to the right and/or left. Flop tops with bottoms. Make Straight Stitches diagonal ones and vice versa. Have fun!

When you can manipulate stitch sizes, rotate the direction, and combine stitches, you are truly a master needleworker. Give it a try; you can do it!

You may wish to turn your sampler into a set design; for example, a calico cat or a rocking horse. (See Plate 44.) Your sampler should be a learning experience and a reference when planning future projects. I suggest that the basic stitches in the box below be included in your sampler (the page number for each follows the name).

Always put your initials—or even better, your name—and the date on your sampler and on every piece you make. It need not be prominent. I like to hide mine in the design somewhere. My friends think it's great fun to find them! If you care to do this,

Straight Stitches
Straight Gobelin, 139
Brick, 142
Hungarian, 148
Bargello, 168

Diagonal Stitches
Basketweave, 180
Continental, 177
Half Cross, 179
Petit Point, 187
Slanted Gobelin, 189
Byzantine #1, 199
Jacquard, 203
Milanese, 205
Oriental, 206

Box Stitches
Mosaic, 210
Diagonal Mosaic, 213
Cashmere, 215
Scotch, 220
Giant Scotch, 220

Cross Stitches
Cross , 235
Spaced Cross Tramé, 240
Upright Cross, 251
Herringbone, 256
Six-Trip Herringbone, 258
Greek, 259
Double Straight Cross, 272
Double Leviathan, 273

Diamond Leviathan, 274
Triple Leviathan, 275
Rhodes, 277
Woven Band, 287

Tied Stitches
Fly, 307

Eye Stitches
Diamond Eyelet, 317
Squared Daisies, 320

Leaf Stitches
Leaf #1, 325
Roumanian Leaf, 328

Line Stitches
Backstitch, 335
Outline/Stem, 335
Couching, 336
Binding, 338
Chain, 339

Decorative Stitches
Buttonhole, 346
Woven Spider Web, 354
Smooth Spider Web, 354
Ridged Spider Web, 355
French Knot, 356
Looped Turkey Work, 359
Japanese Ribbon, 365
Needleweaving, 367

do not place your name or anything else on the very edge. You must remember that the finishing of a piece—whether framing or pillow making or anything else— usually takes up a few rows on the edges.

CLEANING NEEDLEPOINT

Cleaning your needlepoint becomes necessary sooner or later. There are three acceptable methods: vacuum, wash in detergent, or use a commercial needlepoint cleaner. Soap leaves a film.

Hand wash badly soiled pieces. However, wash only when absolutely necessary. The reason for this is that washing removes some of the sizing. You do not want to wash it all out, for it is the sizing that helps to protect the canvas from humidity. Also, red dyes usually run. Place the clean, wet needlepoint between two clean, dry terry cloth towels. Roll. Squeeze out excess water gently. Do not twist. Block immediately. (See page 113.)

There are several commercial needlepoint cleaners that are quite good. I do not, however, recommend them for long stitches that will snag or for stitches worked with delicate fibers, because you must rub the needlepoint with a towel when using some commercial cleaners. A spray cleaner is good for touch-ups and spot removal. I question their use if you are using museum preservation techniques.

I do not trust a dry cleaner to clean my needlepoint correctly. Wool and animal hair fibers cannot be heavily steam-pressed because they shrink and mat when exposed to excessive heat and steam for too long a time. If the cleaning fluid is not clean, the colors in your needlepoint may dull. (This applies to coin-operated dry-cleaning machines also.) If you are **absolutely** sure that your cleaner will change the fluid and that he will **not** press your needlepoint and that he will steam it lightly, then send it to the cleaners. Hope for the best.

Never apply waterproofing or other similar products to your needlepoint. Do not put foam rubber or other synthetic items next to your needlepoint. (See page 130.) They do not allow the yarn to "breathe." (Natural fibers need to breathe.) There have been reports of premature rotting of the yarn.

If you are interested in museum preservation techniques, beware of putting any chemicals or acids on or near your artistry.

LEFT-HANDED STITCHES

The instructions in this book are written for right-handers, but the left-handed stitcher need not despair. It will help tremendously if you turn the book upside-down and work the stitches as you see them. Reverse the words *left* and *right* and *up* and *down* in the written instructions. (See Figure 2-39.)

I have found that most left-handed people have learned methods of their own that enable them to function in a right-handed world. There are nearly as many methods

2-39a, left; and b, right: Left-handers, take diagram shown in a and simply turn it upside down as shown in b, following the numbers of the stitches in reverse order.

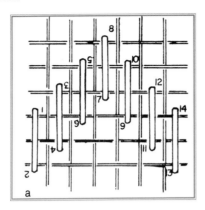

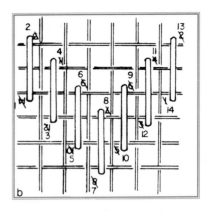

as there are people. This is particularly true of people who have done other things with their hands. If you wish to try my hint or use one of your own, it will not matter so long as the results are the same. Hold the canvas so that it is comfortable; turn it and the book so that you can attack it from the viewpoint that is most logical for you.

When a right-handed person is showing you how to stitch, ask him or her to stand directly in front of you and not beside you. His or her right hand then corresponds to your left and you see it from your viewpoint.

In this chapter I have introduced to you the basic procedures of needlepoint. You can see that it is not a difficult hobby and that with a minimum of effort and a maximum amount of pleasure, you can learn to do something with your time and your hands that will bring you joy and a feeling of accomplishment. In the next chapter we will explore stitching techniques.

2-40 How not to treat your needlepoint!

STITCHING TECHNIQUES

Not only do different yarns and a variety of stitches dress up your needlepoint piece, but there are also different stitching techniques that will enhance your stitchery. For centuries embroiderers have worked an assortment of embroidery techniques on fabrics, with the background showing as part of the design. For just as many centuries, needlepoint required that the background canvas be covered. The lines between the techniques were always distinct. In the last two decades of the twentieth century, these formerly clear lines began to blur. Needlepointers now feel free to incorporate the bare canvas as part of the design, to stitch Black Work and White Work in colors, to use Brazilian Embroidery techniques with yarns other than those native to that technique, and so on. This opens a whole new world to needlepointers!

Methods such as Pulled Thread, Hardanger, Appliqué, and Trapunto (padding) are now applied to needlepoint canvas. Beautiful and interesting effects are also created by cutting the canvas and attaching free pieces of canvas (Detached Canvas technique). Other forms of embroidery translate readily to canvas. They include Assisi, Black Work, Brazilian Embroidery, Candlewicking, Darning Patterns, Diaper Patterns, Filet, Hedebo, Hemstitching, Hardanger, Fagoting, Huck Embroidery, Reticella, Richelieu, and Teneriffe. As a result, needlepoint is an exquisite art form!

SHADING

Shading adds realism to any stitchery. (See Plate 19.) Flat, unshaded colors make a design appear more contemporary. Use light colors for highlights and for areas that would naturally catch light. Dark colors suggest shadows, edges, and recessed areas. A shaded background can be used to represent a sunrise or sunset or a storm.

The stitching technique for shading is not difficult, but knowing where to put the different shades comes only with the study of light and shadow and practice. (If you buy a painted canvas or a charted design, the shaded areas are already marked for you.)

Color selection and value (page 81) are most important in shading. Choose as many colors in your range as you can find. The closer together the colors are, the more effective your shading will be. Lay your chosen yarns on a photocopy machine (labels down) and make a black-and-white copy. Copy your painted canvas too. The values will be so much easier to see. If you cannot get the proper range of colors, **do not attempt to shade.**

For example, let us say that you have selected five colors of Persian yarn to shade a background. Letter the shades A, B, C, D, and E. It takes three areas of each color to advance from one shade to another. Therefore five colors will need thirteen areas to complete this shading process. The first area is for color A. It will take three areas to complete the transition to color B, three areas to color C, three areas to color D, and three areas to color E.

Divide the canvas areas to be shaded into thirteen sections. Follow the basic shape of the object to be shaded. For example, if you are shading an apple, the sections will be delineated by curved lines. If you are shading a sky, the areas may be marked by straight lines. Put them on your canvas with a gray waterproof marker. Start with the lightest color. Fill the first section with a 3-ply yarn of color A. In the second area, stitch with a yarn composed of two plies of color A and one of color B. In the next area, use only one ply of color A and two of color B. The fourth section is worked with three plies of color B. Continue this pattern until you have worked up to a 3-ply yarn of the last color. (See Figure 4-15 for an example.)

The charts in Figure 3-1 show the shading sequence for 3-ply and 4-ply yarns. Many stitches lend themselves to shading, but none does as well as Irregular Continental. The trick is to make the line that divides each area irregular and ragged. Stagger rows and stitches. Interlocking Gobelin, Irregular Continental, and Brick make good shading stitches. The charts at the beginnings of Chapters 8 through 17 list other stitches for shading. I'm sure you can find others.

Hint: Once in a while we all miscalculate and run out of yarn. If your luck runs like mine, the store will be out of your dye lot. When this happens, blend the new shade into the old shade by the same shading technique described above. Follow the charts in Figure 3-1, AAA(A) through BBB(B).

OPEN WORK

Leaving canvas unstitched is a real viable option. This canvas becomes a design element. You may leave it absolutely plain (Plate 47); you may paint it (Plates 5, 6, and 36); or you may add sparsely spaced stitches (Plate 48) or strategically placed stitches (Plate 49). You may also do a Pulled Thread technique (Plates 8 and 38). Consider adding embellishments. You may also use a combination of techniques in one piece.

As a general rule, Open Stitches need open spaces to work well. The cat in Plate 44 is an example of the successful exception. If you choose to leave the canvas plain, the color of the canvas becomes part of your design. Colored canvases provide choices beyond white and tan. Beautiful sunsets can be created by painting on a pale blue canvas. A few sparse horizontal stitches can create wispy clouds or trees, especially when stitched with a slub yarn. (See Figure 6-2.) Distance and depth can be controlled by how closely those stitches are placed. Use your imagination! Have fun!

3-1 Shading charts.

3-Ply Yarn		4-Ply Yarn	
Area		Area	
1	AAA	1	AAAA
2	AAB	2	AAAB
3	ABB	3	AABB
4	BBB	4	ABBB
5	BBC	5	BBBB
6	BCC	6	BBBC
7	CCC	7	BBCC
8	CCD	8	BCCC
9	CDD	9	CCCC
10	DDD	10	CCCD
11	DDE	11	CCDD
12	DEE	12	CDDD
13	EEE	13	DDDD
		14	DDDE
		15	DDEE
		16	DEEE
		17	EEEE

SUPPLIES

You will need Mono canvas for Pulled Thread.

Any yarn you can think of will serve some design purpose. Pearl is a mainstay for open work. Its various sizes make it versatile to work with, and its twist and luster add subtle design touches. It does not have to be laid (page 40), making it easy to work with. Linen does a great job. Slub yarns can make *very* interesting design contributions (Figure 6-2). Remember that the slub needs to fit comfortably through the canvas hole.

Yarn color that is close to the canvas color adds a subtle touch. Darker and contrasting colors are better on pieces whose design is not so busy.

For Open Stitches use a yarn that is decidedly finer than would be used to cover the canvas. I'm sure there are exceptions, but when I see a yarn that *almost* covers, I have to wonder, was it intentional or accidental?

TECHNIQUES

Just a few examples of various stitching techniques are included in this chapter to give you a taste of what is possible.

DRAWN THREAD WORK

Drawn Thread Work is a method of adorning the canvas by removing the canvas threads in one direction only. (See Filet and Hardanger on page 54.) The remaining threads, called bars, are then decorated. **Drawn Thread Work must be done on a frame.**

Hemstitching techniques group the remaining canvas threads in decorative patterns. They are then knotted or tied together. Page 379 has instructions for working one Hemstitching configuration. Group the threads together in any design you like. Embroidery books have many classic Hemstitching patterns in them. Invent your own.

In **Needleweaving,** the remaining canvas threads are covered by weaving over and under them with a yarn. (See page 367.) When combined with wire, a detached canvas look results (see the rabbit's ears in Plate 23). The pattern may be varied to suit your purposes. Many patterns can be created with this technique.

CUT WORK

Cut Work (Figure 3-2a) removes the threads of the canvas in both directions. How the hole is edged and filled—or not filled—and how much of the ground fabric is cut away determine the name of the technique. **Renaissance Cut Work** has the most ground canvas left intact. **Richelieu Cut Work** has more canvas cut away; **Reticella** has the most canvas cut away. **Cut Work must be done on a frame.**

 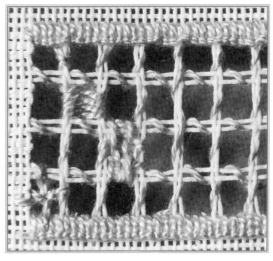

3-2a, left: Cut Work.

3-2b, right: Filet.

In **Hardanger,** the edges are bound with a Buttonhole, Satin, or Straight Gobelin Stitch before the canvas is cut. Then some of the canvas threads are removed and some are left in place. Usually four threads horizontally and four threads vertically are left; they are called bars. The bars and the holes are decorated in various styles; Loopstitch Bars (page 382) is one example.

Filet (Figure 3-2b) is essentially the same as Hardanger, except that only pairs of canvas threads are left to decorate. The threads of the canvas may be cut short at the stitching (page 381) or they can be woven back into the canvas. If you weave them back in, do this before you stitch the edge. In this case you may also opt to leave the edge of the canvas uncovered.

Hedebo, also a cousin of Hardanger, creates rounded and oval shapes. All of the bars are removed and the hole is filled, traditionally with round shapes.

Renaissance Cut Work adds bars of yarn that are then covered with the Buttonhole Stitch. Often the bars are added to odd-shaped areas to help the hole retain its shape and to keep the canvas taut. (See Figure 3-2a.)

Richelieu Cut Work merely decorates these bars with Picots.

Reticella begins like Hardanger, but the squares are quite large and the bars are traditionally decorated with Needleweaving.

STITCHING METHODS

Pulled Thread (sometimes mistakenly called Drawn Thread) is worked by pulling the threads of the canvas together to form holes or open spaces. The resulting geometric patterns give a lacy look to the canvas, as in the walls of the gazebo in Plate 38. This style of stitching can be used for backgrounds as well as designs. See Chapter 17 for instructions on how to work just a few of the many Pulled Thread stitches. Almost any stitch can be converted to a Pulled Thread stitch. Try converting some yourself; experiment with how hard you pull. I took a middle-of-the-road approach; most of the stitches could be pulled more or less hard, if you like.

Candlewicking looks like Turkey Work (page 359). Turkey Work is more dense; Candlewicking makes better fuzzy dots than a background scattered with Turkey Work. Turkey Work is slow; Candlewicking is much quicker to do. Turkey Work is quite secure; Candlewicking will pull out much more easily. This stitch is merely a Running Stitch that has been worked with a lofty yarn such as wool. The long stitches are then cut in the middle, creating a fluffy spot on your canvas. (See page 358.)

Teneriffe is a kind of Surface Darning. Needleweaving is done on yarns (bars) that have been attached to the canvas instead of darning on the canvas threads. In Tenneriffe, the canvas threads are still intact over the design area; they are not removed, as in Needlelace, Hemstitching, and other Cut Work. (See Detached Weaving, page 249.)

A lacy stitch that does not use bars of yarn, such as Hollie Point, then becomes Surface Darning because it does not penetrate the canvas. (When Hollie Point is worked over an area where the canvas threads have been removed, then it is more like a Needlelace technique, below.) Refer to Needleweaving, Needlelace, and other embroidery books for more ideas.

Needlelace fills an open area where all of the canvas threads have been removed. The corners of Hemstitching are filled with Needlelace. Bars of yarn are laid across the opening, and a pattern of stitches (see Loopstitch Bars) or Needleweaving is done on them. Loose tension will result in a lovely open pattern. (See the example pictured with Hemstitching, page 379.) Stitches like Hollie Point can also be worked over this open hole. Books on Needlelace will provide you with more stitches than space allows here.

OPEN STITCHES

Open Stitches are those that are deliberately worked so that the canvas shows through. A painted canvas could become part of the design. Plate 6 shows a background that has been shaded with paint. Shading here was created with one color of yarn! The effect is stunning!

Almost any stitch will be successful when adapted to an open technique. The most prominent exceptions I can think of are highly textured stitches, like some of the decorative stitches.

There are several techniques that work. Experiment and see what you like!

Figure 3-3 shows several stitching methods you can use to make almost every stitch an open stitch. Experiment. Invent your own open stitches!

PATTERN DESIGN

Stitches create pattern. Some pattern groups are named because they share common characteristics. **Black Work** designs create open geometric patterns of varying

3-3a, top left: Work the stitch as is with a fine yarn. This Scotch Stitch sample was worked with sewing thread. Notice that the stitch looks uneven or poorly stitched. If you look closely, you will notice that every other motif looks the same. Each intersection of canvas threads alternates with a horizontal canvas thread and a vertical one. There is an odd number of components in each motif. This means that the same stitch within each motif alternates in crossing horizontal and vertical canvas threads at each intersection. The finer the yarn, the more sensitive it is to the bumps in the canvas threads. These bumps cause the light to be reflected one way when the fine sewing thread hits a horizontal canvas thread and another way when it hits the thread as it covers a vertical thread. A motif with a multiple of an even number of stitches, like Mosaic, would in theory look smoother. Discover for yourself.

3-3b, top right: Omit every other stitch.

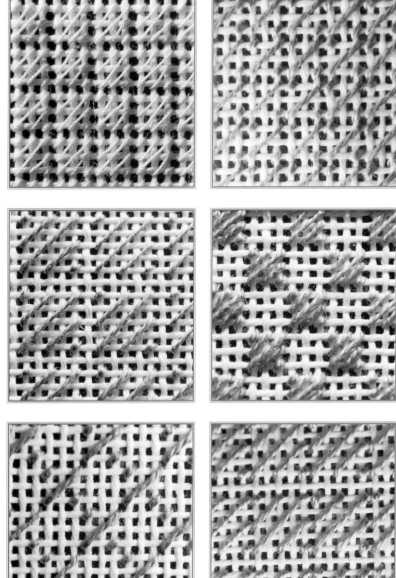

3-3c, middle left: Skip every other canvas thread in the motif and around the motif.

3-3d, middle right: Omit every other motif.

3-3e, bottom left: Omit every other motif and every other stitch in the motif.

3-3f, bottom right: Leave a blank canvas thread between rows of motifs (but not the columns) and skip every other canvas thread in the motif. Notice that three of the motifs in the lower left corner were stitched in a finer yarn than the others in the photo. This gives a finer and even more open look to the area.

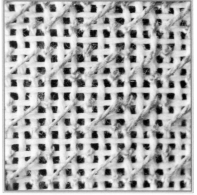

3-3g, top left: Leave a blank canvas thread all the way around each motif, skip every other canvas thread in the motif, and skip every other motif.

3-3h, top right: Skip every other stitch in each motif and leave a blank canvas thread between the rows of motifs, but not the columns. Notice again that the lower left corner was worked in a finer yarn than the rest was.

3-3i, bottom: Skip every other canvas thread in each motif.

density. They are stitched primarily with a Double Running Stitch and a Backstitch. Correctly done, Black Work should be completely reversible. At one time, Black Work was done in colors, then decades later in black on white. Now we stitch these lovely geometric designs in colors again. (See Figure 3-4.)

Laid Filling Stitches are couched yarns that are held in place by tying them down in a variety of patterns. The Lattice Stitch (page 376) is an example. The wonderful colored canvases will blend well with these stitches.

Diaper Patterns are formed when motifs, such as one Scotch Stitch, are combined so that clear visual diagonal lines are formed in both directions. These are created by color, design, and/or texture. One example is a checkerboard. (See the Reversed and Checker Box Stitches.) The lower window in Plate 54 is stitched in a Diaper Pattern.

Pattern Darning is a form of embroidery that is worked in the Running Stitch. Rows run parallel to either the lengthwise canvas threads or the horizontal ones. The length of the stitches is varied so that patterns are formed. Only one or two canvas threads are picked up between the long stitches on the front of the canvas. This produces almost no backing at all. The resulting patterns go by many names, such as Diaper Patterns, Huck Darning, Damask, and Huckaback. (See the Angelis Stitch, page 377.)

This stitch should not be confused with the Double Darning Stitch or the Padded Double Darning Stitch (page 155), which are variations of Pattern Darning.

3-4 Black Work.

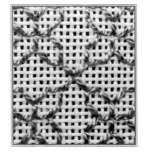

Combine different stitches and then follow the above suggestions. Stitch some areas of the background and not others.

The possibilities are endless.

Remember that every stitch makes a pattern. Please, do *NOT* throw in stitches just to throw in stitches. Each stitch becomes a design element; it needs to work for your design. The cat in Plate 27 uses many different stitch patterns, but each one serves a purpose. The front leg really appears to be in front of the body. The head looks like it is in front of the body too. When viewed from a distance, the cat reads as a whole, the sum of its parts, and not as a random patchwork of patterns.

Too many medium to strong patterns make your work too busy and the design is lost. You could, of course, leave the canvas as is.

Have fun. Nothing is wrong if you like it and it works!

APPLIQUÉ

You are not limited to one size of canvas within a design. It is possible to appliqué a larger size canvas onto a smaller one or a smaller one onto a larger one. For example, a piece worked on Mono 10 may have one or more areas of greater detail if you appliqué a piece of Mono 18 onto it. This way you do not have to work a whole piece in a small-sized canvas just to get one little area of detail. It also adds interest in having two or more different sizes of stitches.

The process is really not as difficult or complicated as you might think. Figure 3-5 gives step-by-step instructions. Fabric was appliquéd onto the canvas with the Blind Stitch (see page 129).

TEXTURE

Texture can be created with stitches, but in order to achieve high relief, you will need more than yarn. The techniques presented below employ various methods to achieve a three-dimensional look. They are fun to do!

3-5a, left: To appliqué another piece of canvas onto your design, first work the background around the spot to be appliquéd, leaving a small area of blank canvas, then block. In this series of photos, a woman's hand is being appliquéd onto a piece of needlepoint designed and stitched by Dodi Maki.

3-5b, right: On another piece of canvas, stitch the design to be appliquéd, leaving 3" of blank canvas all the way around it. After blocking, ravel the canvas right up to the stitches.

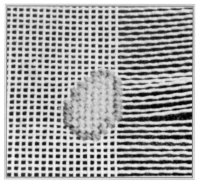

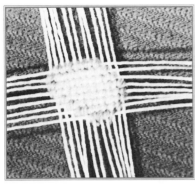

3-5c, top left: Ravel the canvas on the second, third, and fourth sides.

3-5d, top right: Lay the hand in position on the canvas and poke the remaining canvas threads into the background canvas, using a needle if it helps.

3-5e, second row left: This is how the back of the canvas looks after one side of canvas threads has been poked through to the back.

3-5f, second row right: Thread a needle with the loose canvas threads. Work them into the stitches of the background for an inch or so.

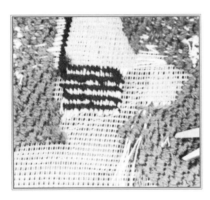

3-5g, third row left: Cut these canvas threads close to the background stitches. In case you have wondered about the dark Continental Stitches worked every other row and about the large area of blank canvas—the woman's dress is to be appliquéd fabric. The Continental Stitches were worked to provide a place to work in the canvas threads from the appliquéd face. They will be covered later by the dress fabric.

3-5h, third row right: When the threads on all four sides are worked in, the right side should look like this.

3-5i, bottom: Work the background stitches right up to the appliquéd stitches, working through both pieces of canvas. Check the canvas threads on the back of the canvas for guidance in keeping the background stitches even.

Brazilian Embroidery creates medium relief with just yarn and stitches. (The Drizzle, Cast-on, and Double Cast-On stitches are examples. See them on pages 370 to 372.) Traditionally it was done with fine yarns on fabric, but you can work these stitches with any size or type of yarn for interesting effects.

Stumpwork is quite dimensional. The bulk of the dimension is achieved through highly textured stitches and Padded Appliqué. Some of the more common Stumpwork stitches are included in this book. See Raised Close Herringbone, Rose Leaf, Raised Rope, Buttonhole on a Knot, and Raised Buttonhole on pages 331, 332, 341, 348, and 350.

Padded Appliqué adds additional interest by stuffing the area that you appliquéd. To do so, the appliquéd piece must be slightly larger than the area where it will be stitched down. Attach it to the canvas as above. Just before closing the last open spot, stuff the area with polyester fiberfill or quilt batting. You may mold and shape an area of texture with multiple layers of differently shaped felt pieces. This form of appliqué is used often in Stumpwork.

Trapunto is a form of quilting; the design area is stuffed, but the background is not. Mono canvas must be used because the canvas needs to give under the tension of the stuffing. To achieve this three-dimensional look, first stitch the needlepoint. Then sew a piece of fabric over the design area to be stitched. Be careful to make your stitches invisible. If you are not already using a frame, you must use one now. Next, slit the fabric so that you can stuff it with polyester fiberfill. Stuff it as much as you think you can. Using a whip stitch, sew the slit in the fabric closed.

With so much padding, the finished piece needs to be stretched on a frame permanently. If it is not, the background may buckle. While it is possible to do Trapunto on fabrics that are not stretched on a frame, it is difficult to do so on canvas. More stuffing is needed for the canvas to give. This added tension will buckle the background when the canvas is taken off the frame. The stomach of the frog in Plate 18 is a wonderful example of this technique.

DETACHED CANVAS

This technique was developed to add a third dimension to needlepoint. It is a fun thing to play with. Very interesting effects can be created (see Plate 2).

You must plan in advance to do this. First, draw a sketch of your final design (Figure 3-6). From this drawing, make *separate* patterns for those components that you would like to stand out. Be sure to indicate where each piece will be attached to the main canvas. Next, make a drawing of the main canvas, minus the stand-out parts, except for where they attach. Transfer this drawing of your main canvas onto any canvas of your choosing. Transfer all of the stand-out component pattern pieces to **Interlock** Mono canvas. Leave a small margin of blank canvas around the stand-out parts.

Stitch the main canvas as you would any other piece—except you must leave blank those areas where the stand-out pieces will attach. Block (see page 113). While the main canvas is drying, stitch the components.

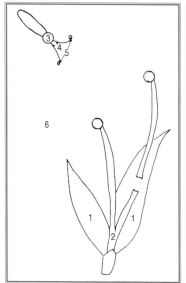  

Still leaving a margin around each stand-out piece, work the needlepoint. Stitch two canvas threads all the way around in Tent Stitch. Work it in a fine yarn if you like. This produces a stronger edge that is less likely to ravel. This also gives you a guide to follow later when working the Buttonhole Stitch. Leave the area to be attached blank. Block. Coat the edges and the back side with a commercial antifraying solution, clear nail polish, or glue made specially for fabric. Allow this to dry **thoroughly.** Use natural glue for museum preservation techniques. Then, **very carefully,** cut the canvas out from around the stitches. Do not cut the yarn or unravel the stitches. Handle the piece gently.

Then work the Buttonhole Stitch around the raw edges, except where the piece is to be attached to the main canvas. It should go in about two canvas threads. When working this Buttonhole Stitch, catch a piece of lightweight wire on the wrong side. This enables you to bend and mold your pieces into pleasing curves. Line each piece with fabric.

There are other things you can do with the free parts. Attach a tip of a leaf to the main canvas. Apply stiffener to the back side of the stand-out part. Mold it into the shape you want before the stiffener dries. You may also apply an iron-on interfacing to the back of each part. (See page 118.) This adds body and a lining. (However, do not do this if your needlepoint stitches are textured. Ironing will flatten them.) Or leave all components free. Or do almost anything you can think of!

Baste the stand-out pieces onto the main canvas with sewing thread matching the threads of the canvas. Do needlepoint in these blank areas, treating the two pieces of canvas as if they were one.

Use this technique for leaves, bows, skirts, hats, feathers, wings, paws, roofs, etc.

This chapter has given you a taste of what can be done on needlepoint canvas. Unfortunately, space does not permit me to go into more detail. Many fine books

3-6a, left: Detached canvas techniques: background.

3-6b, center: Detached canvas techniques: attached elements.

3-6c, right: Detached canvas showing elements superimposed on background. Designed by the author.

on all kinds of embroidery techniques are available in needlework shops and bookstores. Try used bookstores as well; stitching techniques never get old, just recycled and rejuvenated!

Part 1 has described the basic preparations through stitching techniques. Part 2 will teach you color and design so that you may evaluate another's design or do your own. Part 3 will show you how to put it all together, including blocking and finishing of your needlepoint project. Last, but not least, is the most fun part: Part 4, the stitches shown in simple, clear, and effective drawings and photos.

Photo 5—Ball Gown: *stitched by Brenda Hart; designed by Sharon Garmize; yarns and stitches selected by Brenda Hart. [Smith]*

P~~art~~ ~~Two~~ DESIGN AND COLOR

Photo 6—Bear in Birches: *stitched by Gail Bloom; designed by Charley Harper; yarns and stitches selected by Gail Bloom. [Smith]*

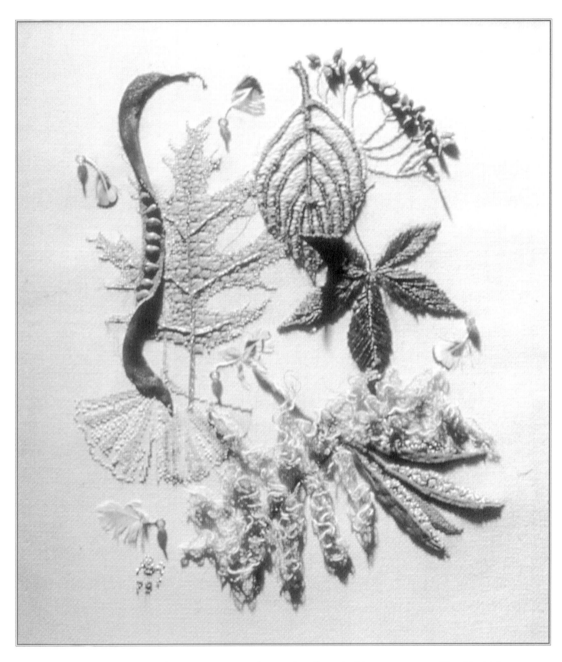

Photo 7—Leaves: *designed and stitched by Bernice Janofsky. [Smith]*

DESIGN

*W*hether you create your own design or buy someone else's, it will behoove you to analyze it. Needlepoint canvases might wind up on the closet floor because there is something about them you don't like. Maybe it's the design, the colors, the stitch selections, a stitching error—or a combination. Analysis of the design and of the color selections before stitching may prevent your canvas from winding up on *your* closet floor.

The following questions need to be answered before you begin:

1. What is to be the use of the finished needlepoint piece?

2. What is the subject matter?

3. What is the shape of the finished design—square, rectangular, round, or irregular?

4. What kind of composition (arrangement of objects) are you considering?

5. Do you like aerial (realistic) or Oriental (decorative) perspective?

6. Do you wish the objects in your design to be modeled (realistic) or flat (decorative)?

7. Do you want shadows (realism)? If so, determine the source of light—from the upper right or left.

8. What is the focal point?

Once you have the answers to these questions, you have some kind of starting point.

Deciding on the shape of the design gives a needed outer confinement. You might later find that the boundaries need to be changed, but you have to start somewhere.

FORM

Form is the basic shape or structure of *all* objects. Everything can be reduced to a sphere, a cube, a cone, or a cylinder (Figure 4-1).

Every good design should have a variety of forms, yet some of them should be repeated. Constant repetition is boring, and constant variety is confusing. Repeated forms add texture (Figure 4-2).

TEXTURE

Texture is important to a design because it adds interest. (See Plates 3, 4, 5, 8, 38, 47, and 49, plus many others.) It creates patterns of lights and darks; heavily

4-1 All things boil down to four shapes: sphere, cube, cone, and cylinder.

textured areas appear darker (Figure 4-3). In needlepoint, most of the texture is added to the design with stitches, fibers, and yarns.

Texture is lost as the design moves farther from the viewer (Plates 3, 5, 7, and 19). The stitches should be reduced in size for background objects. The individual bricks on a brick wall appear less and less distinct as you move farther away. Keep this in mind as you stitch a design. This is an imperative element in realistic design, but it is still important in nonrealistic designs. Attention to this detail makes more attractive compositions. Texture can be added by using yarns or stitches (Plate 51) or both.

UNITY

Unity ties a design together and gives it a focus (Figure 4-4). Such elements as focal point, point of entry, and proportion combine to create a unified design.

4-2a-b Note that all four shapes are represented in this drawing of a boat.

FOCAL POINT

The focal point catches the eye and shows it something of interest. (Figure 4-5). Avoid putting it in the center of the picture. Things that are slightly off to one side are more appealing. A focal point can also be made with color (Plate 6). The focal point on people and animals is most often their faces or what they are doing.

The artist who creates a design should make a pleasing focal point. He or she will create interest several ways. Look for it where the lightest light color (or white)

4-3 Texture.

4-4a Unity—wrong.

4-4b Unity—right.

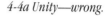

(b)

4-5a Focal point—wrong.   4-5b Focal point—right.

meets the darkest dark color (or black). (See the eyes in the mask in Plate 15, and the cat on the clothesline in Plate 39.) Sometimes a very warm color (see Plates 19 and 20) or a very large area will command the viewer's attention over the strength of a light color next to a dark one.

Squint your eyes and look through your eyelashes—or take off your glasses. If you disregard what you *want* to be the focal point, you will soon see what *really is* the center of interest. Enhancing a focal point—or creating one—can be accomplished with your stitching by adding texture, shine, and pattern. Your choice of fiber and yarn can add texture and shine. Both of these cause objects to come forward. The lack of texture and shine causes things to recede.

The stitches you choose can increase or decrease texture and, thus, attention. They also make patterns. Strong patterns attract attention. (See the stitch charts at the beginnings of Chapters 8 to 15.) If pattern is omitted or reduced in one spot of a busy design, attention will be focused there. (See the lawn in Plate 3 and the bird's nest in Plate 8.) The reverse is also ture.

The focal point that is located in the foreground (the first plane) is much easier to stitch than the one located in the middle ground (the second plane) or the background (the third plane). (See Plate 8.) Any amount of texture, shine, pattern, and warm color can be used to create a focal point—assuming that that amount is compatible with the rest of the design.

Some designs have several planes. Each plane must appear to be in front of the ones behind it or in back of the ones in front of it. So, in order to stitch the focal point with texture, shine, pattern, and warm color, the planes before the focal point must still appear to be in front of the focal point, but still not detract from it. If you want anything (including the focal point) textured in the middle ground or the background, then the items in the planes before it must also be textured. Keep in mind that the most textured plane is the first one, or the foreground. Each plane has less texture as you go back.

The book title in the tote bag on the title page is still the focal point—despite the warm colors, textures, shiny embellishments, and strong patterns in front of it. The warm-colored yarns and the shiny scissors are decidedly in front of the textured basket, which is in front of some yarns, which are in front of other yarns. The black-and-white book title is in the fourth plane, but still it is the focal point.

See Figure 4-18 (page 75) for guidelines on where to place the focal point.

POINT OF ENTRY

A point of entry takes the viewer into the picture (Figure 4-6 and Plate 32). A door, slightly ajar, invites the viewer inside a building (Plate 7). A road, path, or sidewalk leads the viewer to a building, the focal point (Plate 7). A stream entices the viewer to follow it into the picture (Plate 19). A closed gate and a river with no entry point bar the viewer from coming in.

4-6a, left: Point of entry—wrong.

4-6b, right: Point of entry—correct.

4-7a, left: Proportion—wrong.

4-7b, right: Proportion—correct.

PROPORTION

Fill the space given with your design or focal point (Figure 4-7). A too-small object will be lost in a too-large area. Space divided into thirds is generally considered pleasingly proportionate.

BALANCE

Your design should not violate the principle of balance. You can attain either a formal or an informal effect by how you choose to balance the design.

FORMAL OR SYMMETRICAL BALANCE

In pictures that have formal balance, the right side of the picture is a mirror image of the left side (Figure 4-8a). The two sides do not have to be exactly alike, but they should be very similar.

4-8a, left: Formal (symmetrical) balance.

4-8b, right: Informal (asymmetrical) balance.

4-9a Formal (symmetrical) balance.

4-9b No balance.

4-9c Informal (asymmetrical) balance.

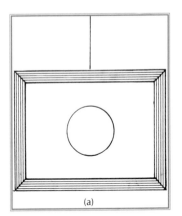

(a)

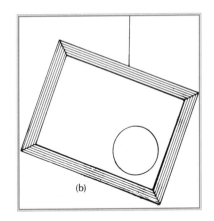

(b)

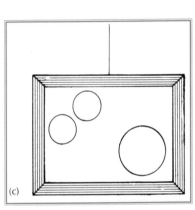

(c)

INFORMAL BALANCE

Informal balance is a little harder to see than formal balance. Visualize a picture of a circle hanging on a string (Figure 4-9a).

When the circle is in the center, the picture is formally balanced. Yet when the circle is moved to the lower right corner, the picture seems to tilt, because that corner looks heavier than the rest of the picture (Figure 4-9b). Now add two smaller circles to the upper left corner. The picture straightens out because it is now informally balanced (Figure 4-9c). It is easier to make an odd number of objects balance informally, although an even number can be made to work (Figure 4-8b).

LINE

The art world uses seven definitions of line. Only five apply to needlepoint:

1. Line carries its own inherent beauty (Hogarth's Line of Beauty) (Figure 4-10a).

2. Line divides or limits an area (Figure 4-10b).

3. Line defines forms (Figure 4-10c).

4. Line catches and guides the eye throughout the design (Figure 4-10d).

5. Line creates design or arrangement (Figure 4-10e).

THE LANGUAGE OF LINE

Lines, by themselves, tell many stories. Each type of line imparts a mood or feeling. Use the type of line you need for your design. Do not use conflicting types of lines. Lines that imply hate and war (conflicting diagonals) should not be used with lines that imply tranquility and calm (horizontal lines). (See Figure 4-11 for examples.)

Figure 4-12 (page 73) tells the language of line.

Every design should have some curved lines, some straight lines, Hogarth's Line of Beauty, and at least one subjective line. A **subjective line** (Figure 4-13, page 73) is one that the eye connects behind an object to complete the line.

Static points (Figure 4-14, page 73) are spots created by line, color, or contrast in values. They hold the eye so that it never leaves that spot to continue to look at the rest of the picture. In Figure 4-15 (page 73), the moon and its corona could create a static point. The corona is very close in color (value) to the moon, so its starkly round outline is not readily apparent. Then the moon and its corona read as one big circle, creating another potential static point. The static point of the doughnut-shaped corona is broken by color; the darker sky is slowly blended into the lighter colored corona. The branch of the tree also breaks the corona's potential static point.

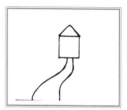

4-10a

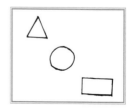

4-10b

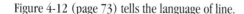

4-10c

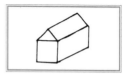

4-10d

4-10e

4-11a, top: Horizontal lines are restful.

4-11b, second row, left: Vertical lines are stately.

4-11c, second row, right: Curved lines are graceful.

4-11d, third row, left: Diagonal lines show action.

4-11e, third row, right: Hogarth's Line of Beauty.

4-11f, bottom left: Conflicting diagonals indicate war and hate.

4-11g, bottom right: Rhythmic curves mean joy and spaciousness.

HORIZONTAL	☰	TRANQUILITY, REPOSE
VERTICAL	⦀	DIGNITY, STATELINESS
DIAGONAL	\\\	DYNAMIC MOVEMENT, INSTABILITY
CURVED	∿	GRACE, BEAUTY
CONFLICTING DIAGONAL	⤫⤫	HATE, WAR, CONFUSION
RHYTHMIC CURVES	ƐƐƐƐ	JOYOUSNESS, SPACE
HOGARTH'S LINE OF BEAUTY	∽	BEAUTY

4-12 The language of line.

4-13 A subjective line is a broken one that the eye automatically connects behind an object. The table continues on the other side of the vase. The rim of the vase is hidden behind the leaf. Can you find other subjective lines in this drawing?

4-15 The static point in this design was broken using shading in the stitching technique. Designed by Cindy Pendleton and stitched by the author.

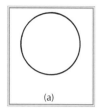 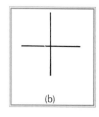

(a) (b)

4-14a-b Avoid these static points in your design. Strong colors can also create static points.

4-16a, left: The horses, and your eye as well, go right out of the picture. This is not good composition.

4-16b, right: Not only does your eye stay inside the picture, but the picture is more interesting as well. This is good composition.

THE DYNAMICS (OR ACTION) OF LINE

The lines of a design can lead the eye out of the picture, never to return (Figure 4-16). Never take a line into the corner of a picture, for the same reason. This *must* be avoided at all costs. Avoid arrows, a road, or any other lines that point out of the picture. This applies to stitches also. The Oriental Stitch (page 206), for example, forms rows of arrowheads. Make them point toward the center of the picture, not its edge. Reverse the stitch if necessary.

There are many devices that you can use to stop this action. A spot of appropriate color just beyond the offending line will do the job. Curve a road or path back inside the picture. Use a hill, a curve, or a tree to stop the action. A house, a fence, or a hat on the end of the baseball bat are also effective in keeping the eye inside the picture. If you do use a fence, there should always be an open gate (page 68) that leads the viewer's eye around the inside of the picture. A building should always have an open door. (See Plate 7.)

Once stitching has begun, other tricks will help correct troublesome lines. Drape leaves, flowers, vines, branches, and such over one or both parallel lines, crosses, and circles. Use a row or a line of dark stitches along one side and the top (or bottom) of a door or gate to imply that it is open. Sometimes just reducing the contrast of light and dark colors is enough to divert attention to a more pleasing focal point. Do this by choosing yarn colors slightly lighter and/or darker than the artist indicated on the design.

Once you start thinking about this problem, you will come up with many solutions of your own.

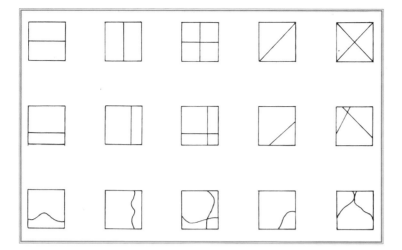

4-17 Space becomes far more interesting as it is divided unevenly and as straight lines are curved.

COMPOSITION

Where you put the objects and lines in your design is considered part of composition.

The **distribution of space** is very important. Figure 4-17 shows how space can be divided. Notice: As the focal point is removed from the center of the picture, the design becomes more interesting. As these lines are curved, even more interest is created.

To find the best spot for the center of interest of your design, divide the length and width of your space into five equal parts (Figure 4-18a). Use any line, horizontally or vertically, but be sure there are two spaces between it and the closest boundary of the picture (Figure 4-18b-e). Where these lines cross is the best place to put your center of interest.

Adding other things to a picture is easier when you have a starting point. Each object that you place in a picture should be tied in with or overlapped with the others. (See Plates 3, 5, 12, 13, 50, and others.)

There are times when you can break all these rules and still achieve an effective design. For example, a successful design may have an element that is not tied in, but it still works.

My mother always told me that I had to learn to make a cake from scratch before I could use a cake mix. You, too, should learn to design by the rules before you break them.

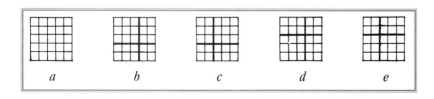

4-18a-e Place the center of interest off-center for more effective composition.

4-19a-b In aerial perspective, all things get smaller as they reach an imaginary vanishing point.

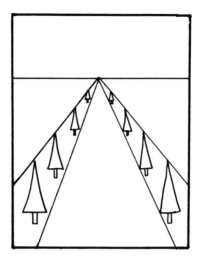

PERSPECTIVE

Perspective can be achieved with line. The creation of perspective through color will be discussed on page 85.

AERIAL PERSPECTIVE

In **aerial perspective,** objects get smaller as they recede into the background. Figure 4-19 shows an imaginary vanishing point. As things approach this spot they get smaller. Proper perspective takes practice to perfect. I have merely introduced you to the subject here. (See Plates 3, 5, 7, 12, 13, 19, 29, and 54 for examples of good perspective.) If you want to go into it further, I suggest you study an art book that deals with perspective.

ORIENTAL PERSPECTIVE

In Plates 10 and 35, all objects seem to be right up front. The size and shape of the objects, as well as the color (page 85), create this illusion, which is known as **Oriental perspective.**

IDEA SOURCES

If you wish to do your own design, there are many idea sources available to you. Sometimes you can copy (for your own use only) directly from children's coloring books, stained-glass pattern books, and appliqué books.

Sometimes you can combine two or more designs to make one. To do this, trace all the design elements that you like and wish to include in your design. Cut them out. On another piece of paper, draw the outer boundaries of your design. Arrange all the loose pieces in a pleasing composition (Figure 4-20). Follow the Design Checklist (page 110) to determine whether you have created a good design (artistically, that is). Tape the design in place before a breeze or a sneeze takes it away.

The design for the belt in Plate 52 was inspired by its buckle. You can find many design ideas from similar sources and from fabric and wallpaper. A photo of something may inspire you. The tree roots stitched in Plate 24 were inspired by a real live tree whose roots were exposed, just as you see them in the needlepoint.

Viewpoint can be the difference between the mundane and the unusual (Plates 24 and 25). It can mean an interesting design where none could otherwise be found. The cat's-eye view in Plate 41 is an excellent example of unusual viewpoint.

Now that you have a design that you like, learn how to color it in the next chapter.

4-20a-c Trace elements from two or more designs (these are by Ed Sibbett, Jr.) and cut them out. Then rearrange them in a pleasing design on another piece of paper.

Photo 8—Angel Annalisa: *stitched by Carol J. Noel; designed by Janice Gaynor; yarns and stitches selected by Carol J. Noel and Nancy Smith.* [P. Christensen]

*I*n most types of needlepoint, you must at least choose the colors of the yarns whether or not you have done your own design. If you have bought a kit that comes with yarn or chosen a charted design, this decision is made for you. Otherwise, the color choice is yours.

In doing needlepoint, the design that you stitch can be done for you, or you may do your own.

COLOR USES

PREWORKED CANVAS

A **preworked canvas** has the design stitched for you. All you have to do is choose the background colors and fill in the background. This may be plain or fancy or somewhere in between. Of course, how difficult the background is to stitch depends on how plain or fancy a background you choose. Remember that the background stitch must be less prominent than the design. Otherwise, your design will be too busy.

A dark background makes colors seem brighter. A light background makes most colors seem softer.

PAINTED CANVAS

A **painted canvas** has a design on the canvas, ready for you to stitch. You can buy this type of needlepoint canvas, or you can paint your own. The color choice is still yours. Sure, it's painted in color—but there are *lots* of reds and *lots* of blues. So— which one? Does it matter? Yes, it matters a lot!

CHARTED DESIGNS

A **charted design** is a design worked out on graph paper; symbols are used to show different colors. To stitch, you start in the center of a blank piece of canvas and the center of the chart. Count the stitches and work them on your canvas. If you can count, you've got it made! Most often the exact colors are specified on the chart. If not, the color choice is yours.

BARGELLO

Bargello, also a charted design, begins with blank canvas. Here, too, you begin in the center of your design and the center of the canvas. Work the main line or framework (page 168) to the right and to the left. Then all you have to do is repeat the pattern. (See "Illusions, Bargello Pillow," front cover.)

FOUR-WAY BARGELLO

Four-Way Bargello is a little bit different from Bargello in spacing and putting the design on canvas. (It is discussed in more detail on page 171.) Its colors are similar to those of Bargello—usually in one family of colors with an accent color. Or the colors can blend from one to another—for example, from orange to yellow with a touch of brown for accent.

COLOR THEORY

Once you understand what color can do to make your design work, you will see why a brief study of color is important. Color can make mountains in the background of a landscape appear to be far away (Plate 50). Color can give objects form or shape by shadows (Plate 17). Color can be used to develop a center of attention in a busy design (Plate 54). Color can also create moods, such as joy and warmth.

THE COLOR WHEEL

The color wheel (Plate 2) should be your guide to selecting and using color. There are three *primary* colors: red, yellow, and blue. The *secondary* colors are orange, green, and violet. The other colors are *tertiary* colors.

Warm colors are those colors on the color wheel from yellow to orange to red-violet. The colors on the other side of the color wheel from yellow-green to blue to violet are *cool*. True yellow and true violet are fairly neutral regarding warmth or coolness.

Even though red is considered a warm color, we can still have a cool red or a warm red. **Color relates to its environment.** When we compare two reds, the one that leans toward violet on the color wheel is cooler than the one that leans toward orange (Plate 1). By the same token, in considering two blues, you can see that the one that leans more toward violet is warmer than the one that leans toward green.

The warmth or coolness of color is an important concept. Warm colors come forward, and cool colors recede. This principle is what makes the houses in Plate 50 appear to be in front of the mountains.

Adding gray to a color also make it recede. This is the technique that is usually used to make mountains and faraway landscapes appear to be distant.

DIMENSIONS OF COLORS

Color has three dimensions: hue, value, and intensity (chroma).

HUE

Hue is simply another word for color. Red, yellow, and blue are hues. Warmth or coolness is a part of hue.

VALUE

Value refers to a color's darkness or lightness. A light green leaf is higher in value than a dark green leaf.

Value is the *most* important of the dimensions of color. To change the value of a color, such as primary red, add white to make a tint. Add black to make a shade. Doing this does not change the hue—only the value changes.

Look at the black-and-white value scale (Figure 5-1). White is at level 1 and black is at level 9. Primary red is at level 6, primary yellow is at level 2, and primary blue is at level 7. It takes only a little black added to red and blue to lower their value, but much white is needed to raise their value. Yellow is just the opposite. It takes very little white to raise the value of yellow and quite a lot of black to lower it. Primary yellow naturally starts out higher on the value scale than primary red and primary blue.

The more skilled artisan works on a wider range on the value scale than the beginner. (See Plates 3, 7, and 19.) Some color schemes will stay primarily at the top of the value scale. We call these *high key* or *high major* (Plates 46 and 47). A snow scene is also a high-key picture. Others will rest mainly in the middle of the value scale. These are referred to as *middle key* or *intermediate major.* Middle values are easiest for beginners to work with. Still others are at the bottom of the scale. These are called *low key* or *low major,* as in "Illusions, Bargello Pillow" (front cover). Imagine a dark, stormy night scene; it is low major.

To determine the key of a picture, consider the overall look. Dark colors can—and should—be found in a picture that is high key and vice versa.

Some types of designs require colors of nearly equal value ("Art Nouveau Frame," front cover). Oriental perspective (page 76) is achieved with colors close in value.

Value is easily seen when you compare black-and-white photographs and color photographs of the same thing. Even though colors are different, they will photograph as the same gray in a black-and-white image if their values are equal. A photocopy machine is invaluable in evaluating your design's color scheme. Make several black-and-white copies of your design. Keep track of color numbers and stitches on one. The others will be useful if you need to change colors or design elements. Feel free to cut and paste.

Put your yarns on a photocopy machine—labels down, so you will know later what you are looking at! Use the resulting black-and-white copy to compare the values of

5-1 Black-and-white value scale.

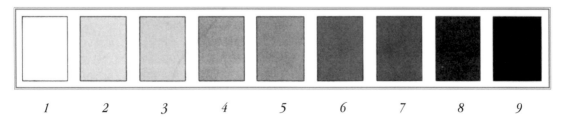

1   2   3   4   5   6   7   8   9

your yarns to the values on the black-and-white copy of your design. The better the values match, the more successful your color choices will be.

INTENSITY

The *intensity* of a color is the strength of pure pigment. To change the intensity of a color, add black, white, or some other color. Colors of lower (darker) intensity recede. When the intensity is changed, the value is sometimes changed.

COLOR SCHEMES FROM THE COLOR WHEEL

The color wheel can be—and should be—very useful in selecting color schemes for your needlepoint. We will discuss five kinds of color schemes in this book. There are others.

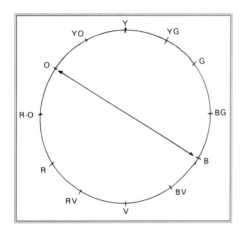

5-2 Complementary color scheme.

COMPLEMENTARY COLOR SCHEMES

The **complementary** color scheme is, perhaps, the one we've all heard the most about (Figure 5-2). Complementary colors are the colors opposite each other on the color wheel (Plate 2). Knowing this doesn't seem to help, you say? Then use the following hint: When complementary colors are used in equal intensity, the result can be jarring to the eye. However, when the primary color's intensity is changed, the result is more pleasing. For example, a pink rose with bright green leaves is very pretty (Plate 48). A complementary scheme is more difficult to work with than the next two.

ANALOGOUS COLOR SCHEMES

The **analogous** color scheme is the one most people seem to prefer. It utilizes three colors that lie next to each other on the color wheel (Figure 5-3). Any group of three may be chosen (Plates 5 and 16). For interest, you may add a small amount of the complement of the main color (Plate 15). In Figure 5-3, that would be violet.

MONOCHROMATIC COLOR SCHEMES

The **monochromatic** color scheme lends itself readily to Bargello designs. It is several colors in the same family—or, in other words, several tints and shades of one color. This color scheme is used in the projects in Plates 25, 27, 46, and 47. An accent color adds interest. Remember, black and white are not colors.

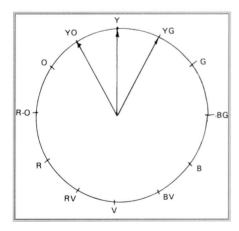

5-3 Analogous color scheme.

TRIADIC COLOR SCHEMES

The **triadic** color scheme uses three colors that are an equal distance apart on the color wheel (Figure 5-4). A line drawn inside the circle from one color to the next forms an equilateral triangle. Red, yellow, and blue are one example; orange, green, and violet are another.

SPLIT COMPLEMENTARY COLOR SCHEMES

The **split complementary** color scheme uses one color on one side of the color wheel and the two neighbors of its complement on the other side. For example, yellow and violet are complements. One split complement would be red-violet, blue-violet, and yellow (Plate 41); another is yellow-orange, yellow-green and violet (Figure 5-5).

By sticking to a color scheme, you avoid busyness in color. You are then limited to two or three colors and their shades (black added) and tints (white added) and mixtures of them.

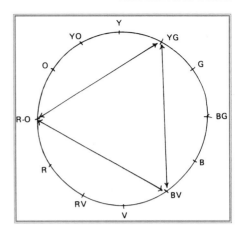

5-4 Triadic color scheme.

CREATING MOODS FROM COLOR

The psychology of color is important because color sets moods. You would not use explosive reds, yellows, and oranges for a quiet, somber mood. Blues and grays will not create a jubilant mood.

Use the chart in Figure 5-6 as your guide to color and mood.

Colors are affected by their environment (Plate 1). *Never* choose colors for your needlepoint without placing them all together to see how they look (see page 80). A red that seems clear and warm may take a turn toward the cooler violets when placed next to blue. The same red can appear to turn toward the warmer oranges when placed next to yellow.

Colors appear bright, bold, and dramatic against a black or dark background. The very same colors will appear subdued when placed against a white or light background.

White or light colors make dark colors stand out more.

Make certain that each area of your design will stand out against the background. A navy blue object will be lost against a black background.

A yellow will look much different surrounded by black than when it is surrounded by white. See other color comparisons in Plate 1. See the Appendix for a detailed diagram of the colors.

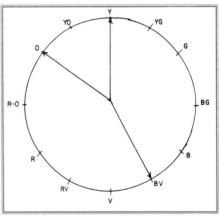

5-5 Split complementary color scheme.

5-6 *Moods created by color.*

MOODS CREATED BY COLOR	
Red	Happy times, Christmas and Valentine's Day; clear red is pleasing with other pleasing colors
Orange	Warmth, friendliness, harvest, Halloween
Yellow	Happiness, warmth, sun, life, cowardice, deceit; gold is also harvest
Green	Nature, plants, outdoors, jealousy, envy, safety
Blue-green	Distance, air, water
Blue	Gloom, somberness (gray-blues), sky, water
Violet	Dark, serious moods, royalty, mysterious feeling
Red-violet	Cheapness, garishness
Cold colors	Mold, decay
Warm colors	Freshness, warmth, and friendliness

LOCAL COLOR

The **local color** of a piece is determined by the color that you've used the most. Usually this is the background color, but not always. If you are designing your own piece, choose the local color first. Then all the other colors will fall into place more easily.

Note: When framing a picture (needlepoint or otherwise), **the frame and mat should match the local color.** This way the picture is of primary importance, not the frame. Once in a while you'll want to emphasize the frame and the picture as a whole. Break this rule then. Use the frame to pick up and thus emphasize a color used in small amounts.

USING COLOR FOR STYLE

The colors you choose for your design will help to determine its style. You should aim for either a realistic or a decorative overall effect.

REALISTIC STYLE

Many people prefer *realism* in design (Plate 19). Several factors must be considered if you are to achieve this effect.

You must strive to get realistic hues, values, and intensities. The best way to do this is to observe nature and then try to match the colors you see with paint on paper and then with yarn on canvas.

SHADOWS

Shadows also contribute to realism and give a subject depth (Plate 17). This, too, should be done throughout the whole piece and not on only one or two items in your picture.

To make shadows on any given design, pick an imaginary light source first. The light must come consistently from one place, as it does in nature. The shadows fall on the opposite side of the light source.

Using tracing paper, trace the design. Then move it to the right and below the design (if the light is coming from the upper left) enough to make a shadow. (See Figure 5-7.) The shadow falls on the side opposite the light source and its color should be a combination of the object's color and the background color. The shadow of a red apple cast on a green leaf will be olive green (the result of a mixture of red and green). You can see this by shining a high-intensity lamp on red yarn. Hold green yarn so that the shadow of the red yarn falls on the green yarn. You will see olive green.

TEXTURE

Texture is created through the use of stitches. Imagine what the various parts of your design would feel like if you could not actually touch them. Try to match that texture to the feel and look of the stitches. For this reason it is handy to have a sampler. Pieces with good texture will give you an overwhelming desire to touch them (Plate 43).

MODELING

Modeling means that shadows give an object a round or three-dimensional look. Realistic objects should be modeled. Highlights also add to this effect (Plate 19). Lack of modeling sometimes gives a feeling of a primitive style (Plate 39).

5-7a-b Making a shadow.

AERIAL PERSPECTIVE

Aerial perspective is another important feature of realism. Objects in the picture *must* appear to recede. A vase must sit *on* a table and the flower stems must be *inside* the vase. Perspective can be created with line as well as color (see page 76).

NONREALISTIC (DECORATIVE) STYLE

Oriental perspective is a prominent feature of decorative designs (page 76). No one item of design component seems to recede ("Art Nouveau Frame," front cover). This is achieved by using colors of the same value. Repeated colors in the foreground, middle ground, and background ensure a flat (not receding) design.

Colors need not be realistic; they may be imaginary, serving the purpose of the design. A tree may be red with violet leaves, yet everyone will know it's a tree. This kind of design is called **abstract**. Many people think of an abstract design as one that is geometric or the like, but in art circles such a design is called a **nonobjective design.**

A nonrealistic design may be textured or not, and objects are usually not modeled.

Triangle Method. When you are trying to decide just where colors should go on a decorative piece, it helps to use the **triangle method** of coloring a design. Figure 5-8 shows how to place colors on a map of the United States. Arrange your colors in a triangle. For example, color Maine, Texas, and Idaho red; California, Minnesota, and North Carolina, blue; and Nebraska, Michigan, and Florida, yellow. The triangle method makes it easier to put a few colors on a large design.

APPLYING COLOR THEORY TO NEEDLEPOINT

When you buy someone else's design, you must always feel free to change either design or color—or both. But when you change design elements or colors, know what is wrong and *why* the change you want will fix the error. If your design and color scheme pass the checklists on pages 110 and 111, any changes you make might make things worse—not better. Don't remove red-violet, for example, from a successful color scheme just because you don't like red-violet. If it works, leave it alone. I don't like mustard, but baked beans without mustard are not as good as those made with it. The complexity of tastes is more interesting, as are the complexities of a successful color scheme.

The best way to choose colors is to take your design to your yarn shop and try to match the colors on the painted canvas as closely as possible. You must re-evaluate the colors you have chosen when you see the yarn stitched into the canvas. Yarn usually stitches up a shade darker, but this may vary with your choice of stitches.

If you decide to change the colors, it is wise to have a colored drawing. A color copy made on a photocopy machine is very helpful in changing colors. Use construction paper or markers to build basic areas of color. Cut pieces the approximate size and shape of each area of color and lay them on your design. Once you have a color that

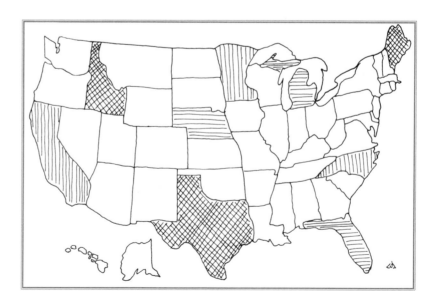

5-8 Use the triangle method of color placement to color many areas with only a few colors.

seems right, paint the design on paper with crayons, colored pencils, markers, acrylic paints, or anything else that will color paper.

Step back and look at your design from a distance often to be sure the colors are falling into place as they should. Continue to do this as you stitch too.

PAINTING THE DESIGN

In painting your design, try to come as close as you can to the color of yarn you wish to use. The following are some hints that will make the painting of the design easier.

1. If you cannot find colored paper that is the color you need, color your paper by using a light wash of acrylic paint over the whole paper. This should be your background color (or local color). Use acrylic paint or watercolors thinned with a *lot of water.* You should be able to see the guidelines of your drawing. Allow it to dry before going on.

2. Use a transparent palette; a piece of untinted tempered glass works well. A side window from a car is perfect. You can get one free (or for a nominal charge) by asking for one at a junkyard. Put a piece of colored paper the color of your local color under your palette. When you choose and mix your colors you will then have a fair idea of what the color will look like before you get it on paper or canvas.

3. Buy the modular colors (premixed) as well as the primary colors. There's really no need to spend hours learning to mix paint.

4. Except for the shadows that are cast, work from dark to light. It will be easier to find colors that fit together.

5. In using, for example, a split complementary color scheme of green, red-orange, and red-violet, you can use those colors *and* the colors that you get by mixing them. Red-orange and red-violet make a red. Red-orange and green make a sort of olive green. Beware when working with a triadic color scheme. Every color can be made from a triad. Too many colors will be too busy.

6. Use warm colors next to cool colors and dark colors next to light colors.

7. Paint highlights and shadows last.

8. No color is as light as it seems or as dark as it seems. No color stands alone. It relates to its environment.

BLACK GLASS

Value is the most important single point to consider. It must be right. A *black glass* (Figure 5-9) aids you tremendously in determining whether your values are correct. It is a sandwich of a piece of clear glass and a piece of sheet metal with tar between the pieces. When the reflection of colored objects is seen on the glass side, the colors that are low in value (dark) will recede and become lost. Colors that are high in

5-9 Use the reflection of your project in the black glass to help you choose the colors for your needlepoint. The needlepoint shown here was stitched by the author from a painting by her father, Luciano Ippolito.

value will stick out like the proverbial sore thumb. This simplifies the analysis of value. To use it, turn your back to your drawing, yarn, or needlepoint piece. Hold the glass up to your shoulder so that the reflection of your work shows in the glass. Study the values. Don't forget that there should be a wide range of values that are in balance throughout your design.

There will be times when you will want certain portions to come forward or to go back. The black glass will show just how much they do come out or go back. In Oriental perspective (page 76), things should come forward or recede very little. The design elements should be relatively flat.

The black glass also helps you with warm colors and cool colors. Remember that warm colors come forward and cool colors recede.

Also use the black glass to look at your skeins of yarn. I always take mine to the yarn shop to help me in choosing yarn.

CONSTRUCTING A BLACK GLASS

Figure 5-10 shows all the steps in making a black glass, which takes less than an hour. You will need to gather together these supplies before you start:

1. A piece of glass from the side window of a car (tinted or not) or a piece of tempered glass *about* 7" x 9". Get it from a junkyard.

2. A piece of sheet metal (any kind) the same size as the glass. A sheet metal place has scraps this size.

3. Roofing tar. The very best tar is the stuff that is a hot liquid found at construction sites. Workers will often give you a couple of cups. Take a tin can along when you go begging! You may also use the stuff that comes in a tube at the hardware store. If you do not have a gun to dispense it, you will need that too. It's the same gun used for caulking.

4. Duct tape (also available in a hardware store).

5. Gasoline (for cleanup).

6. Rags.

7. Scissors to cut the tape.

8. Rubber gloves.

It's wise to have someone to help you whose hands will be clean. But on the other hand, maybe you need someone who doesn't mind getting his or her hands dirty! Better yet—be smarter than I; wear rubber gloves! Don't wear jewelry, either.

Part 1 has helped you with the basic preparations through stitching techniques. Part 2 has taught you the basics of color and design. Now Part 3 will aid you in putting it all together, including blocking and finishing your needlepoint project. Part 4 illustrates how to create each stitch—simply, clearly, and effectively.

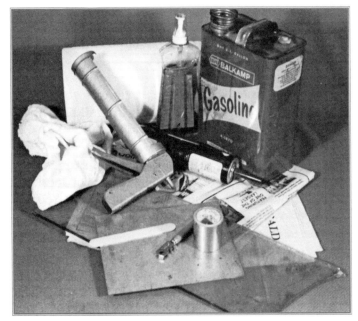

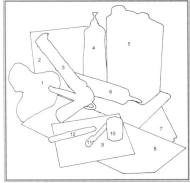

5-10a Materials needed to make a black glass: (1) rags, (2) paper towels, (3) caulking gun, (4) glass cleaner, (5) gasoline, (6) roofing tar, (7) newspaper, (8) safety glass, (9) sheet metal, (10) duct tape, (11) glass cutter, (12) stick to spread the tar, (13) rubber gloves (not pictured).

5-10b Clean a piece of safety glass.

5-10c Mark and cut the glass to size.

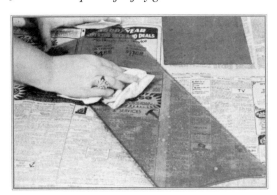

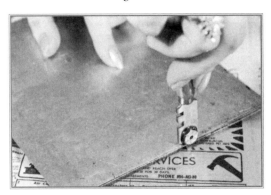

5-10d *Squeeze the tar onto the metal.*

5-10e *Spread the tar around with the stick and, eventually, your fingers.*

5-10f *Put a thick layer of tar evenly on the glass. Smooth out the tar so that there are no little valleys that will cause bubbles when the glass traps the air in them.*

5-10g *Put the glass, tar side down, on top of the tar-coated metal.*

5-10h *The bubbles shown in this photo must be eliminated by picking up the glass and respreading the tar.*

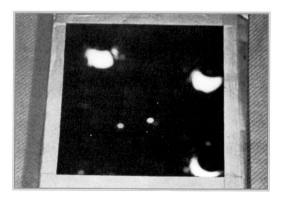

5-10i *Clean the edges with the gasoline and bind them with duct tape.*

PUTTING IT ALL TOGETHER

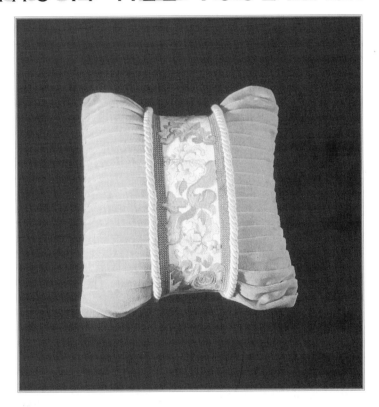

Photo 9—Lily Band Pillow: *stitched by Martha Shevett; designed by Ginger McTeague; yarns and stitches selected by Martha Shevett.* [Smith]

Photo 10—Carousel Horse: *designed and stitched by Jinice Beacon and Vi Etmund. [P. Christensen]*

EVALUATING YOUR DESIGN, COLORS, AND YARNS

he previous chapters have presented a lot of information. So what do you do with it?

Although we have very talented artists creating canvas designs for us all to stitch, not every artist can please everyone. Whether you do your own design or buy one, you will still want to evaluate it carefully. Remember: unfinished needlepoint pieces wind up on the floor of the closet, stuffed in a bag, for four primary reasons: (1) design, (2) color choices (by the stitcher and/or designer), (3) stitch selection, and (4) stitching errors.

Use the Design Checklist and the Color Checklist to give yourself a head start. *Put your canvas on display so you can see it every day.* Move it around every few days. Live with it for two to four weeks. If there is something about the design or the color scheme that will eventually bother you, you will soon see it. You might be able to fix it before you start to stitch.

Then you will be ready to select fibers and yarns. Use the yarn evaluation section of this chapter to help get you started. Put your design on canvas and select stitches. You are ready to go. Once you are through stitching, block and finish your needlepoint.

EVALUATION OF YOUR YARN

Some manufacturers and distributors of yarns provide stitchers with well-labeled products that tell the fiber content and how to use the yarn. If they do not, you *can* figure out *for yourself* just what you need to know in order to stitch with a new yarn.

Many kinds of yarn are merely borrowed from other disciplines, such as knitting, crocheting, weaving, rug making, and tatting, among others, and are not exclusive to needlepoint. Distributors are making them available to stitchers at such a rapid pace that any guide to fibers and yarns is obsolete at printing. It seems to me that the only way around this is to learn to evaluate the yarns ourselves. It is **NOT** as hard as it seems. An engineer I know always says that if you just look and observe carefully, you can learn a lot. She is so right! If we do our observing in a systematic way, noting the findings, we can do it! I'm sure your mother said, as mine did, "If you want anything done right, do it yourself!" So here we go!

ANALYSIS

What is it made of? Knowing the fiber content of yarns is very helpful in evaluating their performance. There is a simple and fun burn test that you can do at home in minutes that will identify some of the most commonly used fibers in yarn construction.

To do the burn test, work with a candle in your kitchen sink. ***HOLD THE YARN WITH A PAIR OF TWEEZERS,*** because some of the fibers burn so quickly that your fingers can get burned before you can drop the yarn. Ask me how I know! Move the yarn toward the flame; observe its reaction. Also note how it reacts while it is in the flame and after you remove it from the flame. The chart in Figure 6-1 will help you identify your yarn's fiber. Have a good time!

BURNING TEST FOR FIBERS

IMPORTANT INSTRUCTIONS: Work with a candle in your kitchen sink. Hold a 2" piece of yarn **WITH TWEEZERS.** Burn both a single ply and the whole yarn. Blends produce both residues.

Fiber	Approaching Flame	In Flame	Out of Flame	Odor	Residue
NATURAL Protein	Curls away from the flame	Burns slowly	Often self-extinguishing	Burning hair	Crushable black bead; silk bead is round and shiny; wool bead is irregular and duller
Cellulose	Ignites readily; does not shrink away from the flame	Burns quickly	Keeps on burning	Burning paper	Fluffy gray ash
TRANSITION Rayon (viscose)	Ignites readily; does not shrink away from the flame	Burns quickly with a blue flame	Keeps burning with an afterglow	Burning wood	Fluffy gray ash, but very small amount
Acetate, triacetate	Melts	Burns quickly	Keeps burning	Vinegar	Hard, irregular black bead
MAN-MADE	Melts and curls away from the flame	Burns very quickly	Self-extinguishing except for acrylic, which keeps burning and melting	Bitter chemical smell	Hard, irregular, shiny black bead

6-1 Burning test for fibers.

Can I get it in lots of colors? The wide range of colors that we stitchers enjoy is possible only in natural fibers and rayon (regenerated cellulose). The natural colors of fibers, their bleachability, and their absorbency will affect this range. For example, cotton is nearly white to begin with, bleachable, and absorbent. Therefore cotton is available in lots of colors. Camel hair is absorbent but not bleachable. This means that its natural color cannot be bleached out and therefore light colors cannot be applied. It can only be dyed colors that are darker than the natural color of camel hair. Vicuña is not bleachable and not absorbent; therefore it must be used in its natural colors. Wool is very absorbent and takes dyes readily, but its lightest natural color is an off-white color, and bleach destroys the fiber. This is why wool cannot be produced in as pure a white as cotton.

Overdyeing a yarn that has already been dyed a solid color can produce interesting results. Natural fibers respond to this technique best. A manufacturer begins with a yarn of solid color and adds more dye, usually by space dyeing (dyeing at intervals and leaving some of the original color.) Synthetic fibers do not, as a rule, handle overdyeing well; the resulting colors are often muddy. See Plate 17 for an outstanding example of a background stitched with an overdyed yarn.

Is it colorfast? Check the fiber properties chart in Figure 1-8 before you wet your yarn. Once you know your fiber can withstand water, testing for colorfastness is easy; wet a piece of yarn thoroughly in warm water. Blot it on a white paper towel. If the color comes off on the paper towel, the yarn is not colorfast. Reds, purples, and blacks are notoriously not colorfast. Anytime you wet yarn, let it air-dry. This test is also used for canvas and fabric.

If the dye is not colorfast, you might be tempted to soak the whole skein in warm water, hoping all of the free dye will run out. Indeed it might, but keep in mind that when colorfastness is tested in a textiles laboratory, those colors that run fade a little *every time* the yarn is wet. So if you block your piece wet, the color might fade even though you soaked the whole skein to get the free dye out. Know that you are taking a risk.

One of the causes of water spotting is the color's migrating to the outer edges of a drop of water. Think twice about using noncolorfast yarns on items that could be near water or rain, such as clothing and tote bags.

It is really important for every piece of needlepoint to be blocked—and preferably a wet blocking, not dry blocking. (See page 113.) **If you mix fibers, your needlepoint item will be only as washable as the least washable fiber in it.** Pieces stitched with colors that are not colorfast must be dry blocked unless you want the colors to run. (See page 114.)

Do I have any limitations on the end use of the project? Needlepoint pieces that do not have great abrasion resistance should not be used for end products that will get a lot of wear, such as chair seats or footstools. Yarns might wear thin and expose the canvas. The nap might wear off unevenly or the fiber might pill. Pills form from the bits of staple fibers that stick out from the twisted yarn (nap). The pills will eventually wear off on natural fibers, but the pills on synthetic yarns do not.

Light might also limit the end use of the project. Some colors fade, not only in water but also in light, especially sunlight. It is probably safest to assume that needlepoint will not stand up to sunlight. Some fibers actually deteriorate in sunlight.

Does this fiber need special considerations for storage? Some fibers are more resistant to mildew, rot, and insects than others. However, our first consideration is for the canvas, because silverfish will eat cotton when it is starched. Canvas is essentially starched cotton. Stored canvas might attract insects. A consideration when creating an heirloom piece is that fibers that are resistant to fungus, bacteria, and vermin may decrease the likelihood that a stored piece of needlepoint will become some critter's dinner. Refer to the chart of fiber properties in Figure 1-8.

How do I care for the finished piece? For the most part, the washability of canvas, fibers, and yarns depends on colorfastness. For all practical purposes, once you mix fibers, consider needlepoint not washable. It then becomes only as washable as the least washable fiber. Most colors fade in sunlight. Because synthetic fibers generally melt when exposed to heat, ironing may not always be possible. If you are ever tempted to iron needlepoint yarns, test a scrap or inconspicuous area first. Most yarns can be *lightly* steamed. This makes dry blocking or steaming a piece of stitchery on a blocking board a real possibility.

Dry cleaning poses new problems. Historical preservationists may consider these chemicals damaging to heirlooms. (See page 49.)

For historic needlework, consider that stitchery worked before 1921 was made from all natural fibers, which are washable—if they are colorfast. But most old dyes were not colorfast, especially those used on silk. (Acetate, the first nonwashable synthetic fiber that was produced, was first commercially manufactured in England in 1921.) Even though an antique embroidery was stitched with washable fibers, its condition may not warrant giving it a bath; the dirt may be all that is holding the piece together! Consult a textile expert before cleaning a very old or threadbare piece of needlepoint. Try calling museums and universities to find textile experts.

YARN CONSTRUCTION ANALYSIS

How easy is the yarn to handle? Several yarn characteristics must be addressed:

Elasticity is a major consideration. Using yarn that is too elastic will make it difficult to get even tension in your stitching. Of course, the prime example is knitting worsted. While it is possible to stitch with it, you need to watch your tension very carefully. It is very easy to get the stitches too tight, thus distorting the canvas. Therefore I do not recommend it, but make your own choice.

The **diameter** of the yarn can be troublesome in novelty yarns. If you want to take the yarn in and out of the canvas, the fattest part of the yarn needs to go through the holes of the canvas easily. In all probability, these yarns will not cover the canvas, although they do work up nicely in an open technique on the right size canvas. See Figure 6-2.

A yarn's **pliability** (flexibility) affects how it needs to be handled. Couching (see page 336) is required for yarns that are too fat to go through the holes of the canvas or for yarns that are too stiff. Of course, it can be done with any yarn for the effect.

Will it cover the canvas? The answer lies in the loft and the ability to strip your yarn. The **loft** of a yarn may enable a seemingly too-fat yarn to go through the canvas easily. Loft describes how much a yarn can be crushed and how much it will spring back to its original diameter. If you want a yarn to cover the canvas, loft will be very helpful. When you stitch with a lofty yarn, you need to select one that is slightly fatter than the canvas holes yet will still go through the holes without distorting the canvas. The canvas threads will squash the yarn, but it will plump out again over the intersection of the canvas. With no loft, this plumping out does not happen (Figure 6-3). Wool is an example of a lofty yarn.

It is **crimp** that produces loft. Crimp is microscopic waviness of a fiber. Only natural *hair* fibers have natural crimp. The other natural fibers do not even retain an artificially induced crimp. Often synthetic fibers are crimped for added loft and more interesting color (page 13).

Stripping plies from a yarn can make a yarn fatter or thinner. Plies of spun yarns and filaments that are loosely twisted together, such as Persian yarn (wool) and embroidery flosses (no matter what fiber), need to be taken apart and put back together again without the twisting. This is called stripping. (See page 32.) To make the yarn thicker, add as many plies as you need; to make the yarn thinner, take away as many plies as you need. Save the extras to assemble other yarns later. Don't forget to keep track of the direction of the nap when you separate the plies. I always place the extras across the arm of my chair with the nap going in the same direction and use them in the next needle. Other people put them across one shoulder or over their frames. You will need to lay (page 40) these loose plies when you stitch.

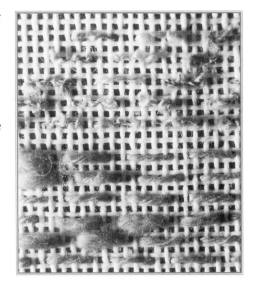

Can I change the texture of the yarn? Generally, no, you cannot change the texture of yarns. However, some yarns can be brushed to raise the nap to its maximum. Use the cat's brush; he won't mind if you borrow it! This will produce a fuzzier nap. All yarns with nap should be run between your fingers before stitching to remove any loose fibers. This will make your work look neater (see page 100).

6-2 Novelty yarn stitched with open stitch.

YARN PERFORMANCE ANALYSIS

Up to this point this self-test has called for little on your part. Now you will need to make a few judgment calls. If you feel too inexperienced to trust your own judgment, don't worry. Everyone is inexperienced at first. Keep at it and you'll do fine!

Comparison is your best tool for understanding differences in things you do not already know. For example, how long is "long" in a staple fiber? Compare two and you will get a handle on which is longer. As you compare more, the notion will gel.

How do I get the wrinkles out of the yarn? Many manufacturers and distributors wrap yarns on cards for sale in shops. These wrinkles may come back to haunt you if you do not get them out before you stitch. There are a few methods:

- Wet washable, colorfast yarns; let them air-dry. Then wrap the yarn around a cardboard tube.

- Stretch the yarn vigorously; some of the kinks may snap out.

- Iron the folds out of those yarns that can stand ironing. (See the fiber properties chart in Figure 1-8.)

How do I keep the yarn from raveling? Some yarns ravel once cut, especially those constructed with

6-3 Left: yarn without loft. Right: yarn with loft.

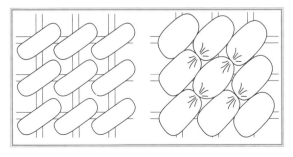

the crocheted chain technique. Several methods can help; some work better on some yarns than on others. Breaking, rather than cutting, crocheted chains helps reduce raveling. Cut the ends of braids, ribbons, and tubes on a severe diagonal. Put a dab of clear nail polish or commercial antifray solution on the ends. Burn the ends of some synthetics. If all else fails, hold the eye of the needle as you stitch to (we hope) keep the raveling at bay. Experiment. With persistence you will find the right way to handle your yarn.

What size needle do I use? Your needle should be able to drop through the holes easily without distorting the canvas. (If your design will benefit from the distortion of the canvas, disregard the previous statement.) True, a bigger hole made by a bigger needle will give the yarn more room and thus less opportunity to fray, but the canvas might be permanently changed. Cutting the yarn shorter can achieve the same results without harming the canvas. The yarn should have room in the eye of the needle to slide through easily.

If the needle is hard to thread, you might need a bigger needle, but first try a few hints to get it threaded. (See page 34.)

Some novelty yarns, like velour, will fit much more snugly in the eye of the needle. The needle might even ruin the yarn where it is abraded by the eye. Experiment to see if this is the case with your yarn. If so, try a larger needle, but if the larger needle is too big for your canvas, place the yarn in the eye of the smaller needle so that there is a very short tail. As a hole wears in the yarn at the eye, move the eye *toward* your stitching (just the opposite from what we usually do). Cut off the damaged piece of yarn.

Other yarns may fit too loosely for tapestry needles. You now have a choice of using a smaller, sharp needle or putting up with the thin yarn in a too-big hole. A thin, slippery yarn will forever come unthreaded. Stitching then becomes a constant battle to keep the needle threaded and a whole lot less fun. Rather than donate blood to your creation while using a small, sharp-pointed needle, use the dull-pointed tapestry needle and make a slip knot (Figure 6-4) at the eye to keep your thin yarn in place. If your thin and/or slippery yarn is washable and colorfast, dampening it slightly may make the yarn behave much better.

What size canvas do I use with this yarn? Whatever you do is right if it works for your design. In this section (and most of the book, for that matter) I will assume that, for the most part, you do not want to distort the canvas. Distorted canvas makes uneven stitches. Figure 6-5 shows you what is *generally* true about the relationships between Tent, Cross, and Straight Stitches on common size canvases.

If you want to cover the canvas, experiment with your yarn on two or three different sized canvases. (See page 33 and 96.) If you do not want to cover the canvas, you will probably be most successful if your attempt really looks like you meant for the yarn not to cover. (See the discussion of Open Stitches on pages 55, 100, and 374.)

6-4 Slip knot.

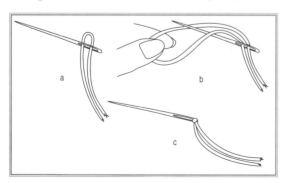

As my son was growing up I always told him to disregard the opinions of movie critics. He is the only judge of what he likes. **Only you know what you like. Trust your judgment.** If you don't like it, it is wrong for you. Period.

What is **the longest yarn I can stitch with?** We all hate to break our rhythm in stitching once we get going really well. Consequently, we are tempted to cut our yarns longer and longer so we won't have to stop as often. Not a good idea! Here's why: As the yarn goes in and out of the canvas, the harshness of the canvas wears it thin by rubbing off the nap, a little at a time. At first the thinning is not noticeable, but eventually the later stitches are thinner than the first ones. The trick is to stop before the stitches get noticeably smaller, unless you can incorporate thinning into your design. Then it becomes a desirable trait. Most of the time we want to avoid it.

RELATIONSHIPS OF TYPES OF STITCHES TO YARN AND CANVAS SIZES			
Straight Stitches and Tent Stitches			
Yarns that will cover this size canvas Æ with a Tent Stitch will *generally* cover this size canvas Ø with Straight Stitches	10	14	18
14	•		
18		•	
22			•
Tent Stitches and Cross Stitches			
Yarns that will cover this size canvas Æ with a Tent Stitch will *generally* cover this size canvas Ø with Cross Stitches	10	14	18
7	•		
10		•	
14			•

6-5 Relationships of types of stitches to yarn and canvas sizes.

What counts here is the number of times the yarn goes in and out of the canvas. Although the size of your canvas is a guide, it is only that—a *guide*. If you are taking long stitches on large canvas, the yarn can be a whole lot longer than if you are working a Tent Stitch on very small canvas, like 24 count Congress Cloth. If you are working with a very delicate yarn like angora, you need a *much* shorter yarn (maybe 8") than you would if working on the same size canvas in the same stitch with the much stronger filament silk.

The best way to figure this out is to see for yourself. Stitch a sample of Basketweave with two very long light-colored yarns—much longer than you think you can get away with. No one is grading you if your guess is way too short or way too long. Stitch with the same continuous yarn until you can readily see that the stitches are becoming thinner.

If your guess was on the short side and you ran out of yarn before it thinned, just repeat this step with a *much* longer yarn right after the first thread, in the same sample of Basketweave. Then repeat the process two or three more times. By now you should be able to see definite lines in your work.

Loss of nap is just one sign of a thread that is too long. Others are fraying and loss of twist, texture, and sheen or luster.

Carefully examine the stitches under a good light and with a magnifying glass if necessary. Mark the first stitch in each yarn on your test sample with a ballpoint pen. Also mark the last good, full stitch on each of your yarns. Next, you get to engage in a stitcher's favorite (ha!) activity—reverse stitching, or ripping! Rip from the first mark to the second mark (the last full stitch) plus a few stitches on each yarn and cut. Measure from mark to mark on each length of yarn. Average them together. You have

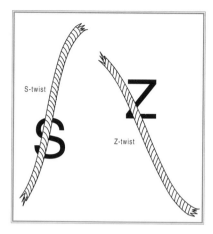

6-6 S-twist. Z-twist.

now figured out how long a yarn you need to stitch Basketweave on the test canvas with the test yarn.

If you are working with Open Stitches, you will need a yarn long enough to go from the beginning, where the yarn is anchored, to another place where you can anchor the other end of the yarn. Sometimes in Open Stitches this can be difficult. The rule of thumb here is still to choose a stitch and a yarn that will do the job without destroying the yarn.

How do I keep the yarn from untwisting? If you want uniform stitches, it is very important to keep the twist of the yarn as close to the original twist as possible. The very best method is to learn to give the needle a slight twist after every two or three stitches. The more damage that is done to the twist, the harder it is to restore it.

Yarn is manufactured in S- and Z-twists (Figure 6-6). Right-handed stitchers find the S-twist much easier to work with, and left-handers can keep the original twist on a Z-twist yarn much more readily.

Do I need to make any adjustments for the yarn's nap? Review the comments on page 31 about nap. Incorporate them in threading your needle.

Doubling the yarn over (Figure 6-7) so that the ends meet gives a thicker thread with the nap of half going in one direction and the nap of the other half going in the other direction. (See Figure 2-11.) This technique of threading the needle will give a fuzzier look to the finished stitches. It is not wrong so long as you are consistent and that look works in your design. Having the fibers run in both directions in each stitch will help in raising the nap by brushing. (See page 97.)

Does the yarn need to be stripped? If the plies of the yarn are readily separated, they *do* need to be stripped. Taking these plies apart and putting them back together again is called **stripping.** This process separates and realigns the plies and makes neater, more even stitches. Strip Persian yarn from top to bottom. With other fibers, pulling each one, straight up, from the end makes the job easier. (See Figures 2-12a and b.)

Does the yarn need to be laid? If you stripped the plies, you need to lay (page 40) them—assuming you want even stitches. If you are stitching with a plied yarn, you need to strip and lay it.

Do I need any other special stitching techniques? Try everything you know. If nothing solves a yarn's aggravating habit, make up something that will solve the problem. Nothing is wrong so long as it works.

YOUR YARN EVALUATION SUMMARY

Don't allow yourself to be intimidated by the unknown. You have a new yarn. Don't know what size canvas it works on? Don't know what to do with it? Don't worry! You *CAN* figure it out!

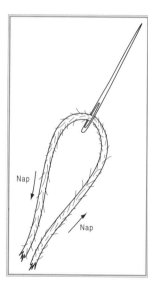

6-7 Doubling the yarn over.

STEP-BY-STEP ANALYSIS OF YARNS

As an example, I have a new hologram yarn—new to me, anyway (Figure 6-8). Let's analyze my new yarn together.

A. Fiber Analysis

1. *What is the fiber content?*

   Even though the distributor put the yarn out on a card with a ton of wonderful information I would like to know, I, of course, got home with only a sample and *not* the card! Sound familiar?

   This is a new, shiny metallic with a play of metallic colors. My general knowledge tells me it **MUST** be a synthetic. The burn test confirms my suspicion that it is a synthetic. So what do I know about holograms? Not much. I've seen hologram pictures at craft fairs; haven't you? If memory serves me well, they are made from a photographic process that adds tremendous depth and movement to a two-dimensional surface. They are gold or silver with the same play of metallic rainbow colors.

2. *Can I get it in lots of colors?*

   My sample is basically silver with a *lot* of colors. It also comes in gold with lots of colors. I don't remember seeing holograms at craft fairs in backgrounds (foregrounds?) other than gold and silver. I saw something on TV recently about holograms. New technology now makes it possible to produce holograms in true colors. Although this yarn is available only in gold and silver now, the future may bring a wider range of colors. But for right now this seems to be it.

3. *Is it colorfast?*

   When I give my sample a bath and blot it with a white paper towel, the colors do not run. No surprise.

4. *Do I have any limitations on the end use of the project?*

   My guess is abrasion resistance is no problem. This looks and feels like pretty sturdy stuff. (But keep reading; I'll soon be proved wrong.)

5. *Does this fiber need special considerations for storage?*

   Bugs, mildew, and rot won't want to dine on it, according to the fiber properties chart.

6. *How do I care for the finished piece?*

   The fiber properties chart (Figure 1-8) tells me synthetics are sensitive to heat. It tolerates the

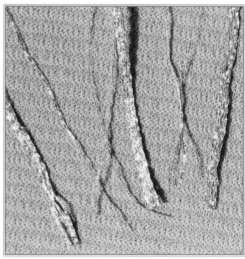

6-8 Hologram yarn. Left to right, yarn with three plies removed, three single plies, full yarn in center, two single plies, yarn with two plies removed.

iron on low when I test it. I have already learned I can wash it (Step A3 above).

B. Yarn Construction Analysis

1. *How is it made?*

Examination under a magnifying lamp reveals that the yarn is a flat braid ⅛" wide. I cut off a 2" piece and unbraided it. There are nine tiny strips or strands. So it looks like the manufacturer cut a hologram into *very* narrow strips that are a little less than ¹⁄₆₄" wide.

2. *Is the yarn pliable (flexible) enough to stitch with? Is it a very elastic yarn?*

It is slightly stiff. It's not elastic at all, but pliable enough to stitch with.

3. *Does the yarn go through the canvas holes?*

The width is even, so I just have to find out what size canvas will fit.

4. *Is it a lofty yarn?*

No, no loft—so I need to get a good fit on canvas size. I cannot depend on loft to help me.

5. *Can I strip this yarn?*

I pull out one strand. It does not strip as easily as floss, but with care, it is definitely strippable! When I stretch the length of the remaining yarn, the result is a very usable braid, ³⁄₁₆" wide! The width is slightly less even, with long, wavy lines on the sides. Pulling a second strand produces another usable braid two hairs wider than ¹⁄₁₆"! There are the same wavy sides.

Wow, what fun! Pulling one more strand gives me a braid a hair wider than ¹⁄₁₆". The width is now more even. Every pulling of a strand makes the ends of the yarn ravel more and makes it a little longer. Each time the braid gets more pliable (flexible) and less dense. By the time there are just three strands left, the braid is too loose to stitch with as one piece. But one, two, or three plies could be used if I laid the plies in stitching with this yarn (page 40). (See Figure 6-9.)

6. *Does it ravel?*

Yes, it ravels. (See page 97 for tricks to slow raveling.) Melting the ends works with this yarn.

7. *Can I brush up the nap?*

No, there is no nap at all (pages 32 and 97).

YARN EVALUATION RESULTS ON HOLOGRAM BRAID				
Number of Plies	Width of Braid	Size of Canvas Needed to Cover Canvas with:		Size of Needle
		Tent Stitch	Giant Brick Stitch	
9	⅛"	12–14	14–18	22–24
6	³⁄₃₂"	16–18	18–22	26–28
3	¹⁄₁₆"	20–22	—	28
1	<¹⁄₆₄"	—	—	28

6-9 Yarn evaluation results on hologram braid.

C. Yarn Performance Analysis

1. *Is this yarn pliable enough?*

   Yes, even though it has a lot of body (stiffness), I can still stitch with it. I test the yarn with Basketweave (page 180) and other stitches.

2. *Do I need to get the wrinkles out of the yarn? How do I do this?*

   There are fold marks where the yarn was wrapped around the card it came on. Snapping the yarn gets rid of some, but it breaks when I snap a little harder. The fold marks will show if I work a very long stitch. Ironing gets rid of them. I use a press cloth.

   The strands that I stripped are crimped. Ironing got rid of most of the crimp, but it doesn't seem to matter. There is so much play of light in the hologram that I cannot tell which strand I ironed.

3. *What size needle do I use?*

   The 22 needle threads easily with no threading aids. To get a 24, 26, and 28 needle threaded, I need to use the paper method (page 34).

4. *What size canvas do I use with this yarn?*

   Experimenting is the best way to find out. The chart in Figure 6-9 shows what I discovered.

5. *What is the longest yarn I can stitch with?*

   Stitching Basketweave (page 180) on 12 count canvas, I take 27 Tent Stitches before one strand on the edge breaks. The length of the yarn is 15"! I thought this yarn looked fairly sturdy, but snapping broke it, and now I can get only 54 passes through the canvas.

6. *Will the yarn untwist easily? Is it an S- or Z-twist* (Figure 6-6)?

   The yarn is not constructed by twisting, so it won't untwist. It is a braided yarn.

7. *Do I need to make any adjustments for the yarn's nap?*

No nap (page 31).

8. *Does the yarn need to be stripped?*

It does not *need* to be stripped, but *can* be.

9. *Does the yarn need to be laid?*

Yes—the twisted braid looks awful and will benefit from being laid (page 40).

10. *Does the yarn have any special characteristics that need other special stitching techniques?*

The Giant Brick Stitches (page 143) look *much* better than the Tent Stitches. Longer stitches show off the play of colors.

Now we have become fairly knowledgeable about what the hologram braid will do and won't do! Taken step by step, the process wasn't very hard.

PUTTING YOUR DESIGN ON CANVAS

SIZE OF DESIGN

Once you have a design you like, it must be made into a size suitable for needlepoint. If you want to use decorative stitches, it is best to work with broad curves and large areas. There are several ways to bring your drawing to the proper scale.

A photocopy machine is your best method of enlarging or reducing a design. If you want to chart a design from a line drawing, put a sheet of graph paper on the top of the machine's paper stack. The machine will print your design on your graph paper!

The **grid method** is a good way to make your design the correct size by yourself. To enlarge your drawing, draw a ¼" grid on the original. If you do not want to draw on the original, trace the design onto tissue paper. Then draw the grid over it. On another sheet of paper draw a 1" grid with the same number of squares, and copy the contents of each square.

This enlarges the drawing four times. Reverse the process to reduce the drawing four times. Juggle the size of the grids to change the original drawing to the size that you need. Transfer the design to the larger grid, square by square. On an intricate design, this can be tedious. However, on most designs suitable for needlepoint, it is not too bad a job.

TRANSFERRING THE DESIGN

Now that you have a design that is the correct size, it is a relatively easy matter to transfer it from paper to canvas. (See Figure 6-10.)

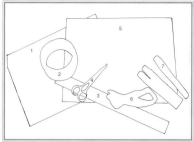

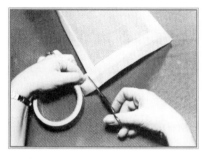

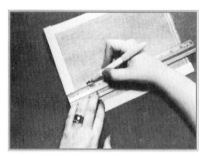

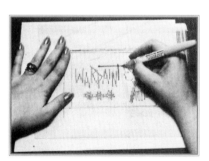

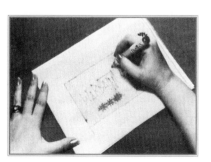

6-10a, first row: Supplies needed to prepare a canvas for stitching: (1) canvas, (2) masking tape, (3) ruler, (4) scissors, (5) drawing of the design, (6) zipper (used in this case to get the correct size for a makeup bag), and (7) waterproof markers—if used instead of acrylic paints. Design by Cindy Pendleton.

6-10b, second row left: Bind the edges of the canvas with masking tape.

6-10c, second row right: Rub the handle of a pair of scissors over the tape to make it stick better.

6-10d, third row left: Draw the margins with a waterproof marker.

6-10e, third row right: Trace your paper drawing with a black marker.

6-10f, fourth row left: Lay the canvas over the design and trace the design onto the canvas with a waterproof gray marker.

6-10g, fourth row right: Your canvas should look like this.

6-10h, fifth row left: Paint the design elements and the background. Let the canvas dry at least an hour or two, even if it seems dry right away.

6-10i, fifth row right: The canvas is now ready to stitch.

First, trace around all the outlines on the paper design with a black felt-tip marker. Using masking tape, tape a large piece of white paper to a tabletop. Tape your design on top of the paper. Center your canvas over the drawing, leaving a 3" margin on all sides. (Most projects need this 3" margin, but some do not. Very large projects need even more. Check Chapter 7, "Blocking and Finishing," before you cut your canvas.) Tape the canvas to the table.

Always use **waterproof** materials when working on needlepoint canvas. Use your gray marker (page 26) to draw the 3" margin all the way around the canvas. (If you are making a picture, see page 120.) Then trace your design onto the canvas with gray or colored waterproof markers. Easy, isn't it?

You may or may not wish to color in the design on the canvas. This can be done by painting with one of two media: **waterproof markers** or **acrylic paints.**

As I see it, there are two advantages and one disadvantage in painting your design. The disadvantage is that it is more trouble than just leaving it in simple outline form. (But if you like to paint, then it's more fun to paint!)

The advantages, however, may outweigh the disadvantage. The painted canvas can become a design element, as in the background behind the pot of flowers in Plate 6. When the canvas is painted in colors that correspond to your yarn colors, stitches that do not **quite** cover will be less noticeable. If the lack of coverage is slight, you may not have to thicken your yarn. Painting could save you time in the long run. There are some stitches that won't quite cover when worked with three-ply yarn. And yet when worked with four-ply yarn, the resulting stitch is so thick that its design is obliterated. When it seems you can't win, paint the canvas and use the thinner yarn.

Following are a few hints for working with acrylic paints. They can be thinned and the colors lightened by adding water. The paint should not be so thin as to soak the canvas, nor so thick as to clog the holes. Ideally, there should not be any paint showing on the wrong side. Use just enough to do the job.

A broad brush will be needed for the larger areas, and a finer one for the small areas. Do not get the brushes very wet. Too much water will dissolve the sizing.

If you make a mistake, paint over it with paint to match the color of the canvas. Then correct your mistake.

Acrylic paint is easily removed **before** it dries, so be sure to wash your brushes immediately after using—in water. Once this paint has dried thoroughly, it should be absolutely waterproof. **But test it yourself.** Run a dry patch under water and blot it with a white tissue or a white paper towel. Just to be sure it won't run, spray the dried paint **and marker** with an acrylic spray. Allow it to dry thoroughly. Test again.

If you are concerned about museum preservation, paint with oils. They are **very** slow to dry. When they **seem** dry they might still be wet at the intersections of the canvas threads—sometimes even after months of drying. Use oils with extreme care. Omit the acrylic spray.

Iron-on transfers are now available, but these, too, must be tested. It would be a tragedy if the colors ran during blocking and spoiled your needlepoint. (See page 118.)

There is one other way to put a design on canvas. A graph or chart, as it is called, gives details, shading, and geometric designs the precision they need (Figure 6-11 and the Appendix). Each color area can be outlined in Continental Stitch (page 177) or a Backstitch (page 334) and filled in with Basketweave (page 180).

For each symbol on the graph chart, make one Continental or Basketweave stitch (page 4). If you can count and you have lots of patience, you have got this technique whipped!

In planning your own chart, you must be aware that the canvas is not perfectly square. If you need 50 canvas threads, count them; do not measure 5" (if, for example, you are working on Penelope or Mono 10 canvas). Work on graph paper that has the same number of squares per inch as your canvas has canvas threads per inch. This will give a finished drawing approximately the same size that your finished needlepoint will be. Color-key your graph with colored pencils or markers.

You could also take a photograph of whatever real-life subject you wish to reproduce. Use film that makes slides. Put the slide in a projector and flash it up on the wall the size you want it to be. Tape paper to the wall and trace the projected image onto the paper. Someone handy with a computer could produce a paper copy of your design from a slide. A photocopy machine could enlarge a photograph of the canvas.

CHOOSING THE STITCHES FOR YOUR DESIGN

An important step in executing your needlepoint design successfully involves the selection of the appropriate stitches for your work. You will learn more about individual stitches in Part 4, but for now a few hints might be in order. (Also, don't forget the design hints in Chapter 3 and Chapter 4, particularly in the sections on shading and shadows, pages 51 and 84.)

First of all, let the stitches do the designing for you. Avoid realism if you plan to use a wide variety of stitches. If you want realism, use Basketweave (page 180) wherever you can. Petit Point (page 187) adds detail. The Continental Stitch (page 177) gets you in and out of tight places. Rely on surface embroidery for very small places, such as eyelashes (page 109). Large stitches need large areas in a design to establish the pattern. Smaller stitches don't need such large areas.

Don't let the stitches take the eye out of the picture (page 74). Work the stitch so that it slants in the opposite direction if that will suit your purpose. To create an illusion of depth, place large stitch patterns in the foreground and smaller ones in the background.

6-11 Graph chart.

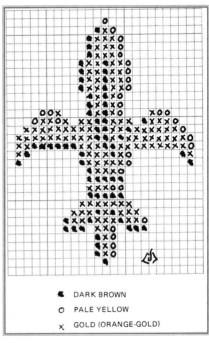

🐾   DARK BROWN

O   PALE YELLOW

X   GOLD (ORANGE-GOLD)

MIXING STITCHES

Be aware of design problems that might arise when you mix stitches. Diagonal stitches and straight stitches do not go together easily, but they can be made to work out reasonably well. Work the Diagonal stitches first and then stitch the Straight ones, sharing the hole (Figure 6-12). Or you can stitch a row of Tent Stitches (page 177) around the Diagonal Stitches in the background colors. Then work the Straight Stitches, sharing the hole.

Each stitch produces a pattern and/or texture. These patterns and textures become integral parts of your design. They *must* be considered, just as you would think twice in mixing prints in interior design or your clothes. Just as gingham and paisley do not go together, many stitches do not mix well. Avoid using a variety of stitches just to use a stitch. Each stitch MUST contribute to the overall design, just as your accessories must complement your outfit. See Plates 12, 20, and 27 for outstanding examples of how many stitches fit together when they are well chosen. Think twice, stitch once.

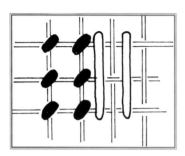

6-12a Diagonal stitches and straight stitches share the hole when they are worked next to each other. Work the diagonal stitches first.

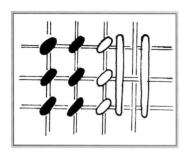

6-12b This alternate method of combining diagonal stitches and straight stitches keeps the diagonal stitches from being swallowed whole. Work a row of Tent Stitches in the same color as the straight stitches.

STITCH USES

Many stitches have several uses related to design effectiveness. Some are better for certain things than others. For example, very large stitches need very large areas for their patterns to show up. There are many special uses for particular stitches that will make your design more striking and pleasing to look at.

LETTERS AND NUMBERS

These can best be worked either in Continental Stitch or Cross Stitch. (See Plate 50.) Follow the chart at the end of the Appendix, a chart from a book of needlepoint or Cross Stitch alphabets, or work your own out on graph paper. Always add your initials and the date of your work. If you wish to incorporate your initials into a fancy monogram, plan it out first on graph paper (Figure 6-13). If you do not wish your initials and the date to be prominent, work them in a color that is just one shade lighter or darker than the background or incorporate them into your design. For example, the date makes a good house number.

Mottoes and sayings are popular additions to samplers. Consider adding one to your work.

BORDER STITCHES

These stitches help to dress up any needlepoint. They make a ready-center piece or a painted canvas more your own. Some suggestions for border stitches are Cashmere, Mosaic, Scotch (and their reversed versions); Stem, Fern, Ray, Bound Cross, Fly, Triangle, Woven Band, Six-Trip Herringbone, Two-Color Herringbone, and Woven Band. There are many more. Check the charts at the beginning of each chapter of stitches. See also Plate 47.

Curved lines are difficult, at best, to work effectively. Couching (page 336 and "Art Nouveau Frame," front cover), Outline (page 335 and Plate 26), and Chain Stitch (page 339 and Plate 36) work better than any others I have found. Any of these can be worked on top of the background stitch or in a space left for them. Van Dyke works, but it cannot get around tight corners and curves. How much relief (texture) you want depends on which method you use. This will vary from design to design.

SURFACE EMBROIDERY

This is stitchery that is worked on top of a background stitch. Surface stitches can add fine detail that cannot be added any other way or they might add high relief. This technique makes it easier to get a background around intricate stitches. (See photograph on page 91.)

Consider using the Lazy Daisy, Straight Stitch, Outline, Spider Webs, many Cross Stitches, Chain, Couching, Thorn Stitch, Detached Weaving, Hollie Point, and many others in this manner.

DISTORTION OF THE CANVAS

Many types of stitches will distort the canvas. This is a nuisance, but it can be compensated for in stitching. Diagonal Stitches that are slanted in alternating directions will lessen canvas distortion. See Reversed Mosaic, Reversed Cashmere, and Reversed Scotch.

The very worst offenders are the Continental Stitch, Jacquard, Byzantine, Milanese, Oriental, Scotch, Mosaic, Cashmere, and most of their variations. Generally they are the Diagonal and Box Stitches (Chapters 9 and 10).

Those stitches that do not distort the canvas are Basketweave, Straight, Cross, Leaf, Eye, Tied Stitches, and others.

Try not to distort the canvas for items other than a picture. The canvas is permanently secured to a stretcher frame in framing a picture. If you do have a distorted canvas and cannot block the distortion out, it must be held rigid with rabbit-skin glue or a commercial substitute. (See page 118.)

SUMMARY

Once you understand the basic principles of creating works of art with your needle, yarn, and canvas, the following lists will give you a quick guide for each new project.

◎ Dark color   ✕ Medium color   ○ Light color

6-13a, top: When planning a monogram, start with graph paper and draw or trace a letter onto it. Then fill in the squares with symbols representing colors.

6-13b, bottom: Monogram stitched on canvas.

DESIGN CHECKLIST

Does your design include the following points?

1. Space that is pleasingly divided? (Plate 52)

2. Lines that create an interesting design or arrangement? (Plate 41)

3. Lines that define forms? Plate 13)

4. Aerial or Oriental perspective (not both)? (Plates 10 and 19)

5. Lines or objects that direct the eye through (not out of) the picture? Keep in mind that the pattern of stitches can lead the eye around too. (Plate 7)

6. Balance (turn your design upside down to check)? (Plate 6)

7. A variety of forms (spheres, cones, cylinders, and cubes), with some repeated? (Plate 33)

8. Objects that relate to their environment (for example, no camels in the house; they should be in the desert)? (Plate 3)

9. No floaters? (Give solidarity by adding a dark line at the bottom of an object.) (Plate 17)

10. Objects that are tied together? (Plate 12)

11. A variety of textures? (Plate 4)

12. One predetermined source of light (if you're using shadows)? (Plate 17)

13. A subjective line? (Plate 31)

14. Hogarth's Line of Beauty? (Plate 24)

15. A combination of compatible lines? (Plate 19)

16. No static points? (Plate 48)

17. No parallel lines? (Plate 17)

18. An *intended*, pleasing focal point? (Plate 31)

Remember that lines are much more than mere outlines. They convey thoughts, feelings, and moods. Creative stitchery *must* begin with creative lines. These creative lines are simply those you choose to draw.

Make any changes on the photocopy of your design first. Have fun; enjoy! You will never know what you can do unless you try.

COLOR CHECKLIST

Use the following checklist to be sure your color scheme works as you intend it to:

1. Have you stayed within the color scheme that you have chosen (analogous, complementary, etc.)? (Plate 41)

2. Have you included some contrast of color (hues)? (Plate 12)

3. Do you have a balance of light and dark areas? (Plate 19)

4. Do areas of color intensity balance? (Plate 36)

5. Are the values (lights and darks), intensities (brightness), and hues (analogous, complementary, etc.) in harmony? (Plate 19)

6. Do you have warm colors next to cool ones? (Plate 6)

7. Do you have dark colors next to light ones? (Plate 6)

8. Do the colors take your eye around the design, just as lines do? (Plate 19)

9. Have you used areas of color to stop the action? (Plate 19)

If the answer to any of these questions is No, use a color photocopy of your design to make any changes. Once you find a color scheme you like, paint it on the canvas.

FIBER AND YARN CHECKLIST

Does your project include:

1. A variety of fibers and yarns, yet not too many? (Plate 5)

2. Fibers and yarns that contribute to the overall design? (Plate 4)

3. Fibers and yarns that enhance the focal point? (Plate 15)

4. Fibers and yarns that don't compete with the focal point? ("Needlepointer's Tote Bag," title page)

5. Fibers and yarns that don't create static points? (Plate 15)

6. Reduced texture and shine in receding planes? (see title page)

7. Texture and shine that guide the eye through—but not out of—the design? (see title page)

STITCH CHECKLIST

Does your project include:

1. Stitches that contribute to the overall design? (Plate 20)

2. A variety of stitches, yet not too many? (Plate 5)

3. Stitches that enhance the focal point? (Plate 8)

4. Stitches that don't compete with the focal point? (Plate 2)

5. Stitches that don't create static points? (Plate 8)

6. Stitches with the largest patterns in the first plane? (Plate 6)

7. Stitches with less and less pattern as the planes recede? (Plate 12)

8. Stitches that lead the eye through—but not out of—the design? (Plate 47)

Many wonderful works of art and stitchery are created that break the rules. If you are a beginner and you want to create art, try to stay within the rules, but don't forget to have a good time!

Photo 11—Eyeglass Case: stitched by LeAnn Bemis; designed by Boots Bailey; yarns and stitches selected by LeAnn Bemis. [Smith]

BLOCKING AND FINISHING

nce the stitching is completed, many people think that their part in doing a needlepoint piece is over; it is not.

BLOCKING

Finishing can make or break your needlepoint. Good finishing can really improve any level of stitching. Poorly done, it can spoil a flawless piece of stitching.

There are plenty of blocking and finishing methods that are more sophisticated than the ones presented here. You can spend a lot more money to accomplish the same end results. The real secret to professional finishing is excellence. Blocking a piece over and over until it is straight. Doing the sewing or framing with meticulous precision until it is right.

It is beyond the scope of this book to go into any appreciable detail on more complex finishing techniques. There are many fine books on finishing that do the subject justice. See the Bibliography.

Every piece should be blocked. Blocking gives a professional, finished look to your needlepoint. Ironing a shirt at home produces an okay finish, but not nearly the polished professional results that the laundry produces. Blocking (well done at home or professionally done) gives your needlepoint the professional look that the laundry gives to a shirt.

Professional blocking is costly, but it is simple enough so that **you** can learn to do it yourself.

The first step is to make a blocking board. Go to the lumberyard and ask for a scrap of insulation board or fiberboard. There seem to be many names for this product. Perhaps it would help to mention that this is the material that some bulletin boards are made of. Pins and staples go into and pull out of it easily. It is porous, and needlepoint dries more quickly on it than on anything else. A piece 2' square should be large enough at the start.

It is absolutely necessary to cover this board. It has a rough finish and a color that bleeds. This cover will protect the needlepoint from stains and snags. There are two good kinds of covers: paper and fabric.

The first is a **paper** cover. Cut a brown paper grocery bag open. Piece it together with masking tape if needed. Place it on the board and tape it in place all the way around the board. This means every inch of both sides, for the board's color can rub off on your clothes. Use very wide masking tape or duct tape to wrap the edges, catching the paper on both sides. Next, draw a grid on the paper with a black **waterproof** marker. The lines must be **exactly** perpendicular and parallel. One-inch squares make it easier to block your needlepoint, although they are not absolutely necessary. I used the width of my yardstick for the size of my squares. It was certainly a whole lot easier than measuring out 1" squares!

When you have drawn all the lines, thoroughly saturate the paper with water. Until it dries it will look like such a mess that you will be certain you have done something wrong. You have not. After it dries, the paper will be taut—honest!

The other cover is **gingham** fabric. Gingham with ½" squares works well, but so do other sizes. The gingham **must** be woven. (If it is, it will look the same on both sides of the fabric.) One hundred percent cotton is best, but a polyester blend also works. Avoid preshrunk fabrics. Do not wash the fabric before using because you want the fabric to shrink on the board so it will be taut.

Tape a brown paper bag over the board, as above. Shrink it by wetting it. Allow the paper to dry. Cover all of the board with the gingham, then secure it onto the board with **rustproof** tacks or small nails. Put them very close together (every ¼"). As you tack, make sure that the lines in the gingham remain perpendicular and parallel. Pull the fabric so it is as tight as you can get it.

The cover on the board should be taut. (If it is not, a tuck could be caught under your needlepoint; this would throw the lines off and then the needlepoint would be crooked.) Pour very hot water over the fabric. Let the excess run off. (The bathtub is handy for this step.) Untreated, nonpreshrunk 100% cotton will shrink, making the fabric cover more taut. **Some** permanent press fabrics may shrink enough; most will not.

Measure the size of your canvas (where the needlepoint design will be) before you even start to stitch. This will be an invaluable help in blocking. The finished piece should be the size of your prestitched design area.

Figure 7-1 shows the steps in blocking a needlepoint piece. A badly misshapen piece will take **lots** of muscle power and two—or sometimes three—people to block it.

Pieces that consist of all flat stitches should be blocked face down. However, many pieces have some textured stitches and/or embellishments; these should be blocked face up. This will prevent crushing these stitches.

If your yarns are washable, it is best to wet the canvas thoroughly with cold water before you block it. Roll it gently in a terry cloth towel to get out the excess moisture. If your yarns are not washable, steam the needlepoint *lightly*. Do not let the iron touch the stitching.

On those pieces that have a blank margin of canvas, use a staple gun to block. In my house we have his and hers staple guns. The lighter weight staple gun works just fine. You can use a hammer and rustproof tacks, but that is a lot of trouble. Place the staples very close together in this area of blank canvas—so close that they nearly touch on a badly distorted piece. Putting the staples at an angle will make it easier to hold a misshapen piece in place without stressing the same canvas thread with all of the torque.

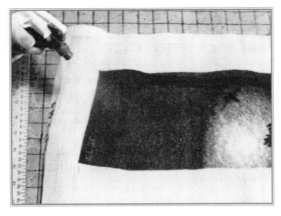

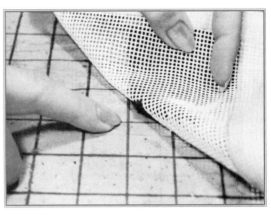

7-1a To block your needlepoint, wet it with a spray of water. Badly misshapen pieces will need a thorough soaking.

7-1b Put one corner of the needlepoint at the intersection of two lines on your blocking board.

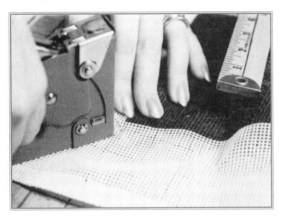

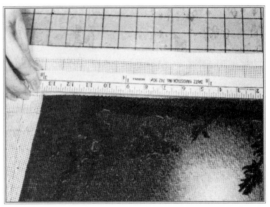

7-1c Staple this corner in place with three or four staples. They will be under lots of tension later.

7-1d Measure along one side, as shown in Figure 7-6, to find the location of the second corner on the blocking board. Mark the blocking board.

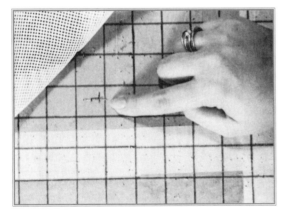

7-1e Your mark should look like this. Pull the needlepoint until it reaches that point and staple the second corner of the canvas in place several times.

7-1f Repeat the previous two steps to find the third corner. Staple the third corner in place.

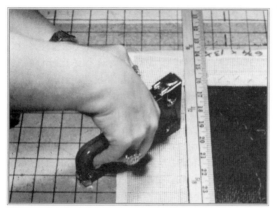

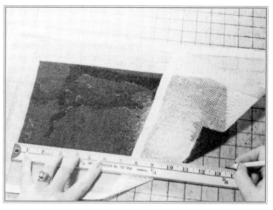

7-1g Then staple between the three corners. Place the staples so each staple is at a slight angle to the canvas threads, and stagger the staples slightly. This way, one canvas thread will not bear all of the tension. Lay a yardstick along the edge of the needlepoint to help you get the sides straight. Start stapling in the middle. Place each staple halfway between two staples every time until the two sides are secure.

7-1h Find the point for the fourth corner by measuring again. Mark this point on the blocking board.

7-1i Pull the fourth corner to meet your mark. If your needlepoint is badly out of shape, you will need one to three people to help you at this point. Staple the corner securely in place. If you worked on a frame, the corners should fall right in place, without any coaxing—one of the many advantages of a frame.

7-1j Staple the last two sides in place as in Figure 7-1g, above. Usually, you can use all the help you can get to block a badly misshapen piece. But with friends like this helping, it takes a longer!

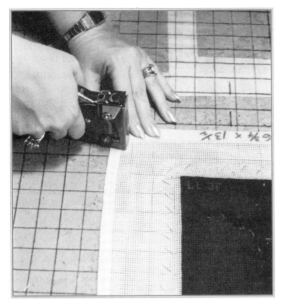

7-1k Staple the corners down so that they will dry flat.

7-1l Sometimes a badly distorted piece will need blocking again. It is a whole lot easier to get it straight the second time around.

For those pieces that do not have a margin of blank canvas, block with stainless steel (not steel plate) T-pins (available in craft stores). The heavier weight ones are necessary because the lighter weight ones will bend under tension. Place the pins ¼" apart and two or three canvas threads in from the edge. Carefully put the pins between the stitches. (Figure 7-2.)

Should your marker, paint, or yarn bleed color when dampened, there are some things that can be done about it. Ripping (page 44) is the least harmful choice. If you don't want to do that, cry a lot first. But while you are crying, do not allow your needlepoint to dry! Put it in a long cold-water soak. Change the water often. The theory here is that if the color will run, given time maybe it will keep running—right out of the yarn. This is not the best choice because it removes all the sizing from the canvas; besides, it does not always work. If it fails, sponge the stain with a mixture of ammonia and water. Use one tablespoon of ammonia per cup of water. Rinse thoroughly. If this doesn't work, the only thing left for you to do is to do the Frog Stitch—ripit, ripit! Then, of course, you must stitch again. The best cure is the proverbial ounce of prevention.

Allow your needlepoint to dry thoroughly. This usually takes twenty-four to forty-eight hours. Sometimes it can take a week or longer. Do not remove the needlepoint from the blocking board until it is **absolutely** dry or it may revert to its previous crooked shape.

Keep your blocking board flat until your needlepoint dries. Do not tilt the board against a wall or anything else. If you do, there might be a watermark on your needlepoint after it dries. I have not found a miracle to remove a watermark. Also, if your needlepoint is not evenly dampened before blocking, a watermark may form.

If there are holes when you take out the T-pins, they can be removed. Hold a steam iron over the holes **briefly.** Then, using a pin or needle, carefully push the yarns back together, closing the hole. **Never touch the iron to the needlepoint.** A **light** dose of steam will fluff textured stitches. Take care not to steam to the point of shrinking and matting wool.

A piece of needlepoint that is somewhat limp can be revived with a dose of spray sizing on the wrong side.

There is just one other problem that might turn up. No matter how precisely you have blocked, some pieces might pop out of shape shortly after being removed from the blocking board. Sometimes several blockings will work. Next time compensate for this in stitching (see page 109).

Pieces that are not badly out of shape can be kept in shape with iron-on interfacing. Choose a heavy weight interfacing. It can be purchased anywhere fabrics are sold. **Do not use it on pieces that have textured stitches.** They will be crushed under the iron.

Badly distorted needlepoint pieces can be straightened only with rabbit-skin or rice glue, which can be bought in art supply stores. Rabbit-skin glue comes in powder form and must be cooked into a gel. Complete instructions come with it. When it cools, it will gel—honestly. I was so sure I had done something wrong when I made

7-2a To block a piece with no margin of blank canvas, use stainless steel T-pins instead of staples. Essentially follow the blocking method above. Start with the three corners, as in the other method of blocking.

7-2b Begin in the middle of one side. Carefully put stainless steel T-pins between the stitches and do one small section at a time. The pins should be ¼" to ½" apart. If one section is more out of shape than the rest, block it first, as I have done here.

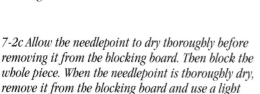

7-2c Allow the needlepoint to dry thoroughly before removing it from the blocking board. Then block the whole piece. When the needlepoint is thoroughly dry, remove it from the blocking board and use a light dose of steam to remove any pinholes that might show.

it for the first time that I started a second batch. It took the first batch about six or eight hours to gel. And three hours after that, my second batch gelled too. I had more rabbit-skin glue than I could use! After a week it smelled as if a rabbit had died in my refrigerator! Be more patient than I was.

To apply, block a piece with flat stitches face down. Allow it to dry. With a knife, spread the rabbit-skin glue on **thinly.** Allow it to dry.

Textured stitches need different treatment. Block first. Build a wooden frame that is larger than the finished needlepoint area (Figure 7-3). This frame does not have to be fancy, but it should be covered to protect your needlepoint from stains and snags. Staple the area of blank canvas onto it. Draw lines on the frame to help you if necessary.

TACKS

NEEDLEPOINT
WRONG SIDE

7-3 Frame for applying rabbit-skin glue to textured stitches.

If you have no margin of blank canvas, your frame must be ¼" smaller on all four sides (inside dimensions) than your needlepoint. For example, if your needlepoint is 8" x 10", the measurement on the inside of your frame should be 7½" x 9½". Unless you have superstrong thumbs, you will not be able to use T-pins for attaching your needlepoint to your frame. Use rustproof tacks and a hammer. Tack the needlepoint in place face down. The thickness of the frame (about ½" to ¾") will be enough to keep the textured stitches from being crushed. Spread the rabbit-skin glue thinly on the wrong side of the canvas. Allow it to dry.

FINISHING TECHNIQUES

I am convinced that poorly finished items detract from the quality of even the best stitching. On the other hand, if your stitching is not quite perfect, it can be dressed up reasonably well by exquisite finishing. Nothing, however, can beat the winning combination of professional-looking finishing and error-free stitching. This is my goal—and it should be yours too. But don't ever forget—this is supposed to be fun!

You can get this professional look at home with proper instructions and some effort. Because whole books have been devoted to finishing techniques, I will consider only a few of the basic types of finishing in this book.

FRAMING A PICTURE

Needlepoint pictures seem to be one of the most popular projects. They can also be the most costly to finish. If you plan your needlepoint so that it fits a standard-sized frame, it will cut your cost considerably.

These frames come already put together and are much more economical than custom-made frames. There are also precut strips of frame molding that come in pairs with hardware and instructions for putting the frame together. Before you cut your canvas, visit local stores and check the exact sizes that frames come in. There are many attractive styles. Choose one that will not detract from your stitching.

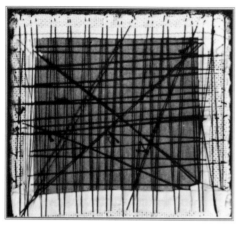

7-4 To wrap a piece of needlepoint around a Masonite board, lace the sides together with heavy thread.

No matter what kind of frame you choose, it will have to be deep enough to accommodate a stretcher frame. If you are not sure, buy the stretcher frame first and test it for fit before buying the frame. The stretcher frame should not stick out beyond the frame on the back.

If, however, you are in love with one frame in particular that is not deep enough, you can still use it. Lace your canvas over a piece of Masonite or foam core with heavy thread, as shown in Figure 7-4. If you use cardboard it will bend under the tension put on it, and you will not be able to get the needlepoint taut. Humidity will eventually do it in.

Canvas board (available in art supply stores) can be cut into ovals or any shape you want. The needlepoint can be stapled on, as it is onto a stretcher frame.

Never put your needlepoint under glass unless you live with a smoker. It will crush your stitches and hide the texture from admirers. Natural fibers also need to breathe. Museum conservation techniques do provide breathing space for needlework. See page 49 for cleaning information.

There is a trick in getting your needlepoint to fit the frame you choose. The trick lies in careful measuring. Allow a 3" margin of blank canvas on all four sides. In other words, if you wish to make a piece that will be 8" x 10" when you are finished, add 3" to both sides of the 8" and the 10": 3" + 8" + 3" = 14" and 3" + 10" + 3" = 16". So you need to cut a piece of canvas 14" x 16" in order to have a finished size of 8" x 10". (See Figure 7-5.)

7-5 Measuring 3" margins for a picture 8" x 10".

At first glance this may seem to be a lot of wasted canvas. Let me assure you, it is not. When it comes time to block, you will be grateful that you have something to hang on to, particularly if your needlepoint is badly out of shape. The framing process will also eat up much of this blank canvas.

Mark your margins next. (See Figure 7-6.) Draw a line to indicate the margins. On size 10 canvas, it should be two canvas threads (one on either side) short of 8" and two canvas threads short of 10". In essence, you have left a blank canvas thread all the way around your finished work. This extra canvas thread is your fudge factor.

If you plan to have a border, remember that the lip of the frame covers ¼" of your needlepoint, or about two canvas threads on size 10 canvas. One of these two canvas threads is the blank canvas thread you have already provided for. The other should be one row of Continental Stitches (page 177). Then comes your border. If you stitch the border right to the edge, ¼" of it will be hidden. On some wide borders this may not matter. However, a border that is only two canvas threads wide can be swallowed whole by the frame.

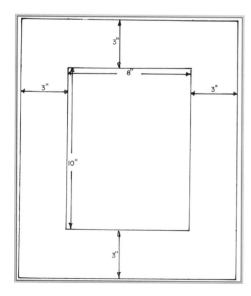

Now stitch your needlepoint and block (page 113).

You will need a **stretcher frame** to stretch your needlepoint. Art supply stores carry stretcher bars that are sold in pairs. They usually come sized only in whole inches and are inexpensive. They are easily assembled (Figure 7-7b). You may need a hammer to tap the stretcher bars in place. Use a square or something else with a 90° angle to be sure that the corners are at exactly 90°. Put the stretcher frame into the frame to be sure that it will fit. (Figure 7-7d).

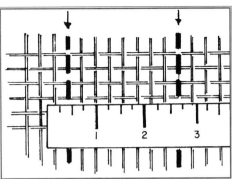

7-6 Measuring margins for a 3" picture. Stitch between the dotted lines.

Staple or tape a piece of **cardboard** onto the front of the stretcher frame. It should be slightly smaller than the stretcher frame. Do not use corrugated cardboard; it is too thick. This cardboard will keep the center of your stitchery from sagging. At this point, you may add a layer of quilt batting if you want a padded look.

Stretch the needlepoint over the stretcher frame. Start at the corners, making them just as perfect as you possibly can, and staple them in place. The extra row of canvas threads you have left now gives you a margin of error.

Under no circumstances should yarn from the worked needlepoint go over the edge of the stretcher frame. There is simply not enough room between the stretcher frame and the frame for any excess materials. Do not worry if that one row of blank canvas shows now. The lip of the frame will cover it.

Staple the rest of the canvas in place. Make sure the needlepoint is perfectly straight. If it is not, do it again and again and again until it is **perfect!** The finishing technique makes or breaks a project. (See page 113.)

Next, put the stretcher frame into the picture frame. Double-check now to be sure it is perfectly stretched. Secure it by stapling or tacking. On a 3" x 5" index card, write your name, the date, and your address. Tape it to the back of the cardboard. It is also nice to include your comments on the design, fibers, yarns, and stitches. This information will be interesting in the future. (Surely your needlepoint will outlive you! This will help historians of the future.)

For a professional look, cover the back with brown paper. A brown paper bag will do nicely. Be sure the paper is a couple of inches larger all the way around than your frame. Run a narrow line of white glue around the outside edge of the back of the frame. Wet the paper thoroughly. Place it over the glue on the back of the frame.

On very large pictures, put the paper on dry and wet it afterward. A large piece of paper that is wet is unwieldy. The extra paper should hang over the edge of the frame. Allow it to dry. As with the blocking board, it will look so bad you will be sure you have done something wrong. But you haven't. In about an hour, you will be in for quite a surprise—that paper will magically shrink and be very taut!

Using a **sharp** single-edged razor blade, trim the dry excess paper away just inside the edge of the frame. **Don't** ruin the finish on the side of the frame by running a razor blade on the edge. Guess how I figured this one out!

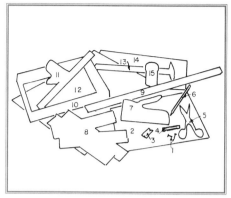

7-7a Equipment needed for framing needlepoint: (1) tacks, (2) cardboard, (3) single-edged razor blade, (4) sawtooth hanger, (5) scissors, (6) pencil, (7) staple gun, (8) stretcher frame, (9) ruler, (10) frame, (11) square, (12) needlepoint, (13) hammer, (14) paper bag, (15) white glue.

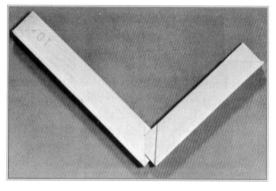
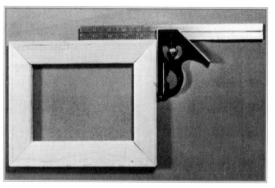

7-7b Stretcher frame pieces fit together at the corners like this. They might need a tap of the hammer to get them all the way together.

7-7c Check to be sure each corner is 90°.

7-7d Try the stretcher frame in the frame for size. Note that there is very little extra room.

7-7e Cut a piece of cardboard a little smaller than the stretcher frame and staple it in place on the stretcher frame. This will prevent your needlepoint from sagging when the humidity gets to it. If you wish, add a layer of quilt batting to make your picture slightly padded.

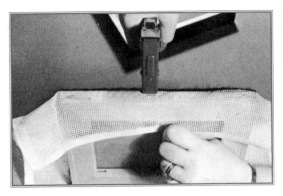

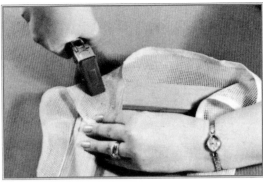

7-7f *Wrap the needlepoint around the stretcher frame so that the cardboard lies next to the needlepoint. Be certain to get the line of stitching absolutely straight. Patience and perseverance will win out! I promise! Staple the corners first, then the sides.*

7-7g *When all the sides have been stapled, miter the corners on the back. To do this, pull the tip of the corner to the wrong side of the stretcher frame and staple it in place.*

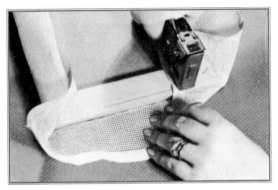

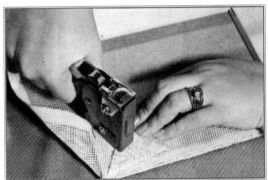

7-7h *Next staple the sides of that same piece.*

7-7i *Fold one side of the canvas to the back to form one half of the mitered corner. Then fold the other side back and staple it. Repeat on the other three corners. Next, staple the sides between the mitered corners.*

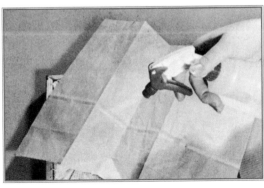

7-7j *Put the stretcher frame into the frame. Staple or nail the stretcher frame in place.*

7-7k *Wet a piece of paper for the backing.*

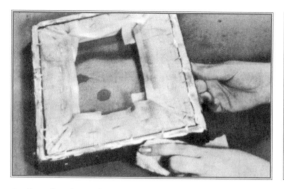

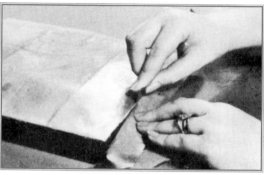

7-7l Apply white glue to the edge of the back of the frame. Wipe away the excess glue with a damp paper towel.

7-7m Place the paper over the back of the picture frame and trim away the excess paper with a single-edged razor blade. Again, wipe away excess glue.

7-7n Find the center of the picture frame and attach the sawtooth hanger. The paper will dry and shrink to a taut dust cover. You will have a picture that looks better than many professionals can do it!

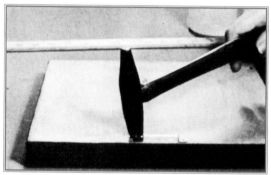

Attach a sawtooth hanger and you are ready to receive compliments!

If you are interested in museum preservation techniques, be sure that all paper and cardboard are acid free. Use a wire hanger instead of a sawtooth hanger.

PILLOWS

The pillow is another popular item, yet expensive to have finished. If you sew, even just a little bit, you can make your own. You will need a sewing machine, fabric, and polyester fiber stuffing (this is more washable than cotton batting and more durable than foam rubber).

When you stitch your needlepoint, work two extra rows of Continental Stitch (page 177) all the way around the finished design. When you machine-stitch later, sew between these two extra rows and your design (Figure 7-8). This gives much-needed strength and stability to the seam. Block.

THE INNER PILLOW

Make an inner pillow that is **1" larger** than your needlepoint; for example, if your needlepoint is 14" x 14", make the finished size of your inner pillow 15" x 15". Use a sturdy, but not heavy, machine-washable fabric for the inner pillow.

Preshrinking. Before you make it, preshrink the inner pillow fabric by washing in the washing machine with water just as hot as the fiber will allow. Dry in the dryer at the hottest setting that the fiber will allow. Cut to size. Leave a 5/8" seam allowance. Stitch all four corners and three sides, leaving an opening through which you can stuff (Figure 7-9). Stuff with polyester batting, which can be purchased at fabric shops. Make a plump pillow with **fully stuffed corners.** Stitch the fourth side closed on the sewing machine. (This inner pillow is machine washable and dryable as it is.)

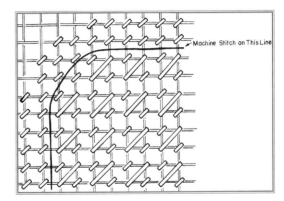

7-8 Stitching the Continental Stitch in the seam allowance for a pillow.

BACKING

In selecting a fabric for a pillow backing, you must consider several points: (1) durability of the fabric, (2) elegance that will set off your needlepoint, and (3) washability.

Because needlepoint is so long-wearing, you will want to choose a backing with equal **durability.** And you certainly do not want to downgrade your needlepoint, so select fabric with **elegance.**

If the rest of your pillow is washable (either by hand or machine), you might want to make the backing fabric also **washable.** This is not absolutely necessary. However, if you do select a washable fabric, preshrink it according to the instructions given above.

The fabric that I recommend is high-quality synthetic suede that is actually washable—and it does not water spot! It comes in a remarkable variety of colors. Look for it at fabric shops.

No-wale corduroy gives the look and feel of velveteen, yet it, too, is washable and much less expensive than quality synthetic suede. Velvet is hardly the most durable fabric, but it feels s-o-o-o good!

7-9 Stitching the inner pillow.

TRIMMING

It is at this point that you must decide how you want to trim the pillow once it is finished.

Cording. Although this is a popular choice, I cannot recommend it unless you are an experienced seamstress. As a seamstress myself, I still find cording difficult because I don't do it often. It is something that must be practiced. For that reason I am not including instructions for cording here.

Twisted Cord. This resembles cording, yet it is quite a bit easier to make—and it is prettier, I think. It takes two

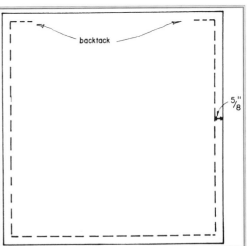

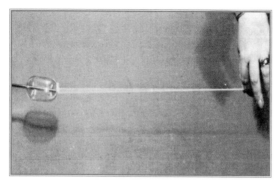

7-10a To make a twisted cord, tie the yarns together with one knot in the center of the strands. Then tie one end of your yarn to the beater of an electric mixer or to a hook or give one end to a friend.

7-10b Holding the yarn tightly, twist the yarns until the resulting cord kinks when you release the tension.

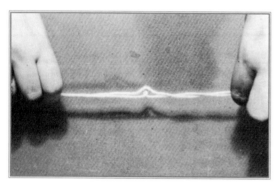

7-10c Bring the ends together while you place the center knot on a hook or a friend's finger. Starting at the center knot, slowly release the tension. The two twisted pieces will twist together.

7-10d Tie the ends together so they will not untwist.

people to make a twisted cord—or one person and a cup hook. Measure the distance around the outside of your pillow. Multiply this number by 3. This is the length of yarn you will need to make one twisted cord long enough to go all the way around your pillow. For example, if your pillow is 14" x 14", the circumference is 56", which you then multiply by 3 to obtain 168".

Cut six yarns 168" long. (How many yarns you choose determines the thickness of your cord. Six makes a nice-sized cord for a pillow.) You will need an uncut skein of yarn to do this.

Knot the yarns at both ends. Put a knot through all yarns in the middle so you can find it easily later. Put a pencil between the yarns at each end. (See Figure 7-10.) You hold one pencil and give the other to a friend—or hook one end on a cup hook. Twist until the yarn kinks. Keeping the yarn taut, hook the center knot over a hook (or a chair back or a finger). Give your pencil to the person holding the other pencil. (He or she now holds both pencils.) Keep the yarn taut.

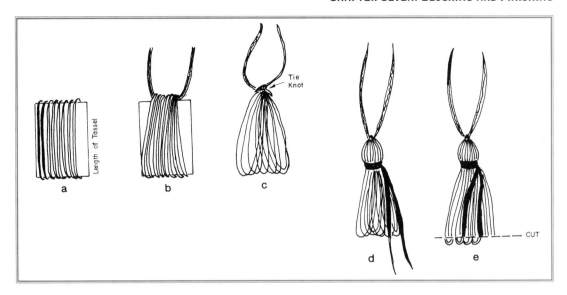

Length of Tassel

Tie Knot

CUT

a   b   c   d   e

Remove the center of the yarn from the hook. Slowly release the tension. The two pieces will now twist together. If you go too fast, the twist will be uneven. (This uneven twisted cord makes a very interesting vine to couch onto your needlepoint garden trellis.) Tie the ends together with another yarn so the twisted cord will not untwist. Hand-sew it in place along the seam of the finished pillow, using an invisible stitch. Tuck the ends in. See how the twisted cord is used in Plates 43 and 48.

Tassels. These make a nice finish for a pillow, although they do not have as formal a look as cording. To make tassels (Figure 7-11), wrap yarn around a piece of cardboard about 4" long. Using a piece of yarn about 6" long, tie the yarn together at the top of the card. Leave the strings hanging. Remove the yarn from the card. About ¾" to 1" down, wrap a yarn around all of it several times and tie. Let the ends of the yarn hang down. Cut through the loops at the bottom of the tassel. Trim the ends of the yarn that are hanging down even with the rest. Bead the top if you like.

Once you have chosen your backing fabric, **machine-stitch** it to the needlepoint. Place right sides together. Put the tassels between the two pieces, pointing toward the center. Let the free-hanging yarns at the top fall in the seam allowance. (Figure 7-12.) Catch these when you stitch the seam. Tassels also give a festive touch to a Christmas stocking (Plate 22). Instructions for very fancy tassels with beaded and crocheted caps and other embellishments can be found in books, magazines, and craft and fabric stores.

Fringe. Fabric stores have a very wide variety of fringes that can dress up your needlepoint. These are usually attached in the seam allowance when you sew the pillow together. (See "Illusions, Bargello Pillow," front cover.)

Other Finishing Techniques. Photo 8, "Lily Band Pillow" (page 91), shows an imaginative way to finish a pillow.

7-11a-e Making a tassel.

7-12 Inserting a tassel in a seam.

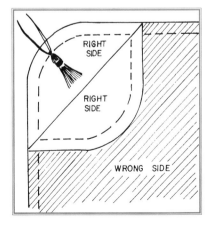

RIGHT SIDE

RIGHT SIDE

WRONG SIDE

7-13 Stitching a pillow. (The drawing is not to scale, so the curves are exaggerated.)

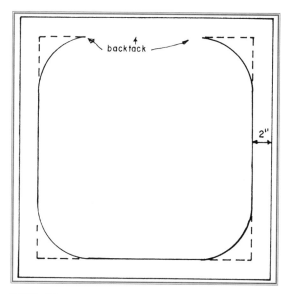

backtack

2"

FINAL SEWING

Now stitch between the two rows of Continental Stitches and your pillow's needlepoint (Figure 7-8). Round the corners as you stitch the backing on (Figure 7-13). (If you plan for this when you stitch the needlepoint, it will be better. In other words, stop your needlepoint where the corners will be rounded. If you did not plan ahead, it is not disastrous; you can make up for it now.) Be sure each corner has the same gentle curve.

Again, stitch all four corners and three sides. Back-tack well at the beginning and end of your machine stitching. Trim the seam to within ⅝" of the stitching on the rounded corners, even if you have to cut the needlepoint. (See Figure 7-**13**, *NOT* Figure 7-9.) Zigzag the raw edges together all the way around, except for the opening you have left. Zigzag those raw edges separately. Turn, making sure the corners are fully turned.

Put the inner pillow into the needlepoint cover. Remember that the inner pillow is bigger than the needlepoint cover. Be careful not to break the machine stitching at the edges of the opening. Push the inner pillow into the corners well. (Limp corners cry "Homemade!" not "Handmade!") If necessary, take a wad of polyester batting and stuff it into the corners, between the cover and the inner pillow.

When you are satisfied with the way the pillow looks, pin the fourth side, tucking in the fabric ⅝". Hand-sew using the Blind Stitch, as shown in Figure 7-14. Run the needle in the fold of the fabric. Bring it out every ¼" to ⅜". Pick up one thread of canvas and reinsert the needle into the fabric. This makes a stitch that does not show—hence the name, Blind Stitch.

PINCUSHIONS AND CHRISTMAS TREE ORNAMENTS

Nearly the same procedures are used in making pincushions as are used in making pillows. But there are two differences. First, pincushions are smaller. Second, they

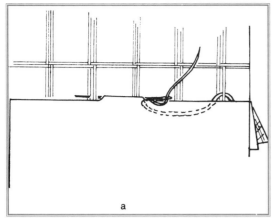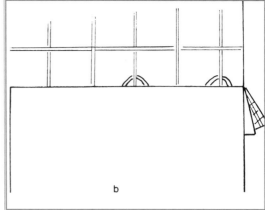

are stuffed with steel wool wrapped in polyester batting. This is to protect your needlepoint in the remote event that the steel wool rusts.

7-14a-b Blind Stitching the fourth side of pillow.

Christmas tree ornaments may be made in this way too, but no inner pillow is needed. Stuff only slightly. They may also be made flat, lined, and finished with a twisted cord.

TWO-STEP EDGE FINISHING

Two-step edge finishing is a dandy method I use to finish projects that stand alone (without frames or backing). Belts, eyeglass cases, needle books, brick doorstops, scissors cases, checkbook covers, and book covers may be finished using this method.

Two-step edge finishing leaves no raw edge of canvas with which you must contend. It also sews a seam as it finishes if you so desire.

When planning a project, note that you need only five or six canvas threads all the way around beyond your design. Use five pairs of threads for Penelope canvas and six threads for regular and Interlock Mono canvas (Figures 7-15a and b).

Put your design on the canvas. Before you take even one stitch, turn four threads (four pair on Penelope) under and leave the fifth and sixth on Mono canvas (the fifth pair on Penelope) on the edge. Match the threads up perfectly and baste in place.

Double-check yourself by inserting the needle under the fifth thread on Mono (fifth pair on Penelope) when the canvas is flat. Then turn the four threads (or pairs of threads) under. The needle will automatically keep the correct threads on the edge (Figure 7-15c). Baste, being very careful not to let the canvas slip.

There will be four layers of canvas at the corners. Stitch through all of them as well as you can. It really isn't as bad as it sounds. Do not cut the canvas. Hard wear will cause these corners to ravel if you cut them.

Work your needlepoint stitches through all thicknesses just as if they were one. Stitch right up to the two threads that are on the edge (Figure 7-15d).

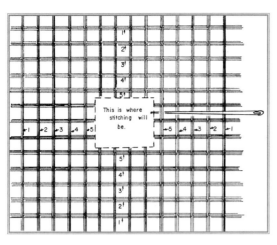

7-15a *Finding canvas threads on Penelope canvas for the Binding Stitch.*

7-15b *Finding canvas threads on Mono canvas for the Binding Stitch.*

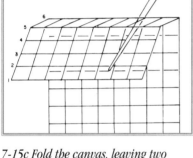

7-15c *Fold the canvas, leaving two canvas threads on the edge for the Binding Stitch.*

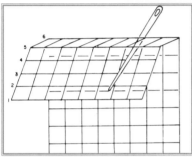

7-15d *Stitch right up to the edge through both layers of canvas as if they were one.*

Block, following the directions for blocking with no margin of blank canvas (page 117). When the needlepoint is thoroughly dry, remove it from the blocking board. Allow it to sit overnight if you have used stitches that distort the canvas. The piece will lose its shape overnight if it is going to. If it does go out of shape, apply rabbit-skin glue (page 118) or iron-on interfacing (page 118) at this point. Next, stitch the Binding Stitch on the blank threads (see page 338).

BOX TOP

A box top (Plates 21 and 47) is finished by wrapping your needlepoint around a piece of ¼" plywood. It may have quilt batting on it (Figure 7-16), as in Plate 47, or it may be flat, as in Plate 21. Staple in place as you did with a picture on a stretcher frame.

Make or purchase a wooden box with a lid that will allow the needlepoint to be inserted from the inside. The plywood should be about ¼" smaller than the lid. For example, if the lid is 4" x 6" (inside dimensions), cut the plywood to 3¾" x 5¾". Insert the needlepoint into the lid from the back. Replace the back of the box top that should have come with your box.

Line the box with synthetic suede, satin, moiré, velvet, or velveteen. Cut pieces of cardboard that are slightly smaller than the sides, bottom, and top of the box. Using fusible webbing bond, fuse your lining fabric to the cardboard and miter the corners, as shown in Figure 7-17 (page 132).

Fit the pieces into the box. Glue them in place.

 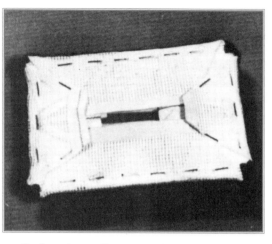

7-16a To attach a piece of needlepoint to the top of a box, start with a box with a deep lid. Cover a piece of ¼" plywood with a piece of quilt batting. A piece of lightweight fabric over this will make it easier to handle, but it really is not necessary.

7-16b Place the needlepoint on the box lid as you did on the stretcher frame in Figure 7-7g-j.

Cut a piece of felt slightly smaller than the box and glue it to the bottom. Or cut circles of felt and glue one in each corner.

UPHOLSTERED ITEMS

Upholstered items should always be worked on Penelope or Mono (not Interlock) canvas for strength and durability.

Unless you have had experience in upholstering furniture, I would advise you to have a professional mount your needlepoint for you. Also, you should consult the professional **before** you begin to stitch. Take the piece of furniture you wish to cover to him. Ask him to make you a **muslin** pattern—not paper. Paper does not go around curves well, and precision is lost. Trace this pattern onto your canvas. Allow at least a 3" margin of blank canvas. Take your needlepoint to the upholsterer **after** *you* have blocked it.

PLASTIC CANVAS

Plastic canvas simplifies finishing. There are no raw edges to ravel. It can be cut into almost any shape you want. There is no blocking involved, either. Simply work the Binding Stitch around the edge and you are finished. (See Plate 50.)

Linings must be sewn by hand, however—unless you would like to melt the canvas by ironing on a lining! Turn the edges under about ¼" and stitch it to the wrong side of your needlepoint with a Blind Stitch (Figure 7-14).

Plate 50 shows you that plastic canvas can make an easy, inexpensive, and effective wall hanging.

Part 1 has guided you from the basic preparations through stitching techniques. Part 2 has helped you with color and design, and Part 3 has discussed all aspects of putting it all together, including blocking and finishing of your needlepoint project. Part 4 will show you how to create each stitch—simply, clearly, and effectively.

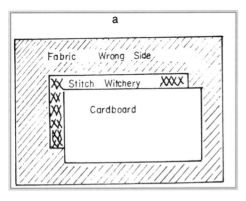

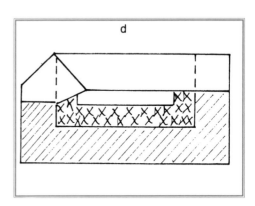

7-17a-f Lining for box.

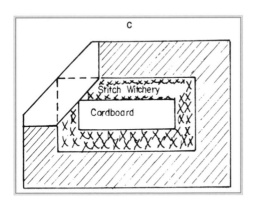

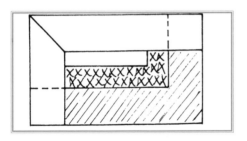

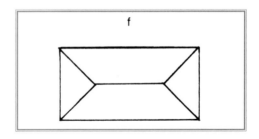

Part Four

THE STITCHES

Photo 12—Horace, Rocking Horse: *stitched by Martha Shevett; designed by Marlene Webb; yarns and stitches selected by Martha Shevett. [Smith]*

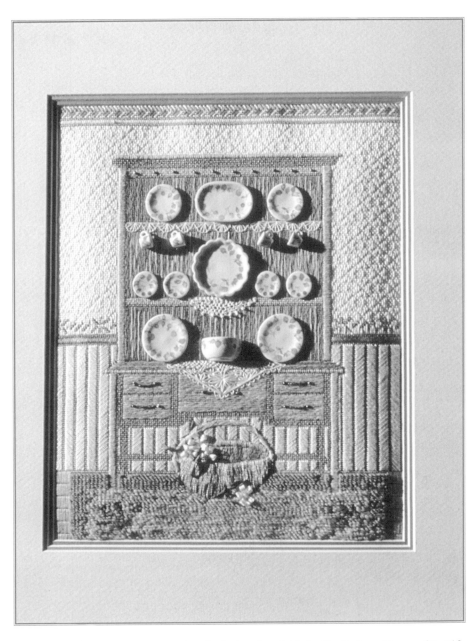

Photo 13—Country Hutch: *designed and stitched by Barbara Elmore.* *[Smith]*

HOW TO READ THE DIAGRAMS

Before you even start to stitch, you will need to know the definition of the symbols used in the drawings. ⟨ʋ⟩ and ⅌ show the location of the beginning of the stitch. In stitches that are done in steps, the starts are identified by ⟨ʋ⟩ 1, ⟨ʋ⟩ A, ⟨ʋ⟩ a, ⟨ʋ⟩ AA, and ⟨ʋ⟩ aa and also by ⅌ 1, ⅌ A, ⅌ a, ⅌ AA, and ⅌ aa, in that order.

Arrows alone outside the grid of the canvas indicate a row change with no turning of the canvas. Arrows accompanied by a clock show a turning of the canvas:

T ⟲ means, "Turn 90° to the right."

T ⟳ means, "Turn 180°."

T ⟲ means, "Turn 90° to the left."

Where it would complicate things, these arrows and clocks have been omitted. However, you can still tell where to turn the canvas. Simply turn the book so that the numbers are upright. Turn your canvas the same way and stitch.

The numbering has been arranged so that the best backing is created. Economical yarn use usually creates a poor backing. On the front, the stitches do not look as smooth (see Figure 2-29.) This poor backing also reduces the durability of needlepoint.

When several stitches go into the same hole, the numbers have been omitted because there simply is not room for all of them. (See the Eye Stitches, Chapter 13.)

A change of color is indicated by darkening the stitches, but the use of a second color is not absolutely necessary. Sometimes this darkening was added merely to help you to see the next row more clearly. Other colors (third, fourth, etc.) are indicated by different symbols within each stitch. When working with two colors that cross each other, put the darker color on the bottom. Work the lighter colors last.

Two other types of arrows have been used to help you stitch from the diagram. In some stitches, this arrow —||⟶ is used to indicate that you are to slip the needle under the crossing stitch before the needle penetrates the canvas.

Dotted arrows are used on the Pulled Thread Stitch diagrams to show you where and in which direction to pull. The numbering also communicates this information. Gray arrows and numbers mean pull **under** the canvas. Black ones mean pull on **top** of the canvas. For example, – – – – – –⟶ 2 a means after you penetrate the canvas at #2, pull **under** the canvas in the direction of the arrow. After pulling in that direction, if there is a 2b, then pull in that direction. Similarly, – – – – – ⟶ 3 a means after you penetrate the canvas at #3, pull on **top** of the canvas in the direction of the arrow. Again, after pulling in that direction, if there is a 3b, then pull in that direction.

135

The canvas pictured is the canvas used for the particular stitch. Generally, all stitches can be worked on Penelope canvas; Mono canvas does have some restrictions on types of stitches that can be used. These have been pictured on Penelope canvas. (These restrictions do not exist on Interlock Mono canvas.) Renumbering the stitches may help some of them. For the sake of consistency and continuity, I have not made a concerted effort to do this. Feel free to experiment.

The rest of the stitches have been drawn on Mono canvas for simplicity and clarity. See also page 195.

Photo 14—T. S. Nicholas: stitched by Sandy Z. Brown; designed by Leslie Storman and Karen Damskey; yarns and stitches selected by Barbara Budlow. [Smith]

STRAIGHT STITCHES

Straight Stitches are those stitches that cover the canvas vertically or horizontally. A vertical stitch covers two to six horizontal canvas threads and lies entirely between two vertical canvas threads. A horizontal stitch covers two to six vertical canvas threads and lies entirely between two horizontal canvas threads.

A single strand of both tapestry and Persian yarn, when worked in Straight Stitches, covers Mono 14 canvas well. On Penelope or Mono 10 or 12, you will have to thicken your yarn.

Straight Stitches make beautiful patterns and good backgrounds, as a rule. They work up quickly and can give a good backing if you plan on it.

Many of the Straight Stitches depend on color for their splendor, especially Bargello. (See page 168.) Straight Stitches do not distort the canvas when you stitch. I recommend them for everyone, but especially for beginners and children.

STRAIGHT STITCHES	Border	Good Backing	Poor Backing	Background	Design	Accent	Fast	Slow	Geometric Pattern	Shading	Yarn Hog	Snags	Snag-Proof	Little Texture	Medium Texture	High Relief	Flower Stitch	Weak Pattern	Medium Pattern	Strong Pattern	Distorts Canvas
Straight Gobelin	•	•		•	•				•				•	•				•			
Straight						•	•					•		•							
Satin		•			•	•	•					•		•				•			
Renaissance		•		•	•				•				•		•			•			
Split Gobelin		•		•	•			•		•	•		•	•				•			
Interlocking Straight Gobelin		•		•	•			•		•			•					•			
Brick		•		•	•				•	•			•	•				•			
Padded Brick		•		•	•				•	•			•			•		•			
Giant Brick		•		•	•		•		•	•		•		•					•		
Double Brick		•		•	•		•		•					•					•		
Horizontal Brick		•		•	•		•		•	•		•		•					•		
Horizontal Double Brick		•		•	•		•		•	•				•					•		
Shingle		•		•	•		•							•					•		
Parisian		•		•	•		•		•	•				•					•		
Double Parisian		•		•	•		•		•					•					•		
Giant Horizontal Parisian		•		•	•		•		•	•	•			•					•		
Parisian Stripe		•		•	•				•					•				•			
Pavillion	•	•		•	•		•		•					•						•	
Hungarian	•	•		•	•	•	•							•						•	

STRAIGHT STITCHES	Border	Good Backing	Poor Backing	Background	Design	Accent	Fast	Slow	Geometric Pattern	Shading	Yarn Hog	Snags	Snag-Proof	Little Texture	Medium Texture	High Relief	Flower Stitch	Weak Pattern	Medium Pattern	Strong Pattern	Distorts Canvas
Horizontal Hungarian	•	•		•	•	•	•		•					•					•		
Hungarian Ground	•	•		•	•		•		•					•					•		
Double Hungarian Ground	•	•		•	•		•		•					•					•		
Double Hungarian		•		•	•	•	•		•			•		•					•		
Pavillion Diamonds	•	•		•	•	•	•		•			•		•						•	
Old Florentine		•		•	•		•		•			•		•					•		
Horizontal Old Florentine		•		•	•		•		•			•		•					•		
Beaty	•	•		•	•		•		•			•		•					•		
Wild Goose Chase	•	•		•	•		•		•					•					•		
Willow		•		•	•		•		•			•		•					•		
Horizontal Milanese		•		•	•	•	•		•			•		•						•	
Vertical Milanese		•		•	•	•	•		•			•		•						•	
Upright Oriental		•		•	•		•		•			•		•						•	
Double Darning		•			•	•		•				•	•					•			
Padded Double Darning		•			•	•		•		•		•			•				•		
Diagonal L		•		•	•	•		•	•			•		•						•	
Roman II		•		•	•			•	•					•					•		
Lazy Roman II		•		•	•			•	•					•					•		
Roman III		•		•	•			•	•					•					•		
Lazy Roman III		•		•	•			•	•					•					•		
Gingham		•		•	•				•					•					•		
Patterned Threes		•		•	•				•					•					•		
Framed Pavillion		•		•	•	•	•	•	•			•		•					•		
Pavillion Steps		•		•	•		•		•	•		•		•						•	
Pavillion Boxes		•		•	•		•		•			•		•						•	
Jacquard Palace Pattern		•		•					•			•		•						•	
Darmstadt Pattern		•		•	•	•			•			•		•						•	
Jo-Jo		•		•	•	•	•		•			•		•						•	
Sutherland		•		•	•	•	•		•			•		•						•	
Frame		•		•	•	•	•		•	•		•		•						•	
Palace Pattern		•		•	•				•			•		•						•	
Princess	•	•		•	•	•	•		•			•		•						•	
Indian Stripe	•	•		•	•	•	•		•			•		•						•	
Victorian Step		•		•	•				•					•						•	
Triangle Variation	•	•		•	•	•			•			•								•	
F-106	•	•		•	•	•	•		•			•		•						•	
Woven Ribbons		•		•			•		•			•		•						•	

STRAIGHT STITCHES	Border	Good Backing	Poor Backing	Background	Design	Accent	Fast	Slow	Geometric Pattern	Shading	Yarn Hog	Snags	Snag-Proof	Little Texture	Medium Texture	High Relief	Flower Stitch	Weak Pattern	Medium Pattern	Strong Pattern	Distorts Canvas
Bargello Line Pattern		•		•	•		•		•	•		•		•						•	
Split Bargello		•		•	•			•	•	•	•	•		•					•		
Bargello Framework Pattern		•		•	•		•		•	•		•		•						•	
Four-Way Bargello		•		•	•		•		•	•		•		•			•			•	
Medieval Mosaic		•		•	•		•		•					•						•	
Jockey Cap	•	•		•	•		•					•		•						•	

This stitch can be worked over any number of canvas threads, up to six.

STRAIGHT GOBELIN

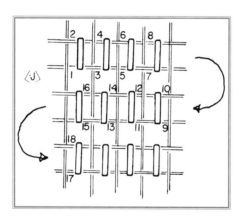

STRAIGHT

Any stitch that is made by placing the yarn between two points is a Straight Stitch. Place them anywhere they are needed. They are particularly useful on top of a background stitch to create fine detail.

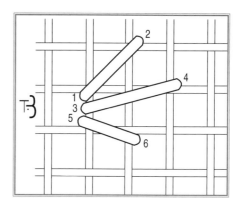

SATIN

This is a stitch borrowed from embroidery. Fill any irregularly shaped area with parallel stitches, disregarding the canvas threads.

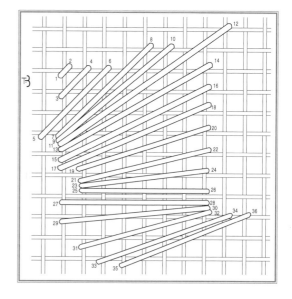

140

The Renaissance Stitch is Straight Gobelin over a tramé of one ply of Persian yarn. This gives subtle texture.

RENAISSANCE

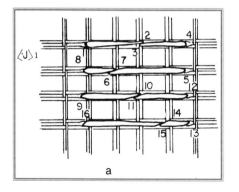

a

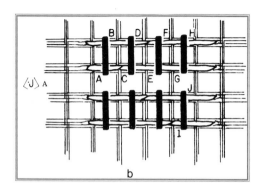

b

This stitch is based on embroidery's Split Stitch. It is particularly good for shading. Work this stitch over two to five canvas threads.

SPLIT
GOBELIN

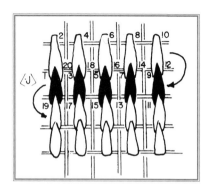

INTERLOCKING STRAIGHT GOBELIN

This Gobelin Stitch, too, may be worked over two to five canvas threads. Thicken your yarn if your stitch is over two canvas threads tall. It is particularly good for shading.

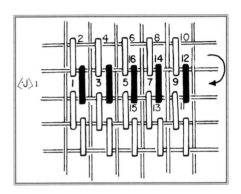

BRICK

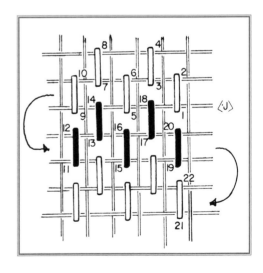

This stitch has a horizontal tramé like the Renaissance Stitch that gives it a subtle texture.

PADDED BRICK

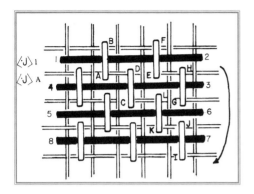

This stitch may be worked over four or six canvas threads with an even step. (See page 168.)

GIANT BRICK

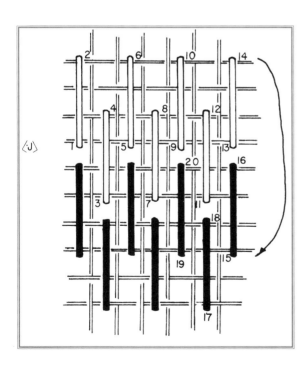

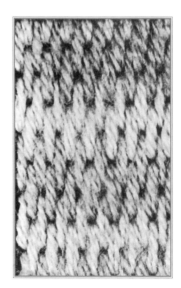

DOUBLE BRICK

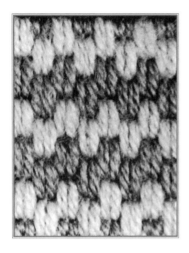

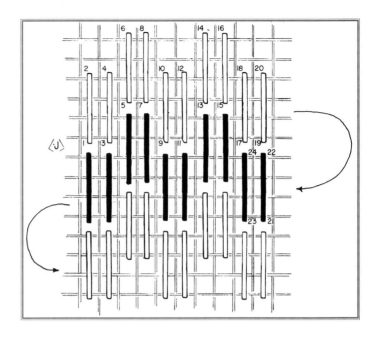

HORIZONTAL BRICK

HORIZONTAL DOUBLE BRICK

This stitch can be worked over two or four canvas threads. The photo shows Horizontal Brick; the drawing shows Horizontal Double Brick. Work it either way.

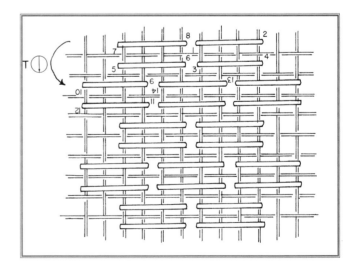

This arrangement of Straight Stitches reminds me of shingles on a roof.

SHINGLE

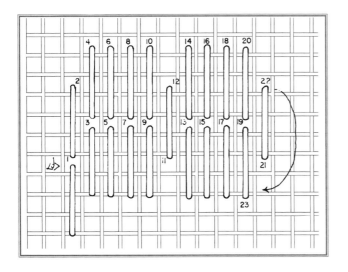

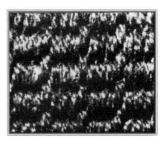

Parisian is a combination of long and short stitches (over two and four canvas threads). The tall stitches are over the short ones.

PARISIAN

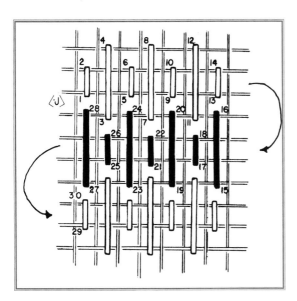

DOUBLE PARISIAN

This may be worked small (2,2,4,4,2,2,4,4, etc.) as in the photograph, or large (4,4,6,6,4,4,6,6, etc.).

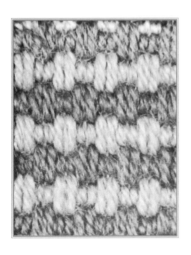

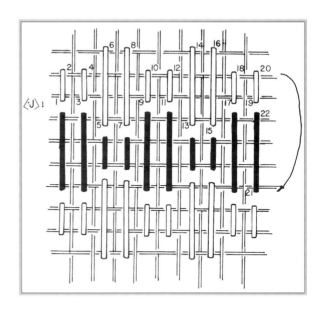

GIANT HORIZONTAL PARISIAN

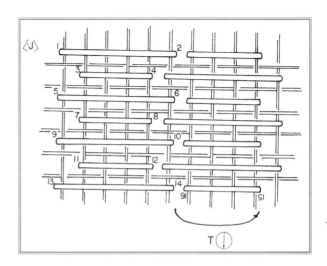

PARISIAN
STRIPE

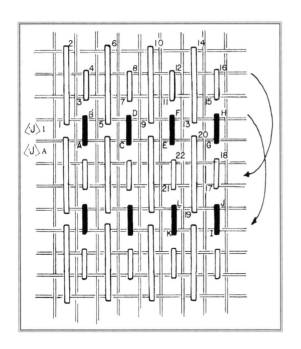

The diamonds share the short stitch.

PAVILLION

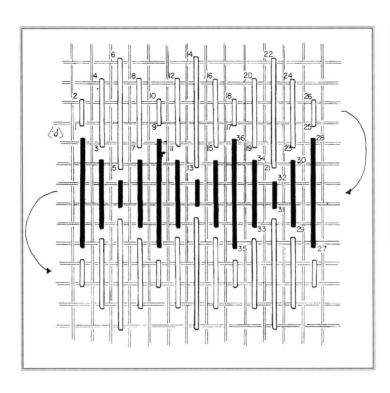

HUNGARIAN

This vertical stitch establishes a diamond pattern. It is good in two colors, although it is stunning in one color.

It is a set of three stitches—2,4,2. Skip a space. Repeat 2,4,2. Skip a space under the long stitch. Continue the pattern—2,4,2, then skip, then 2,4,2, etc. The long stitch in the second row fits in half of the space left in the first row.

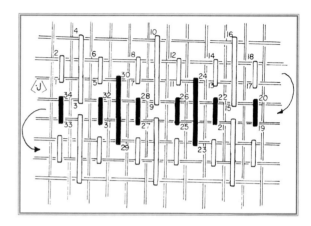

HORIZONTAL HUNGARIAN

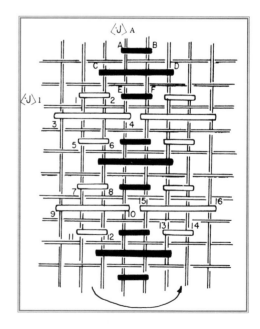

HUNGARIAN GROUND

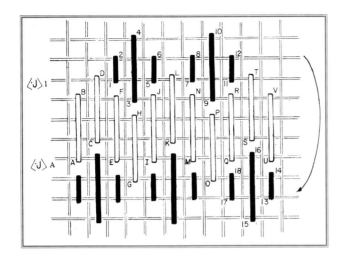

DOUBLE HUNGARIAN GROUND

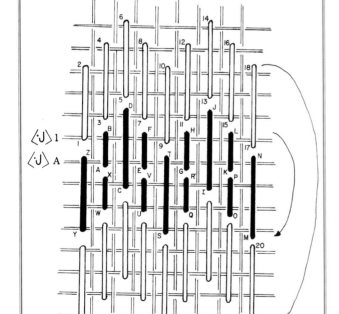

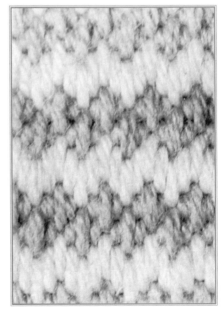

DOUBLE HUNGARIAN

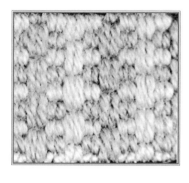

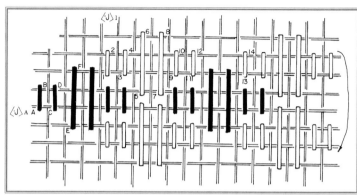

PAVILLION DIAMONDS

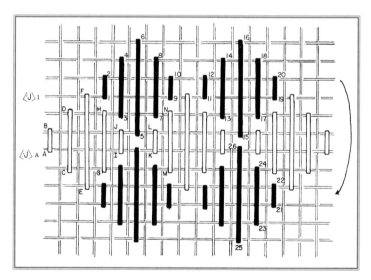

OLD FLORENTINE

Short:short:long:long:short:short. The short stitch goes over the long. The smallest version is 2,2,6,6,2,2; the largest is 3,3,9,9,3,3.

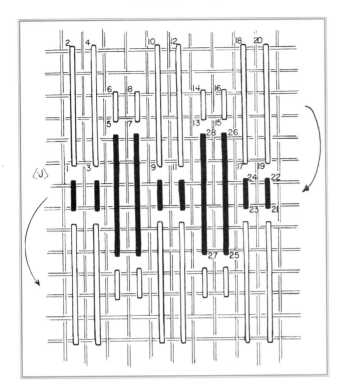

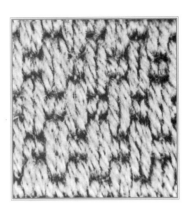

HORIZONTAL OLD FLORENTINE

When all the short stitches are worked in a second color, the stitch resembles a woven basket.

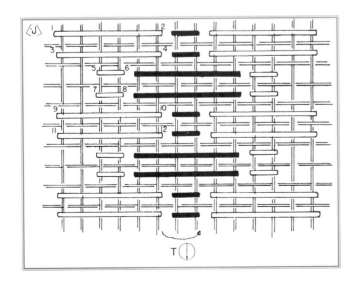

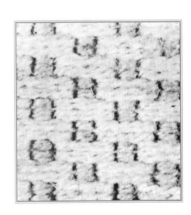

BEATY

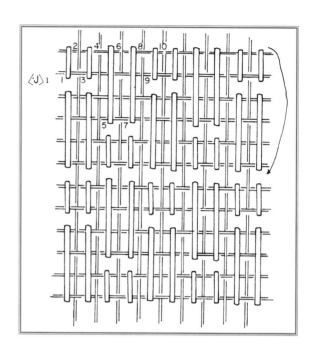

WILD GOOSE CHASE

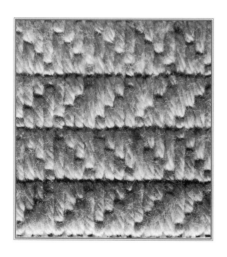

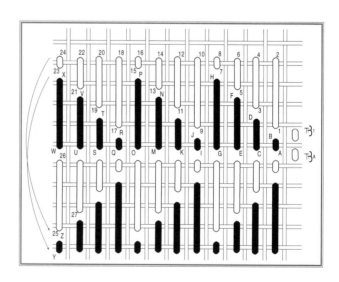

This is like Old Florentine, except there are three sets of stitches, 2,2,2,6,6,6,2,2,2.

WILLOW

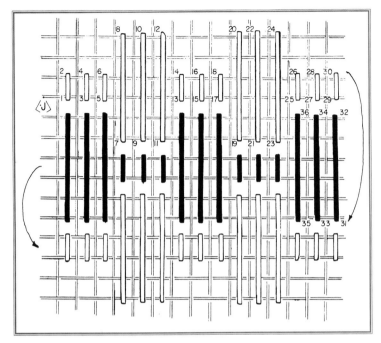

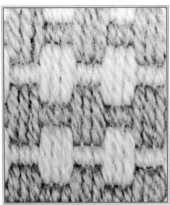

HORIZONTAL
MILANESE

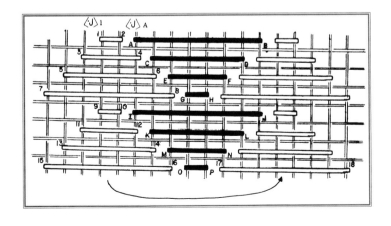

VERTICAL
MILANESE

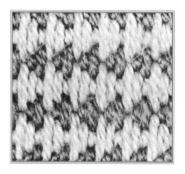

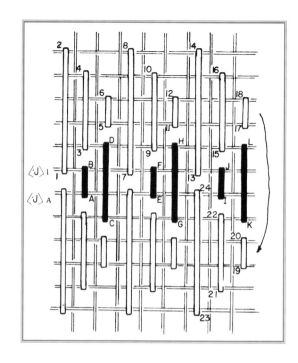

UPRIGHT
ORIENTAL

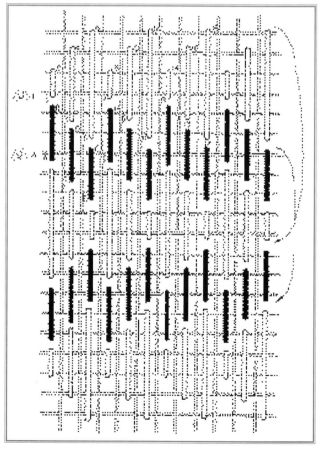

Darning patterns are created by working a Running Stitch in geometric patterns. Usually the canvas threads show where the yarn goes under them. (See the Angelis Stitch, page 377.) In this case, they are covered by making two trips across the canvas between the same canvas threads. This stitch can be worked in a varying pattern of over and under stitches. The stitch gives a bumpy look. In shorter stitches, it could look like gravel.

DOUBLE DARNING

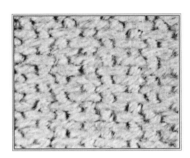

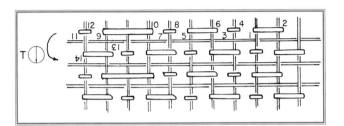

This fills an area that is similar to the Double Darning Stitch (see above), except that it is padded. If you are stitching with wool, make four trips across Penelope 10 and only two on Mono 14 to produce this thickly padded stitch. Experiment with other fibers to see how many trips you need to make across the area to duplicate the effect.

It makes a good sidewalk, wall, or other solid area. Vary the number of canvas threads that you go over and under.

PADDED DOUBLE DARNING

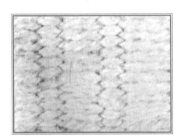

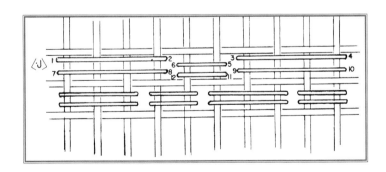

DIAGONAL L

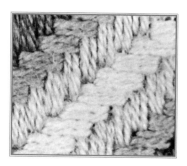

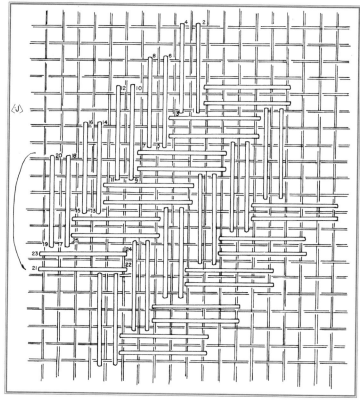

ROMAN II

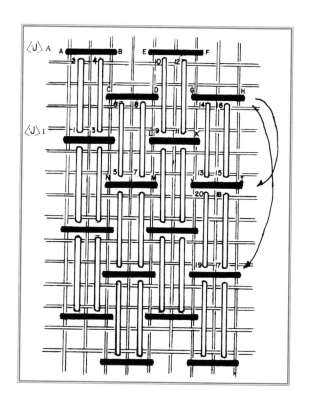

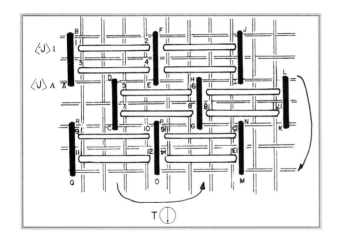

LAZY ROMAN II

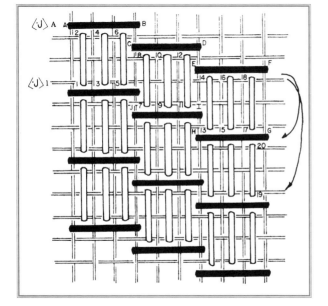

ROMAN III

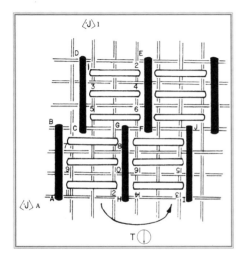

LAZY ROMAN III

GINGHAM

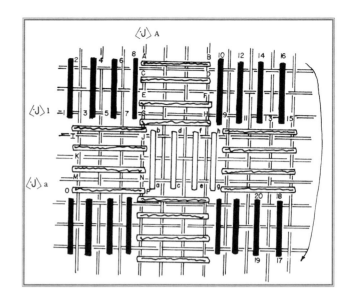

PATTERNED
THREES

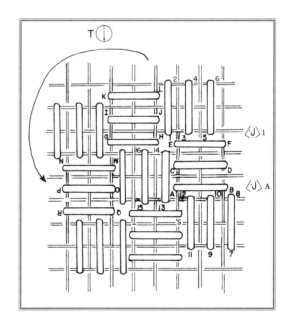

FRAMED PAVILLION

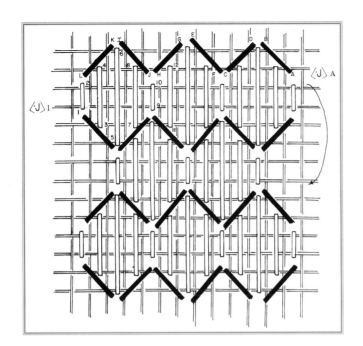

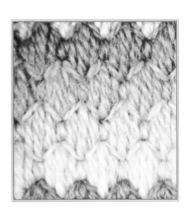

To get the three-dimensional look, always use three colors.

PAVILLION STEPS

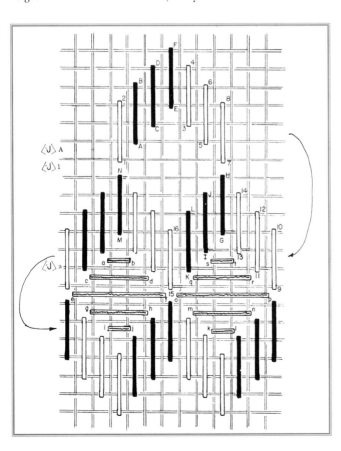

PAVILLION
BOXES

Use thinner yarn for the diagonal stripes.

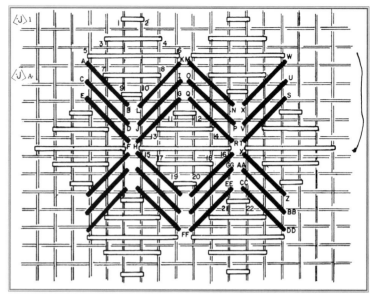

JACQUARD
PALACE
PATTERN

Use thinner yarn for the Frame Stitch.

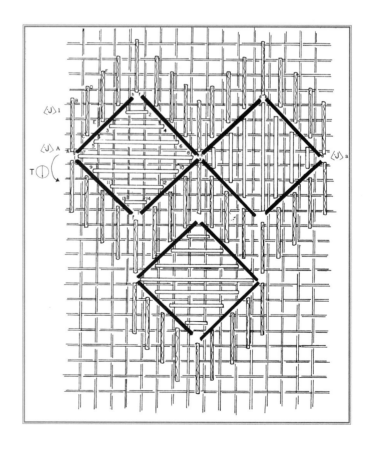

This stitch makes good butterfly or insect wings.

DARMSTADT PATTERN

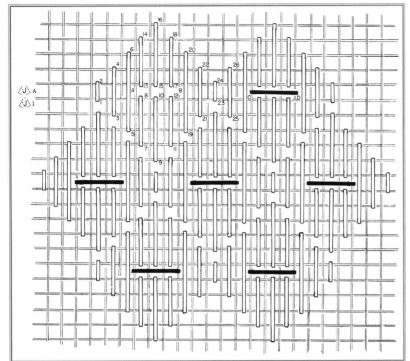

JO-JO

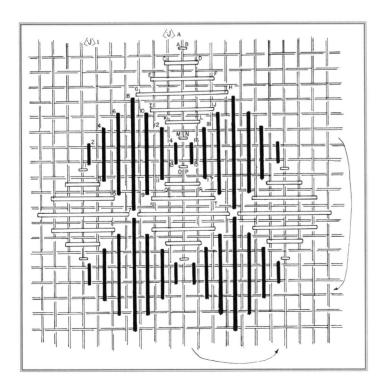

SUTHERLAND

You might want to thin your yarn. Note how the color variations change the look of the stitch.

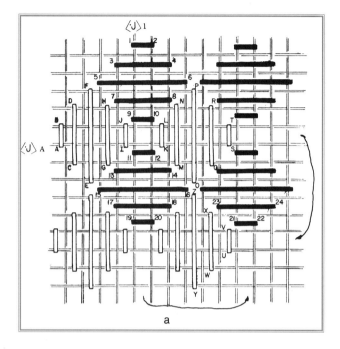

a

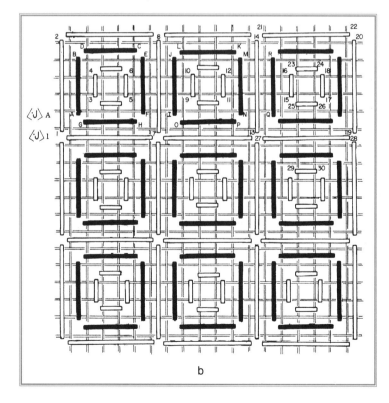

b

When working large stitches first, it is very easy to pull too tightly. Be careful. If, however, you wish to begin with the small stitches, watch the placement of them. It is not difficult to get them wrong. Work the dark shades in the center and the light colors on the outside for a three-dimensional look.

FRAME

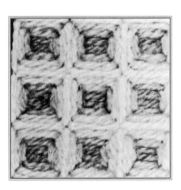

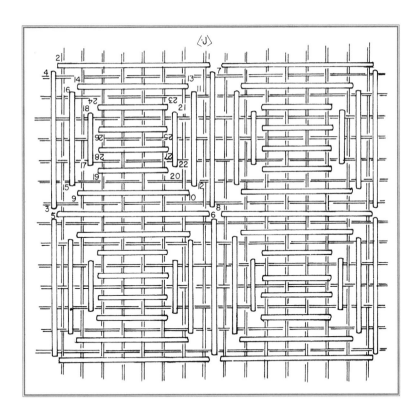

PALACE
PATTERN

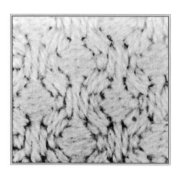

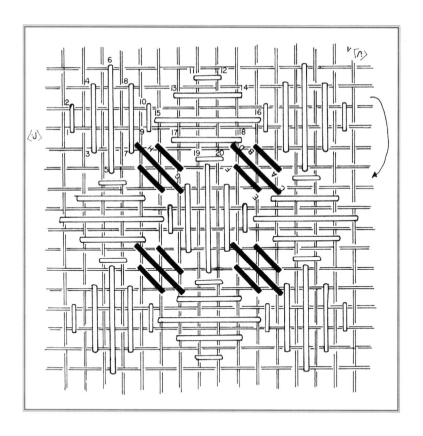

PRINCESS

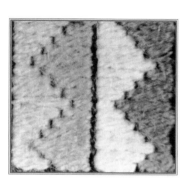

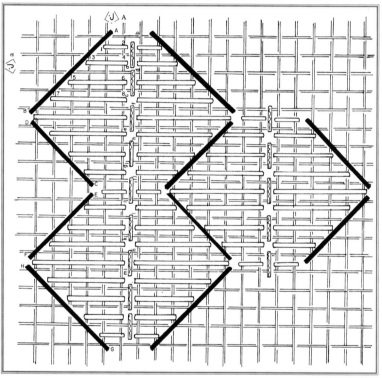

INDIAN
STRIPE

This stitch is best as a single stripe; however, if you want to do a whole area in Indian Stripe Stitches, alternate the rows to make them fit.

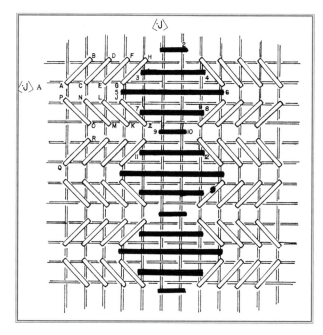

VICTORIAN
STEP

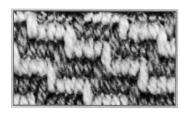

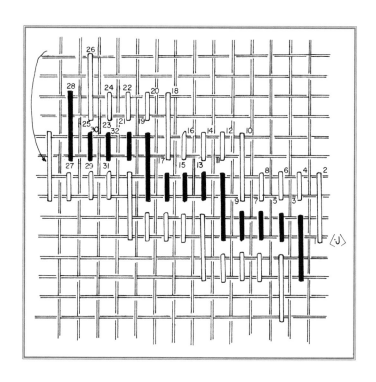

Portions of this stitch can be used for a sail on a boat.

TRIANGLE
VARIATION

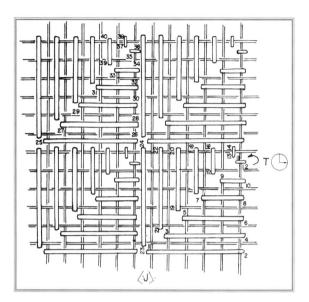

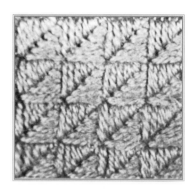

F-106

Various color combinations make this stitch look different. This stitch was
named for a delta-wing aircraft.

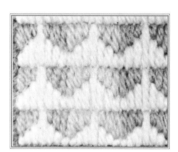

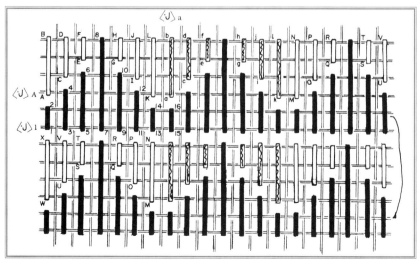

WOVEN
RIBBONS

Work the compensating stitches last.

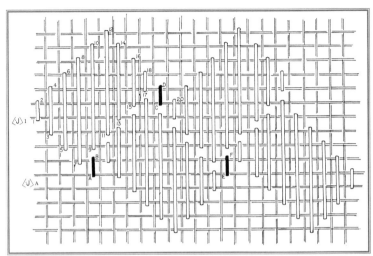

BARGELLO

Bargello is Straight Stitches worked in a geometric pattern. These stitches can vary in size from two canvas threads tall to six canvas threads tall. When stitches are placed next to each other in a zigzag line, the distance between the **top** of one stitch and the **top** of the next one is called a **step.** It is referred to by number—for example, "4:2." The "4" indicates how many canvas threads tall the stitch is; the "2" tells us how many canvas threads in the step. A "4:2" stitch is the most common in Bargello. The smaller the step number, the more gradual the incline (a). The larger the step number, the steeper the incline (c).

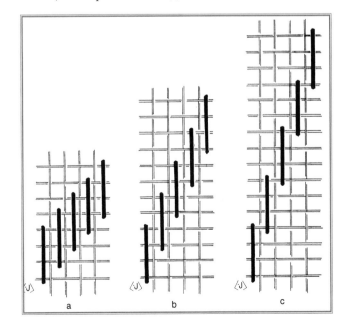

A line pattern is a zigzag of stitches. Both the stitch size and the step number may vary within one line. Split Bargello (page 170) is one example of a line pattern.

To produce arcs or curves, place more than one stitch on the same step (4:0). The more stitches there are on one step, the broader the curve (Bargello Line Pattern, below). These arcs or curves may be combined with a zigzag line for a more interesting pattern.

A framework pattern can be made by turning a line pattern upside down. (See page 170.) Fill in the center with a secondary pattern of your choice.

Bargello has limitless variations, both in stitch and in color. There is much more to learn about Bargello. There are lots of other kinds of patterns. Refer to any of the many good books on Bargello.

Note: In working a whole piece in Bargello, start the pattern in the middle of the canvas to achieve balance.

This is an example only. Both stitch size and step number may vary within one line.

BARGELLO LINE PATTERN

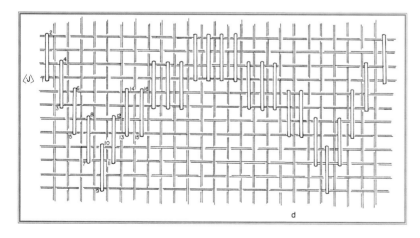

SPLIT BARGELLO

This stitch is wonderful for shading. In working this stitch you cannot start with the main line. You must start with compensating stitches. Use any line pattern. This is an example only.

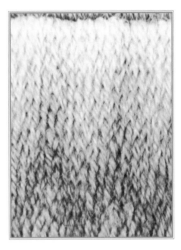

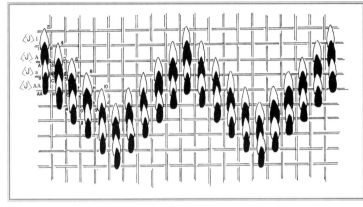

BARGELLO FRAMEWORK PATTERN

Try working the framework in the darkest color and lighter ones in the center. This is an example only. Try your hand at creating other patterns.

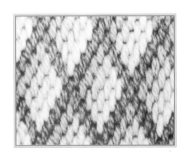

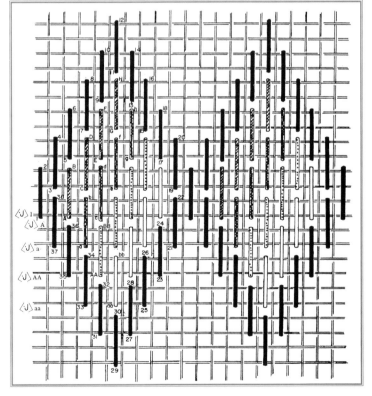

FOUR-WAY BARGELLO

Draw lines from the center to each of the four corners. It is on these lines that you change from vertical to horizontal stitches. I find it easier to turn the canvas at these lines.

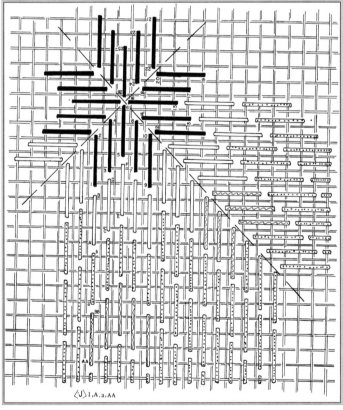

⟨J⟩ 1, A, a, AA

MEDIEVAL MOSAIC

This sample was stitched with the yarn going against the nap. See how uneven the stitches are! See page 31.

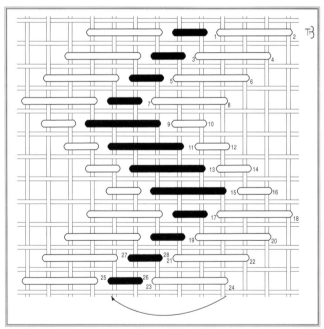

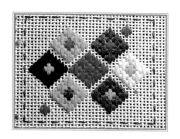

Plate 1—Color Relationships

Color relates to its environment. Notice how the colors change when surrounded by different colors. The lone square on the left seems red when viewed alone. So does the one on the right. Yet, when compared with true red in the center, they seem more orange and more violet, respectively. The same colors when used in different amounts (but still with the same colors) appear different. The yellow seems more vivid and intense in small amounts and against darker colors. [Smith]

Plate 2—Four Seasons in the Color Wheel

Designed and stitched by Margaret Brique. [P. Christensen]

Plate 3—Chaplain's Garden

Stitched by Eve Ingraham; designed by Marty Bell; yarns and stitches selected by Eve Ingraham. [Smith]

Plate 4—Gardening

Stitched by Pauline Hansen; designed by Mary Margaret Waldock; yarns and stitches selected by Jill Rigoli and Shirley McClure. [Smith]

Plate 5—Grampian Mountains in Summer

Designed and stitched by Margaret Brique. [P. Christensen]

Plate 6—Bachelor Buttons

Designed and stitched by Lani Silver. (also shown on front cover) [Smith]

Plate 7—Open-Door Cottage

Stitched by Marsha Olshin; designed by Marcy Covington; yarns and stitches selected by Martha Shevett. [Smith]

Plate 8—Floral Wreath with Bird's Nest

Stitched by Bernice Abernathy; designed by Barbara Post Elmore; yarns and stitches selected by Bernice Abernathy. [Smith]

Plate 9—First Thanksgiving

*Stitched by Pat Fifield-Saenz;
designed by Carol Gantz and Sandy
Steere; yarns and stitches selected by
Pat Fifield-Saenz. [P. Christensen]*

Plate 10—Spice Angel

*Designed and stitched by Judy Dalvit.
[Smith]*

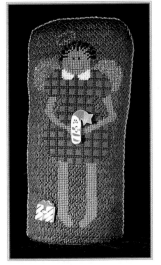

**Plate 11—Clara, Angel of Missed
Stitches**

*Stitched by Sharon Snyder; designed
by and yarns and stitches selected by
Debbie Stiebler. [Smith]*

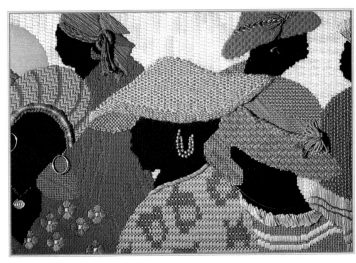

Plate 12—Territorial T'ing

*Stitched by Sherrill Collins; designed
by Lisa Etre; yarns and stitches
selected by Sherrill Collins.
[P. Christensen]*

Plate 13—Far Horizons

Stitched by Vera Holland; designed by Tish Holland; yarns and stitches selected by Vera Holland. [Smith]

Plate 14—Christmas Ribbons

Designed and stitched by Ruth Schmuff. [Smith]

Plate 15—Mardi Gras Mask

Stitched by Lucenda A. Ichioka; designed by Teresa Lee; yarns and stitches selected by Lucenda A. Ichioka and Susan Portra. [P. Christensen]

Plate 16—Halloween Pumpkin

Designed and stitched by Ruth Chow. [Smith]

Plate 17—Crystal Santa

Stitched by Christine C. Chrystal; designed by Joan Thomasson; yarns and stitches selected by Christine Chrystal. [P. Christensen]

Plate 18—Tudor Frog Prince

Stitched by Judy M. Greer; designed by Shiela S. Corey; yarns and stitches selected by Judy M. Greer. [Smith]

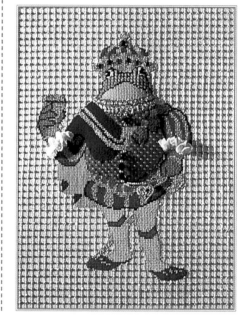

Plate 19—Hunt Scene

Stitched by Jogina Picariello; designed by Claire March; yarns and stitches selected by Martha Shevett. [Smith]

Plate 20—Sunflower Doll

Stitched by Kelly A. Doyle; designed by Sandy Jenkins; yarns selected by Kelly A. Doyle; stitches selected by Kelly A. Doyle and Sandy Jenkins. [P. Christensen]

Plate 21—Scissors Box

Stitched by Pat Fifield-Saenz and Elaine Maffie; designed by Sharon Garmize; yarns and stitches selected by Pat Fifield-Saenz. [P. Christensen]

Plate 22—Santa and Critters

Stitched by Patty Cwalinski; designed by Liz Goodrick-Dillon; yarns and stitches selected by Patty Cwalinski and Nancy Laux. [P. Christensen]

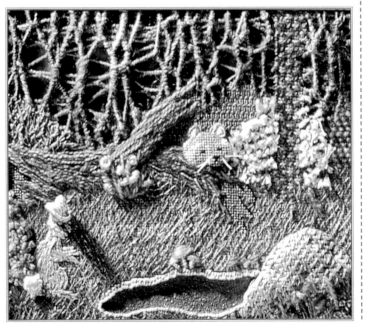

Plate 23—All Creatures

Designed and stitched by Cyndi Parker. [Smith]

Plate 24—Cliff Hanger

Designed and stitched by Davie
Hyman.(idea from a photo,
near right) [P. Christensen]

Plate 25—White Coat

Stitched by Susan Simons; designed
by Charley Harper; yarns and stitches
selected by Susan Simons.
[P. Christensen]

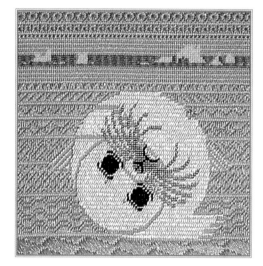

Plate 26—Feathers and Lace

Stitched by Jogina Picariello;
designed by Clarice Bethel; yarns
Martha Shevett. [Smith]

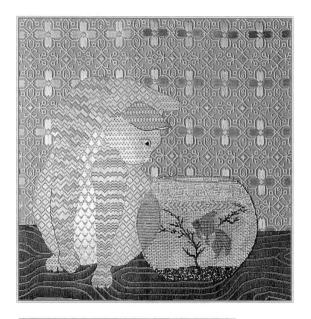

Plate 27—Cat and Fish Bowl

Designed and stitched by Susan Dawson. [P. Christensen]

Plate 28—Mr. M. Fibian

Designed and stitched by Brenda Stofft; yarns selected by Brenda Stofft; stitches selected by Dede Ogden. [Smith]

Plate 29—Bola Tie and Name Tag

Designed and stitched by Sally Ann Licocci. [Smith]

Plate 30—Colonial Quintet

Stitched by Gail Bloom; designed by Genny Morrow; yarns and stitches selected by Genny Morrow. [Smith]

Plate 31—Queen Elizabeth Tea Cozy

Stitched by Diana Bosworth; designed by Susan Burge and Margy Richardson; yarns and stitches selected by Diana Bosworth. [Smith]

Plate 32—Easter Egg Diorama

Stitched by Mary Kay Whaley; designed by Karen McVean; yarns and stitches selected by Mary Kay Whaley. [Smith]

Plate 33—Farmer's Delight

Stitched by Carol M. Hester; designed by Davie Hyman; yarns and stitches selected by Davie Hyman and Carol M. Hester. [P. Christensen]

Plate 34—March Angel

Stitched by Gale Martin; designed by Ricki Henry; yarns and stitches selected by Gale Martin. [Smith]

Plate 35—Lady with Red Flower

Stitched by Helen Veronin; designed by Clarice Bethel; yarns and stitches selected by Helen Veronin.
[P. Christensen]

Plate 36—Hot-Air Balloon

Stitched by Barbara Budlow and Karen Funk; designed by Linda Kovac Johnson; yarns and stitches selected by Barbara Budlow. [Smith]

Plate 37—Dreidel

Designed and stitched by Jill Rigoli. [Smith]

Plate 38—Gazebo

Designed and stitched by Cyndi Parker. [Smith]

Plate 39—Cats and a Dog

Stitched by Susan Simons and Leah Powers; designed by Christine Kulie; yarns and stitches selected by Susan Simons. [P. Christensen]

Plate 40—Collegiate Snowman

Stitched by Sue D. Jennings; designed by Carol Dupree; yarns and stitches selected by Sue D. Jennings. [Smith]

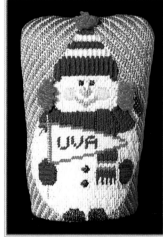

Plate 41—Cat and Feet

Stitched by Vicky DeAngelis; designed by Terry Enfield; yarns and stitches selected by Vicky DeAngelis. [Smith]

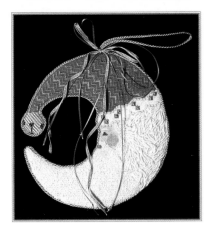

Plate 42—Crescent Santa

Designed and stitched by Jill Rigoli. [Smith]

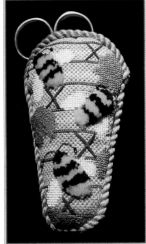

Plate 43—Scissors Case

Stitched by Aurora A. Grosse; designed by Lani Silver; yarns and stitches selected by Aurora A. Grosse. [Smith]

Plate 44—Mollie, the Calico Cat

Designed and stitched by Amy Wolfson. [Smith]

Plate 45—Jacket

Designed and stitched by Shirley McClure. [P. Christensen]

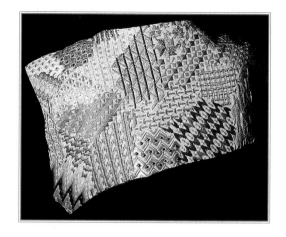

Plate 46—Winter Lambscape

Designed and stitched by Fay Thiebaud. [P. Christensen]

Plate 47—Columbines and Lace

Designed and stitched by Joan-Marie Duff. [P. Christensen]

Plate 48—Rose Heart

Stitched by Mary Brandon; designed by Terry Enfield; yarns and stitches selected by Mary Brandon. [P. Christensen]

Plate 49—Akiko

Stitched by Amy H. Bunger; designed by Marjorie Hunter; yarns and stitches selected by Amy H. Bunger. [Smith]

Plate 50—Southwestern Houses in the Desert

Stitched by Jackie Beaty; designed by Ann Christmas; yarns selected by Ann Christmas, Jackie Beaty and the author; stitches selected by Jackie Beaty. [Smith]

Plate 51—Celtic Fantasy

Designed and stitched by Carole H. Lake. [Smith]

Plate 52—Edwardian Belt

Stitched by Martha Shevett; designed by Pat Smith; yarns and stitches selected by Martha Shevett. [Smith]

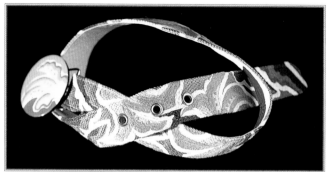

Plate 53—Forest of Lights

Designed and stitched by Kathy Holicky. [Smith]

Plate 54—Persian Fantasy

Designed and stitched by Ann Strite-Kurz. [P. Christensen]

You may save yourself some ripping if you study this stitch before you begin working. This is true for all stitches, but especially for this one. Look at the photo to see how inattention to nap and twist can affect the look of the stitch.

JOCKEY CAP

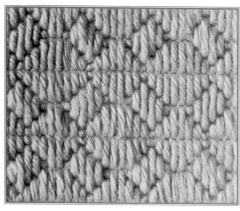

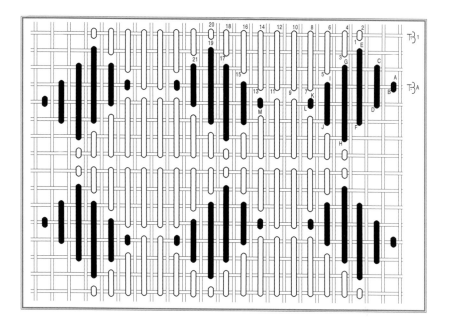

Photo 15—Last Tango: *designed and stitched by Bernice Janofsky. [Smith]*

Diagonal Stitches are those that cover the canvas by crossing junctions of canvas threads rather than by going between them. In referring to these slanted stitches, I have designated the angle or slant they take by two numbers. The first number refers to the number of canvas threads that you go up or down. The second number refers to the number of canvas threads that you go over. For example, a 1 x 1 stitch is a Tent Stitch (Basketweave, Continental, or Half Cross). A 1 x 3 stitch is shown below, as are a 3 x 1 and a 3 x 3. For those stitches where both numbers are the same, you may count, diagonally, the junctions of canvas threads, instead of counting up three and over three. Whether you go up or down (for the first number) is shown in the sketch that accompanies each stitch.

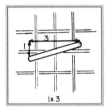 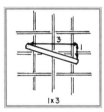 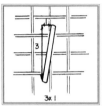 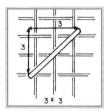 

DIAGONAL STITCHES	Border	Good Backing	Poor Backing	Background	Design	Accent	Fast	Slow	Geometric Pattern	Shading	Yarn Hog	Snags	Snag-Proof	Little Texture	Medium Texture	High Relief	Flower Stitch	Weak Pattern	Medium Pattern	Strong Pattern	Distorts Canvas
Half Cross			•										•	•					•		•
Continental		•			•					•			•	•					•		
Basketweave		•		•	•								•	•					•		
Irregular Continental		•		•	•					•		•		•						•	•
Alternating Continental		•		•	•	•		•					•	•					•		
Padded Alternating Continental		•		•	•	•		•					•	•					•		
Chottie's Plaid	•	•		•	•								•	•					•		
Rainbow Plaid	•	•		•	•								•	•					•		
Petit Point		•		•	•	•		•		•			•	•				•			•
Rep		•		•	•	•		•		•			•	•				•			•
Diagonal Stripe		•		•	•	•			•					•					•		•
Slanted Gobelin		•		•	•		•		•					•					•		•
Slanted Gobelin, 2 x 2	•	•		•	•		•		•					•					•		•
Slanted Gobelin, 5 x 2				•	•		•		•		•			•					•		•
Padded Slanted Gobelin		•		•	•		•	•								•			•		•
Split Slanted Gobelin		•		•	•			•		•			•	•				•			•
Interlocking Gobelin		•		•	•			•					•					•			•

DIAGONAL STITCHES	Border	Good Backing	Poor Backing	Background	Design	Accent	Fast	Slow	Geometric Pattern	Shading	Yarn Hog	Snags	Snag-Proof	Little Texture	Medium Texture	High Relief	Flower Stitch	Weak Pattern	Medium Pattern	Strong Pattern	Distorts Canvas
Giant Interlocking Gobelin				•	•		•			•		•		•				•			•
Oblique Slav			•	•	•		•			•		•		•						•	•
Encroaching Oblique				•	•					•		•		•						•	•
Bunger	•		•	•			•					•		•						•	•
Diagonal Beaty				•	•		•					•		•						•	
Nobuko		•		•	•					•		•		•						•	•
Kennan		•		•	•					•		•		•						•	•
Knitting		•		•	•									•						•	
Lazy Knitting		•		•	•								•	•				•			
Giant Knitting				•	•		•					•		•						•	
Diagonal Knitting		•		•	•									•						•	
Kalem		•		•	•									•						•	
Lazy Kalem		•		•	•								•	•				•			
Stem	•	•		•	•									•						•	
Diagonal Stem	•	•		•	•									•						•	
Byzantine #1		•		•	•		•			•		•		•						•	•
Byzantine #2		•		•	•		•			•		•		•						•	•
Byzantine #3		•		•	•		•					•		•						•	•
Byzantine #4		•		•	•		•					•		•						•	•
Byzantine #5		•		•	•		•					•		•						•	•
Irregular Byzantine		•		•	•		•					•		•						•	•
Byzantine-Scotch		•		•	•		•					•		•						•	•
Jacquard		•		•	•									•						•	•
Irregular Jacquard		•		•	•		•					•		•						•	•
Swirl		•		•			•					•		•						•	•
Diagonal Hungarian Ground		•		•	•		•							•						•	•
Staircase		•		•	•									•						•	•
Milanese		•		•	•	•						•			•					•	•
Milanese Color Variation		•		•	•	•						•			•					•	•
Oriental		•		•	•	•						•		•						•	•
Mixed Milanese		•		•	•	•		•			•	•			•					•	•
Arrowhead		•		•	•	•		•						•						•	•
Criss-Cross Hungarian	•	•		•	•	•	•								•		•			•	

TENT STITCHES

Tent Stitches are a group of three stitches—Half Cross, Continental, and Basketweave—that look essentially the same on the right side of the canvas. They are 1 x 1 diagonal stitches. The primary difference among them is the direction in which they are stitched. Continental is worked from right to left; Half Cross is stitched from left to right; and Basketweave is done on diagonal rows.

Of these, Basketweave is king. It covers the canvas well, with distinct stitches and without distorting the canvas. Its downside it that it is not maneuverable; it does not get into and out of tight spaces easily. Continental does. It also has pretty, well-defined stitches, but it puts a lot of torque on the canvas. Sometimes this distortion cannot be straightened out. Half Cross is the stepchild of the three. Its stitches are not as distinct as the others and it also distorts the canvas. Every once in a while a Half Cross Stitch is needed to get out of a small area of the design. Otherwise it is not recommended. See the full discussions of all three stitches below.

CONTINENTAL

The Continental Stitch has the next best backing and is the next most distinct stitch of the Tent Stitches. Its main drawback is that it pulls the canvas badly out of shape.

You really should use Basketweave wherever you can. But Continental will get the very small areas that Basketweave cannot.

If you insist on using Continental instead of Basketweave, you should try to make the stitches as even and uniform as possible. You may work

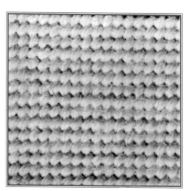

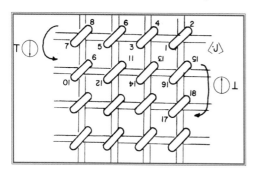

For horizontal rows, work left to right.

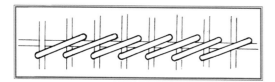

Reverse side of Continental worked horizontally. Compare this to the reverse sides of Basketweave and Half Cross.

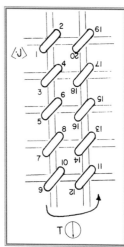

For vertical rows, work top to bottom.

Outlining with Continental.

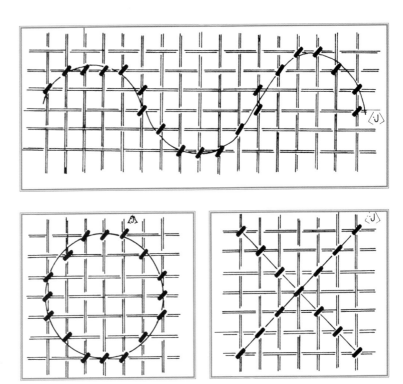

Continental either horizontally or vertically (see page 177). Choose the direction that best fills the area you have.

Always work this stitch from right to left or from top to bottom. If you are filling a large space, do not turn the canvas upside down for the second row; cut the yarn and begin the second row below the first on the right. If you do not, there is enough of a slight difference in the shape of the stitches to reflect the light differently; this will show as a flaw in your final product (see photo on page 177).

If you bury the tails of your yarn at the beginning of each row, there will be a noticeable area of extra thickness at the beginning and end of each row of stitching. Notice that, in the photo, I did not start and stop each row at the beginning of the row but that I buried the tails wherever I was when the yarn ran out. Even though the wool that I stitched with is resilient (see page 36), there is still a bump where I buried each tail. The camera does magnify errors, so these flaws are not nearly so visible when viewed directly. Still, if I had used a Waste Knot or an Away Knot in the margin of blank canvas, it would have been better.

Half Cross has the poorest backing of the Tent Stitches. It will not wear well because of this. It also uses less yarn than the other two Tent Stitches, but this is not a good place to save a little money. Besides, each stitch is not distinct, and it distorts the canvas. I strongly suggest that you replace it with Basketweave—or Continental if you cannot use Basketweave.

HALF CROSS

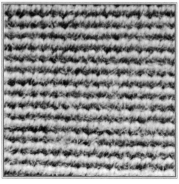

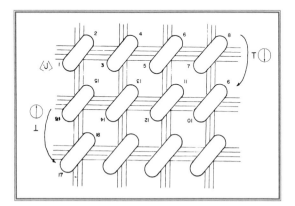

To work Half Cross in horizontal rows, stitch from left to right.

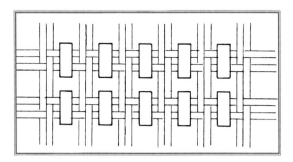

Reverse side of Half Cross stitched horizontally. Compare this to the reverse sides of Basketweave and Continental.

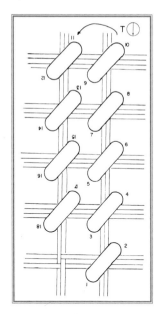

To work Half Cross in vertical rows, stitch from bottom to top.

BASKETWEAVE

Basketweave is one of the most used and misused stitches in needlepoint. It is an excellent stitch to know and use. A durable backing, resembling a woven pattern, is created. This makes it a "must" for chairs, footstools, and other items that will receive lots of wear.

The finished piece is not distorted, but still needs blocking to help even out the tension on each stitch and to reset the sizing in the canvas. (See more about blocking on page 113.) It can be worked without turning the canvas. Because the stitch lacks maneuverability, it is not a good stitch for designing in very small areas. This is when the Continental comes in handy.

Study the figure below. Note that, basically, the stitch fills the canvas in diagonal rows, starting at the upper right corner. These rows interlock, sort of like the teeth of two gears. Some students find learning Basketweave easier if they start with a longer row, rather than starting in the corner and learning how to turn rows before they have the hang of making each basic unit. If this appeals to you, start with the 7-8 stitch in the diagram below and work an up row until you are comfortable with it. Cut the yarn and repeat the process for a down row, beginning with the 13-14 stitch. Once you understand how the rows progress upward and downward, start in the corner, at the 1-2 stitch, and learn how to turn rows.

As you work you will notice that a pattern is developing. In making an up row, the needle always goes straight across under two canvas threads. In making a down row, the needle always goes straight down under two canvas threads. Notice that the first of these two canvas threads is covered by a stitch in the preceding row. It is a very common error to go across or under three canvas threads by not counting the covered one.

At the end of each row there is what many students refer to as a turn stitch. Actually it is the first stitch of a new row. If it helps you to consider it a turn stitch, then do so. At

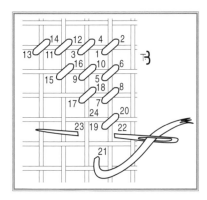

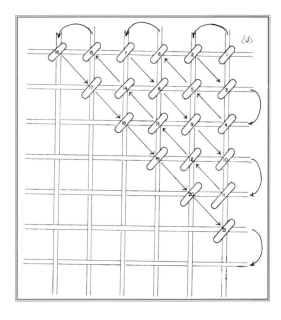

Sequence of stitches.

the end of the up row this turn stitch is a horizontal Continental Stitch, and at the end of the down row this is a vertical Continental Stitch. The common error here is to leave the turn stitch out or get carried away and make two turn stitches. If you have made an error somewhere, check to see if this is it.

When your yarn runs out and you must start another one, be sure to start **exactly** where you left off. If you do not, a line will show on the right side of your work. For example, if your yarn runs out at the end of an up row, do not start the new yarn at the bottom of the up row that you just finished, thus starting another up row. Instead, you should be at the top of that last up row, ready to begin a down row. Most people tend to put their work away for the day when they have finished working the yarn on a needle. It might help you to end in the middle of a row, so that you can tell at a glance whether you are stitching an up row or a down row.

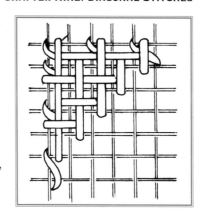

Reverse side of Basketweave; last row is a DOWN row.

When working Basketweave on Regular Mono canvas, note that at the intersections of the canvas threads in a horizontal row, the vertical canvas threads alternate between being on top of and underneath the horizontal canvas threads. However, on the diagonal, the vertical canvas threads are always on top or always underneath the horizontal canvas threads. If you will take care always to cover the vertical intersections of canvas threads with a down row and to cover the horizontal intersections of the canvas threads with an up row, you will produce a stitch that is very even in appearance on the right side and that stabilizes the junctions of the canvas threads. This hint will also help you keep track of up rows and down rows. (See page 182.)

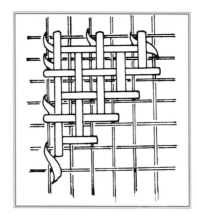

Reverse side of Basketweave; last row is an UP row. Compare this with the reverse sides of Half Cross and Continental.

A Waste Knot works well with Basketweave. If you work the beginning and ending tails under diagonally, a ridge will form that will show on the right side.

When this stitch is done on a frame, it does not produce exactly the same weave on the back as it does when it is worked in continuous motion. On a frame, the needle splits the back of each stitch slightly; this makes a tighter area for weaving tails in. In this case, refrain from weaving the tails in and out of the existing stitches, even in resilient wool.

Sometimes an objectionable diagonal pattern and/or uneven stitches are discernible in areas of Basketweave. Several easily avoidable things cause this:

1. Stitching an up row on the canvas where a down row should be and stitching a down row on the canvas where an up row should be causes less than even stitches. (See page 182.)

2. Stitching with a too-long yarn causes some stitches to be too thin. If you will notice, you can see that the rough canvas wears the yarn thin. If your yarn is too long, stitches at the beginning of a new yarn will be pleasingly plump; those at the end, too thin. When you start a new yarn, a plump stitch will be next to a thin one. Cutting your yarn shorter avoids this. (See page 30.)

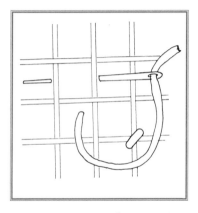

Correct *up row. At each intersection of canvas threads, horizontal canvas threads and vertical ones meet. The one that is on top alternates at each junction of the canvas threads. In this example the vertical thread will correctly be sandwiched by a horizontal canvas thread on the front of the canvas and by a horizontal yarn on the back of the canvas. This arrangement adds stability to this intersection and a smoother look to your stitching.*

3. Overtwisting the yarn as you stitch causes the yarn to get thinner. Thinner stitches do not cover well. Try to keep the yarn's original twist as you stitch. (See page 39.)

4. Losing the yarn's original twist makes a fat, sloppy yarn. The stitches will be uneven and messy looking. Again, keeping the yarn's original twist will cure this problem.

5. If your yarn is not quite thick enough to fill the holes, you will be able to see at a glance whether the thin yarn slants up or down toward the next stitch. Before you stitch, experiment to be sure your yarn is of the optimum thickness. (See the section on thickening and thinning yarns on page 33.) The best solution for Basketweave is to choose another size of canvas or another yarn.

6. Weaving tails of yarn under existing stitches in diagonal rows causes a diagonal line on the front.

Basketweave is not really frightfully complicated. It may take some study on your part, but once you get the hang of the stitch you will enjoy working it. It has a certain rhythm that develops easily. You can achieve a perfection with this stitch that is unique and valued. When the area is absolutely too small, and when outlining, use the Continental Stitch.

Incorrect *up row. Note how the stitch will cover the* vertical—*not the horizontal—canvas thread at the intersection of the canvas threads. This vertical thread will not be stabilized by sandwiching the top canvas thread and the yarn. Also the stitches will not look as smooth as they could.*

This stitch is excellent for shading. In working it, be sure to keep it a 1 x 1, 2 x 2, 3 x 3, 4 x 4, or 5 x 5 stitch. Count the junctions of the canvas threads diagonally (page 175). The rows will be irregular. The drawing and photos are examples only. Do your own.

IRREGULAR CONTINENTAL

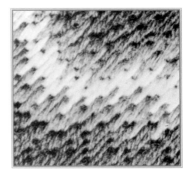

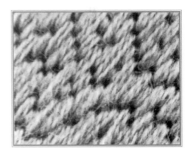

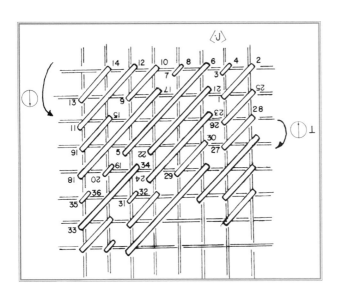

Work this stitch randomly or in a pattern with one color or more than one. It fits into a small area.

ALTERNATING CONTINENTAL

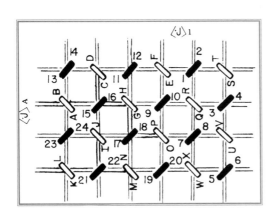

183

PADDED ALTERNATING CONTINENTAL

Work this stitch in three colors.

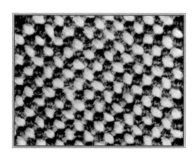

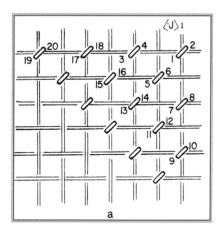

a

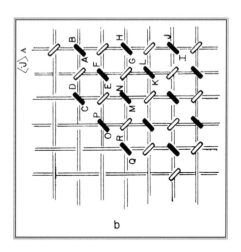

b

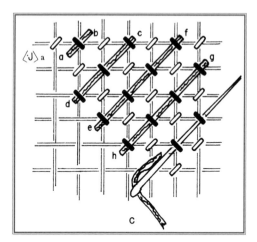

c

CHOTTIE'S PLAID

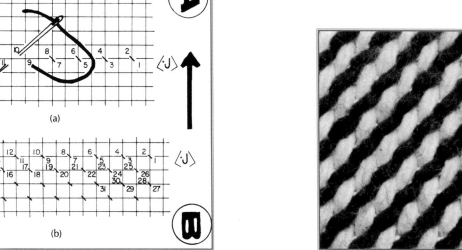

FOUNDATION

(a)

(b)

You can make up your own plaid! Choose as many or as few colors as you like. Too many get busy, unless you have a real pattern to them (like the Rainbow Plaid on page 186). Four colors work well. A plaid is made up of a repeat count called a *sett*. Choose how many times you would like to repeat each color in your sett. It is interesting to use a date to help you do this. The example below uses the date October 12, 1963 (10-12-6-3).

IMPORTANT: The stitches are worked lying in a nontraditional slant; that is, lower right to upper left. You will have to turn the canvas while you work so that the finished piece will have the stitches slanting properly.

To do this, determine the top left and top right corners of your canvas. Mark the top left corner with an A and the top right corner with a B. Turn your canvas 90° so that A and B are on the right side. Now line up your canvas to match the A on the page below with the A on your canvas and so that the Bs match. Stitch according to the diagram. Diagram *a* shows the method of working the stitch; Diagram *b* shows four rows of foundation worked.

Working every other stitch on every other row (as the diagram shows), stitch the foundation in your sett pattern. Color A will be repeated ten times; B, twelve times; C, six times; and D, three times. This makes

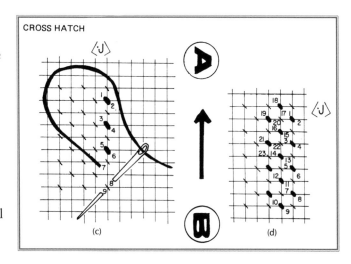

CROSS HATCH

(c)

(d)

your sett. (Once you have determined your count and colors for a particular plaid, stick with it. If you don't repeat the count, you won't make a plaid.) Note that diagonal rows of worked stitches are formed and that diagonal rows of unworked stitches are also formed.

Cross-hatching is the filling in of the unworked stitches that you skipped when laying the foundation. To do the next step, turn the canvas 90°. Then your stitches will slant in the correct direction for a Tent Stitch. Fill in the blank areas with the same stitch technique in the same 10-12-6-3 pattern. Keeping the same directions for the A and B corners in mind, follow the diagrams on page 185. Work ten rows of color A, twelve of color B, six of color C, and three of color D. Continue in this count until you have finished the area. When you have finished stitching Chottie's Plaid, the stitches will lie in the traditional Tent Stitch slant; that is, lower left to upper right.

If you are working Chottie's Plaid correctly, your piece will be reversible; that is, it will look the same on both sides—except where you tied on and off. If you really want it to be reversible (for instance, on a handbag flap or a coaster), tie the yarn on and off in the margins of blank canvas. If you don't care whether the piece is reversible, bury the ends as usual.

It's easy to slip into working a regular Continental Stitch, but if you do, you have lost the whole plaid.

RAINBOW PLAID

This version of Chottie's Plaid produces a beautiful plaid of the colors in the color wheel. Follow the colors listed below to re-create this lovely effect. Stitch one row of each color for the foundation. These colors must run in the sequence in which they are listed. Repeat the entire sequence as many times as you wish. Cross-hatch in the

same count and color sequence (one row for each color of the cross-hatching). This is a large pattern, and it requires a good-sized area to show it off. It makes a lovely pillow or tote bag.

You can use any brand of yarn and any fiber, but you do need to run the colors in families (dark, medium, and light of the same color) or the plaid will not come out right.

COLORS FOR RAINBOW PLAID			
Yellow	dark	Violet	dark
	medium		medium
	light		light
Yellow-orange	dark	Blue-violet	dark
	medium		medium
	light		light
Orange	dark	Blue	dark
	medium		medium
	light		light
Red-Orange	dark	Blue-green	dark
	medium		medium
	light		light
Red	dark	Green	dark
	medium		medium
	light		light
Red-violet	dark	Yellow-green	dark
	medium		medium
	light		light

Split the vertical canvas threads of Penelope canvas and work Continental or Basketweave. Thin your yarn. This is difficult to get even and smooth on Penelope canvas. Use it only if one or two small areas of your design demand Petit Point. For a whole Petit Point picture, use Petit Point canvas (page 9).

PETIT POINT

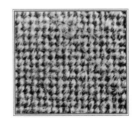

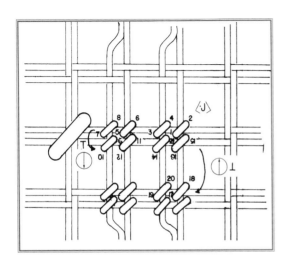

REP

This makes a nice, small, vertical stripe. This is a good stitch in one color. Work it vertically in two colors and make a pin-striped fabric. Thin your yarn.

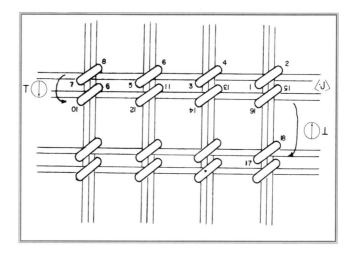

DIAGONAL STRIPE

The color arrangement can make this stitch appear as two different ones. Suit the color selection to your needs. Notice how this example resembles Box Stitches (see Chapter 10).

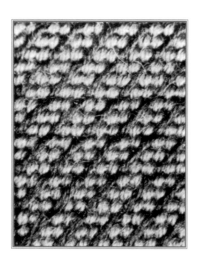

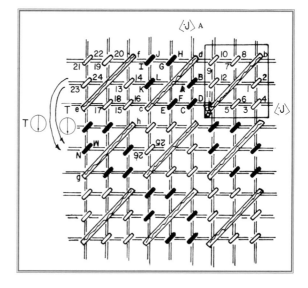

SLANTED GOBELIN

This stitch is quite versatile, for it can be worked between two and six canvas threads tall and one or more canvas threads wide. When the stitch is taller than two canvas threads or wider than three, you will probably need to thicken your yarn.

Slanted Gobelin makes a horizontal row. It is good for dresser drawers, borders, or anything in rows.

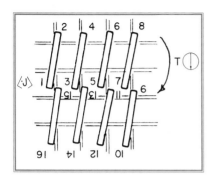

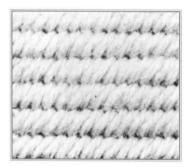

SLANTED GOBELIN 2 X 2

This stitch works well as a divider on your samplers.

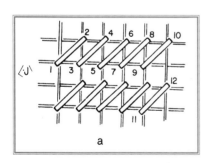

a

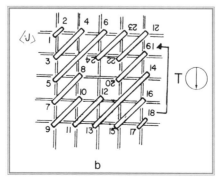

b

SLANTED GOBELIN 5 X 2

Thicken your yarn.

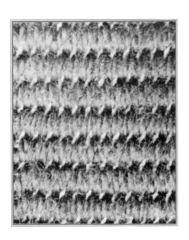

Slanted Gobelin, (top to bottom) 2 x 2, 3 x 2, 4 x 2, 5 x 2.

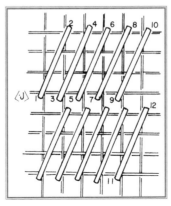

Slanted Gobelin, 4 x 2.

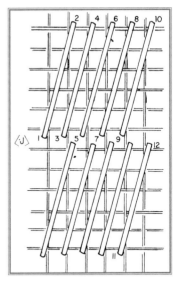

Slanted Gobelin, 5 x 2.

PADDED SLANTED GOBELIN

The tramé adds a padding to Slanted Gobelin. Use it when you want a subtle texture.

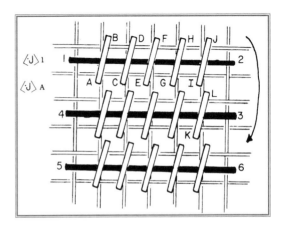

This stitch is reminiscent of embroidery's Split Stitch. Use it for shading. It is tedious to work, but very pretty.

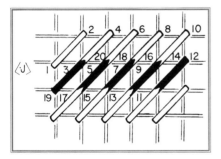

This stitch is similar to Split Gobelin. However, it does not split the stitch on the row above; the stitches of the second row merely rest beside those in the first row. This stitch, too, can be worked two to five canvas threads tall and one to two wide.

INTERLOCKING
GOBELIN

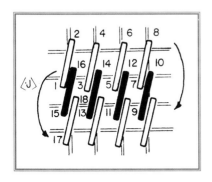

GIANT INTERLOCKING GOBELIN

Thicken your yarn.

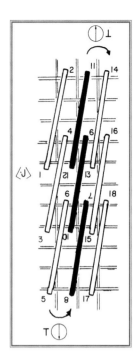

OBLIQUE SLAV

You will probably have to thicken your yarn for this stitch. There are two canvas threads between stitches and two canvas threads between rows.

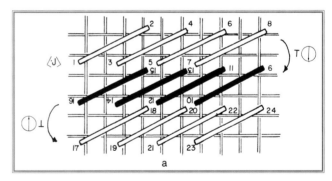

a

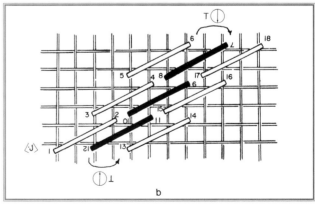

b

This stitch is Interlocking Gobelin turned on its side. Thicken your yarn.

ENCROACHING OBLIQUE

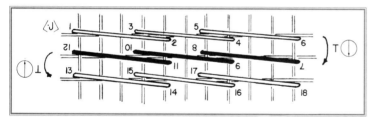

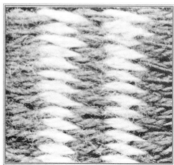

BUNGER

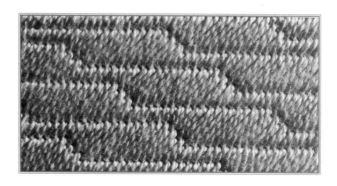

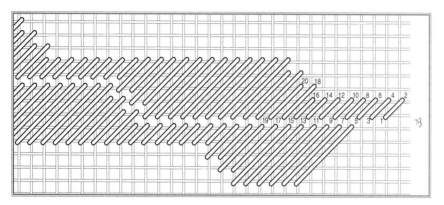

DIAGONAL
BEATY

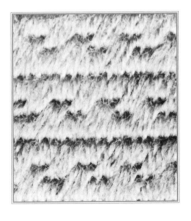

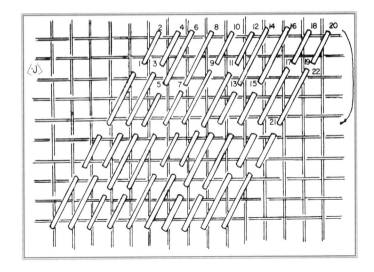

NOBUKO

Do you see the light streak in the upper left? That is not a hot spot in the photo; it is in the yarn. I ripped about three or four stitches and continued to stitch with the same yarn! The loss of some of the nap by an extra passing through the canvas caused the yarn to be a slightly lighter color. I learned from this experience that velour is more delicate than I had originally thought.

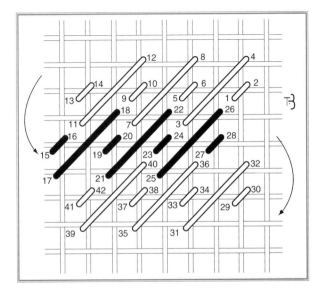

KENNAN

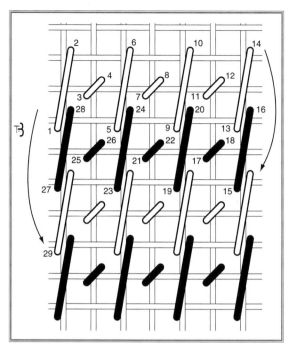

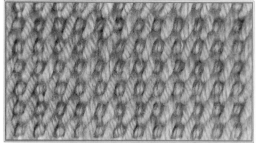

Take great care to get the tension even; otherwise it will look sloppy.

KNITTING

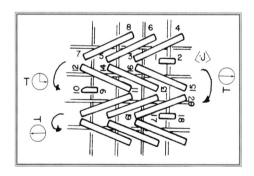

LAZY
KNITTING

Do not confuse the stitch with Alternating Continental Stitch; it's not quite the same.

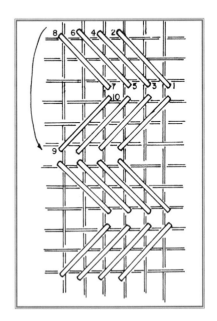

GIANT
KNITTING

You will have to thicken your yarn.

DIAGONAL
KNITTING

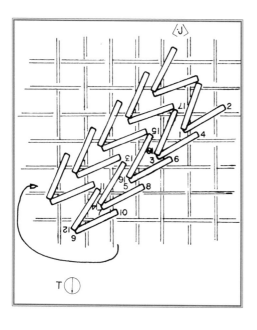

The Kalem Stitch looks like knitting (on sweaters). Be sure the tension is even.

KALEM

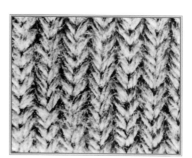

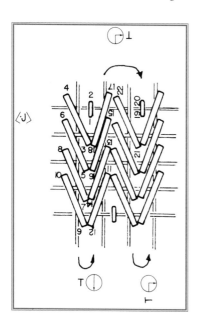

LAZY
KALEM

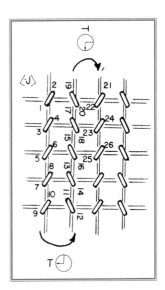

STEM

Needlepoint has its own Stem Stitch and embroidery has its own Stem Stitch. They are different. This is needlepoint's Stem Stitch. See Outline/Stem Stitch for embroidery's Stem Stitch (page 335).

The Stem Stitch is usually best with two colors. Use a thinner yarn for the Backstitch. Complete one column of stitches at a time. Do a vertical Backstitch in a second color between the columns. This stitch makes good fences, columns, etc.

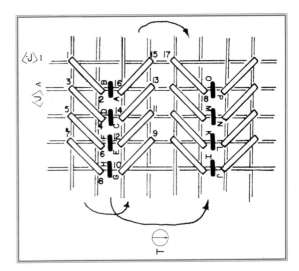

DIAGONAL
STEM

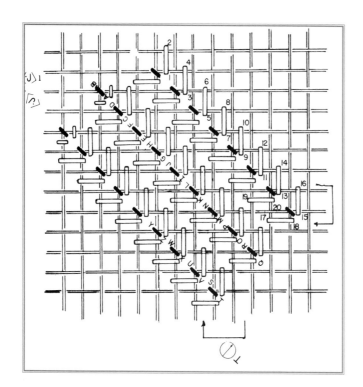

Byzantine makes good stair steps; it fills in diagonally shaped areas well.

BYZANTINE #1

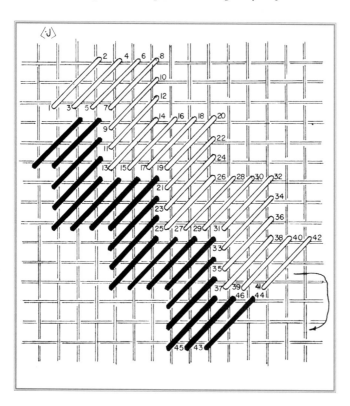

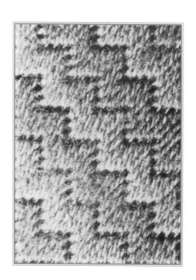

BYZANTINE #2

When covering the canvas with a stitch in a diagonal row, work generally from the upper right to the lower left, as you do Basketweave. This helps you to avoid snagging the yarn in the row before as you stitch.

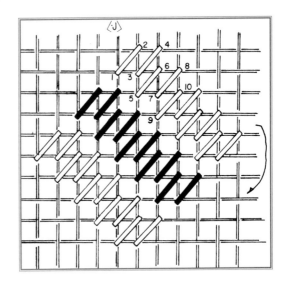

BYZANTINE #3

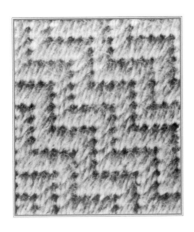

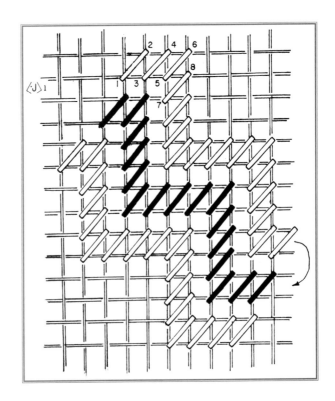

BYZANTINE #4

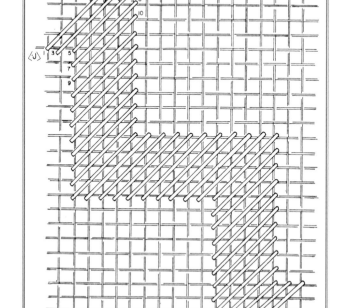

BYZANTINE #5

IRREGULAR BYZANTINE

Work rows of Byzantine 1 x 1, 2 x 2, 3 x 3, and 4 x 4 in order or mix them up. This stitch needs a very large area to establish the pattern.

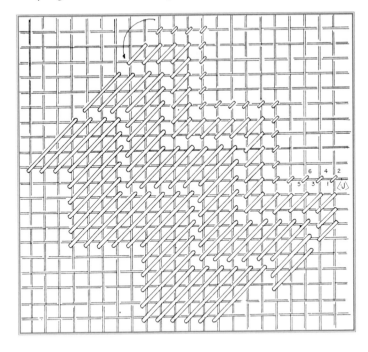

BYZANTINE-SCOTCH

Fill between the Byzantine steps with a Scotch Stitch. This is a larger version of Diagonal Hungarian Ground.

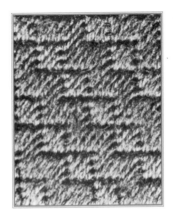

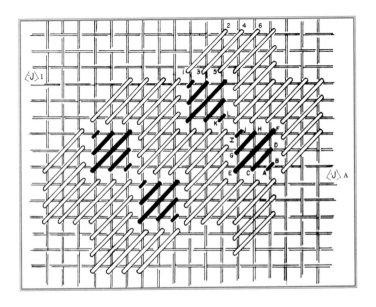

Jacquard is very much like the Byzantine Stitch with a Continental Stitch divider.

JACQUARD

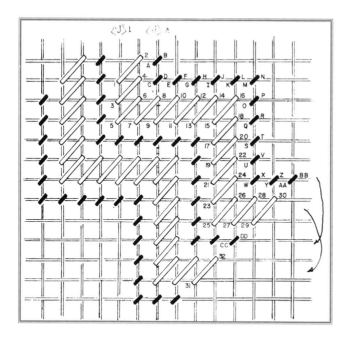

Do as many stitches as you want before turning the corner, but be consistent. Mix up the length of the stitches (2 x 2, 3 x 3, 4 x 4) or stitch them in order. This stitch needs a very large area to establish the pattern.

IRREGULAR JACQUARD

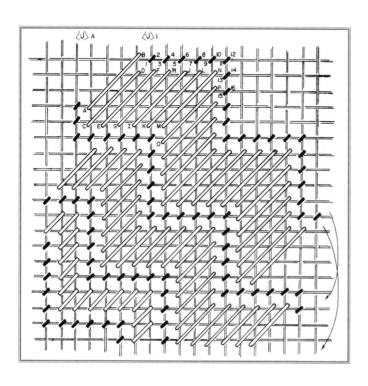

SWIRL

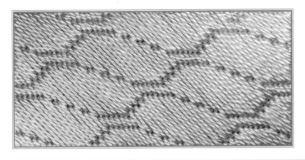

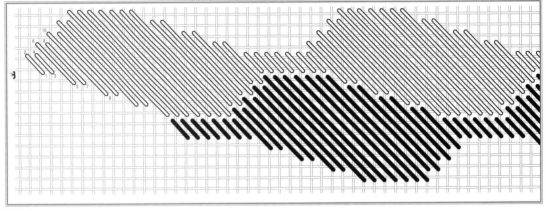

DIAGONAL HUNGARIAN GROUND

Work this stitch in two colors, or work a very large uninterrupted area in one color. The pattern will be lost in one color in a small area.

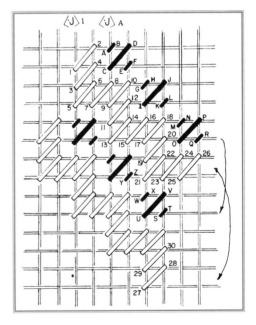

This stitch, too, needs a large area so the pattern can be seen if it is worked in one color. It is also effective in two colors. This stitch is a variation of the Diagonal Hungarian Ground.

STAIRCASE

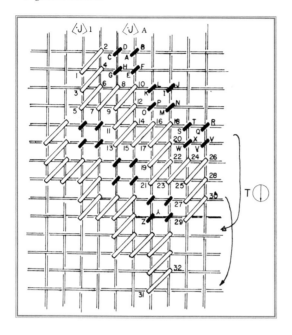

This is an especially pretty stitch, but it is difficult to work around lots of letters. It helps to count out every other row and stitch it. Then you can fill in the rows you skipped without counting. Otherwise, you have to count out every stitch around the letters.

MILANESE

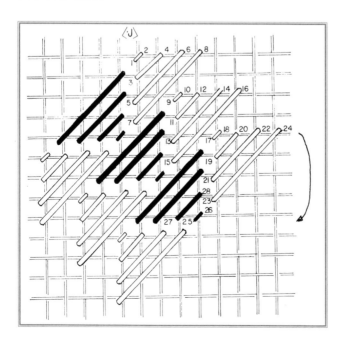

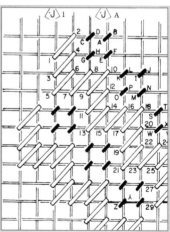

MILANESE COLOR VARIATION

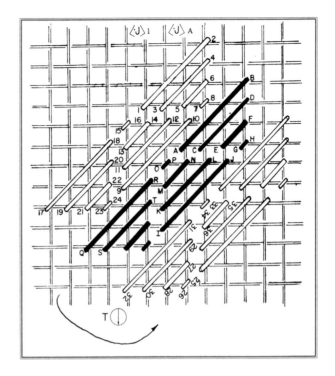

ORIENTAL

The Oriental Stitch is a good background in one color. It looks entirely different in two colors. Few stitches undergo such a change in appearance. Try it both ways.

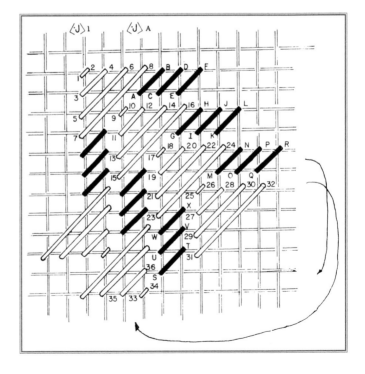

206

Mixed Milanese is easy to lose track of if you don't follow it carefully. It is a beautiful stitch, but it uses a lot of yarn.

MIXED MILANESE

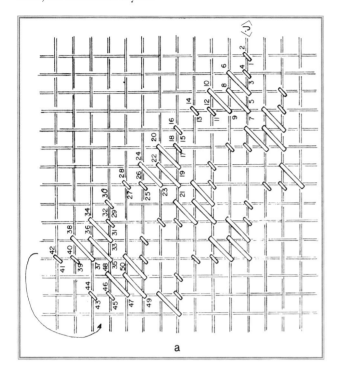

a

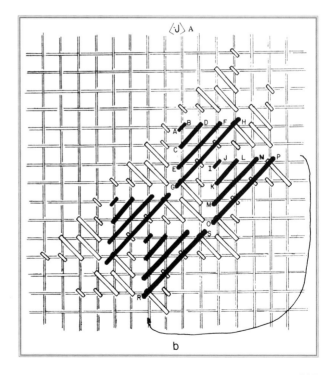

b

207

ARROWHEAD

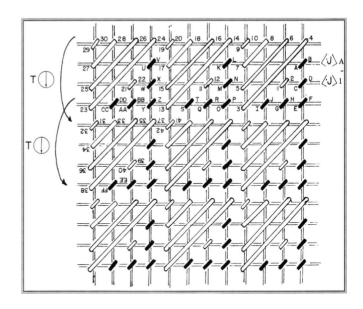

CRISS-CROSS
HUNGARIAN

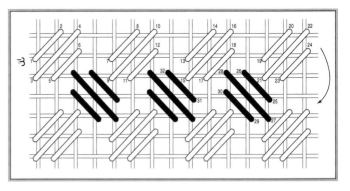

BOX STITCHES

ox Stitches are a series of diagonal stitches that form squares or boxes. These boxes are laid out in horizontal, vertical, or diagonal rows. The diagonal Box Stitches are simply boxes laid in a diagonal line, with the corners overlapping. (See the Diagonal Scotch Stitch on page 228.) Note how the short stitch is shared.

Most of these stitches make excellent borders. They lend themselves to beautiful geometric patterns in several colors. I have gone into only a few color variations, for there are whole books that discuss color variations of just a few stitches.

The Box Stitch samples were worked on Penelope 10 canvas, although they could have been done on Mono 10 canvas. Tapestry yarn was used throughout—and for all forty stitches, I did not have to thicken or thin the yarn.

BOX STITCHES	Border	Good Backing	Poor Backing	Background	Design	Accent	Fast	Slow	Geometric Pattern	Shading	Yarn Hog	Snags	Snag-Proof	Little Texture	Medium Texture	High Relief	Flower Stitch	Weak Pattern	Medium Pattern	Strong Pattern	Distorts Canvas
Mosaic	•	•		•	•		•		•				•	•				•			•
Mosaic Checker	•	•		•	•		•		•				•	•				•			•
Reversed Mosaic	•	•		•	•		•		•				•	•						•	
Framed Mosaic	•	•		•	•				•				•	•						•	•
Diagnoal Mosaic		•		•	•		•		•	•			•	•				•			•
Four-Way Mosaic		•		•	•		•		•				•	•						•	•
Mosaic Stripe		•		•	•				•				•	•						•	•
Giant Diagonal Mosaic		•		•	•		•		•	•		•		•				•			•
Cashmere	•	•		•	•		•		•				•	•				•			•
Staggered Cashmere	•	•		•	•		•		•				•	•						•	•
Cashmere Checker	•	•		•	•		•		•				•	•						•	•
Reversed Cashmere	•	•		•	•		•		•				•	•						•	
Framed Cashmere	•	•		•	•				•				•	•						•	•
Elongated Cashmere	•	•		•	•		•		•				•	•				•			•
Horizontal Cashmere	•	•		•	•		•		•				•	•				•			•
Diagonal Cashmere		•		•	•		•		•	•			•	•						•	•
Framed Diagonal Cashmere		•		•	•				•				•	•						•	•
Scotch	•	•		•	•		•		•					•				•			•
Giant Scotch	•	•		•	•		•		•		•			•				•			•
Dotted Scotch	•	•		•	•				•				•	•						•	•
Half-Framed Scotch	•	•			•			•	•				•		•				•		•

209

BOX STITCHES	Border	Good Backing	Poor Backing	Background	Design	Accent	Fast	Slow	Geometric Pattern	Shading	Yarn Hog	Snags	Snag-Proof	Little Texture	Medium Texture	High Relief	Flower Stitch	Weak Pattern	Medium Pattern	Strong Pattern	Distorts Canvas
Woven Scotch	•	•			•	•		•	•	•			•		•					•	•
Continuous 2-4 Woven Scotch	•	•			•	•		•	•	•			•		•					•	•
Divided Scotch	•	•		•	•				•		•			•					•		•
Scotch Checker	•	•		•	•		•		•					•					•		•
Framed Scotch	•	•		•	•		•		•										•		•
Reversed Scotch	•	•		•	•		•		•					•				•			•
Framed Reverse Scotch	•	•			•		•	•	•				•		•				•		
Framed Scotch Variation	•	•		•	•	•	•		•					•					•		
Windowpane Scotch	•	•		•	•		•		•					•					•		
Triangular Scotch	•	•			•		•		•					•					•		
Diamond Scotch	•	•		•	•		•		•					•					•		
Point Russe # 1	•	•			•	•		•	•				•		•				•		
Point Russe # 2	•	•			•	•		•	•				•		•				•		
Diagonal Scotch		•		•	•		•							•				•			•
Framed Diagonal Scotch		•			•			•	•				•		•				•		•
Giant Diagonal Scotch		•		•	•		•		•				•		•			•			•
Moorish		•		•	•		•		•					•					•		•
Wide Moorish		•		•	•		•		•					•					•		•
Giant Moorish		•		•	•		•		•			•		•					•		•

MOSAIC

Mosaic is the smallest of the Box Stitches. It is just three diagonal stitches: short, long, short. It makes a box two canvas threads by two canvas threads. When short and long stitches are combined within a stitch, the longer stitches often need a tighter tension than the shorter ones. Inattention to this detail will cause the light to reflect differently on the long ones than on the short ones. Your work will then look sloppy.

Mosaic is an excellent background or design stitch. This stitch is a good background to work behind Continental letters. It can be worked horizontally, vertically, or diagonally.

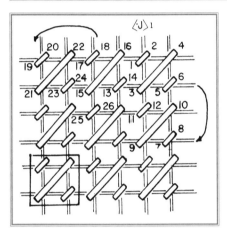

Mosaic stitched horizontally.

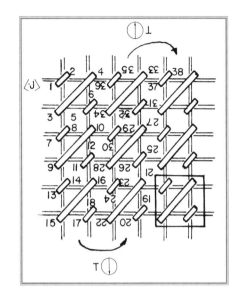

Mosaic stitched vertically.

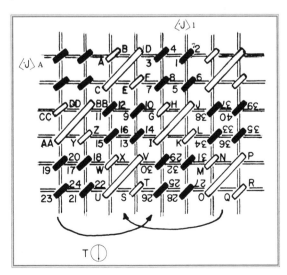

Mosaic stitched diagonally.

Mosaic Checker must be worked in two colors. Do the Mosaic boxes in one color and fill in between them with Basketweave in another color. The Basketweave Stitches are lost if this stitch is worked in one color. This stitch wears well and creates a pretty pattern.

MOSAIC CHECKER

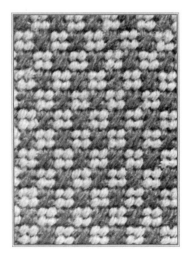

REVERSED MOSAIC

This stitch is worked most easily by doing it in a diagonal row from upper left to lower right. Then turn the canvas 90° so that the upper right becomes the upper left. Work the same type of diagonal row, filling in the blank spaces. I think this stitch looks best in one color.

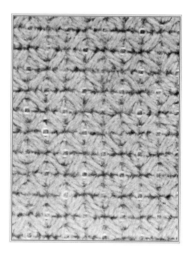

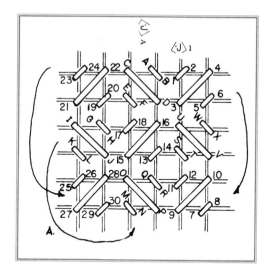

FRAMED MOSAIC

This stitch is simply a Mosaic Stitch with a frame of Continental all the way around. Work this stitch in one or more colors.

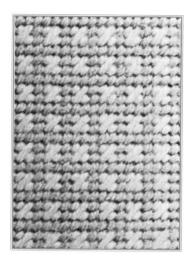

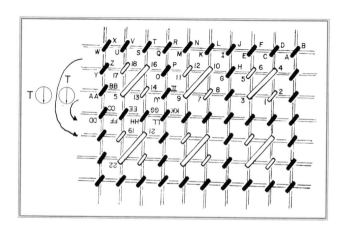

CHAPTER TEN: BOX STITCHES

When Mosaic is worked diagonally, it becomes merely a line of short and long stitches. For this reason, you might like it for shading. Do this stitch in one or more colors.

DIAGONAL MOSAIC

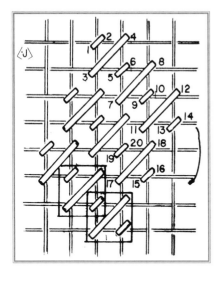

Combine Diagonal Mosaic with Reversed Diagonal Mosaic (above) to make a Four-Way Mosaic. This stitch is most successful if two or more colors are used.

FOUR-WAY MOSAIC

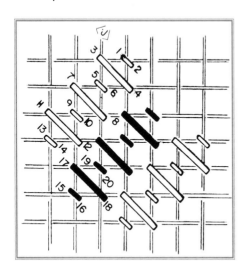

213

MOSAIC
STRIPE

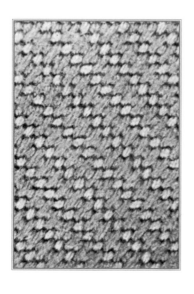

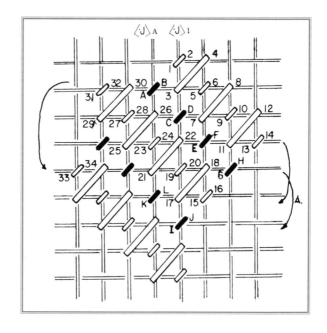

GIANT
DIAGONAL
MOSAIC

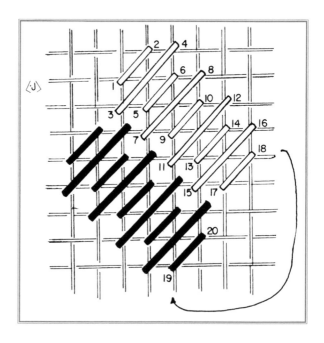

Cashmere is a rectangular Mosaic Stitch. It can be worked horizontally, vertically, or diagonally.

CASHMERE

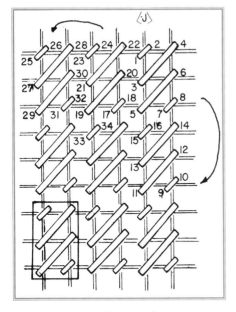

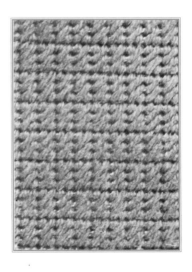

Cashmere stitched diagonally.

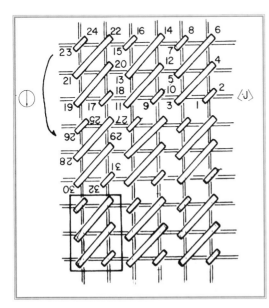

Cashmere stitched horizontally.

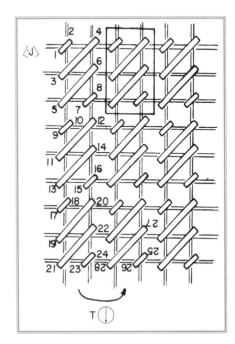

Cashmere stitched vertically.

STAGGERED CASHMERE

Instead of the rows making a checkerboard pattern, the boxes are staggered from row to row. Don't forget that you may also stagger the Mosaic, Scotch, and many other stitches.

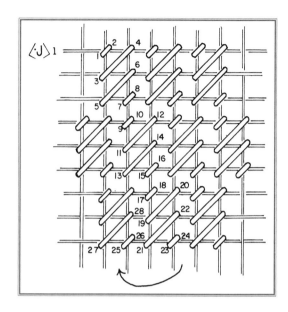

CASHMERE CHECKER

Work Basketweave in the areas between the Cashmere Stitches. Again, keep your eye on the tension of the longer stitches in relation to the short ones, as you did in the Mosaic and Scotch Stitches.

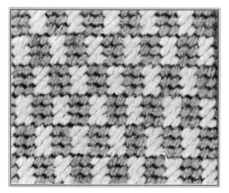

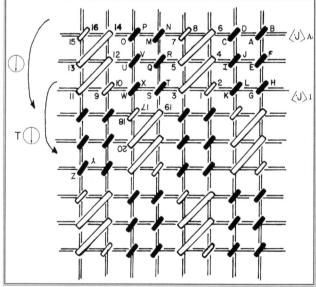

Work this stitch in diagonal rows. Turn the canvas 90° for the next row. Start with the widest part of the area to be filled.

REVERSED CASHMERE

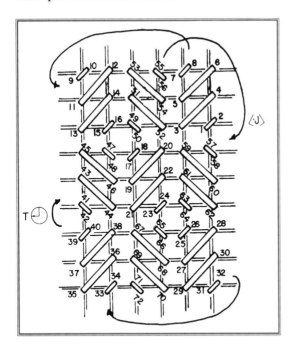

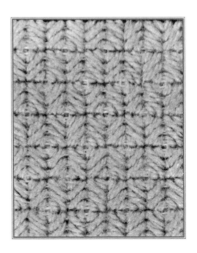

The Continental Stitch is used between the Cashmere boxes.

FRAMED CASHMERE

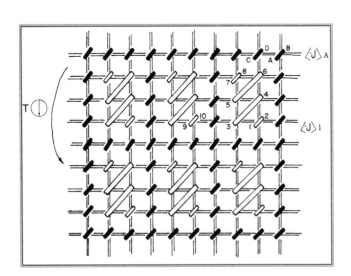

217

ELONGATED CASHMERE

Elongated Cashmere is just an extra-long Cashmere box. In alternating rows, it reminds me of the siding on a barn. The number of long stitches may vary.

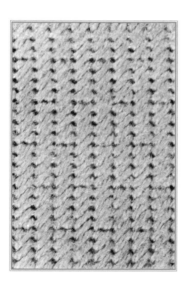

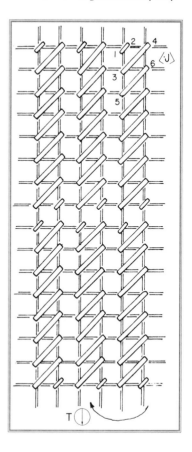

HORIZONTAL CASHMERE

Turn Cashmere on its side and lengthen a little, but not as much as Elongated Cashmere. The drawing shows Horizontal Cashmere; the photo shows staggered Horizontal Cashmere. When the boxes are staggered, this makes nice brick. Frame it with the Continental Stitch in white and you have even more realistic bricks.

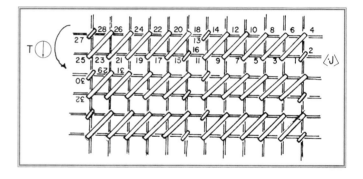

The second row of Diagonal Cashmere is a bit tricky to work; I try to remember that the first long stitch in the second row is diagonally below the last short stitch. After I have taken that stitch, I go back and pick up the first short stitch in the second row until I get the hang of it.

DIAGONAL
CASHMERE

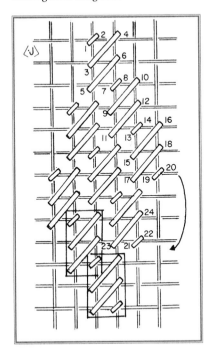

FRAMED
DIAGONAL
CASHMERE

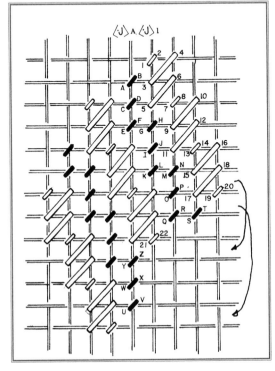

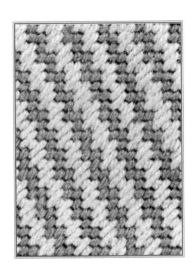

219

SCOTCH

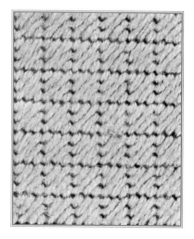

The Scotch Stitch is merely a wider Cashmere Stitch. It has many lovely variations. This stitch can also be worked three ways. (See the Mosaic and Cashmere Stitches.) Pull the longer stitches more tightly than the shorter ones.

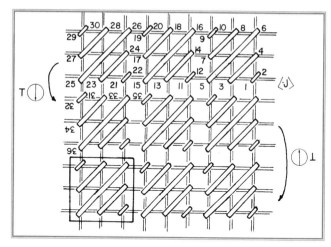

GIANT SCOTCH

The Scotch Stitch can be worked in many sizes: five-stitch, seven-stitch, nine-stitch, and eleven-stitch. Keep in mind that the longer stitches may need a slightly tighter tension. Even with this tighter tension they are more likely to snag than the shorter ones.

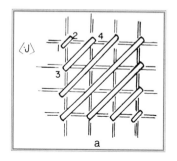

a

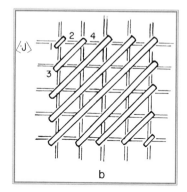

b

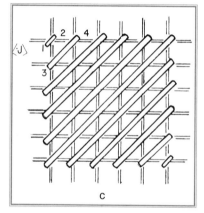

c

There are three Continental Stitches across the widest part of the Scotch Stitch. This cuts down on the snagging possibilities while adding interest.

DOTTED SCOTCH

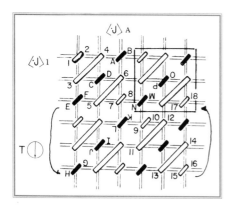

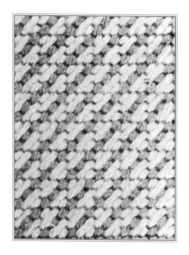

The small Straight Stitches make a most interesting pattern.

HALF-FRAMED SCOTCH

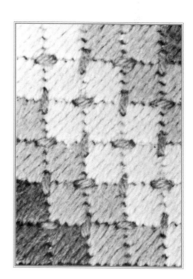

WOVEN SCOTCH

This stitch is worked like a regular Scotch Stitch, except that the contrasting-colored yarn is woven under the first, third, and fifth stitches.

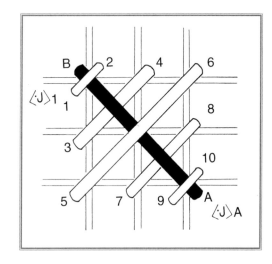

CONTINUOUS 2-4 WOVEN SCOTCH

Weave a contrasting color under the second and fourth stitches for a whole diagonal row, coming up at A and going down at B.

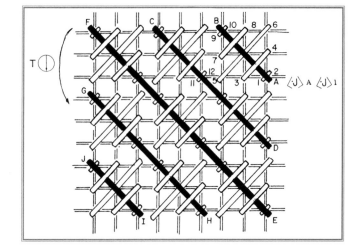

I like this stitch in one color, although it may be worked with more.

DIVIDED SCOTCH

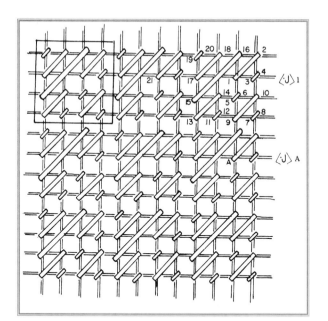

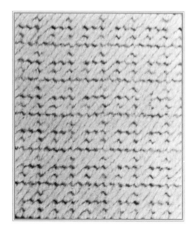

This stitch is pretty in one or two colors. Fill in between each Scotch box with Basketweave.

SCOTCH CHECKER

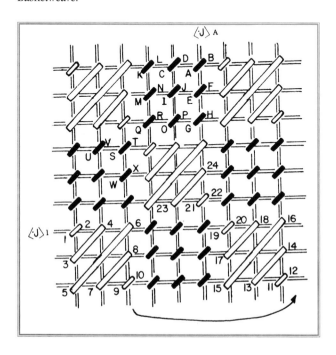

FRAMED SCOTCH

Stitch the frame in the Continental Stitch. Work all the horizontal rows of the frame first. Then work the vertical rows next, skipping the stitches that have been worked. Stitch a portion of the vertical rows to ease turning the corner to the next row. Work the missed areas as convenient.

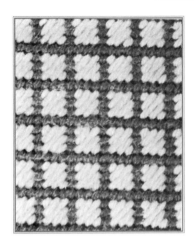

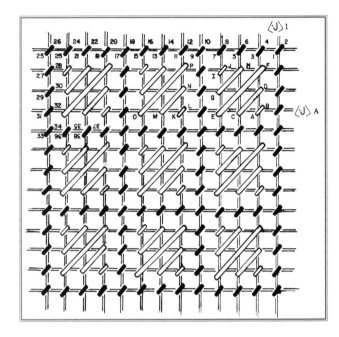

REVERSED SCOTCH

Try this stitch in one color. See Reversed Mosaic for hints on working Reversed Scotch.

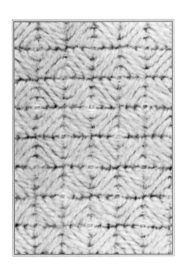

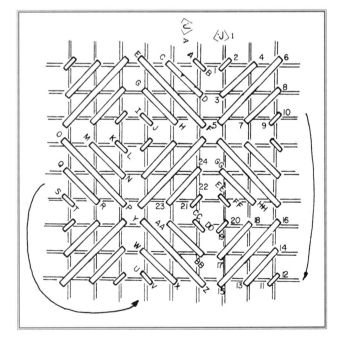

Work a ground of Reversed Scotch and then frame it. This frame is merely a Backstitch around each Scotch box.

**FRAMED
REVERSE
SCOTCH**

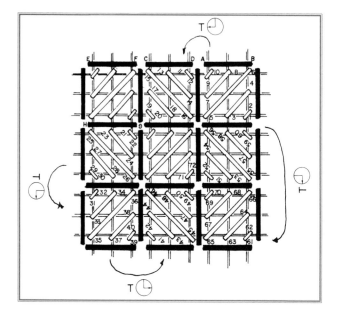

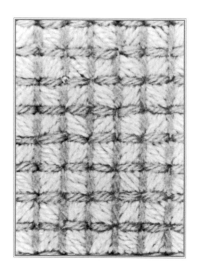

This is only one stitch of the many that can be made by combining Scotch, Frame, and Filling Stitches with color. Experiment and see how many pretty patterns you can come up with.

**FRAMED
SCOTCH
VARIATION**

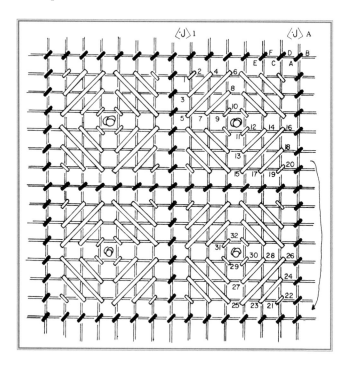

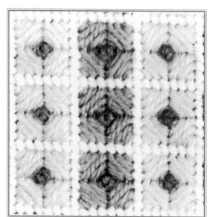

WINDOWPANE SCOTCH

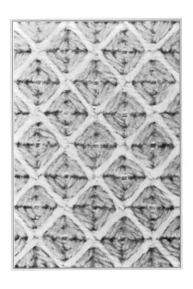

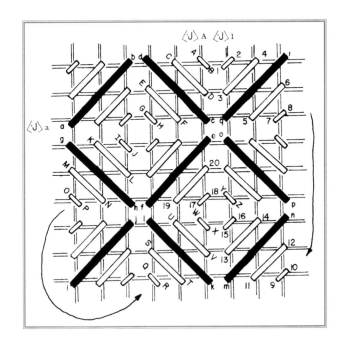

TRIANGULAR SCOTCH

This is merely a Reversed Scotch Stitch with a triangle of color used for a different look.

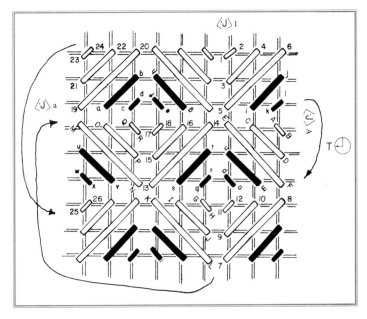

DIAMOND SCOTCH

This, again, is a Reversed Scotch Stitch with a triangle created by a second color.

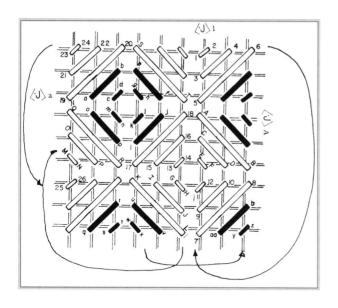

POINT RUSSE #1

This stitch needs at least three colors in order for its pattern to show up.

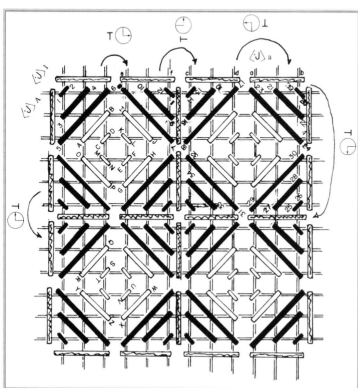

POINT RUSSE #2

This stitch shows off its interesting pattern when worked in a minimum of three colors.

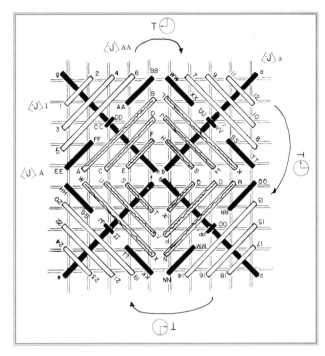

DIAGONAL SCOTCH

Share the short stitch when making the next box.

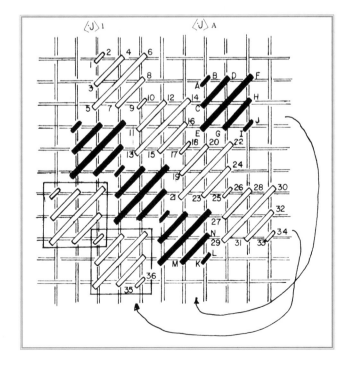

FRAMED
DIAGONAL
SCOTCH

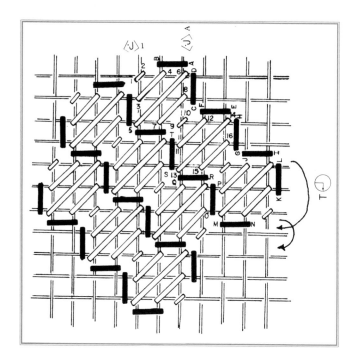

Omit the 1 x 1 short stitch of the Scotch box and share the 2 x 2 stitch.

GIANT
DIAGONAL
SCOTCH

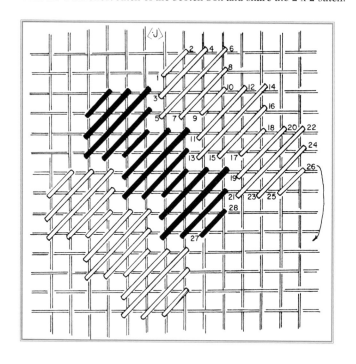

MOORISH

This is simply a Diagonal Scotch with a separating row of Continental Stitch. It resembles stairs; it can also be used for rooftops and geometric designs.

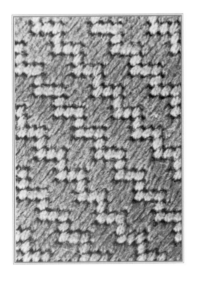

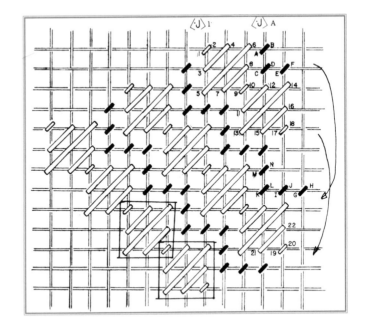

WIDE MOORISH

A 2 x 2 Slanted Gobelin separates the rows of Diagonal Scotch.

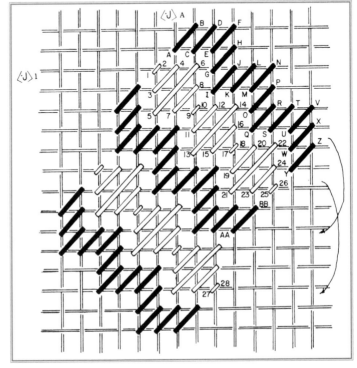

GIANT
MOORISH

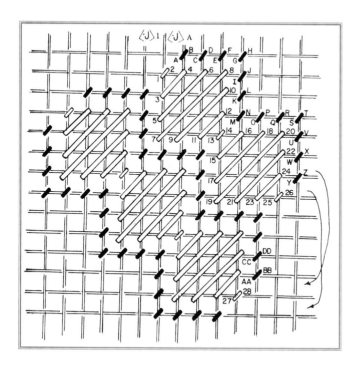

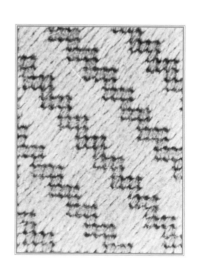

Eleven

CROSS STITCHES

*C*ross Stitches make pretty filling, design, and border stitches. They often stand alone to represent flowers. Many of the large Cross Stitches could lend themselves readily to open canvas techniques (page 55).

When worked on Regular Mono canvas, the Cross Stitch must be crossed as you go. Watch the numbering throughout this chapter. Traditionally, the left arm is on top, but it really does not matter whether you cross the right arm over the left or the left arm over the right—as long as you are consistent.

It often does not matter whether you stitch a row of half of the cross and go back and cross them or you cross each half as you go, unless you are working on Mono canvas. There is little difference in the finished stitch. Sometimes the fiber does cause a difference. Experiment and decide for yourself. If the fiber I'm using is forgiving, I find it easier to be consistent when I work the whole area in half of the cross first. Then I go back and cross those stitches. I manage ro ruin it every time if I don't do this.

The Cross Stitch samples were worked on Penelope 7 canvas with Persian yarn. Many of the Cross Stitches did not need thickening; however, some did. When the Cross Stitch is worked on smaller canvas, it is necessary to thin your yarn or choose another fiber so the stitches will be distinct. Larger crosses can be worked successfully on smaller canvas.

CROSS STITCHES	Border	Good Backing	Poor Backing	Background	Design	Accent	Fast	Slow	Geometric Pattern	Shading	Yarn Hog	Snags	Snag-Proof	Little Texture	Medium Texture	High Relief	Flower Stitch	Weak Pattern	Medium Pattern	Strong Pattern	Distorts Canvas
Cross					•	•			•	•	•		•	•				•	•		
Dotted					•				•	•			•	•						•	
Triangle	•	•		•	•	•			•			•		•						•	
Triangle Color Variation	•	•		•	•	•			•			•		•						•	
Three-Stitch Cross					•	•			•				•		•		•		•		
Crossed Mosaic	•	•			•				•					•					•		
Double Cross Tramé	•				•	•			•					•				•			
Raised Cross					•	•			•	•		•				•				•	
Oblong Cross					•	•			•					•				•			
Oblong Cross Color Variation					•	•			•	•				•				•			
Spaced Cross Tramé, 1 x 1					•	•			•					•				•			
Spaced Cross Tramé, 1 x 3					•	•			•			•		•				•			
Oblong Cross Tramé					•	•			•					•				•			

CROSS STITCHES	Border	Good Backing	Poor Backing	Background	Design	Accent	Fast	Slow	Geometric Pattern	Shading	Yarn Hog	Snags	Snag-Proof	Little Texture	Medium Texture	High Relief	Flower Stitch	Weak Pattern	Medium Pattern	Strong Pattern	Distorts Canvas
Sleeping Oblong Cross				•	•				•			•		•				•			
Alternating Oblong Cross				•	•				•	•		•		•				•			
Flying Cross				•	•				•			•			•				•		
Hourglass Cross				•	•				•			•			•				•		
Raised Knot	•				•	•	•		•		•		•			•	•		•		
Italian Cross	•				•	•			•			•		•				•			
Roman Cross				•	•				•			•		•				•			
Floral Cross					•				•	•		•		•						•	
Double				•	•				•						•	•			•		
Staggered Crosses				•	•				•					•					•		
Barred Square	•			•	•	•	•		•			•		•					•		
Woven Square	•			•	•	•	•		•				•	•						•	
Detached Weaving/Teneriffe			•		•	•	•							•					•		
Bound Cross	•			•	•	•			•			•		•						•	
Braided Cross	•		•	•	•	•	•		•			•		•					•		
Upright Cross				•	•				•	•		•	•					•			
Long Upright Cross				•	•	•			•					•					•		
Diagonal Upright Cross				•	•				•					•						•	
Cross Diagonal				•	•				•					•					•		
Mini-Cross Diagonal				•	•				•			•	•					•			
Checkerboard Cross				•	•				•					•					•		
Combination Crosses				•	•				•			•	•					•			
Slanted Cross	•			•	•				•					•				•			
Fern			•	•	•		•			•					•				•		
Plaited			•	•	•		•			•				•					•		
Diagonal Fern			•	•	•		•				•				•				•		
Herringbone			•	•	•			•		•				•					•		
Herringbone Gone Wrong			•	•	•			•						•						•	
Two-Color Herringbone	•		•									•		•					•		
Six-Trip Herringbone	•		•					•		•		•			•				•		
Greek	•		•	•							•			•					•		
Diagonal Greek			•	•	•			•						•					•		
Plaited Gobelin	•		•		•					•	•			•					•		
Plaited Ray	•		•		•	•	•		•		•		•			•	•			•	
Waffle	•		•			•					•	•				•				•	
Crescent	•		•			•	•	•			•					•	•			•	
Jessica	•		•			•	•	•			•					•	•			•	

CROSS STITCHES	Border	Good Backing	Poor Backing	Background	Design	Accent	Fast	Slow	Geometric Pattern	Shading	Yarn Hog	Snags	Snag-Proof	Little Texture	Medium Texture	High Relief	Flower Stitch	Weak Pattern	Medium Pattern	Strong Pattern	Distorts Canvas
Amadeus	•		•			•		•	•		•					•	•			•	
Arrow Amadeus	•		•			•		•	•		•					•	•			•	
Walneto	•		•			•		•	•		•					•	•			•	
Double Cross				•	•	•			•			•			•		•		•		
Trellis Cross				•	•	•		•	•			•		•			•		•		
Windowpane Cross				•	•	•			•			•			•		•			•	
Fancy Cross				•	•	•		•	•			•			•		•			•	
Slanting Star						•			•			•			•		•		•		
Double Straight Cross				•	•	•						•			•		•			•	
Leviathan	•			•	•				•			•			•		•			•	
Double Leviathan	•					•		•	•		•	•				•	•			•	
Diamond Leviathan					•	•		•	•		•		•			•	•			•	
Triple Leviathan					•	•		•	•			•		•			•			•	
Medallion						•			•			•	•				•			•	
Snowflake						•						•	•				•			•	
Rhodes	•	•				•		•			•	•				•	•			•	
Cross Rhodes	•	•				•		•			•	•				•	•			•	
Triple Cross						•			•			•				•	•			•	
Triple Oblong Cross				•	•	•			•			•			•					•	
Windmill						•			•			•				•	•		•		
Tied Windmill						•			•			•			•		•			•	
Double Layered Cross					•	•			•		•	•				•	•		•		
Smyrna Cross	•			•	•	•			•			•				•	•			•	
Reversed Smyrna Cross	•			•	•	•			•			•				•	•			•	
Horizontal Elongated Smyrna	•			•	•	•			•			•				•	•			•	
Vertical Elongated Smyrna	•			•	•	•			•			•				•	•			•	
Alternating Smyrna				•	•	•			•			•				•	•			•	
Long-Arm Smyrna	•			•	•	•			•			•				•	•			•	
Patterned Crosses	•			•	•	•			•			•			•					•	
Patterned Scotch Crosses	•			•	•	•			•			•			•					•	
Woven Cross	•			•	•	•			•		•	•			•			•		•	
Double Plaited Cross	•			•	•	•			•			•			•			•		•	
Point de Tresse	•			•	•	•			•			•			•					•	
Woven Band	•											•	•							•	
Railway	•			•								•	•							•	

On Mono canvas, the first half of each cross must be crossed right away. Usually they look alike. Sometimes the fit of the fiber to the canvas hole will cause the two methods to produce two different results. In this case, one is usually superior to the other. Experiment with your fiber. See what you like.

Try your hand at renumbering the stitches on Mono canvas. Other numbering patterns will allow you to lay half of the crosses and then go back and cross them if you like.

CROSS

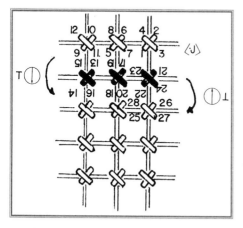

Stitching method for Cross Stitch on all canvases.

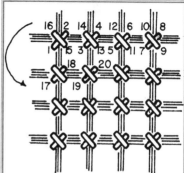

Stitching method for Cross Stitch on Penelope, Interlock Mono, and Plastic canvas. Does not work on Mono canvas.

Stitch the cross in a different color for the full effect of the dots. Note that the stitch pattern is basically Basketweave.

DOTTED

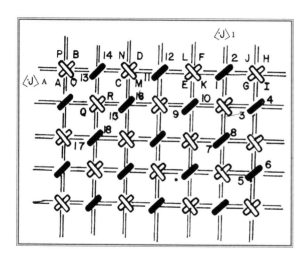

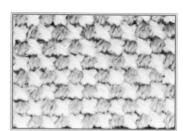

TRIANGLE

It does not matter whether you cross the right arm of a Cross Stitch over the left or the left over the right—as long as you are consistent. Keep this in mind when putting in the crosses.

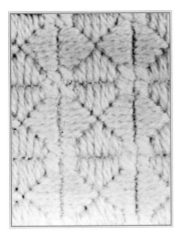

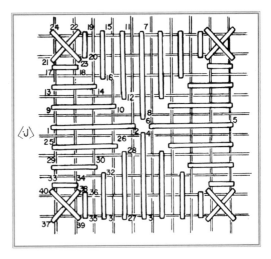

TRIANGLE COLOR VARIATION

When doing two or more colors mixed up like this, the back cannot be super neat. Avoid lumps. Always cross the Cross Stitches consistently. (See the Triangle Stitch.)

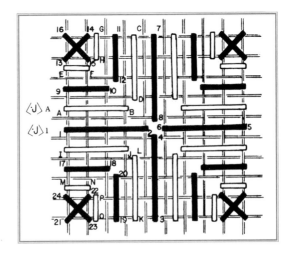

You may need a tramé to cover the canvas.

THREE-STITCH CROSS

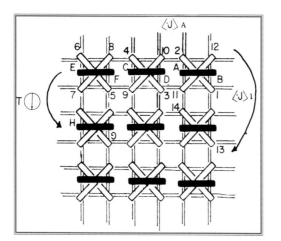

CROSSED MOSAIC

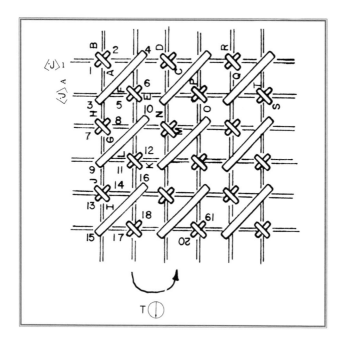

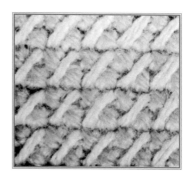

DOUBLE CROSS TRAMÉ

The tramé is needed to cover the canvas.

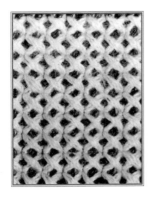

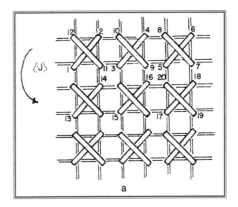

a

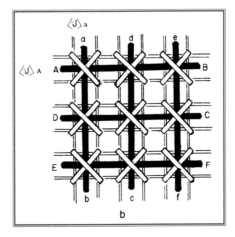

b

RAISED CROSS

Thicken the yarn for the vertical stitches. Three colors are very effective in bringing out the pattern.

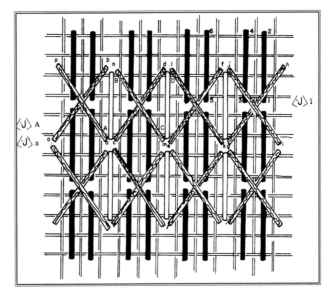

OBLONG
CROSS

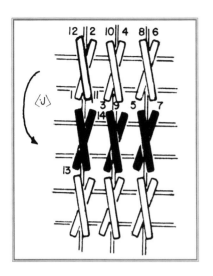

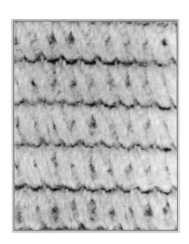

This is just one way to show how color can vastly change the looks of a stitch.

OBLONG
CROSS
COLOR
VARIATION

SPACED
CROSS
TRAMÉ, 1 X 1

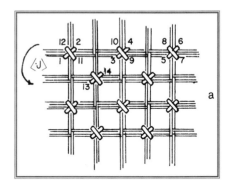

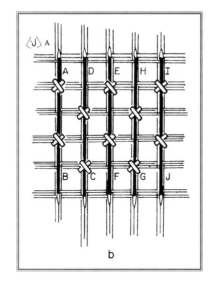

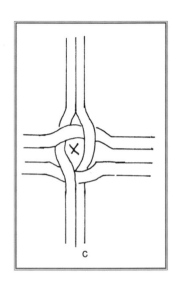

This stitch is worked most easily by stitching a checkerboard pattern of Oblong Cross Stitches first and then running a tramé under them. When the tramé is worked in a dark shade of green and the Oblong Cross in a lighter shade of green, this stitch resembles grass. The tramé and Cross Stitches may run horizontally or vertically. Suit it to your needs.

SPACED CROSS TRAMÉ, 1 X 3

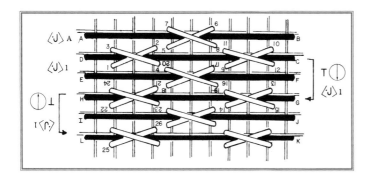

You might need to thicken the yarn for the tramé.

OBLONG CROSS TRAMÉ

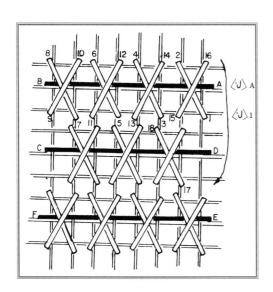

SLEEPING
OBLONG CROSS

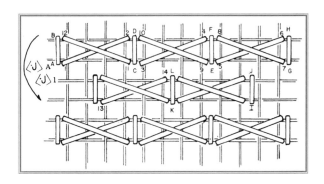

ALTERNATING
OBLONG CROSS

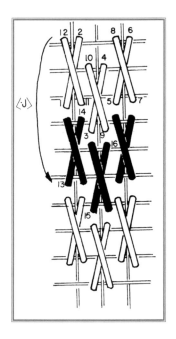

Thicken the yarn to cover the canvas.

FLYING CROSS

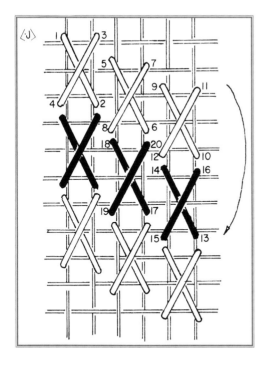

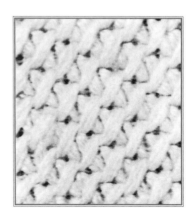

HOURGLASS CROSS

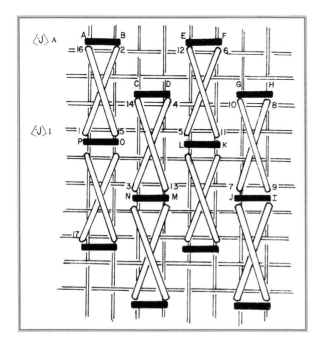

RAISED KNOT

Once the cross is made, bring the needle to the right side of the canvas near the center. Without penetrating the canvas, slide the needle under the center of the cross and wrap each leg of the cross. Take the needle to the wrong side of the canvas near the center of the cross, under your stitches.

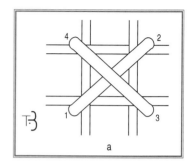

a

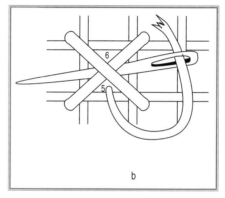

b

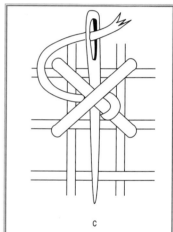

c

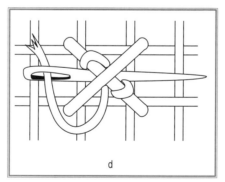

d

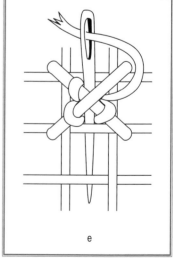

e

Work this stitch 4 x 4, 3 x 3, or 2 x 2.

ITALIAN CROSS

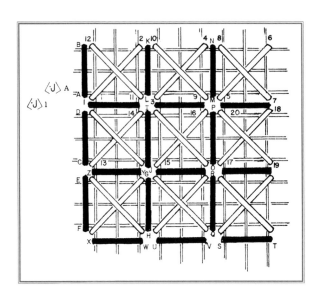

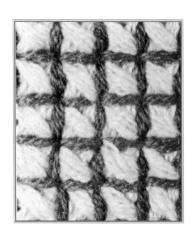

ROMAN CROSS

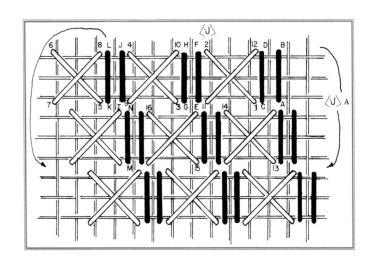

FLORAL
CROSS

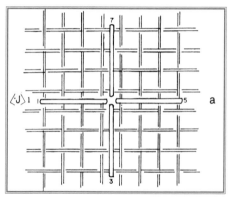

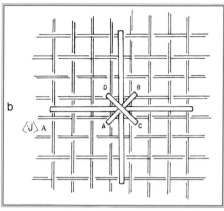

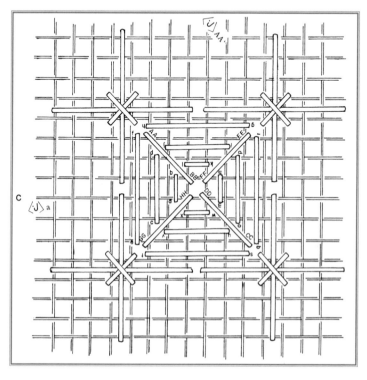

This is a good stitch for bumpy texture. When worked in one color, it resembles tree bark. Worked in two colors, it makes good polka dots.

DOUBLE

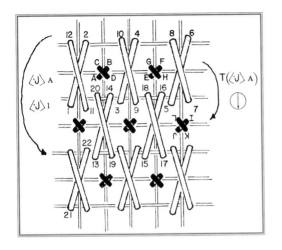

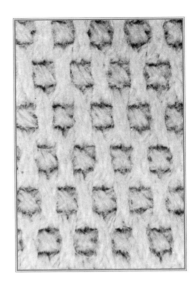

STAGGERED CROSSES

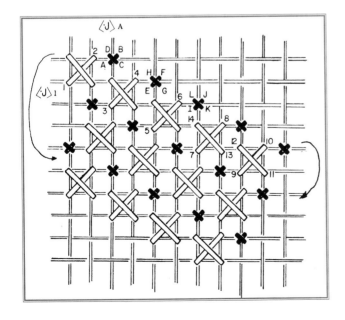

BARRED SQUARE

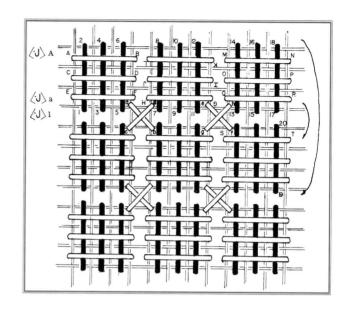

WOVEN SQUARE

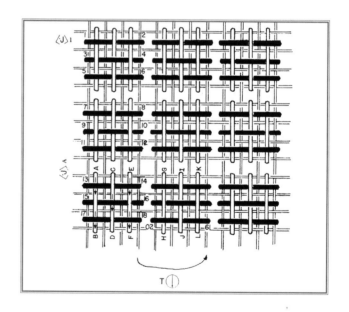

This is really Teneriffe, an embroidery technique, which is the laying of yarns on top of the canvas in one direction and then weaving another yarn over and under them at 90°. All of the yarns penetrate the canvas only at the edges of the area. Weave any shape you like. I have shown you two.

DETACHED WEAVING/ TENERIFFE

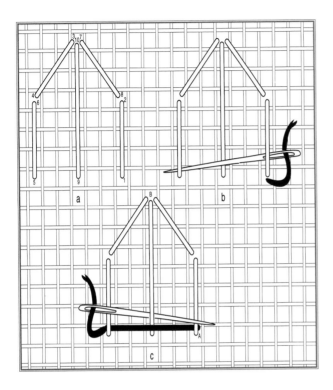

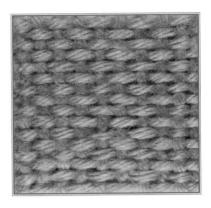

BOUND
CROSS

You can alternate the direction of crosses for a checkerboard effect.

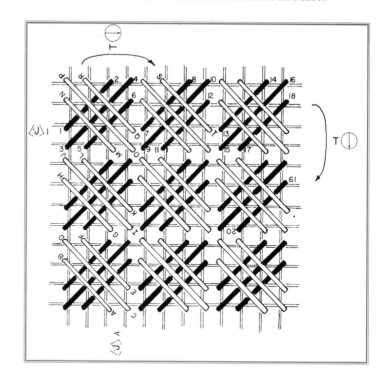

BRAIDED
CROSS

Thicken your yarn for this stitch. The French Knot in the center is purely decorative. It could be easily omitted, leaving the bare canvas to create an Open Stitch. If you do want an open look, do not thicken the yarn for this use.

In going from #5 to #6, slip the needle under the 1-2 stitch. In going from #7 to #8, slip the needle under the 3-4 stitch.

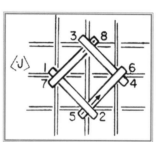

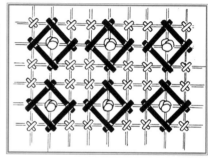

UPRIGHT CROSS

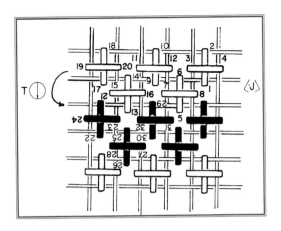

LONG UPRIGHT CROSS

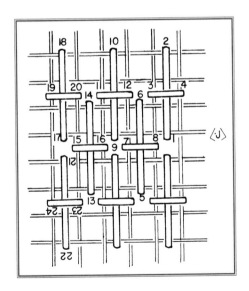

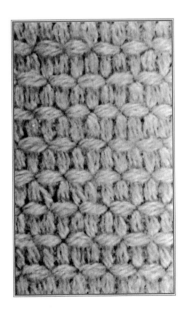

DIAGONAL UPRIGHT CROSS

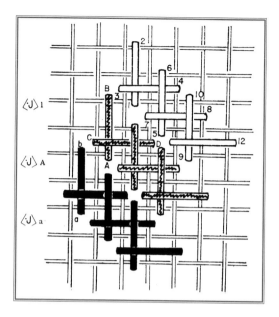

CROSS DIAGONAL

The diagram shows the stitch with half of the diagonals worked; the photo, with the diagonals completed. Use it either way.

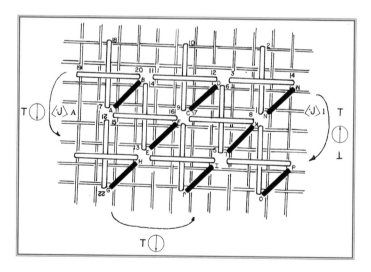

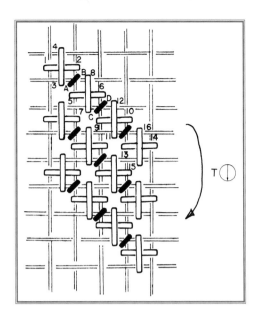

MINI-CROSS
DIAGONAL

This stitch resembles a basket.

CHECKERBOARD
CROSS

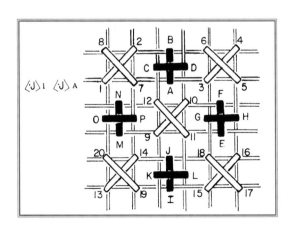

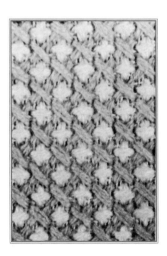

COMBINATION CROSSES

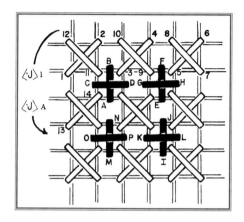

SLANTED CROSS

The first part of the stitch is the same as the Cross Stitch, but the return is like Straight Gobelin.

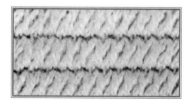

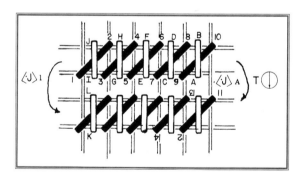

FERN

Work this stitch in vertical columns from top to bottom only. Do not turn the canvas upside down for the next row. It makes a fat, neat braid. The compensating stitch (page 43) is a Cross Stitch. Use the columns individually or together.

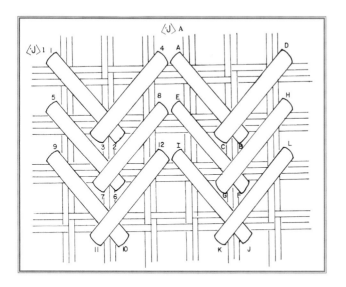

PLAITED

The Plaited Stitch is worked in the same way as the Fern Stitch, but with overlapping rows. It covers Penelope 7 in wool better than the Fern Stitch does. When finished, it looks somewhat like Herringbone, and it is done less painfully.

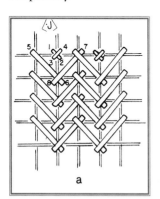

a

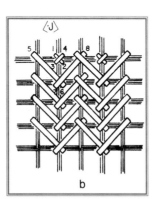

b

DIAGONAL FERN

Thicken your yarn to stitch the Diagonal Fern. This is one of those stitches that is easier to start with compensating stitches.

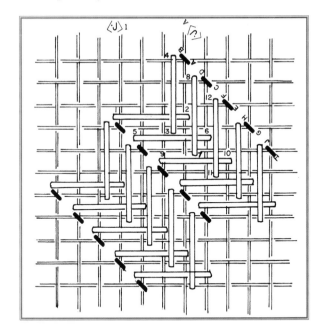

HERRINGBONE

Work Herringbone from left to right only. Cut the yarn at the end of the first row and begin the second row directly beneath the first stitch of the first row, one canvas thread below. You will have to move the yarn in the row above with your finger or a laying tool in order to find the holes for the second row. This stitch is very tedious to work—but, oh, so pretty.

The common error is skipping a row. If you are having trouble, check to be sure every hole is filled along the edge of the stitch.

This stitch is worked like Herringbone except that you turn the canvas upside down to work the second row.

It is easier to learn if you end each row with a stitch that slants upward. You will still have to move the yarns in the row below to find the holes for the second row.

As with the Herringbone, it is a common error to skip every other row.

HERRINGBONE GONE WRONG

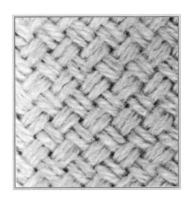

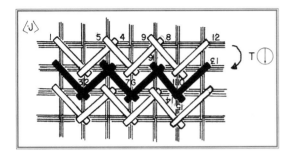

Stitch the darker color first.

TWO-COLOR HERRINGBONE

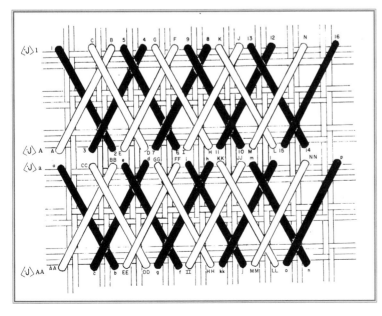

SIX-TRIP
HERRINGBONE

This is an excellent border stitch. Work it on Interlock Mono or Penelope canvas only—use all one color or many shades of one color (a family of colors). Put the darkest color down first. With only five colors, make the first and second trips in the darkest color.

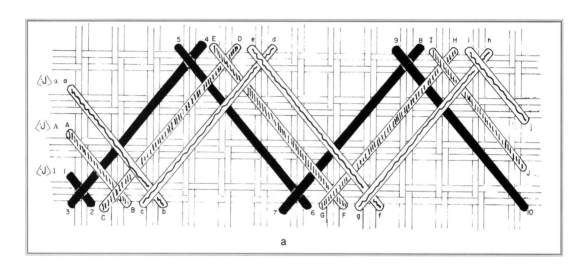

a

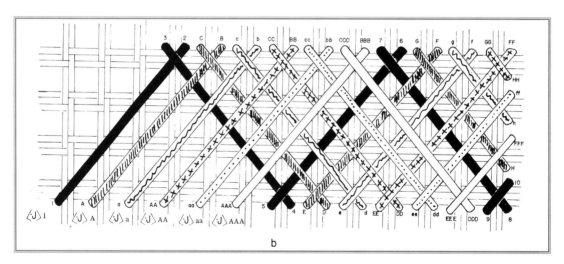

b

Work the Greek Stitch from **left or right only.** Break the yarn at the end of the row and begin again below the first stitch. It is actually a Cross Stitch with one short arm and one long arm. Each cross is overlapped with the next one.

GREEK

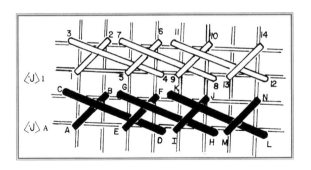

Work from lower left to upper right only.

DIAGONAL
GREEK

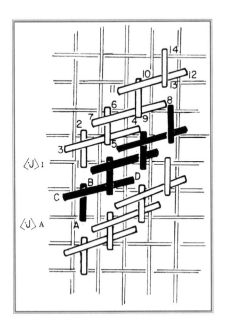

PLAITED GOBELIN

Be sure your yarn will cover the canvas. Experiment. Use your thumb or a laying tool to push the yarn back to find the holes for the next stitch. Work from top to bottom only. Cut the yarn at the end of the first row and begin the second row at the top. Do the compensating stitches last if you need to.

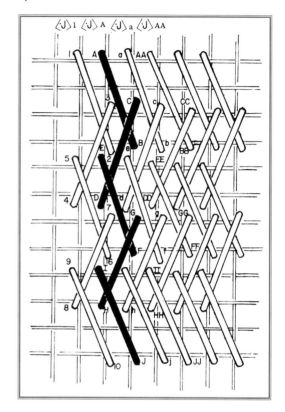

PLAITED
RAY

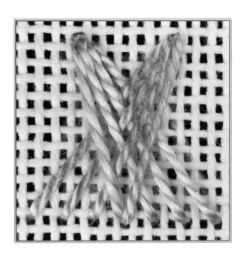

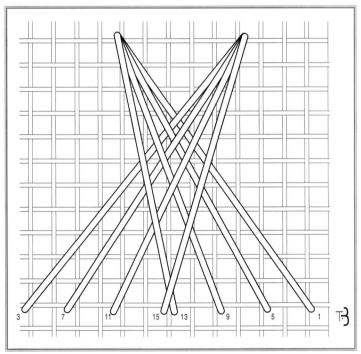

WAFFLE

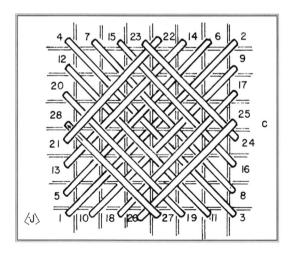

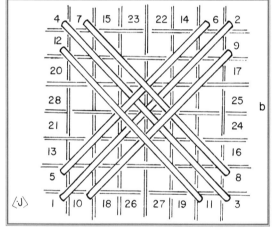

CRESCENT

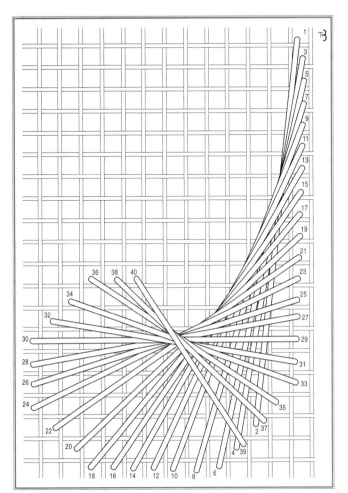

JESSICA

The diagram shows one Jessica inside the other. It is easier to see the pattern on the larger one. Beginning with stitch #20 on the big Jessica, watch for the arrows that indicate where to slip the needle under existing stitches. On the small Jessica in the center, this action is shown by darkening the portion of the stitch that is to be slipped under previous stitches. Starting with stitch 39-40, slip the yarn under the 1-2 stitch. See the charts below for all of the movements.

Large Jessica	
Stitch #	slips under stitch #
25-26	1-2
27-28	1-2, 3-4
29-30	1-2, 3-4, 5-6
31-32	1-2, 3-4, 5-6, 7-8

Small Jessica	
Stitch #	slips under stitch #
39-40	1-2
41-42	1-2, 3-4
43-44	1-2, 3-4, 5-6
45-46	1-2, 3-4, 5-6, 7-8
47-48	1-2, 3-4, 5-6, 7-8, 9-10

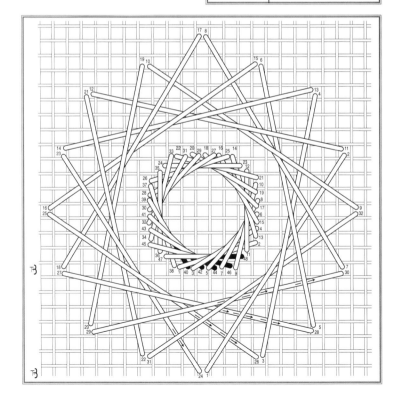

AMADEUS

Use your thumb or a laying tool to move the already stitched yarns aside so you can see better. Each motif can be placed singly or in groups, fanning to the right and/or the left.

Vary all of the components (number of stitches, space between the stitches, angle of the stitches, length of stitches) to create different shapes and curves. See Arrow Amadeus, Crescent, and Walneto.

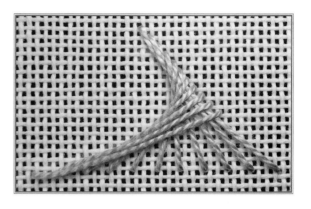

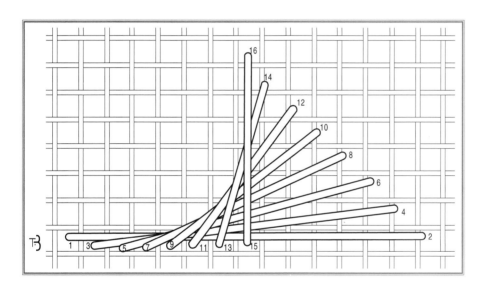

ARROW
AMADEUS

See the Amadeus for information about this stitch.

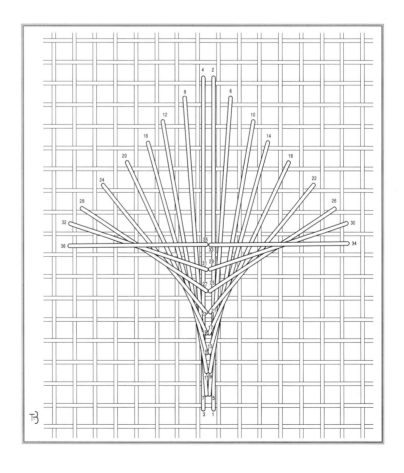

WALNETO

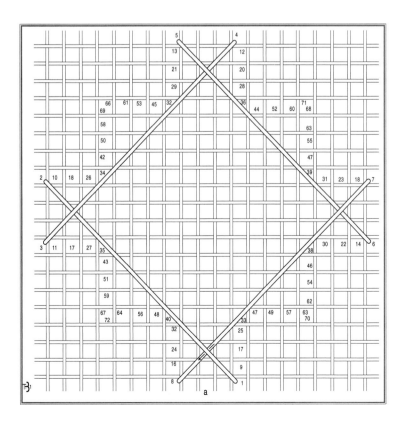

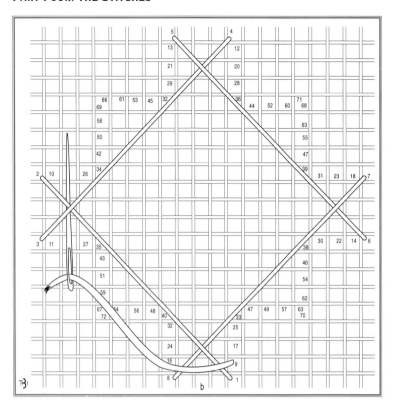

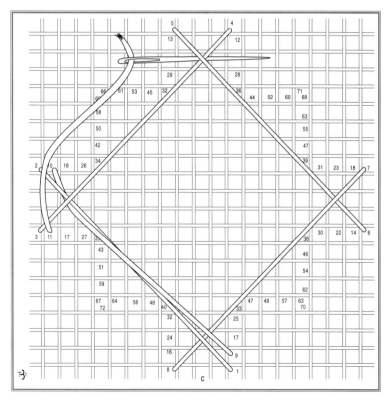

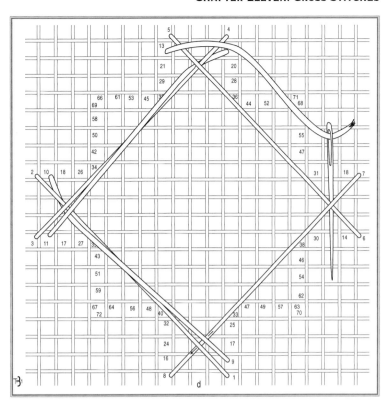

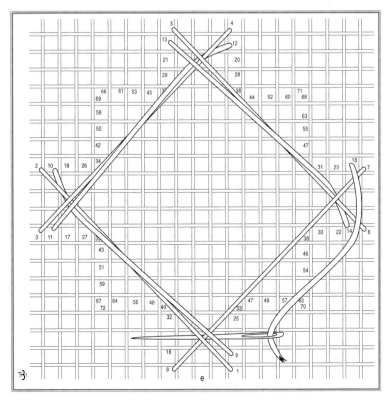

DOUBLE CROSS

This stitch makes a woven basket look.

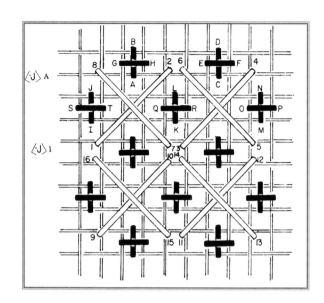

TRELLIS CROSS

This stitch resembles a basket.

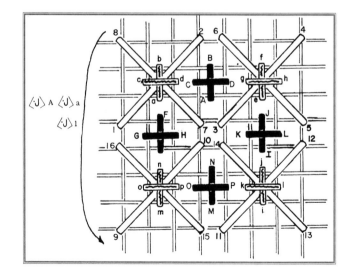

WINDOWPANE CROSS

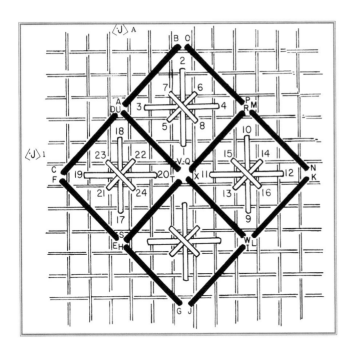

You may need a tramé to make this stitch cover the canvas.

FANCY CROSS

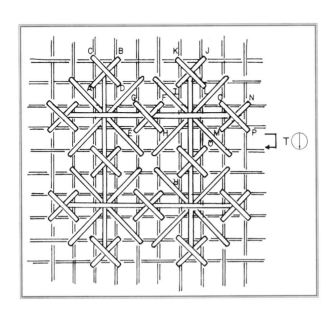

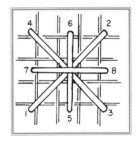

SLANTING STAR

The Slanting Star stands alone on a ground of Cross Stitch, Basketweave, or other simple stitches; it also works well on open canvas. It is actually an Upright Cross with a Knotted Stitch superimposed on it.

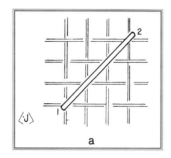

a

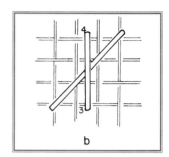

b

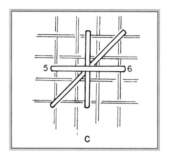

c

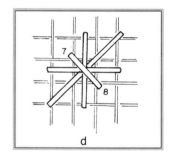

d

DOUBLE STRAIGHT CROSS

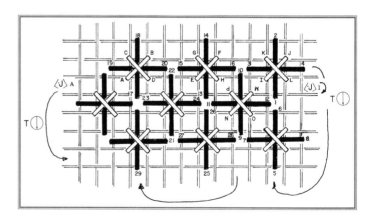

272

LEVIATHAN

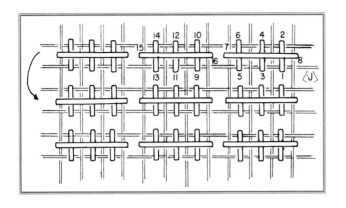

DOUBLE
LEVIATHAN

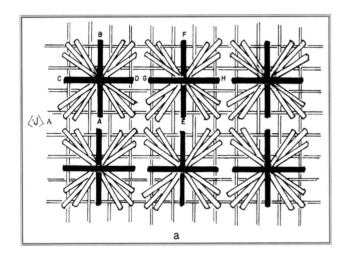

a

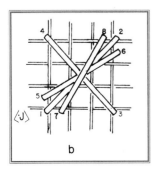

b

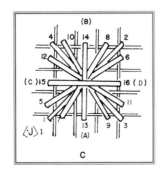

c

DIAMOND
LEVIATHAN

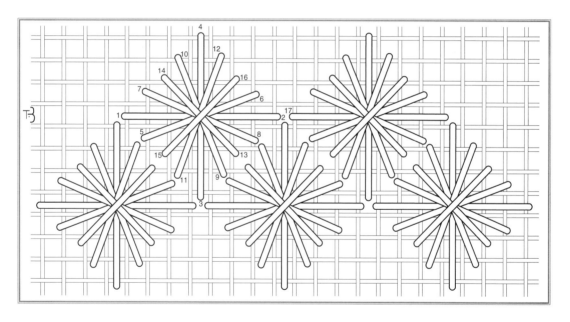

TRIPLE LEVIATHAN

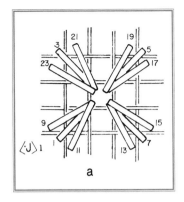

a

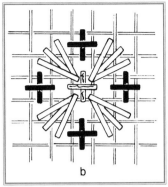

b

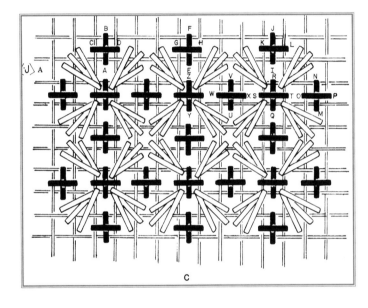

c

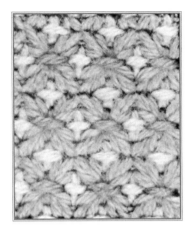

MEDALLION

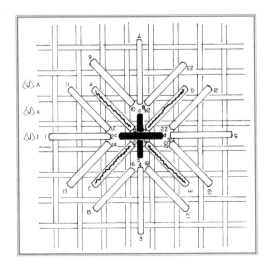

SNOWFLAKE

This stitch stands alone and serves well as an accent.

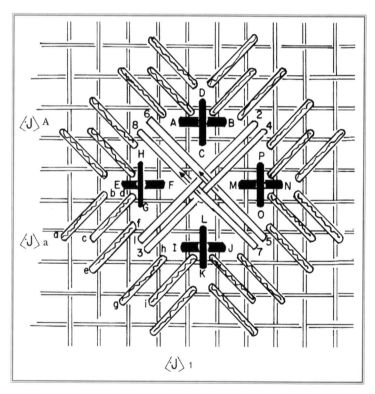

This stitch adds a fantastic texture to a needlepoint piece. Work it in varying sizes and shapes. Compensating stitches are pretty much impossible.

RHODES

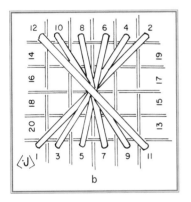

a

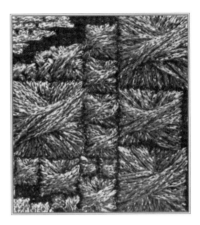

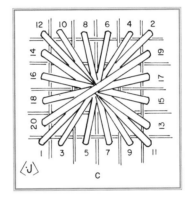

b

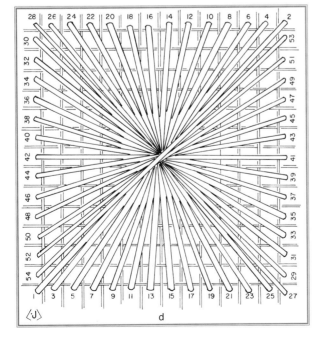

c

d

CROSS
RHODES

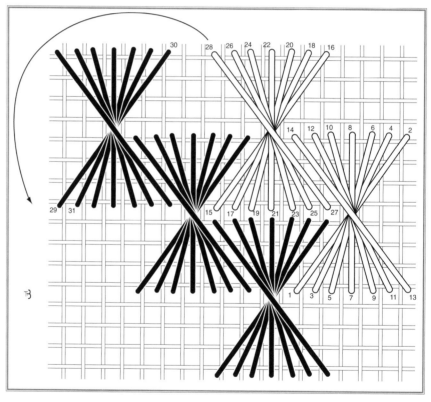

TRIPLE CROSS

Triple Cross stands alone, as Slanted Star does.

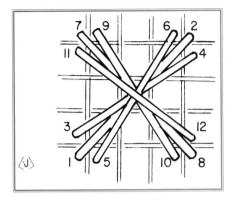

TRIPLE OBLONG CROSS

This stitch can be worked with differently shaped crosses and still give the same effect. The drawing shows a cross and the photo shows an oblong cross.

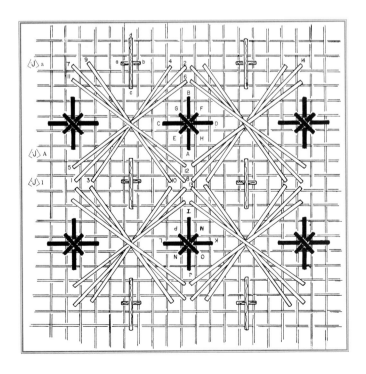

WINDMILL

This is another stitch that stands alone. Place it on a background of Cross Stitch, Basketweave, or open canvas.

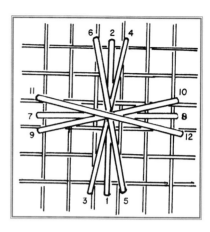

TIED
WINDMILL

The Tied Windmill also stands alone. See the Windmill, above.

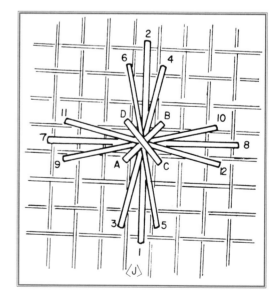

280

DOUBLE LAYERED CROSS

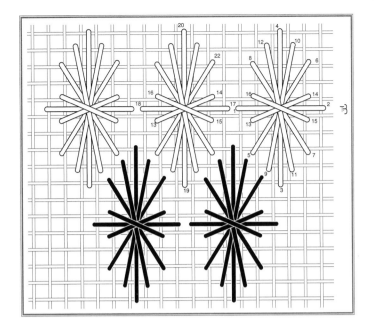

Make the x first, then the +. Smyrna Cross makes a good solid bump. When the + is worked in a light color and the x in a darker one, the stitch resembles hot cross buns. It is good for buttons, polka dots, cobblestones, and more.

SMYRNA CROSS

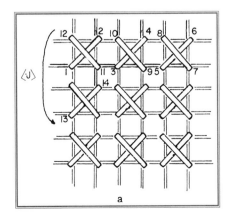

a

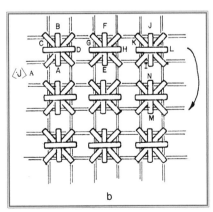

b

REVERSED
SMYRNA
CROSS

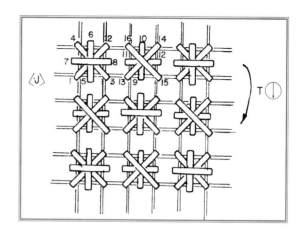

HORIZONTAL
ELONGATED
SMYRNA

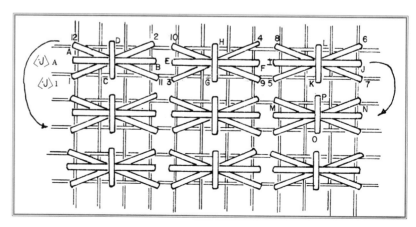

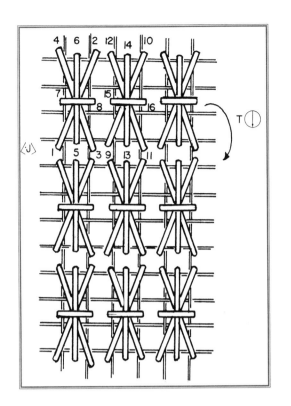

VERTICAL ELONGATED SMYRNA

ALTERNATING SMYRNA

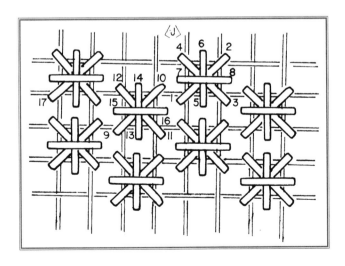

LONG-ARM SMYRNA

The last stitch of the + covers two Smyrna Crosses, giving an interesting reflection of light.

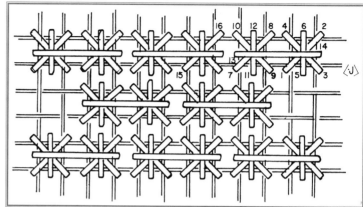

PATTERNED CROSSES

This stitch and the Patterned Scotch Crosses are examples of Diaper Patterns. These are combinations of stitches. Use these or make up your own. The number of effects is infinite.

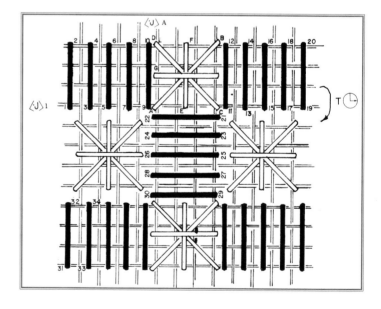

This is another example of a Diaper Pattern. See Patterned Crosses.

PATTERNED SCOTCH CROSSES

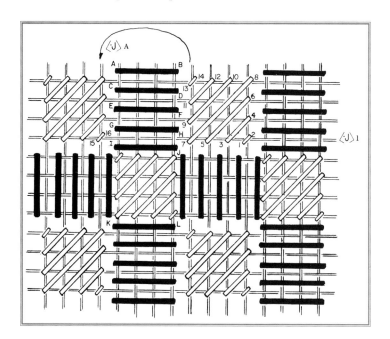

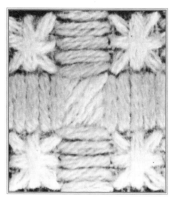

The yarn from #15 is slipped under stitch 9-10 on its way to #16. Compensating stitches cannot be readily done.

WOVEN CROSS

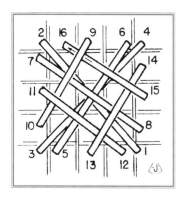

DOUBLE PLAITED CROSS

When making the 7-8 stitch, slip the needle under the 1-2 stitch. Do so on every motif at the same point.

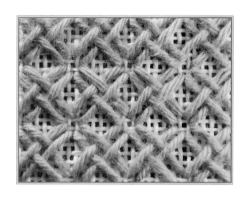

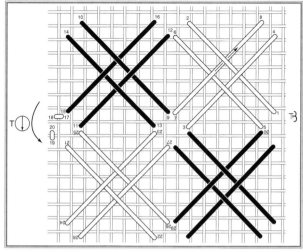

POINT DE TRESSE

This makes a long column that will stand alone, suitable for a border.

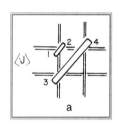

a

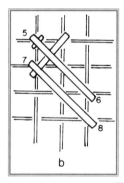

b

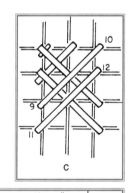

c

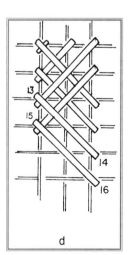

d

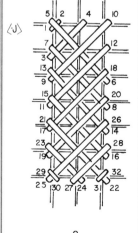

e

This is an excellent border. Each lettered stitch is woven under every other numbered stitch, except the first and last corners.

WOVEN BAND

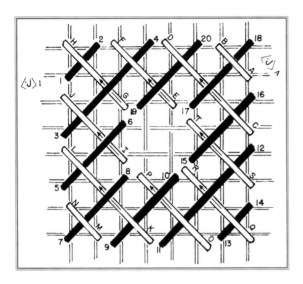

Each lettered stitch is woven under every other numbered stitch. This, too, makes an excellent border.

RAILWAY

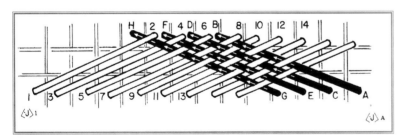

The Tied Stitches are pretty, and many are good stitches for shading. The Periwinkle Stitch was especially designed to be accented with beads.

These stitches are somewhat slow, but they are worth your while. They give good backings with little snagging on the right side of the canvas. It is most important that you tie each stitch or group of stitches as you go. Each of the drawings is numbered; follow them closely until you get the hang of it.

The samples of the Tied Stitches were worked on Mono 10 with a full strand of tapestry yarn. Some of the stitches did not cover completely. Thickening the yarn made them bulky; for them I recommend a smaller canvas, perhaps Mono 12 or 14. A thinner fiber would make the stitches look better too. Remember, this decision is yours, because it depends on the yarn's fiber, construction, color, and brand, as well as the canvas. Test each stitch you plan to use. You might also consider painting the canvas (page 106) or leaving the canvas bare. Enjoy experimenting.

TIED STITCHES	Border	Good Backing	Poor Backing	Background	Design	Accent	Fast	Slow	Geometric Pattern	Shading	Yarn Hog	Snags	Snag-Proof	Little Texture	Medium Texture	High Relief	Flower Stitch	Weak Pattern	Medium Pattern	Strong Pattern	Distorts Canvas
Wicker		•	•				•		•			•		•					•		
Omega		•	•						•			•		•					•		
Tied Pavillion	•	•		•	•	•	•		•			•		•						•	
Knotted		•		•	•			•		•			•	•					•		
Diagonal Roumanian				•	•					•			•	•					•		
Long and Short Oblique	•	•		•	•	•			•			•		•					•		
Interlocking Parisian Cross		•	•	•	•			•		•		•		•					•		
Tied Cashmere	•	•			•	•		•	•			•			•					•	•
Tied Scotch	•	•			•	•			•			•			•				•		•
Crossed Scotch	•	•			•	•		•	•			•	•		•					•	•
Crossed Tied-Down Scotch	•	•			•	•		•	•	•			•		•					•	•
Rice	•				•	•		•	•				•				•		•		
Giant Rice	•				•	•		•	•			•					•		•		
Straight Rice	•				•	•		•	•			•		•			•		•		
Tied Oblong Cross					•	•			•							•			•		
Giant Tied Oblong Cross					•	•			•			•		•					•		
Double Tied Oblong Cross					•	•		•	•			•		•					•		

TIED STITCHES	Border	Good Backing	Poor Backing	Background	Design	Accent	Fast	Slow	Geometric Pattern	Shading	Yarn Hog	Snags	Snag-Proof	Little Texture	Medium Texture	High Relief	Flower Stitch	Weak Pattern	Medium Pattern	Strong Pattern	Distorts Canvas
Hitched Cross	•			•	•	•			•				•						•		
Knotted Cross	•				•	•		•	•		•		•			•			•		
Slashed Cross				•	•	•			•			•				•	•		•		
Butterfly	•			•	•	•			•	•		•				•			•		
Tied Star				•	•	•			•	•		•				•	•			•	
Lone Tied Star						•										•	•		•		
Interlocking Roumanian				•	•					•		•		•					•		
Bokhara Couching			•	•	•	•	•	•		•		•		•					•		
Roumanian Couching			•	•	•	•	•	•		•		•		•					•		
Paris		•		•	•				•				•	•					•		
French		•		•	•				•	•			•	•					•		
French Variation				•	•				•				•	•					•		
Periwinkle				•	•				•								•			•	
Rococo		•		•	•	•			•				•	•					•		
Long Rococo		•		•	•	•			•				•	•					•		
Giant Rococo		•		•	•	•			•				•	•					•		
Fly				•	•									•					•		
Arrowhead Fly	•			•	•	•			•				•	•					•		
Wheat	•	•		•	•	•			•				•		•				•		
Alternating Wheat		•		•	•	•			•				•		•				•		
Interlocking Wheat		•		•	•	•			•				•		•				•		
Diagonal Wheat		•		•	•	•			•				•		•				•		
Rounded Wheat Columns		•		•	•	•			•						•				•		
Alternating Rounded Wheat Columns		•		•	•	•			•						•				•		
Shell	•	•			•	•			•		•	•				•				•	
Web					•	•			•	•			•	•				•			

WICKER

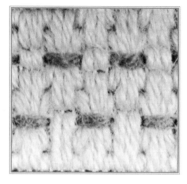

As the name suggests, this two-color stitch resembles wicker. It will look different if you use three colors. Make other color variations by stitching in diagonal stripes and horizontal stripes of another color. It is lovely in one color too.

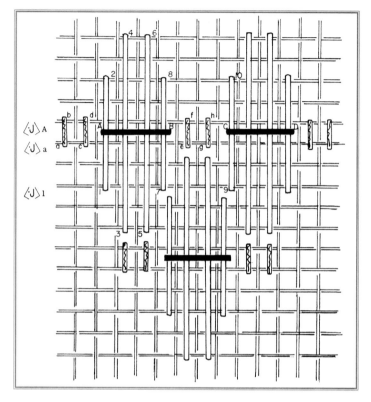

OMEGA

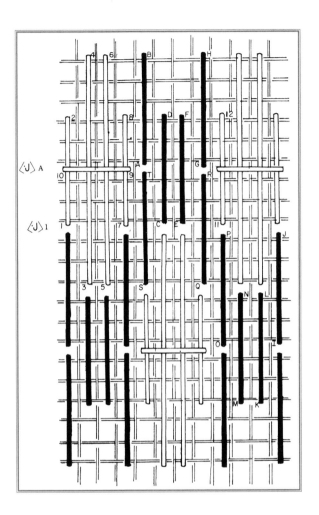

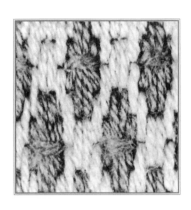

TIED
PAVILLION

The long stitches need to be pulled slightly tighter than the short ones. The tie is over two canvas threads. Backstitch in between the diamonds to cover the canvas if necessary.

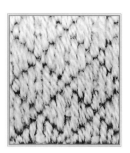

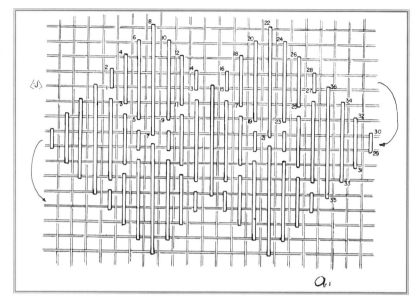

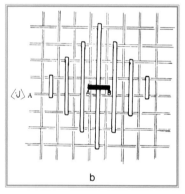

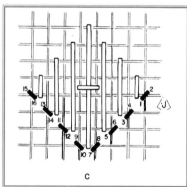

KNOTTED

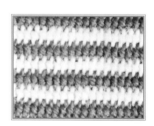

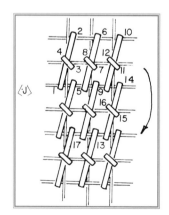

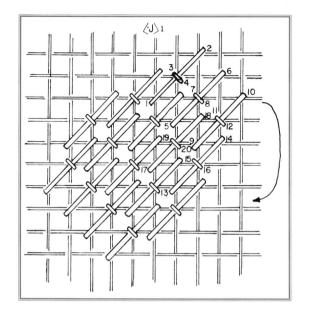

DIAGONAL ROUMANIAN

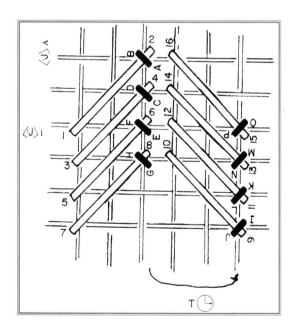

LONG AND SHORT OBLIQUE

INTERLOCKING PARISIAN CROSS

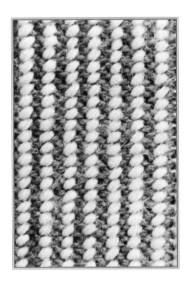

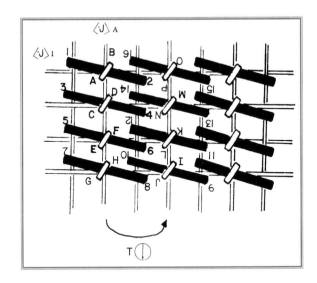

TIED CASHMERE

Tie the two long stitches together. Use your thumbnail or a laying tool to move the yarns aside to see just where your needle must go. This tie creates a slight bump.

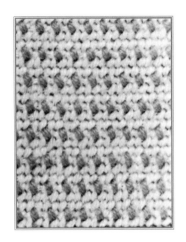

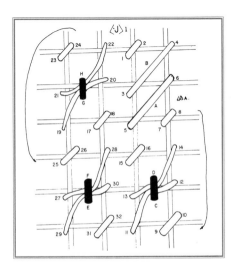

The tie is worked in the center of the longest stitch. This tie adds a bump and also reduces the likelihood of snagging.

TIED
SCOTCH

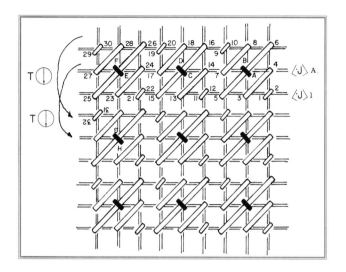

In working the basic foundation of the Scotch Stitch, omit the first and last stitches. Cross each Scotch box by coming up at A and going down at B. Without the shortest stitches in the Scotch box, it is easy to miss the right hole. Study the drawing carefully. The A-B line is merely a large Backstitch (see page 335).

CROSSED
SCOTCH

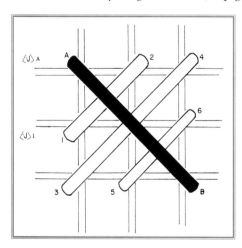

CROSSED TIED-DOWN SCOTCH

This stitch must be done in steps. First, work every other stitch (1-2, 3-4, and 5-6). Next, cross the whole thing. Then fill in the rest of the Scotch Stitch over the crossed stitch.

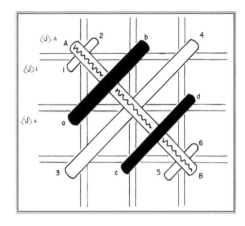

RICE

Use this stitch for a border of varying widths.

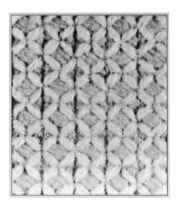

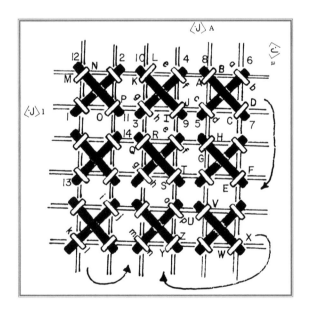

GIANT RICE

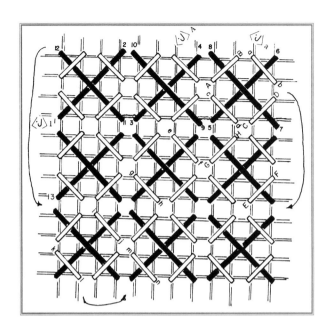

STRAIGHT RICE

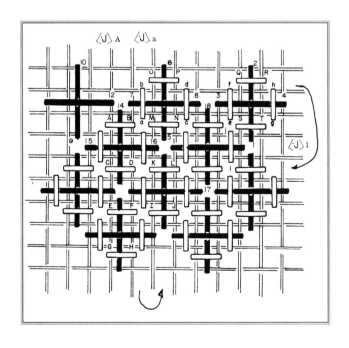

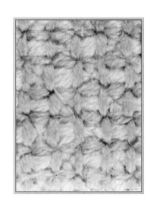

TIED
OBLONG
CROSS

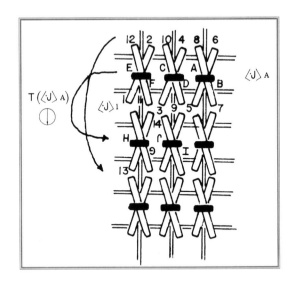

GIANT TIED
OBLONG
CROSS

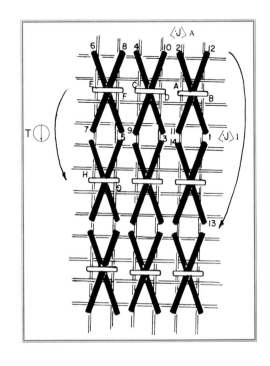

Cross and tie each cross before going on to the next motif.

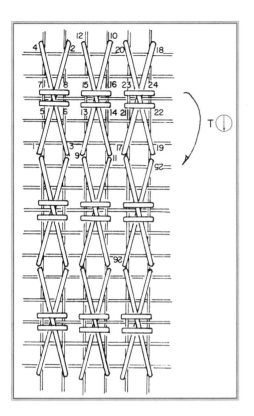

DOUBLE
TIED
OBLONG
CROSS

HITCHED
CROSS

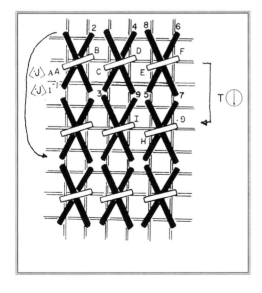

KNOTTED CROSS

This stitch is quite slow to do, but well worth your while for its texture. You will most likely need to use a stabbing motion, rather than a continuous motion, when stitching. Cross and knot each stitch as you go.

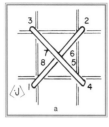

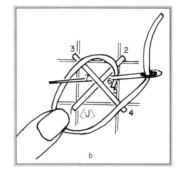

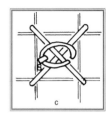

SLASHED CROSS

You will have to use your finger or a laying tool to move the yarns to find where to place the difficult-to-see second row. A single motif can stand alone.

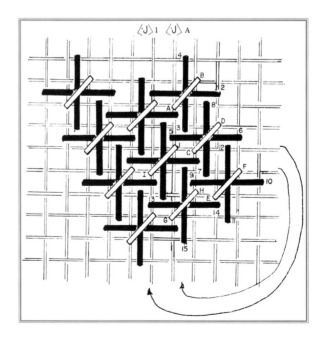

BUTTERFLY

The Butterfly Stitch looks like a basket. When stitch E-F is worked in the same color as the numbered stitch and the A-B and C-D stitches are on top, it reminds me of a butterfly.

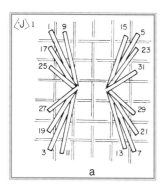

a

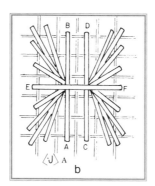

b

TIED STAR

Use this stitch diagonally in both directions.

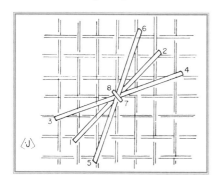

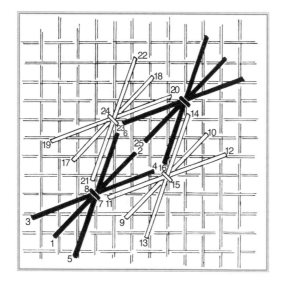

LONE TIED STAR

This stitch stands alone. You may place it on a ground of stitches or on bare canvas. See the Slanted Star. This stitch resembles a bow or a bow tie.

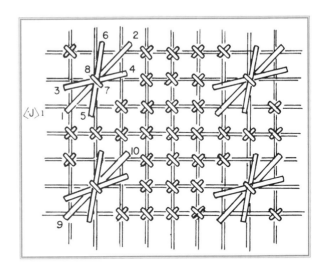

INTERLOCKING ROUMANIAN

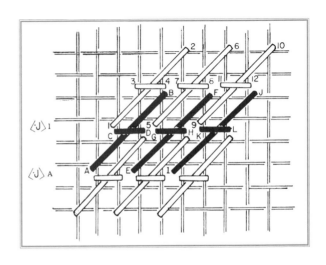

BOKHARA COUCHING

Use the tie stitch to create any pattern, regular or irregular, that you like.

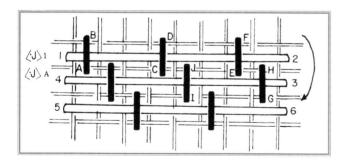

ROUMANIAN COUCHING

You may vary the placement of the ties, but every tie stitch is always a 1 x 3 stitch.

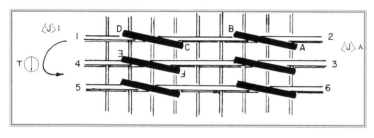

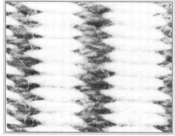

PARIS

Try this stitch when you need a woven basket look.

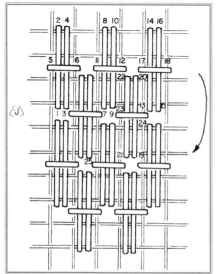

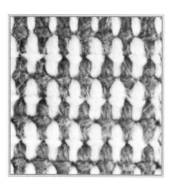

FRENCH

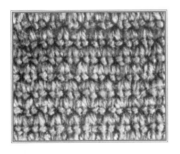

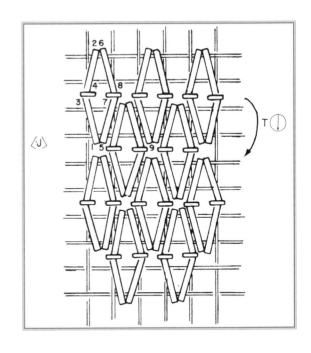

FRENCH
VARIATION

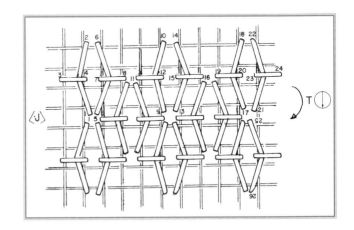

PERIWINKLE

Because this stitch was designed to be used with beads, it does not cover the canvas unless beads are used. Use long, thin beads; one round, large enough to cover; or three, as I have done. Sew the beads on with strong silk sewing thread after stitching the needlepoint stitch. It is also effective to let the blank canvas show through.

This stitch would make a particularly attractive background for an evening purse, especially if worked with metallic yarns.

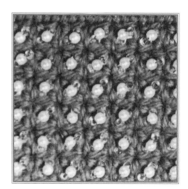

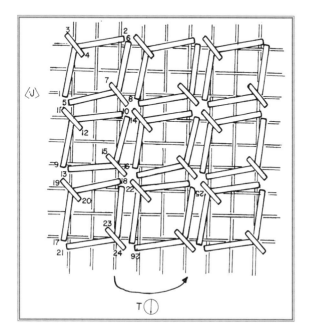

ROCOCO

When used alone, this stitch makes a good ball, balloon, button, or anything else round. When turned 90° (on its side), and with a stem added, the Rococo becomes a nice replica of a musical note.

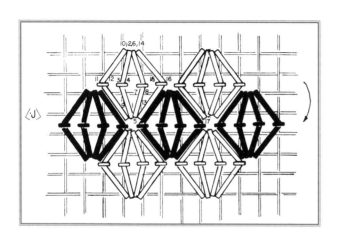

LONG
ROCOCO

Lengthening the Rococo Stitch makes it a diamond shape.

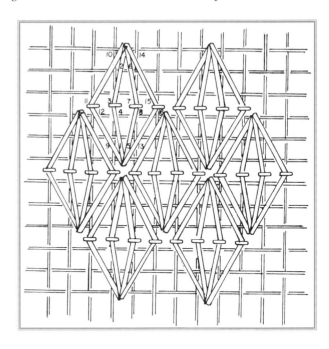

GIANT
ROCOCO

Make the Rococo any size you wish. Simply add a stitch on the far right of the center and on the far left of the center. For every pair of stitches you add, add one canvas thread at the top and one at the bottom. This technique will keep the Rococo round. When extra stitches are not added, the Long Rococo results.

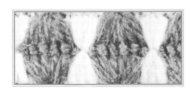

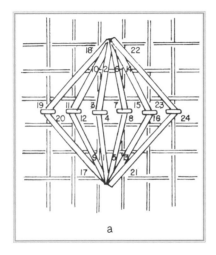

a

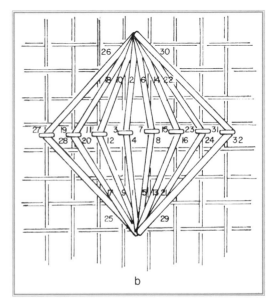

b

FLY

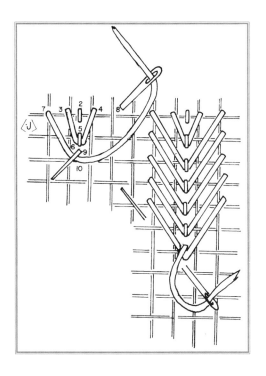

Two arrowheads placed in a vertical column and/or in a horizontal row make an attractive border. This stitch is very similar in construction to the Fly Stitch, above.

ARROWHEAD FLY

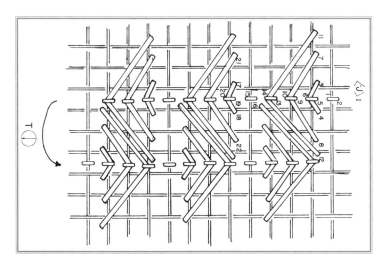

WHEAT

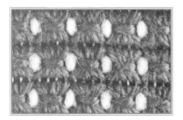

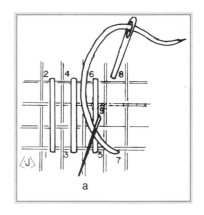

a

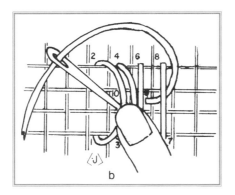

b

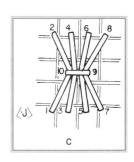

c

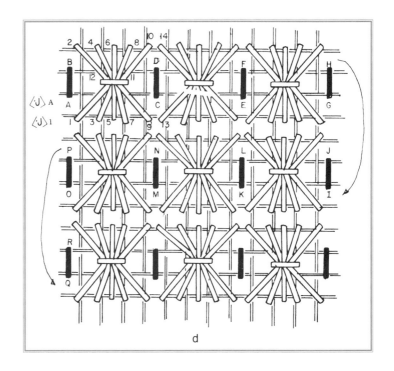

d

ALTERNATING WHEAT

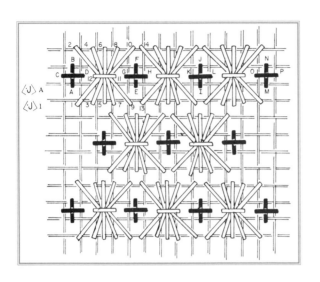

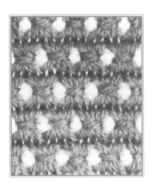

INTERLOCKING WHEAT

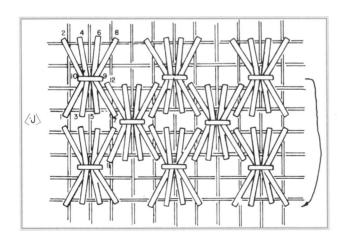

DIAGONAL WHEAT

Diagonal Wheat may slant both ways.

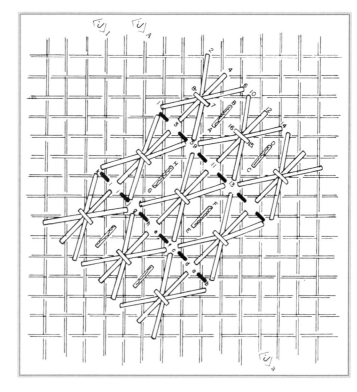

ROUNDED WHEAT COLUMNS

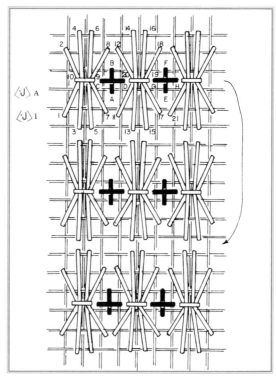

ALTERNATING ROUNDED WHEAT COLUMNS

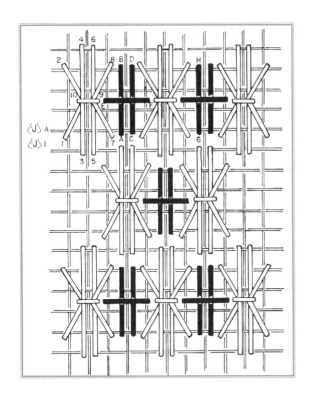

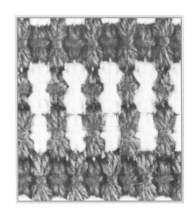

SHELL

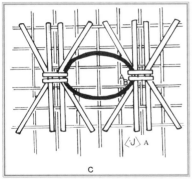

a

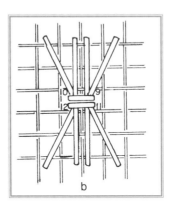

b

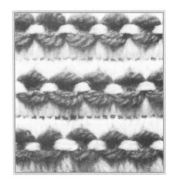

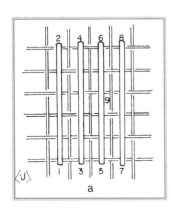

c

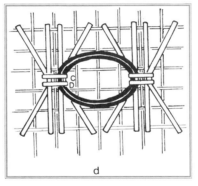

d

311

WEB

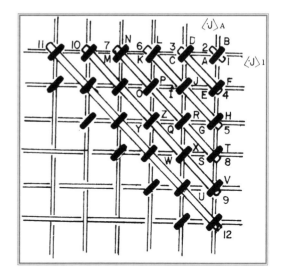

*E*ye Stitches are those that are made by putting several stitches into one hole. This technique creates a hole, a dimple, or an eye.

The samples of Eye Stitches were made on Interlock Mono 10 using a full strand of tapestry yarn (except for Algerian Eye, which needed a 2-ply yarn).

Eye Stitches are very pretty and interesting to do but slow to work up. In stitching them, work from the outside to the center and **always** go **down** into the center. This will prevent splitting or snagging the yarn of the stitches that you have already worked.

As you put what seems an impossible number of stitches into one small hole, take care that each of these stitches goes into the hole smoothly. If you are working on Regular Mono canvas, this task will be a little easier, because the canvas threads will move a little to accommodate so many yarns in one hole. It is a great help to enlarge the center hole by poking the point of a pair of embroidery scissors into it. Spread the canvas threads gently. This works **only** on Regular Mono canvas. (See the photo below.) Use 2-ply Persian yarn on other kinds of canvases.

You may need to pull the yarn more tightly as each eye forms. This helps to make the stitch lie smoothly and evenly around the center hole. Be careful not to pull the canvas out of shape, unless you intend to do so as a Pulled Thread Stitch (page 54). On a well-stitched eye, you should not be able to tell which was the last stitch taken.

Note that Eye Stitches usually begin with an Upright Cross, going from the outside into the center. Next, one stitch is taken in each quadrant in a circular motion until all of the remaining stitches have been taken, The even-numbered stitches are all in the center of the eye, and because they do not fit easily, they have been omitted.

Eye Stitches lend themselves to broad borders, background, and pillows. Single motifs or clusters of two or three eyes make lovely flowers.

Because the Eye Stitches have good backings, most of them will wear well. Those that will not are those that have long yarns, such as Triangular Ray and Square Eyelet. (See the section on thickening and thinning of yarns on page 33.)

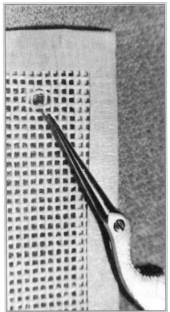

EYE STITCHES	Border	Good Backing	Poor Backing	Background	Design	Accent	Fast	Slow	Geometric Pattern	Shading	Yarn Hog	Snags	Snag-Proof	Little Texture	Medium Texture	High Relief	Flower Stitch	Weak Pattern	Medium Pattern	Strong Pattern	Distorts Canvas
Starfish					•	•								•					•		
Star	•	•			•	•		•	•					•			•		•		
Framed Star	•	•			•	•		•	•			•			•		•		•		
Double Star	•	•			•	•		•	•						•		•		•		
Algerian Eye	•	•		•	•			•	•				•	•				•			
Square Eyelet	•	•			•	•		•	•		•	•		•				•			
Diamond Eyelet	•	•		•	•	•		•	•			•			•				•		
Triangular Ray	•	•			•	•		•	•			•		•					•		
Crossed Diamond	•				•	•		•	•						•		•			•	
Double Crossed Diamond	•				•	•		•	•						•		•			•	
Squared Daisies	•	•		•	•	•		•	•						•		•			•	
Ringed Daisies	•	•		•	•	•		•	•						•		•			•	
Crossed Daisies	•	•		•	•	•		•	•						•		•			•	
Milanese Pinwheel		•		•		•	•		•			•			•		•			•	

STARFISH

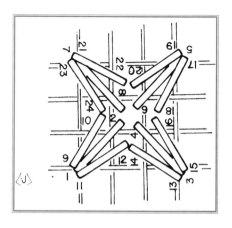

Without the frame, this is simply the Star Stitch. When stitched in wool, the frame is necessary to cover the canvas, except on Mono 14.

STAR/ FRAMED STAR

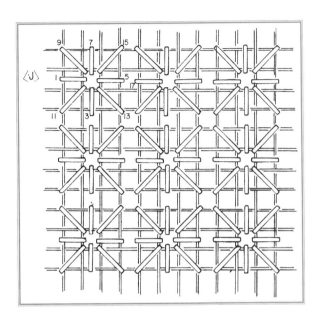

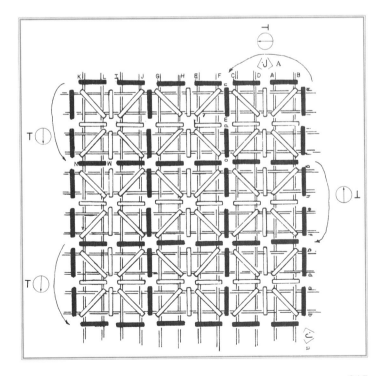

DOUBLE STAR

This stitch is actually a framed Reversed Mosaic. I think you will find it easier to get a smooth finish if you follow the numbers given. This stitch is particularly attractive in two colors.

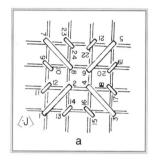

a

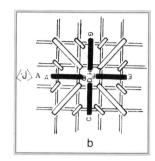

b

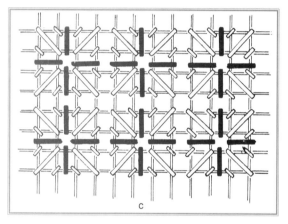

c

ALGERIAN EYE

You may find it necessary to thin your yarn to work this stitch.

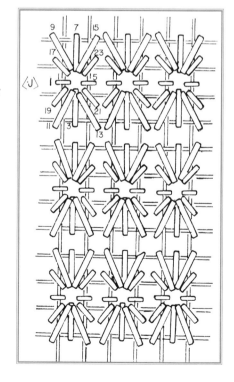

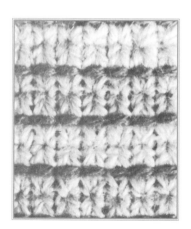

The Square Eyelet Stitch shown here covers an area of ten canvas threads by ten canvas threads. It may also cover a 6 x 6 or an 8 x 8 area. Notice in the photo that I should have pulled my last stitch tighter. It is better for all of the stitches to go smoothly into the center and with equal tension.

SQUARE EYELET

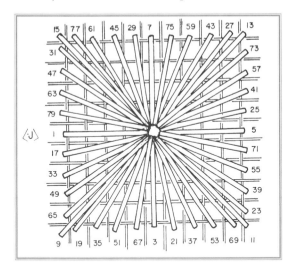

Diamond Eyelet lets you put a pearl or a bead in the center. The Backstitch and a Frame Stitch fill in between the diamonds. This stitch makes a good border, background, or geometric design with many color possibilities.

DIAMOND EYELET

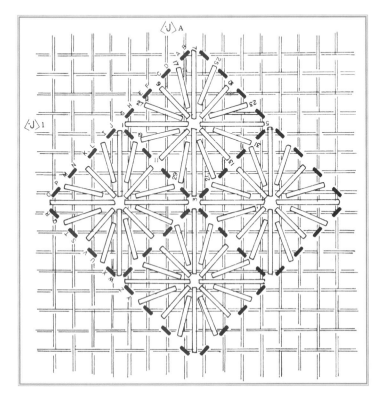

TRIANGULAR RAY

This stitch makes a nice border. Arrangement of color can create rickrack. Use a Backstitch to cover the canvas.

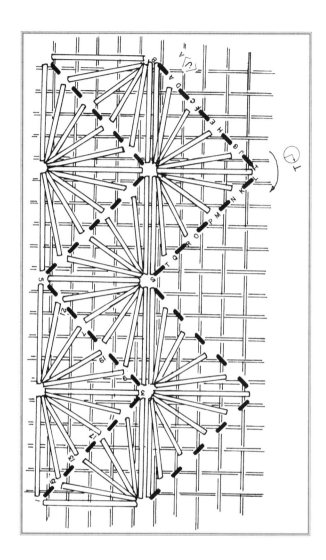

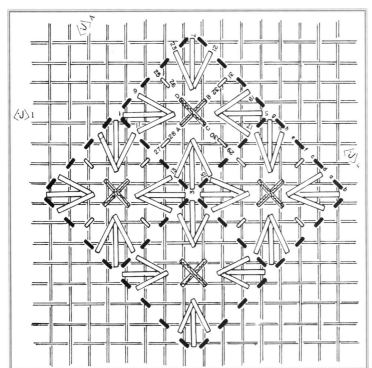

CROSSED DIAMOND

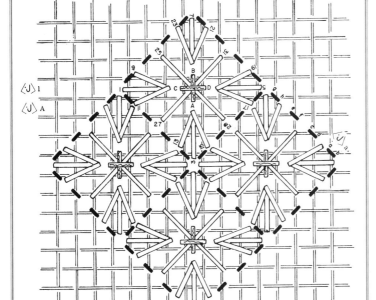

DOUBLE CROSSED DIAMOND

SQUARED DAISIES

You may need to thin the yarn for this stitch. Use a Backstitch to cover the canvas.

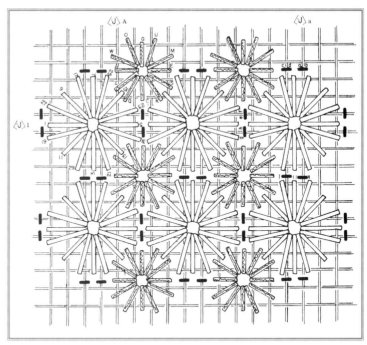

RINGED DAISIES

This is the same round eye as in Squared Daisies, except that the areas between the eyes are filled differently. This gives a changed look to the stitch.

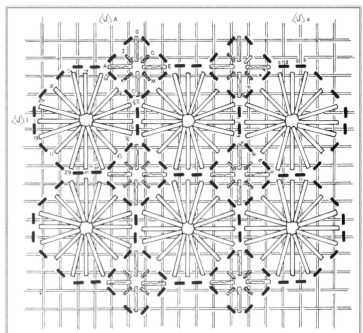

Here again is the round eye, but this time alternate rows instead of columns.

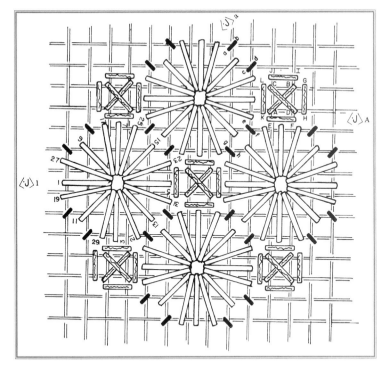

CROSSED DAISIES

Use each pinwheel singly or in groups to cover a large area. Work the center area like the diagram (see page 322) or like the photo. You might find another pretty way if you try.

MILANESE PINWHEEL

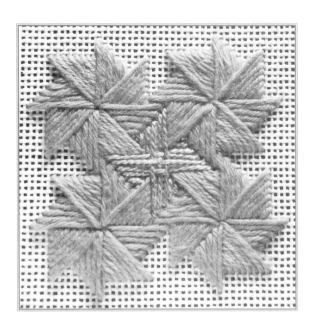

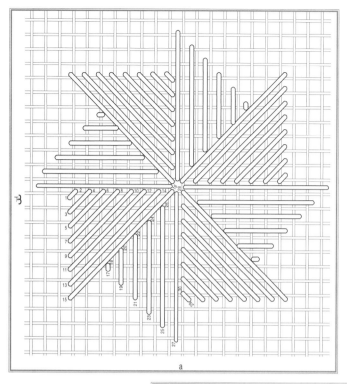

a

b

322

Fourteen

LEAF STITCHES

*L*eaf Stitches have a charm all their own; they complement lovely flowers. Some of them can even be used to make flowers. Given on the following pages are a few of those you can use. Mix them up, use one or two favorites, or make up your own.

Use the Leaf Stitches as overall patterns, singly, or in pairs. Turn Leaf Stitches sideways or upside down to make feathers. The veined stitches may be worked in three ways and are labeled #1, #2, and #3, accordingly:

1. From the top, one stitch to the right, one stitch to the left, etc.

2. From the bottom, one stitch to the right, one stitch to the left, etc.

3. From the bottom, up one side and down the other.

The samples pictured were worked on Penelope 10 with tapestry yarn.

These stitches will also work well in geometric patterns. Most lend themselves well to shading. Have fun with color!

LEAF STITCHES	Border	Good Backing	Poor Backing	Background	Design	Accent	Fast	Slow	Geometric Pattern	Shading	Yarn Hog	Snags	Snag-Proof	Little Texture	Medium Texture	High Relief	Flower Stitch	Weak Pattern	Medium Pattern	Strong Pattern	Distorts Canvas
Diamond Ray		•	•	•	•				•	•					•		•				
Mini Leaf	•	•			•	•			•	•	•				•		•		•		
Ray	•	•				•			•	•		•				•	•		•		
Leaf #1	•	•		•	•	•			•	•			•		•				•		
Leaf #2	•	•		•	•	•			•	•			•		•				•		
Leaf #3	•	•		•	•	•			•	•			•		•				•		
Diamond Leaf		•		•	•	•			•	•			•		•				•		
Four-Way Leaf		•				•			•	•	•		•						•		
Diagonal Leaf		•		•	•	•			•	•			•		•				•		
Roumanian Leaf	•	•				•	•				•				•				•		
Diagonal Roumanian Leaf		•				•	•				•				•				•		
Cretan	•					•	•				•				•					•	
Close Herringbone						•					•					•			•		
Raised Close Herringbone						•					•	•				•			•		
Free-Form Van Dyke						•					•	•				•				•	
Rose Leaf						•		•	•	•	•					•				•	

DIAMOND RAY

The Diamond Ray Stitch makes a most interesting pattern and has a good backing. I generally like something faster to work up for a background, but you might want to use it that way. The longest stitch is not likely to snag.

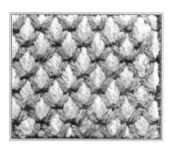

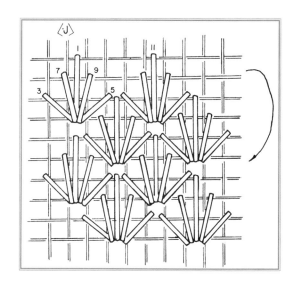

MINI LEAF

The Mini Leaf is just a small version of the Leaf Stitch.

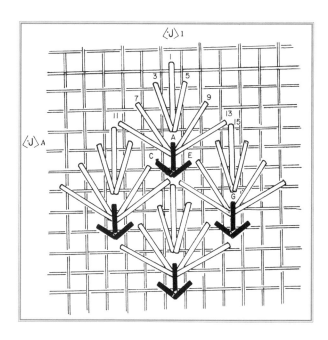

The Ray Stitch is also very slow to work up, and it is hard to get the needle through the canvas in wool. Try spreading the base hole with a pair of scissors as described in the Eye Stitch chapter on page 313. In spite of its drawbacks, this stitch is worthwhile, for it is lovely when finished. It makes a good, bumpy border.

RAY

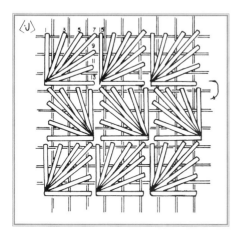

These Ray Stitches were stitched in one color. Isn't it interesting that the light makes it seem like two colors?

This is the basic and most familiar Leaf Stitch. It makes an interesting pattern and is lovely when shaded within each leaf. An optional vein may be added as in Leaf #3. This stitch has a good backing, and it makes a pretty border or vertical stripe.

LEAF #1

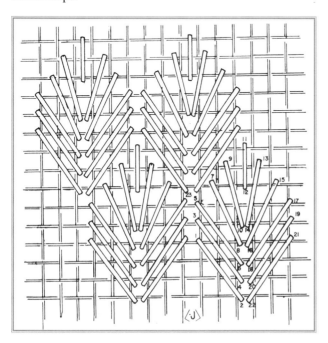

LEAF #2

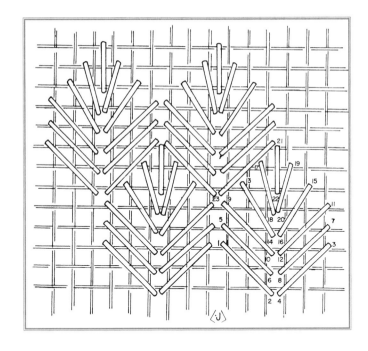

LEAF #3

Do the vein last in another color if you wish.

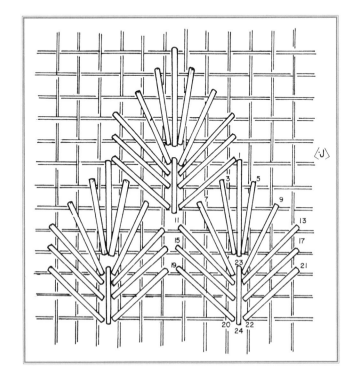

DIAMOND LEAF

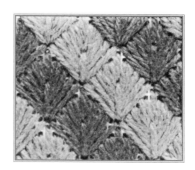

Fill in around the leaves with Basketweave or leave them on a ground of open canvas. When placed in an arrangement of several leaves, a pretty overall pattern with good backing occurs.

FOUR-WAY LEAF

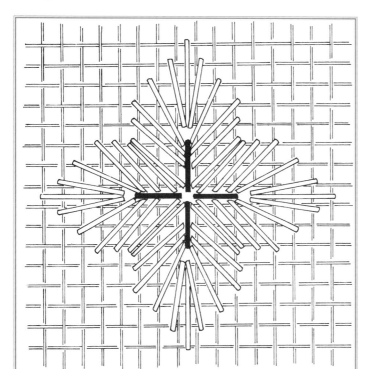

DIAGONAL LEAF

Use this Leaf Stitch in groups or singly. The resulting pattern is pleasing to the eye.

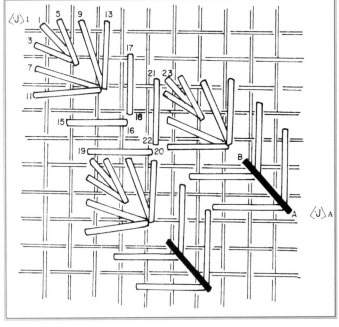

ROUMANIAN LEAF

The Roumanian-type stitches (Roumanian Leaf; Diagonal Roumanian Leaf, below; and Fly Stitch, page 307) are fast and fun to work. Shading within the leaf can be done, but then the speed of the stitch is lost.

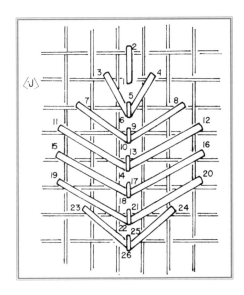

In order to give this more of a leaf shape, two stitches share one of the center stitches. Stitch #7 slips under stitch 5-6 and goes down into the canvas at #8. The pattern is then resumed.

DIAGONAL ROUMANIAN LEAF

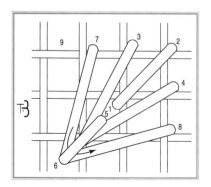

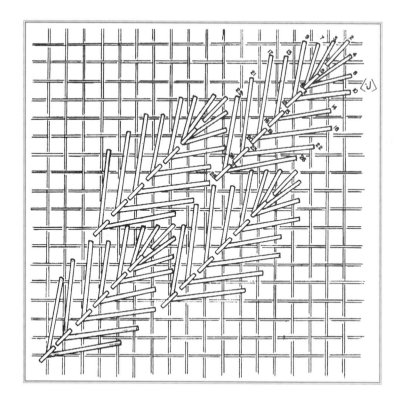

CRETAN

This stitch forms a neat braid down the center. It can be worked with long or short spaces from the center to the edges. This is a very pretty Leaf Stitch. It is usually used singly. There is no backing behind the braid.

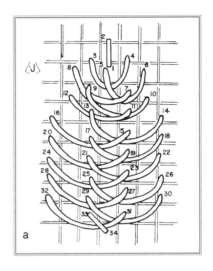

CLOSE HERRINGBONE

This makes a slightly raised leaf with the stitches crossed over each other. There is some backing, but not a great deal. This stitch stands alone and makes a long, smooth leaf.

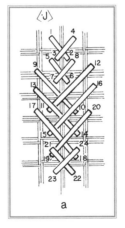

RAISED CLOSE HERRINGBONE

This leaf is quite three-dimensional and is interesting to work. It is worked in steps that produce a fair backing. Again, this Leaf Stitch is used alone as an accent for a design. The needle penetrates the canvas only along the sides as you stitch and at the rear only when you are finished. Only the first stitch at the base goes through the canvas. The rest of the stitches go under the first stitch on top of the canvas. The size and shape can be readily varied.

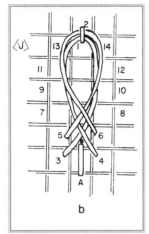

a b c

FREE-FORM VAN DYKE

The Van Dyke can be worked in just about any slant or curve you wish. I have pictured a traditional leaf shape for you, but you may work it on top of your background in a looser arrangement that resembles a fern leaf. The size can be varied too.

This stitch is fun to work and goes quickly. It is used alone or in groups. A pretty raised braid is formed down the center.

Slip the needle from #6 to #7, #10 to #11, etc., without penetrating the canvas.

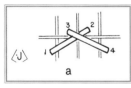

a

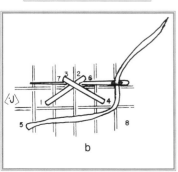

b

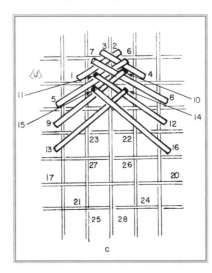

c

ROSE LEAF

The Rose Leaf Stitch looks more difficult than it really is. If you follow the diagrams and instructions step by step, I don't think you will have any trouble.

1. Fold over a piece of lightweight cardboard that is 1" to 2" wide after folding. You will use this to help you keep the size of the loops of yarn consistent; the size of the loops will determine the size of the leaf. The thickness of your yarn will also make a difference in the final size of your leaf. Stitch a few leaves on scrap canvas and experiment with the size of the loops.

2. As you take your needle from #1 to #2 and from #3 to #4, etc., wrap it over the cardboard. When you have made all the stitches, carefully remove the cardboard.

3. Using a crochet hook or your finger, pull the loops, one at a time, through the "tunnel," so that their order is reversed.

4. Arrange the loops so that they resemble a pointed leaf with a broad base. Tack the last loop in place with a short stitch.

5. Using a Straight Stitch, make a vein.

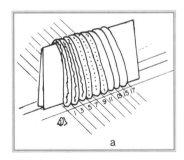

a

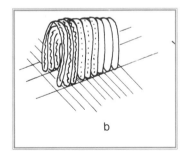

b

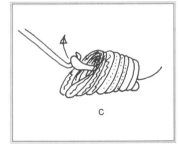

c

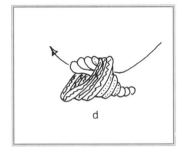

d

e

f

*L*ine Stitches are those long, relatively thin stitches that can be curved easily. They have an infinite number of uses. They can be fat or thin, long or short. When worked side by side, they can fill in an area nicely. Line Stitches can also be stitched on top of other stitches, beside other stitches, and on bare canvas. For the most part, they are easy to do.

The stitches that follow are not related in construction techniques, as are the stitches in other chapters; but they are related in final appearance—an easily curved line. The examples were stitched on a variety of sizes of canvas with a variety of yarns.

LINE STITCHES	Border	Good Backing	Poor Backing	Background	Design	Accent	Fast	Slow	Geometric Pattern	Shading	Yarn Hog	Snags	Snag-Proof	Little Texture	Medium Texture	High Relief	Flower Stitch	Weak Pattern	Medium Pattern	Strong Pattern	Distorts Canvas
Running			•	•	•	•	•							•				•			
Double Running		•			•	•						•		•				•			
Backstitch		•				•								•				•			
Outline/Stem					•	•	•									•		•			
Couching		•			•	•						•		•				•			
Thorn		•				•		•				•		•						•	
Van Dyke	•	•	•		•		•		•			•		•					•		
Binding	•							•								•			•		
Chain	•	•			•	•								•					•		
Open Chain	•	•			•	•						•		•					•		
Twisted Chain		•				•		•				•				•			•		
Raised Rope		•			•	•						•				•	•		•		
Whipped Line		•			•	•		•								•			•		
Chain of Grain		•			•	•										•	•			•	
Zigzag Braid		•			•	•					•					•	•			•	

RUNNING

The Running Stitch is made by plunging the needle into and out of the canvas many times in succession and in a line. The number of canvas threads covered on top of the canvas and underneath the canvas can vary from stitch to stitch within one line.

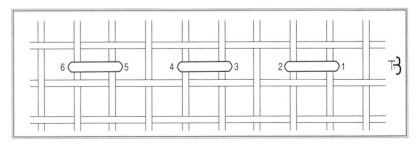

DOUBLE RUNNING

To make a Double Running Stitch, first stitch a Running Stitch. Then go back over the same area with another Running Stitch when a line of Running Stitches has been completed. This time, carry the yarn on the canvas where it was below the canvas last time. This stitch is one of the basic stitches of Black Work. See page 55.

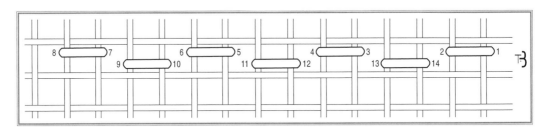

BACKSTITCH

This simple little stitch often is used alone and in combination with other stitches to form new stitches.

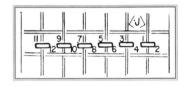

OUTLINE/ STEM

These two stitches are grouped together for two reasons: (1) they are closely related, and (2) to avoid confusion with needlepoint's Stem Stitch (page 198).

These two stitches are made in almost the same way. When stitching the **Stem Stitch** from left to right, the thread is carried *below* the line of stitching and *below* the needle. When stitching the **Outline Stitch**, the thread is carried *above* the line of stitching and *above* the needle. Diagram a shows the Stem Stitch and Diagram b shows the Outline Stitch.

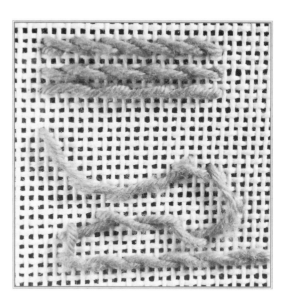

The roll of the worked stitches pitches down with the Stem Stitch (top two rows of stitching in the photo) and up with the Outline Stitch (third row of stitching from the top in the photo). Which name goes with which stitch really isn't important. What is important it their correct use. Which one you use is driven by your design. When stitching an S curve you need to switch from one to the other in mid-line, as shown in the photo. You can see in the photo that my curve is not very neat. I should have taken smaller stitches around the curves. I'm sure that you can do better!

You may place many lines side by side. This makes the Encroaching Oblique Stitch (page 193).

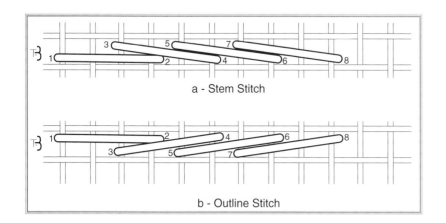

a - Stem Stitch

b - Outline Stitch

COUCHING

Couching is the laying of one yarn where you want it and tying it down with another yarn. It curves well. It's easier to work if you thread two needles and work both yarns at more or less the same time. Usually you will want to try to tack the laid yarn down at even intervals. Couching in a pattern is also possible. See Roumanian Couching and Bokhara Couching on page 303.

This stitch is the perfect way to add an interesting yarn to your design when the yarn is too stiff, too fat, too brittle, or too fragile to go through the canvas's holes and endure its harshness.

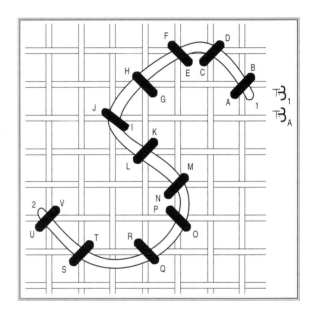

Although the diagram shows the Thorn Stitch worked in a straight line, you may curve it, as shown in the photo.

THORN

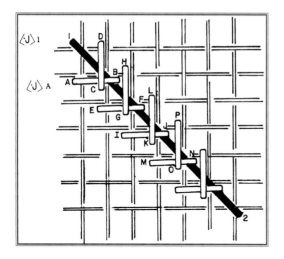

Always start the next row at the top. End and cut the yarn each time. This stitch makes great stripes or columns when used alone.

VAN DYKE

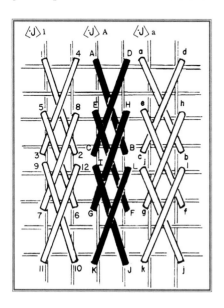

BINDING

Correct *method of stitching the Binding Stitch.*

The Binding Stitch is not only useful; it is attractive too. It finishes edges and sews seams (page 129). It is worked only on the edge of canvas. You will need two threads of the canvas to secure it properly. On Penelope this is one canvas thread; on Mono, two canvas threads.

Play around with the spacing, as I did. The diagram at the top of page 339 shows my favorite version of the Binding Stitch. If you want the stitch to cover the canvas completely, use the version in the diagram at the bottom of this page.

It is worked much like the Fern Stitch, and it, too, produces a braid.

Incorrect *method of sewing a seam with the Binding Stitch.*

Correct *method of sewing a seam with the Binding Stitch.*

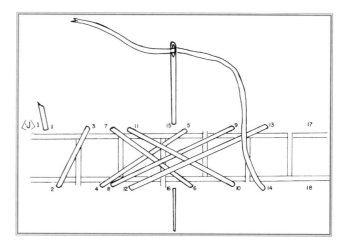

Stitching method that produces a tight braid.

338

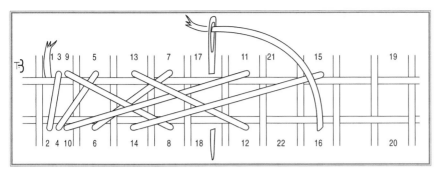

Stitching method that produces a more widely spaced braid.

The Chain Stitch is another versatile stitch. You may work it on top of the background, leave a space in the background to work the Chain Stitch, or lay it on blank canvas. This stitch is easier to work if you turn the canvas so that you are working horizontally and from right to left. Put one chain over two or three canvas threads.

This stitch will cover an area solidly if the lines of Chain are worked side by side. Curving the lines within an area gives it motion. Shape an animal's haunches and shoulders by doing this.

CHAIN

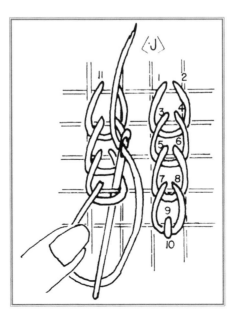

OPEN
CHAIN

This stitch may also be worked on top of the background. Leave a space in the background to work the Chain Stitch or lay it on blank canvas. It may be worked side by side to fill an area.

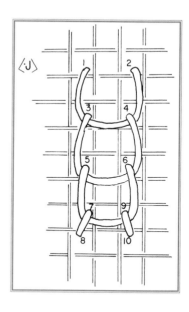

TWISTED
CHAIN

This stitch can be worked in a single row and curved to meet your purpose, just like the others in this chapter. It may also be worked side by side to fill an area. It is **imperative** that your tension be even. Work from the top to bottom only.

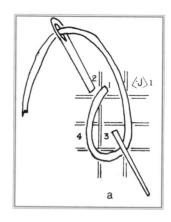

a

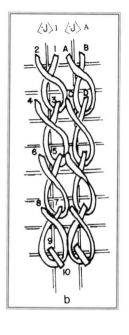

b

Work the stitches very loosely. They will automatically form a ridge. Curve the stitch as you need to. This stitch works particularly well in a circle. It may also be worked side by side to fill an area.

RAISED
ROPE

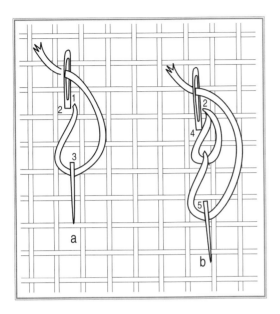

WHIPPED LINE

This same method may be used to wrap any Line Stitch, such as Backstitch, Chain, and Running Stitch. In wrapping the yarn with the threaded needle, never penetrate the canvas until the end of the line. Wrap the yarn snugly or loosely for different effects.

Whipped Backstitch

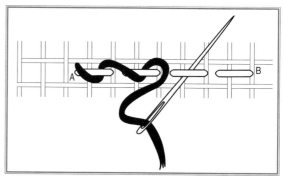

Whipped Chain

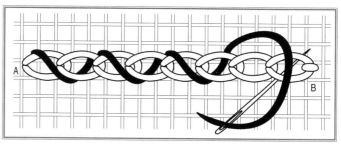

Whipped Running.

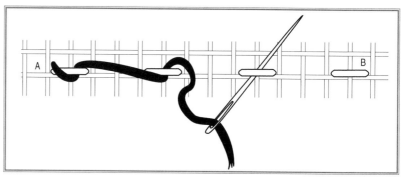

CHAIN OF GRAIN

This is one of several Line Stitches that can be curved or angled. Study the diagram carefully. Note where the needle goes over and under the canvas threads.

Wrap yarn around a laid stitch that hugs the canvas. In wrapping, do not pierce the canvas with the needle. The wrapping around each laid stitch doesn't go in the direction I thought it would. If you do it differently from the diagram the result is an indistinct lumpy line. Feel free to vary your tension on the wrapping stitches for a different look.

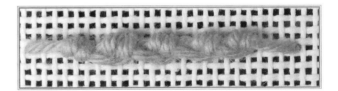

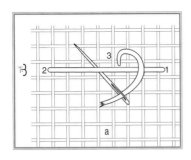

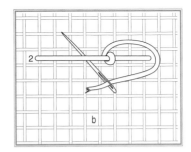

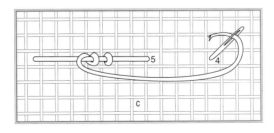

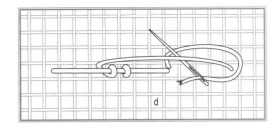

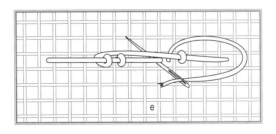

ZIGZAG BRAID

This is a fun line that makes good wheat, flowers, borders, trim on clothing, and other accents. Tension is essential. A too-loose tension makes a mess, and the pattern is lost. A too-tight tension distorts the canvas.

Curve the line if you wish. Make it wider or narrower. Stitch it in different yarns! Have fun!

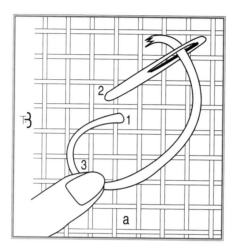

a

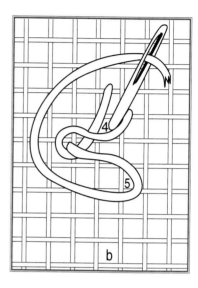

b

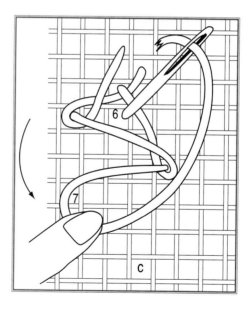

c

DECORATIVE STITCHES

These Decorative Stitches have many uses, some quite specialized and some more broad. They are not related in appearance or construction technique.

These samples were worked on Interlock Mono 10 with tapestry yarn. I did not have to thicken or thin the yarn for any of the stitches in this section.

DECORATIVE STITCHES	Border	Good Backing	Poor Backing	Background	Design	Accent	Fast	Slow	Geometric Pattern	Shading	Yarn Hog	Snags	Snag-Proof	Little Texture	Medium Texture	High Relief	Flower Stitch	Weak Pattern	Medium Pattern	Strong Pattern	Distorts Canvas
Buttonhole/Detached Buttonhole	•			•	•	•			•			•		•				•			
Buttonhole in Half-Circle				•	•	•		•	•			•			•					•	
Buttonhole on a Knot			•			•		•				•									
Raised Buttonhole			•		•			•		•	•				•					•	
Raised Buttonhole on a Raised Band			•		•			•		•	•					•				•	
Laced Chain			•	•	•			•			•		•	•				•			
Diagonal Chain	•		•			•	•							•				•			
Perspective	•		•	•	•	•		•	•			•		•						•	
Reverse Basketweave	•	•		•	•									•						•	
Woven Spider Web			•			•		•			•					•	•			•	
Smooth Spider Web			•			•		•			•					•	•			•	
Ridged Spider Web			•			•		•			•					•	•			•	
Wound Cross			•			•		•			•					•	•			•	
French Knot			•			•		•					•		•	•	•		•		
French Knot on Stalks			•			•		•				•			•		•		•		
Colonial Knot			•			•		•					•		•		•		•		
Bullion Knot			•			•		•		•	•					•	•			•	
Candlewicking			•		•	•		•		•	•					•	•	•			
Looped Turkey Work			•	•		•		•		•	•	•				•			•		
Cut Turkey Work			•	•	•	•		•		•	•	•				•	•	•			
Surrey			•	•	•	•		•		•	•	•				•	•		•		
Velvet			•		•	•		•			•	•				•	•			•	
Loop			•		•	•	•				•	•				•	•			•	
Lazy Daisy			•		•	•							•	•	•		•		•		
Twisted Ribbon			•			•						•				•	•			•	
Japanese Ribbon			•			•						•				•	•			•	
Ribbon Loop			•			•						•				•	•			•	

345

DECORATIVE STITCHES	Border	Good Backing	Poor Backing	Background	Design	Accent	Fast	Slow	Geometric Pattern	Shading	Yarn Hog	Snags	Snag-Proof	Little Texture	Medium Texture	High Relief	Flower Stitch	Weak Pattern	Medium Pattern	Strong Pattern	Distorts Canvas
Needleweaving			•		•	•						•				•	•			•	
Woven Picot	•		•		•	•		•								•	•			•	
Hollie Point			•		•	•		•		•	•	•			•		•		•		
Spiral			•			•		•				•				•	•			•	
Drizzle			•			•		•				•				•	•			•	
Cast-On			•			•		•				•				•	•			•	
Couble Cast-On			•			•		•				•				•	•			•	
Shisha			•			•		•					•			•	•			•	

BUTTONHOLE/ DETACHED BUTTONHOLE

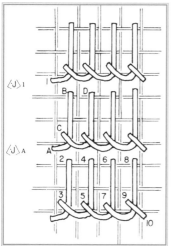

The Buttonhole Stitch has many variations. Only two are given here.

This stitch creates a smooth area and a ridge. Arrange these areas to suit your purposes. You may disregard the grid that the canvas threads create. Treat the canvas as if it were fabric, and stitch. When the Buttonhole Stitch is worked as shown here, horizontal stripes are created.

Work it completely detached from the surface of the canvas, as in Detached Weaving (page 249) except for the edges of the stitched area, and it becomes Detached Buttonhole. The top of each stitch in the second and subsequent rows loops through the bottom of the stitches in the previous row. Stitch it in any shape. Make it flat or increase stitches so that it is fuller in some places than others.

Stitch the rows from bottom to top and from left to right. To change from one strand of yarn to the next, you will need two needles threaded with the same color yarn. If, for example, your yarn runs out at #8 on the drawing, insert the needle into the canvas at #8, leaving the yarn from #7 to #8 a little loose. Let this needle dangle on the wrong side of the canvas. Bury the tail of the yarn on the second needle on the wrong side or use any other method of starting a yarn (page 36). Bring the needle up at #9. Let this second needle dangle. Adjust the tension on the first needle and bury the tail. Continue with the second needle of yarn.

This stitch makes a lovely filler for a field of faraway flowers or very distant trees.

Make sure that the stitches that go into the middle are even. (See the Eye Stitches in Chapter 13.) If you need a whole circle, just keep stitching.

Work it in any size circle. When you turn the stitches so that the loops face the inside of the circle instead of the outside, as here, it is now handy for securing gems and found objects onto your canvas (page 22). Use as many rows as you need to attach the object firmly. Work the stitch as loosely or as tightly as the need dictates.

As you can tell, this is a very versatile stitch. Enjoy using it in a wide variety of ways.

BUTTONHOLE IN HALF-CIRCLE

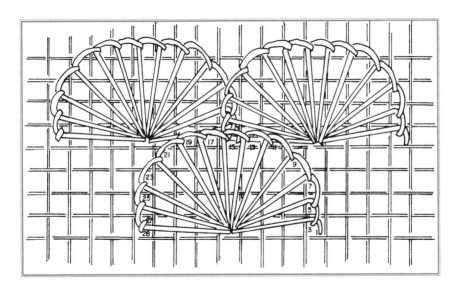

BUTTONHOLE
ON A KNOT

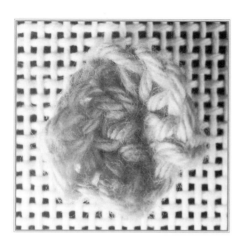

To make a cup, bring your yarn up from the wrong side of the canvas. Tie a loose knot and put your needle back into the canvas. Bring it up again. Secure it in the middle with a tiny Pin Stitch. This is the last time your needle will penetrate the canvas until you are finished. Work a Buttonhole Stitch on each of the loops of the knot.

Keep working Buttonhole Stitches around and around the loops that the Buttonhole Stitch created. Increase the number of Buttonhole Stitches in each loop for a flat circle. When you stop increasing the number of stitches in each loop and make the same number on each row, the yarn will begin to form a cup. Adjust the size and shape to your needs. End the yarn by weaving the yarn in and around the center. Take the yarn to the wrong side of the canvas and secure it. The Buttonhole on a Knot Stitch makes magnificent three-dimensional flowers.

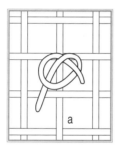

a

b

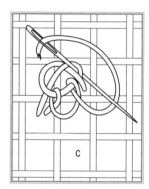

c

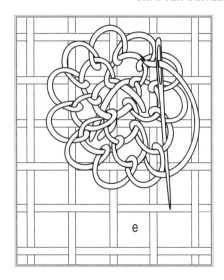

Knot d & e: Work two stitches in each loop of the first row of loops to begin with. Then increase the number of stitches in each trip around the center knot to keep the motif flat. Make as many rows around the knot as you like. Leave it flat or make a cup, as in the next drawing and the photo.

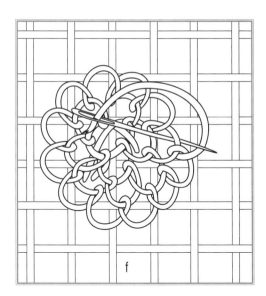

Knot f: To make the motif cuplike in shape, stop increasing the number of stitches in each round. Stitch the same number in each round. The number of rounds will determine the height of the cup. Make as many rounds as you like. To make the cup narrow as it gets taller, skip a loop in a regular pattern.

RAISED BUTTONHOLE

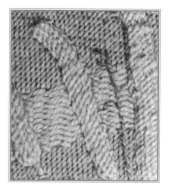

Work the vertical rows of this stitch from top to bottom. Work the rows from left to right for a compact stitch; work them from right to left for an open, lacy look.

When working the buttonhole portion of the stitch from left to right, pull the thread with your nondominant hand, keeping it taut until the next stitch is taken. Use your fingernail or a laying tool to push the vertical rows together. This helps to pack the yarn in for the raised texture.

This stitch makes nice tree bark.

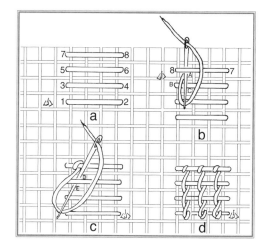

RAISED BUTTONHOLE ON A RAISED BAND

This is the same stitch as the preceding one, except for the bed over which the stitch is worked. The fatter the padding you lay down, the higher the stitch will be. Lay as many stitches as you need. Build up the center for a rounded look. Stagger the start and stop of padding stitches to get a smooth, long look. After you have laid the padding, refer to the Raised Buttonhole to continue working the stitch.

This stitch is **very hard** to rip! Be sure it is what you want before you put it in.

It makes particularly nice tree trunks and limbs.

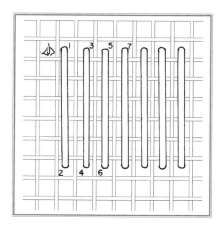

Laced Chain is a snagproof stitch that is fun to work. After the first row of Straight Gobelin is worked, the rest is simply lacing one Chain Stitch onto the one above it in the preceding row. NOTE: the rows are worked **horizontally**, not vertically.

LACED CHAIN

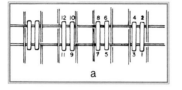

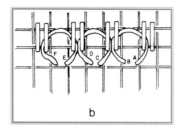

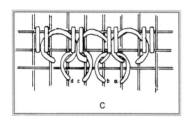

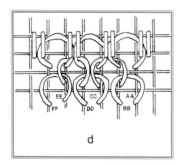

DIAGONAL CHAIN

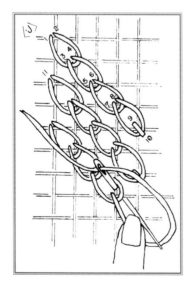

PERSPECTIVE

Make a Diagonal Stitch, 2 x 2, upward and to the right. Place two more similar stitches below the first. From the holes where the first three stitches ended, begin three more diagonal stitches—this time downward and to the right. You will have a three-stripe chevron pointing up. With a second color, superimpose another three-stripe chevron—this time pointing down. See the diagram below for their placement. A box, seen in perspective, is created. This makes an interesting geometric pattern.

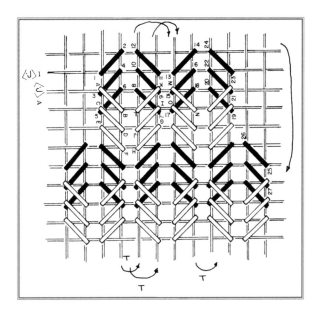

REVERSE
BASKETWEAVE

If you work on a frame, follow the numbering in the diagram. If you use a continuous motion, you can get the same results by turning your canvas over and carefully stitching Basketweave. Bury the tails on the opposite side of the canvas from Basketweave, of course.

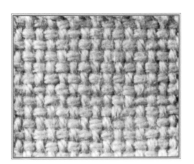

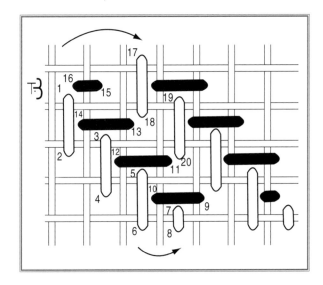

SPIDER WEBS

There are some instructions for working Spider Webs that are basic to all three versions.

Lay one of the foundations shown in the diagram below. Only the Woven Spider Web **must** have an odd number of spokes. If these spokes are not ***well secured,*** the whole thing will come undone.

Bring the needle up as close to the center as you can without actually coming through the center. Work this yarn in the pattern of the stitch you are doing. Do not penetrate the canvas until you are through. Keep going around and around until the spokes are no longer visible. When you think you cannot possibly get one more round in, do two more—**then** you are through.

If you space only a few yarns over the spokes, the stitch will make a great spider web.

To make a high ball, pull the yarn tightly, but not so tightly that the spokes become misshapen. As you take each stitch, pull the yarn toward the center. This helps to tighten the stitch and make it higher.

You may change colors or techniques midstream. For example, you can make a wheel by working Woven Spider Web (for the hub), Ridged Spider Web (for the spokes), and Smooth Spider Web (for the rim).

Use Spider Webs for grapes, apples, other fruit, wheels, balls, buttons, flowers, ladybugs, spiders, and other insects—anything round.

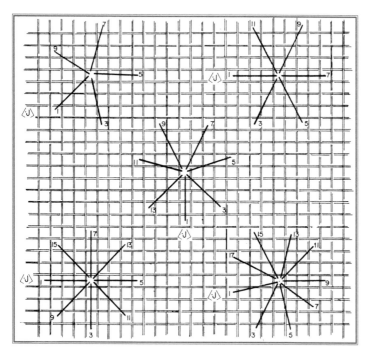

Spider Web foundations.

WOVEN SPIDER WEB

Lay the spokes. You must have an odd number. Weave the yarn over and under the spokes, pulling the yarn toward the center every now and then. When you think you cannot possibly get one more row in, do two more. Then you are through. See Spider Webs, page 353, for more instructions.

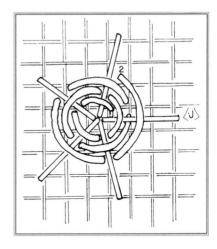

SMOOTH SPIDER WEB

Go over two spokes and back under one; over two, under one; and so forth. See Spider Webs, page 353, for more instructions.

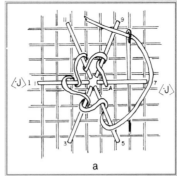

a

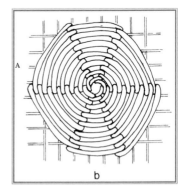

b

Reverse the process of the preceding stitch. In other words, go under two spokes and back over one; under two, over one. See Spider Webs, page 353, for more instructions.

RIDGED
SPIDER WEB

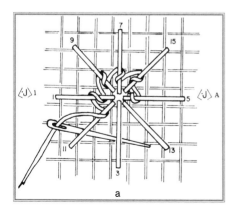

a

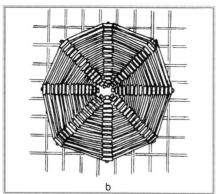

b

This is another good round stitch. Make it as fat and as big in diameter as you like. Wind the yarn under all the spokes without penetrating the canvas.

WOUND
CROSS

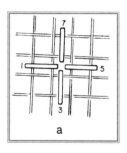

a

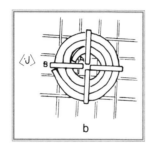

b

FRENCH KNOT

French Knots are handy. They fill bare canvas and make polka dots, flower centers, whole flowers, beards, sheep's fleece, and other design elements.

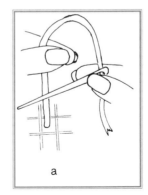

a

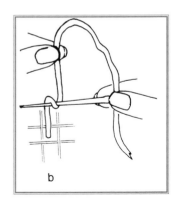

b

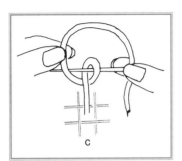

c

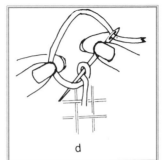

d

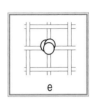

e

FRENCH KNOTS ON STALKS

These are an expanded version of the French Knot. They make lovely flowers on stems, beards, and hair.

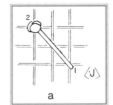

a

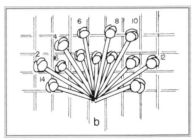

b

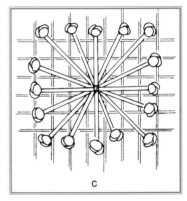

c

Pull this knot tight or leave it loose. It is just as handy as French Knots.

COLONIAL
KNOT

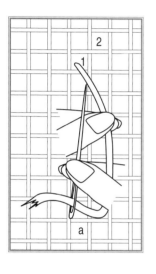

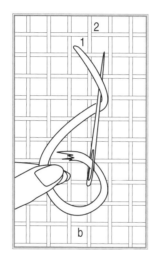

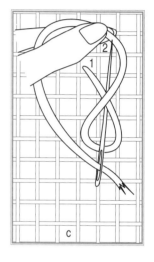

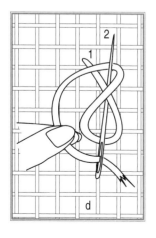

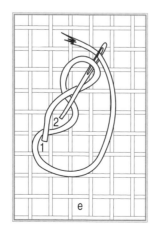

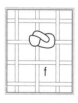

BULLION KNOT

This is an alternate construction technique for the Bullion Knot. I think it's a whole lot easier to make and control. It is worked by laying a thread and wrapping a yarn around it—without penetrating the canvas. Be sure that the tail is well secured. Pull tightly and the stitch will curl. Worked loosely, this stitch resembles finger curls.

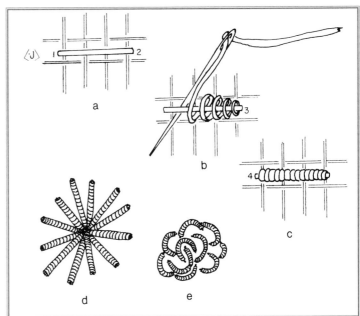

CANDLEWICKING

Turkey Work and Candlewicking give a similar finished appearance. Use lofty yarn for the maximum benefit. The more lofty the yarn, the more secure the stitch and the fuzzier the look. You want the canvas threads to squeeze the yarn at its insertion point and then fluff out when it is free. See page 55 for more information about Candlewicking.

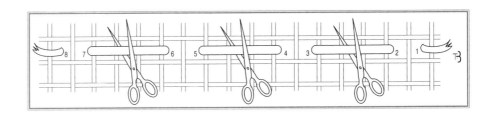

LOOPED TURKEY WORK

Turkey Work is a fun, highly textured stitch! It creates rows of loops that make great beards for Santa and flowers. This stitch does not work on Regular Mono canvas, but the Surrey Stitch, page 361, will.

Stitch the **bottom** row first and work **up**. Work from left to right only. This means that you must cut your yarn at the end of every row. You may bury the tail or incorporate it as part of the stitch. You may skip a row every now and then on a small canvas if it is too crowded. You may alternate the placement of the loops for a diagonal line of loops.

Use a drinking straw, a pencil, or a strip of paper or light cardboard to help you get the loops even (see the drawing with Cut Turkey Work). In working Looped Turkey Work, try not to run out of yarn in the middle of a row.

Turkey Work should be worked on an even number of canvas threads. However, when you get to the end of a row, there often is one canvas thread left over. In this case, work the last three canvas threads by taking an extra big stitch over three canvas threads. You are actually skipping over an extra canvas thread before going back into the canvas.

Work the whole design first, then put in this stitch. If you do not, you will never be able to move this stitch aside to get the others in.

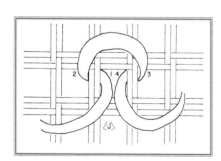

Turkey Work

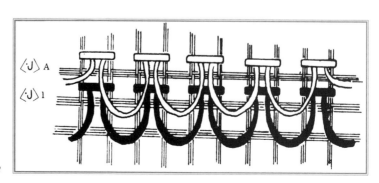

Looped Turkey Work

359

CUT
TURKEY
WORK

When trimmed closely, columns become apparent. While usually considered a flaw in stitching technique, they could possibly be incorporated into the right design.

This is the same stitch as the previous one, only the loops have been cut. This makes an entirely different look. It's nice and fuzzy!

Work this stitch just as in Looped Turkey Work, but cut the loops as you go. After working Row 2, clip Row 1; after working Row 3, clip Row 2; etc. If you cut each row immediately after it is worked, the pieces can be easily caught in the next row as you stitch it. However, if you wait until you have completely finished the area, it is quite hard to do a good cutting job. Cut as shown in Diagram b, below, for an even finish. For a rougher finish, snip through each loop separately.

Cutting the loops too short causes the rows to show. This is fine if this look works for your design. See the top photo (no rows) and the bottom photo (with rows). If you would like an even fluffier look, brush the area with a toothbrush. It does not matter if you end a yarn in the middle of a row. The tail will just become a part of the fuzz. Persian yarn makes a fluffier Cut Turkey Work than tapestry yarn.

As with Looped Turkey Work, stitch your whole design first, then put in this stitch. If you don't, you will not be able to get the other stitches in the surrounding areas.

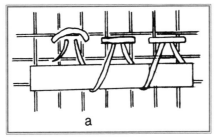

a

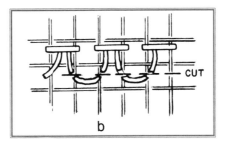

b

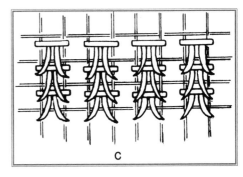

c

SURREY

This stitch is similar to Turkey Work, but it is done diagonally. This makes it ideal for Regular Mono canvas. Stitch it from the bottom up and from left to right. Leave the loops or cut them, as in Cut Turkey Work.

Also work the whole design first, then this one. It spills onto adjacent areas and that makes it hard to stitch those areas.

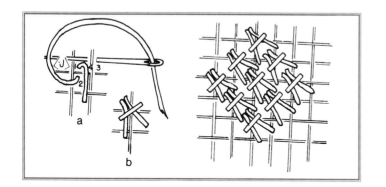

VELVET

This stitch is worked like Turkey Work—bottom up and left to right—**except** that you must bury your tails on the wrong side of the canvas. Skip one canvas thread between rows. If you lift your thumb off the loop before the x is completed, it will all come apart. Cut it or leave it looped.

This stitch lies flatter than Turkey Work. For this reason, it makes a nice thatched roof or a flapper's fringe. If the loops are cut it makes a good shag rug for a dollhouse.

Work your whole design first. See Turkey Work for more instructions.

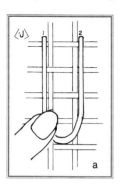

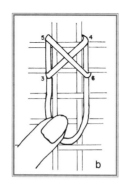

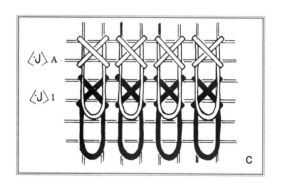

LOOP

This stitch reminds me of Austrian drapes. Two rows of it, the second placed between the loops of the first, make a nice ruffle or lace trim. You might want to make the loops longer in this case.

As with the stitches on pages 359–361, work from the bottom up and from left to right.

In going from #5 to #6, slip the needle under the horizontal bar created by stitch 3-4. The next stitch begins at #6. Let the loop hang down three or so canvas threads between #5 and #6. Place subsequent rows in the next holes up.

Work your whole design first so that it will be easier to get in the stitches in the space next door to this one.

Work this stitch on top of a background stitch or on blank canvas. It can serve as flower petals, leaves, and many other things.

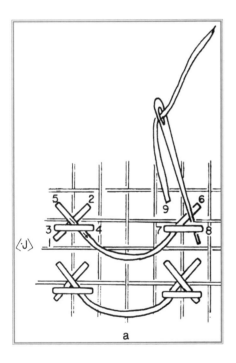

a

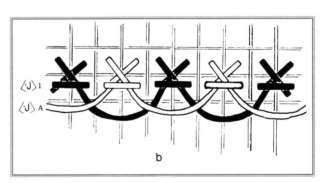

b

See page 19 for more instructions in stitching with ribbon.

LAZY DAISY

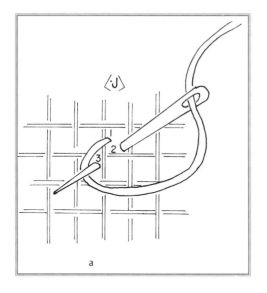

a

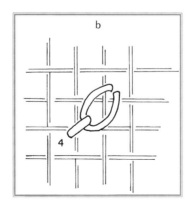

b

TWISTED RIBBON

This essentially a Lazy Daisy Stitch, except that the ribbon is folded at the top of the loop. Use a chenille needle (page 23). Hold it in place with your finger or a laying tool. It makes great leaves and flower buds.

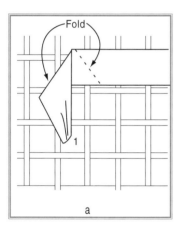

a

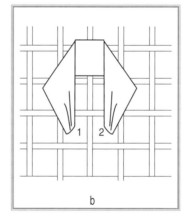

b

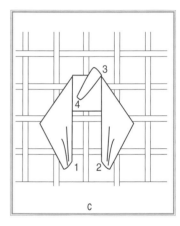

c

JAPANESE RIBBON

Ribbon stitches are unique to stitching with ribbon. See pages 19 and 366 for more instructions in stitching with ribbon.

This stitch must be worked with ribbon and a chenille needle. The wider the ribbon, the more exaggerated the effect. Overdyed ribbon is especially effective in making leaves and flowers.

Lay the ribbon flat on the canvas. Insert the needle into the center (width-wise) of the ribbon. Pull the needle *gently* through the canvas and the ribbon. A fold will naturally happen if you do not pull the stitch too tightly. Place motifs at random on your canvas in varying sizes to make many effects, including buds and leaves.

Notice in the photo how varying the tension caused the stitch to lose that little fold that is characteristic of the stitch.

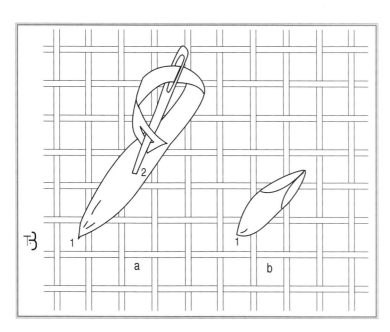

RIBBON LOOP

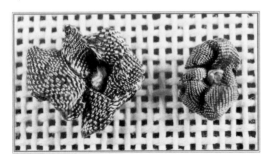

This is a stitch for use with ribbon. See page 19 for more instructions.

Use a chenille needle when working with ribbon. Make a needle eye lock stitch to reduce raveling of the ribbon (below).

If you pull too hard, there will be no loop. Use your laying tool, a straw, a pencil, or another tool to help size the loops. You will also need a stitch of some kind to secure the loops. A French Knot in ribbon, floss, or pearl is ideal if you are making a flower. You may also use another ribbon stitch or embroidery stitches.

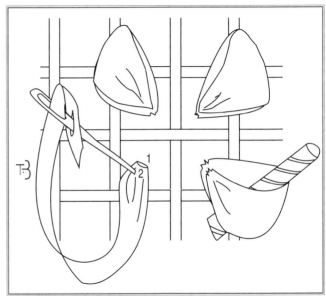

NEEDLEWEAVING

Technically, Needleweaving is the over and under weaving of a yarn on canvas threads whose cross threads have been removed. (See the sections on Needleweaving, Reticella, and Teneriffe on pages 53–56.) However, the term Needleweaving has come to mean any weaving process done on canvas threads or on yarn laid on top of the canvas or fabric.

The Needleweaving discussed here is a kind of Surface Darning or embroidery. The yarn penetrates the canvas only at the outer edges of the area covered in Needleweaving. Any pattern you wish may be woven. The space is quite interesting when some holes are left, as in the photo. The area can be linear, as shown in the drawing, a geometric shape (square, circle, etc.), or a free-form shape.

See Hemstitching (page 379) and Hardanger Cut Work (page 381) for more information on Needleweaving on the canvas threads.

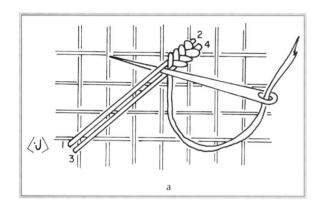

a

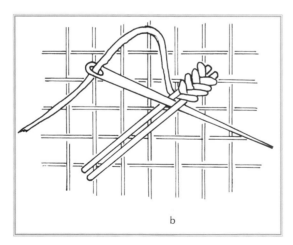

b

WOVEN PICOT

This stitch is completely detached from the canvas except at the base of the triangle. Place a pin or another needle at the far side of the Picot (at what will become the point of the triangle). Secure it by sticking the point of the pin into a small piece of Styrofoam on the wrong side of the canvas. Make the legs of the Picot as shown below. Beginning with Diagram b, weave over and under the legs of the Picot without penetrating the canvas. Remove the pin when you are finished.

This Picot makes great flower petals, leaves, and lace edging. Shape the Picots by twisting or bending. Tack in place. Using fabric-covered wire for the legs of the Picots allows you to shape the pieces without tacking the point down, and it allows more freedom in shaping them, as well.

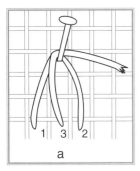

a

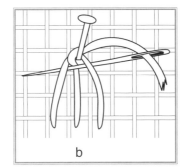

b

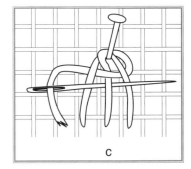

c

HOLLIE POINT

Hollie Point is an interesting stitch to work, and it makes a pretty Surface Darning pattern. When it is worked over a hole in the canvas (where the canvas threads have been removed), this stitch becomes Needlelace (page 55).

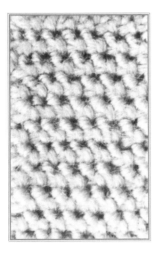

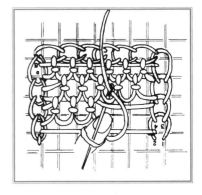

SPIRAL

This is a wonderful stitch for flowers. Bring the yarn to the right side of the canvas. Unthread the needle; turn the needle upside down. Place a piece of Styrofoam under the canvas. Put the point of the needle partway into the canvas and Styrofoam. The Styrofoam becomes your third hand. Wrap the needle, from the canvas up, with the yarn. Rethread the needle and pull the needle through the canvas. Make the tension tight or loose to create different looks. The wrap needs to be just loose enough to pull the needle through the spiral of yarn. (See the Cast-On Stitch, page 371.) The tip of the stitch should hang loose.

If you want a tighter stitch, use a milliner's needle or other needle where the eye of the needle is the same diameter as the rest of the needle. Milliner's needles don't come in big sizes, so you'll need to use finer yarns to get a tight stitch.

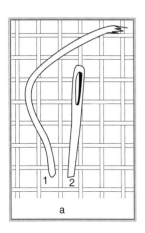

a

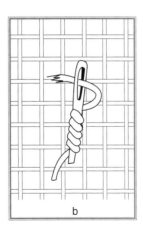

b

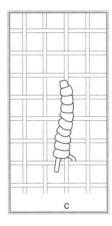

c

DRIZZLE

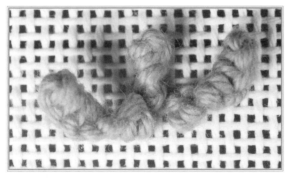

This is a terrific flower stitch! Just as you did in working the Spiral Stitch, bring the needle to the right side of the canvas. Unthread the needle and turn it upside down. Put a piece of Styrofoam under the canvas. Push the point of the needle into the canvas and Styrofoam, leaving half or more of the needle sticking out.

Use the Lick-the-Bowl method (see the diagram) to cover the needle, from the canvas up, with yarn. You may also use the knitting technique of casting-on stitches. Rethread the needle and pull the needle through the canvas carefully. Keep the tension tight enough for the yarn to hug the needle evenly, yet loose enough for the needle to pull through. (See the Cast-On Stitch, below.) The tip of the stitches should hang free.

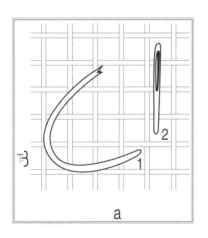

a

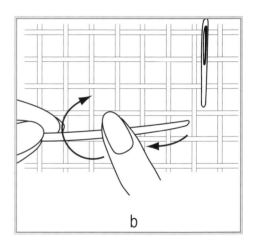

b

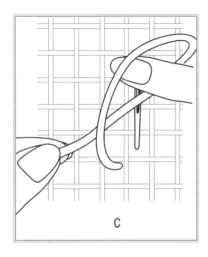

c

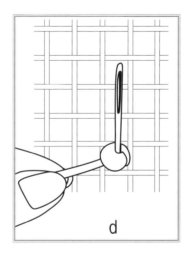

d

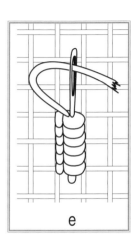

e

CAST-ON

This stitch makes a loop, scallop, or circle—whichever you need. At #2, do not pull the yarn all the way through the canvas. Pull just enough at #3 to get to the next step. Pull the needle part of the way through the canvas. Place a piece of Styrofoam under the eye of the needle to stabilize the needle while you cast yarn on the needle or use the Lick-the-Bowl method of putting stitches on the needle, as shown in the diagram below.

When you have enough stitches on the needle, pull the needle out of the Styrofoam and through the canvas. Place the needle back into the canvas anywhere you need for it to go. Place several loops together to form a flower. Beware of tension that is too tight; you will not be able to pull the needle through the Cast-On Stitches. A needle that is the same diameter for its whole length (like a milliner's needle) makes this easier. The eyes on milliner's needles will accept only fine threads, however; a tapestry needle works if you are careful.

Work these stitches in a variety of lengths; group them together to make flowers. Loosen the tension for a different effect.

a

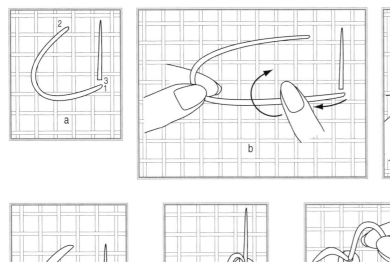

b

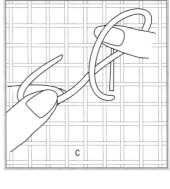

c

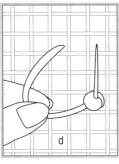

d

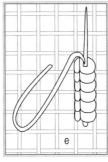

e

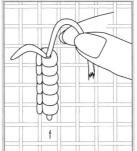

f

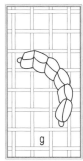

g

DOUBLE CAST-ON

This stitch is very similar to the Cast-On Stitch. Begin with a yarn doubled over the eye of the needle and with both ends knotted together. Using an Away Knot, follow the diagram. When it comes time to cast the stitches onto the needle, alternate the right and left yarns. This stitch makes great leaves and flower petals.

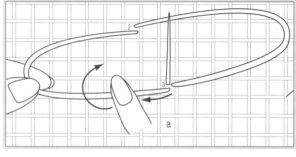

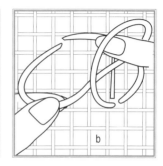

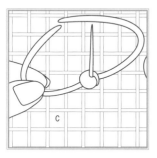

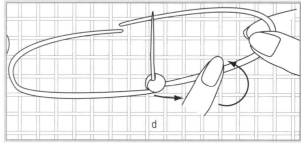

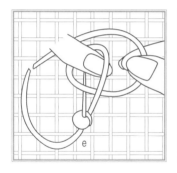

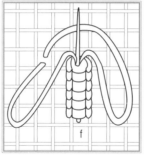

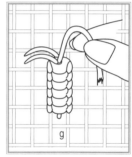

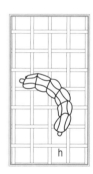

This stitch is good for attaching such embellishments to the canvas as mirrors and gems. It does better with flat things, but items with some height or thickness may be secured with it.

SHISHA

In the diagram, stitches #1 to #16 form holding threads. Steps A to H begin with processes of covering the holding threads with decorative stitches. Continue the steps shown in F and G all the way around the circle.

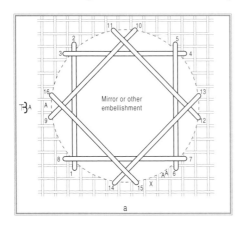

a

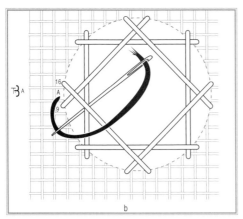

b

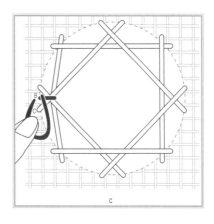

c

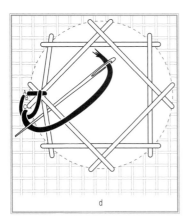

d

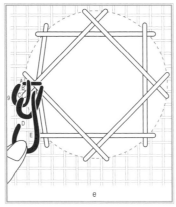

e

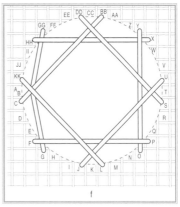

f

Seventeen

OPEN STITCHES

*L*etting areas of blank canvas show is a very effective design tool. Adding some kind of interest to this blank area is even more effective. This area may or may not be painted. Stitching a shaded area can produce a beautiful finished product, but another equally lovely result is to let a background that has been shaded with paint show through Open Stitches. Plate 6 shows how the paint and one color of yarn work together to produce a stunning effect.

Some particular groups of stitches are already Open Stitches. These include Black Work (combinations of Double Running Stitch and Backstitch), Laid Filling Stitches (couched yarns that are held in place by tying them down in a variety of patterns), and Pattern Darning (rows of Running Stitches that produce geometric patterns). Some stitching techniques produce Open Stitches. These include Pulled Thread, Needlelace, Hemstitching, and Hardanger Cut Work.

You can adapt almost any stitch to an open technique, although I don't think that the highly textured stitches, like some of the Decorative Stitches, would adapt so well. Perhaps you will find other exceptions, but most stitches will convert to Open Stitches.

The possibilities are endless, so I can only make suggestions. Figure 3-3 (on page 56) shows several ways you can convert almost every stitch to an Open Stitch. The Eye Stitches can be easily stitched with a Pulled Thread technique (page 54), thus making them into Open Stitches. Many of the larger Cross Stitches need thickened yarn and the addition of an Upright Cross, a Frame Stitch, a Backstitch, or another stitch to cover the canvas. Leave those fillers out and the canvas will show. They may be just what you need. Experiment. Invent your own Open Stitches!

There are some problems unique to Open Stitches that need to be considered before you begin to stitch. They are addressed at various points in the earlier chapters in this book. Please refer to the sections on yarn selection and yarn color choice for Open Work on page 52. Stitching with Open Stitches demands a longer yarn (page 100), a different way to secure your yarn (page 37), and a different way of carrying the yarn from one place to another (page 385). Of course, mending a cut canvas for Open Work needs another technique; it is described on page 45.

OPEN STITCHES	Border	Good Backing	Poor Backing	Background	Design	Accent	Fast	Slow	Geometric Pattern	Shading	Yarn Hog	Snags	Snag-Proof	Little Texture	Medium Texture	High Relief	Flower Stitch	Weak Pattern	Medium Pattern	Strong Pattern	Distorts Canvas
Lattice	•		•	•	•	•	•		•			•		•						•	
Angelis		•		•	•		•		•			•		•						•	
Stephens	•	•		•	•		•		•					•						•	
Fagoting			•		•			•	•			•			•					•	
Hemstitching	•		•	•	•			•				•			•					•	
Hardanger Cut Work	•		•		•	•		•	•						•					•	
Loopstitch Bars	•		•		•	•		•	•						•					•	
Diagonal Drawn Filling	•		•	•	•			•	•				•	•					•		
Double Fagot Ground	•			•	•			•	•				•	•				•			
Checker Filling	•		•	•	•			•	•						•					•	
Window Filling	•		•	•	•			•	•					•						•	
Double Window Filling	•		•	•	•			•	•					•						•	

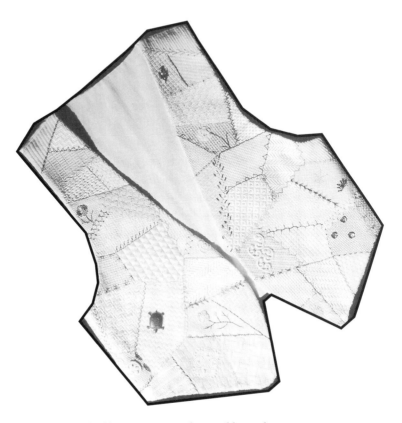

Photo 16—Crazy Quilt Vest: *stitched by Jenny Reves; designed by Ruth Weistart; yarns and stitches selected by Jenny Reves and Ruth Weistart. [Smith]*

LATTICE

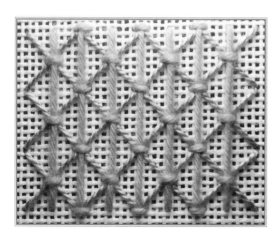

This is an example of a Laid Filling Stitch. As a group, they are useful as open background stitches and design accents. Embroidery books have many other stitches in this group. They are easily adapted to canvas.

On the 19-20 stitch, slip the needle under the 17-18 stitch. This will keep the carried thread (from the end of one row to the beginning of the next) from showing too much.

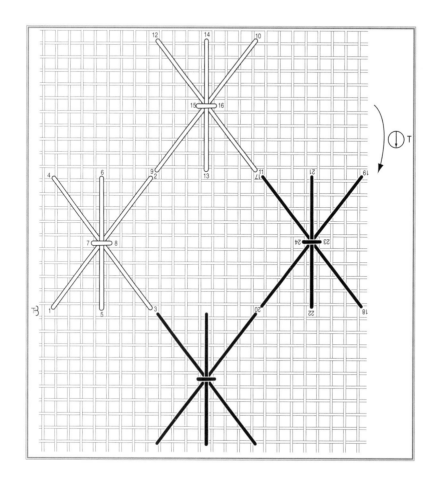

Darning Patterns are essentially the Running Stitch worked in patterns. This stitch is just one of an endless variety of designs that can be created. Try to design your own.

ANGELIS

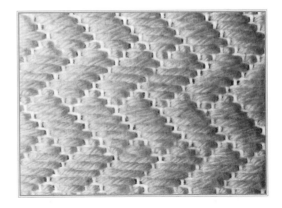

STEPHENS

This Open Stitch was inspired by the F-106 Stitch (page 167) and the Princess Stitch (page 165). The triangles can be spaced farther apart if you want more canvas to show. If you do not want the canvas to show, add an Upright Cross in the bare spot.

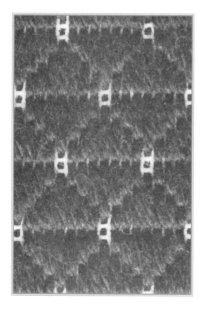

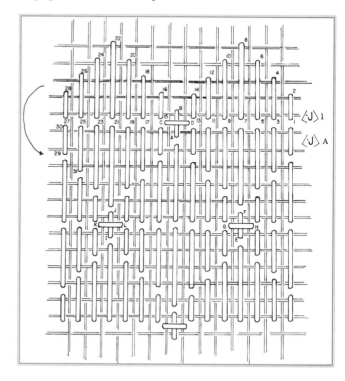

FAGOTING

Two pieces of canvas can be joined with this stitch. It is one of embroidery's Insertion Stitches. When working Insertion Stitches on needlepoint canvas, use the Two-Step Edge Finishing Method on page 129 for more detailed instructions. The drawing here just suggests the method.

Refer to an embroidery book for other Insertion Stitches.

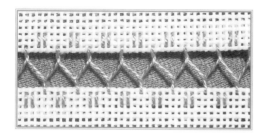

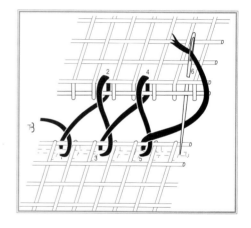

HEMSTITCHING

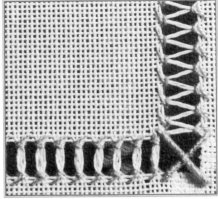

Hemstitching is a Drawn Thread technique (page 53). Cut the canvas thread to be removed in the center. Using your needle or a laying tool, carefully unweave the canvas thread. Then thread the needle with the freed canvas thread and weave it back into the blank canvas at the ends of your rows for about an inch. Ravel one thread and reweave it before you go to the next.

The area of secured threads can be covered with stitching or it can be left as is. If you do decide to let it show, then it becomes a design element. In that case, you will want to consider its shape and size. Vary the lengths of the cut canvas threads to form a pattern and make it more interesting.

The canvas threads that are left are called bars. Oven and under weaving of these bars is called Needleweaving, but when the bars are grouped together—rather than simply covered with Needleweaving, the result is called Hemstitching. There are many patterns for tying these bars together; unfortunately, limited space prevents the reporting of them here. Once the bars are secured to form a pattern, you may then simply wrap them or cover them with Needleweaving.

Filling the corners with decorated bars is a Needlelace technique (page 55). Bars are extended across the open area and are then adorned with stitches. The photo shows only a suggestion. See embroidery books for more ideas.

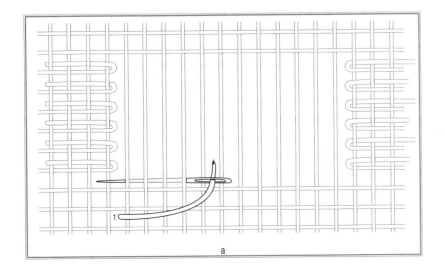

a

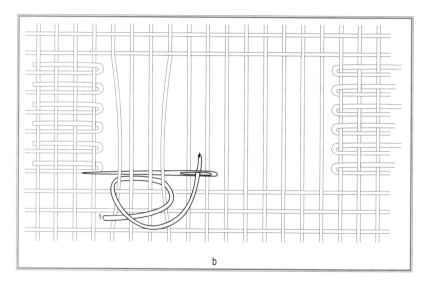

b

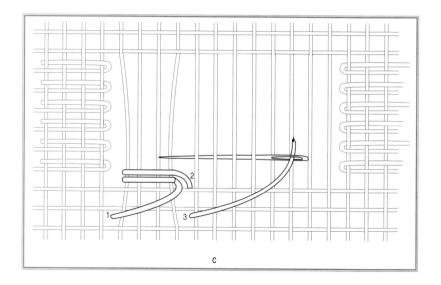

c

HARDANGER CUT WORK

In this stitching technique, threads are raveled out and cut away in a set pattern. Some canvas threads are left; they are called bars. These bars are then decorated with different stitches.

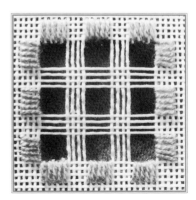

Stitch Straight Gobelin or Buttonhole around the areas to be cut **before** you cut the canvas. Then **carefully** cut the canvas threads on the dotted lines, as shown in Diagram a. With the tip of your needle or a laying tool, ravel the canvas threads. If you move the thread to loosen the sizing, this job will be a lot easier. The result will be an area that resembles the photo.

Once the threads have been raveled, cut them closely. Cut the two that will pull back the farthest on top of the canvas, as shown in Diagram b; they are the canvas threads that are on top of the cross canvas thread that will remain in place. Cut the other two from the wrong side of the canvas, also shown in Diagram b. Ravel and cut one section at a time before you go to the next section. As you can see from the photo, the ends of the cut canvas will show if this is not done carefully. I should have used a magnifying glass when I cut the canvas threads; I thought I had done it well until the photo came back from the developer!

The raveled canvas threads may also be rewoven into the canvas. See Hemstitching, above and page 53, for more information.

Then decorate the bars or leave them bare. The Loopstitch Bar Stitch (below) is only one of the many stitches that can be used to fill the empty corners.

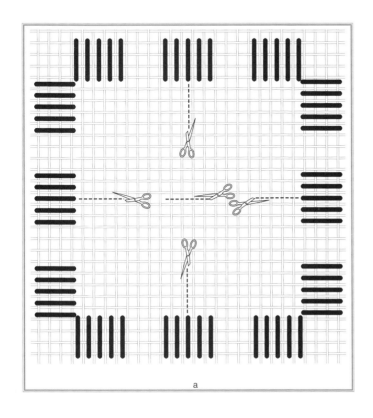

a

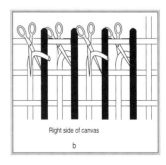

Right side of canvas

b

LOOPSTITCH
BARS

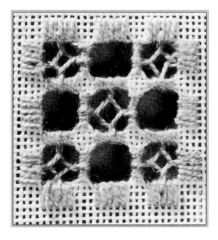

This is a Needlelace Stitch (page 55). It is worked across an area where the canvas threads have been removed in both directions.

A ground of Hardanger Cut Work (above and on page 54) must be laid first. Then decorate the bars by wrapping them in a stair step pattern, moving from lower left to upper right. On every other row, work a pattern of loops in each empty square. Begin the loop when three-and-a-half sides of the square have been bound in stitches. Carefully begin and end your yarn where it will not show.

Consult books on Hardanger, Needlelace, and Needleweaving for other stitches to cover the bars and holes. Invent your own!

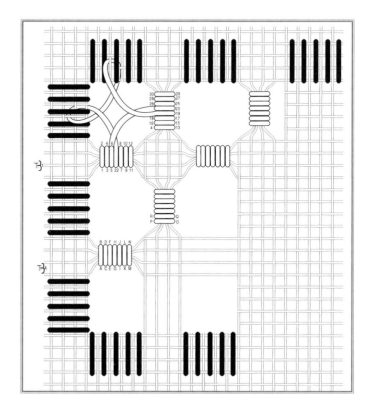

Note the Running Stitches outside the stitch area. That is where I ran the yarn that I carried to the next row. It is out of the way and does not show through the open canvas in this Pulled Thread Stitch.

Soften the canvas with half a drop of water. Congress Cloth waterspots if you get too much water on it. (See more on Canvas and Pulled Thread on pages 7 and 54.) Save yourself ripping later; enlarge the holes with your needle now. The pattern will become readily apparent; errors will show up before stitching. Pull harder than I did and the design will be more pronounced.

DIAGONAL DRAWN FILLING

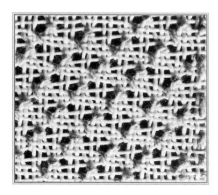

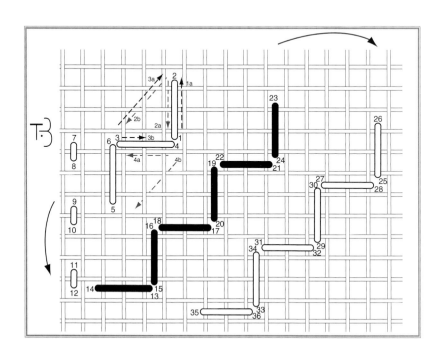

DOUBLE FAGOT GROUND

On this Pulled Thread Stitch, wrap each pair of canvas threads twice, pulling each time.

Note the Running Stitches outside the stitch area. These are there to make sure that the yarn that you carry to the next row does not show through the open canvas.

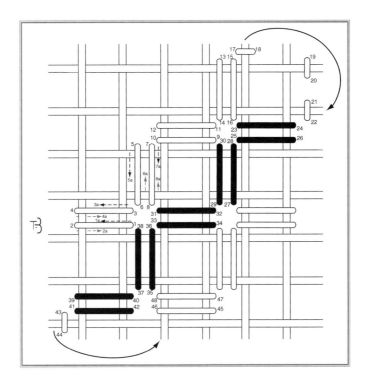

CHECKER FILLING

To make this Pulled Thread pattern easier to see, enlarge the holes before you stitch. This is easier if you moisten the canvas threads with half of a drop of water. (See the hints for Pulled Thread on page 54.) Using your needle, enlarge the holes by spreading the canvas threads apart. Then stitch. Pull each stitch in the direction the stitch just came from **and** in the direction it is going.

The Running Stitches outside the stitch area ensure that the yarn that you carry to the next row does not show through the open canvas.

The first step makes a pretty diagonal pattern all by itself. Notice that I miscounted the pattern. Had I taken the next step, I would have gotten another new stitch!

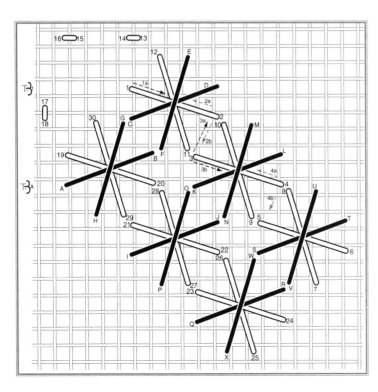

385

WINDOW FILLING

One canvas thread between stitches creates the Window Filling Stitch; two canvas threads creates the Double Window Filling Stitch (below). I suppose three would make a Triple Window Filling Stitch. Experiment yourself. See what you like.

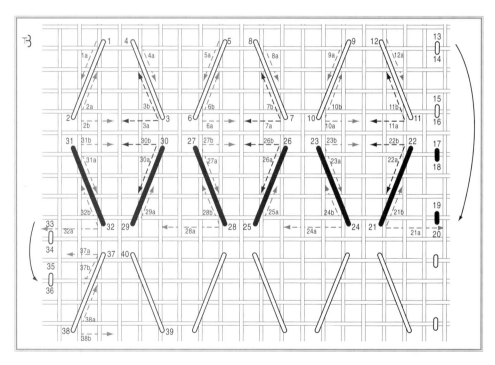

DOUBLE WINDOW FILLING

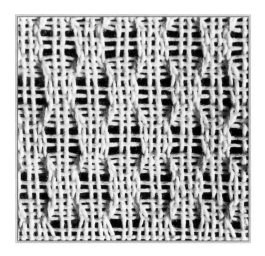

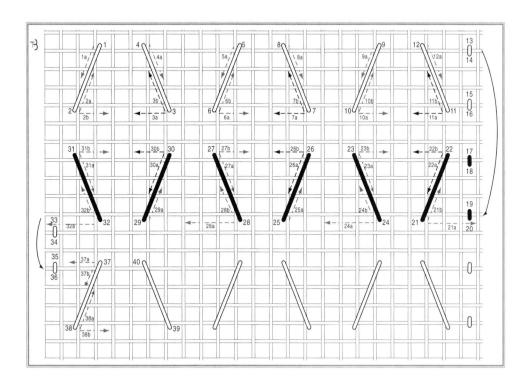

APPENDIX

The drawings in this section identify the various stitches used in the completed needlepoint projects illustrated in the color plates and black-and-white photos. They are identified by their plate numbers (#1–54) and photo numbers (#1–16). Many of the painted canvases, graph charts, and kits may be available for sale at your local needlework shop.

PLATE 1   *Color Relationships*

(1) Warm red
(2) Cool red
(3) True red
(4) Yellow
(5) Blue
(6) Black
(7) White

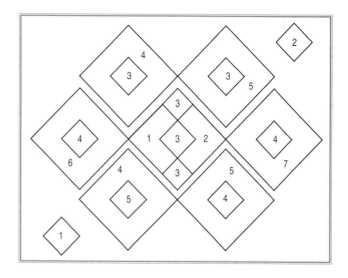

PLATE 2   *Four Seasons in the Color Wheel*

(1) Rhodes
(2) Cashmere
(3) Plaited Double Cross
(4) Waffle
(5) Cross Rhodes
(6) Oriental
(7) Milanese
(8) Leaf
(9) Diagonal Fly
(10) Diagonal
(11) Large Mosaic
(12) Wide Moorish
(13) Moorish
(14) Encroaching Straight Gobelin
(15) French Knot

(16) Straight
(17) Chain
(18) Couching
(19) Turkey Work
(20) Star
(21) Tied Windmill
(22) Stephens
(23) Diamond Ray
(24) Rice
(25) Smyrna Cross
(26) Alternating Continental
(27) Backstitch
(28) Binding
(E) Embellishments

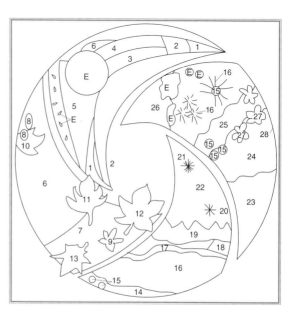

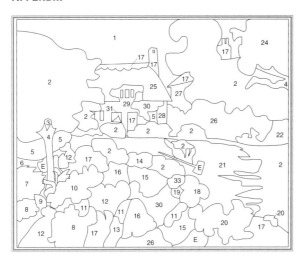

PLATE 3 *Chaplain's Garden*

(1) Woven Plait
(2) French Knot
(3) Detached Twisted Chain
(4) Encroaching Oblique
(5) Padded Satin
(6) French Knots on Stalks
(7) Zigzag Braid
(8) Japanese Ribbon
(9) Chain of Grain
(10) Cast-on
(11) Double Cast-on
(12) Petit Point
(13) Woven Picot
(14) Bullion Knot
(15) Loop Ribbon
(16) Lazy Daisy
(17) Straight

(18) Looped Turkey Work
(19) Ridged Spider Web
(20) Buttonhole on a Knot
(21) Giant Brick
(22) Slanted Gobelin
(24) Cut Turkey Work
(25) Interlocking Gobelin
(26) Raised Knot
(27) Willow
(28) Reversed Scotch
(29) Double Brick
(30) Straight with Twisted Ribbon
(31) Hollie Point
(33) Drizzle Stitch
(E) Embellishments

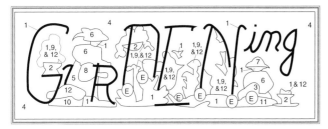

PLATE 4 *Gardening*

(1) Tent
(2) Brick
(3) Parisian
(4) Darning Pattern
(5) Hungarian
(6) Diagonal Beaty
(7) Woven Spider Web

(8) Diagonal Stem
(9) Lazy Daisy
(10) Herringbone Gone Wrong
(11) Elongated Cashmere
(12) Ribbon stitches, varied
(E) Embellishments

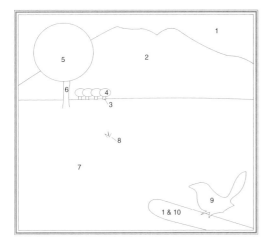

PLATE 5 *Grampian Mountains in Summer*

(1) Detached Buttonhole
(2) Tent
(3) Needleweaving
(4) Turkey Work
(5) Looped Couching
(6) Stem
(7) Straight
(8) Fly
(9) Split
(10) Diagonal Mosaic

PLATE 6   *Bachelor Buttons*

(1) Straight
(2) French Knot
(3) Japanese Ribbon
(4) Couching
(5) Cross
(6) Giant Brick
(7) Satin
(8) Padded Alternating Continental
(9) Tied Oblong Cross

PLATE 7   *Open-Door Cottage*

(1) Encroaching Gobelin
(2) Upright Cross
(3) Slanted Encroaching Gobelin
(4) Tent
(5) Smyrna Cross
(6) Rice
(7) Outline
(8) Diamond Ray

(9) French Knot
(10) Chain of Grain
(11) Bullion Knot
(12) Cross
(13) Turkey Work
(14) Brick
(15) Web
(16) Colonial Knot

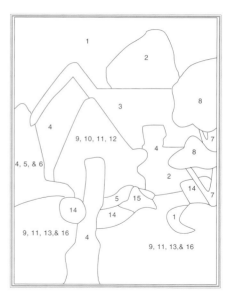

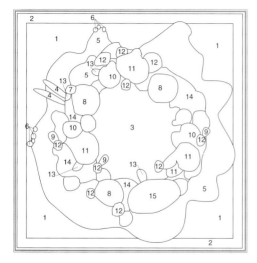

PLATE 8   *Floral Wreath with Bird's Nest*

(1) Herringbone,
     open version
(2) Herringbone
(3) Double Window
(4) Van Dyke
(5) Straight
(6) Japanese Ribbon
(7) Tent
(8) Split
(9) Bullion

(10) Woven Spider Web
(11) Ribbon Spider
     Filling
(12) Ribbon Loop
(13) Lazy Daisy
(14) French Knot
(15) Free-form
     placement of
     yarns

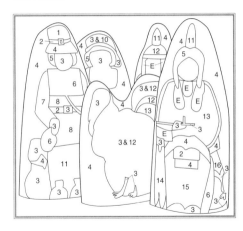

PLATE 9   *First Thanksgiving*

(1) Diagonal Cashmere

(2) Cashmere

(3) Tent

(4) Byzantine #2

(5) Interlocking Gobelin

(6) Slanted Gobelin

(7) Brick

(8) Criss Cross Hungarian

(9) Woven Plait (not visible)

(10) Smyrna Cross

(11) Leaf

(12) Satin

(13) Diagonal Mosaic

(14) Staggered Cashmere

(15) Mosaic Stripe

(16) Straight Gobelin

(E) Embellishments

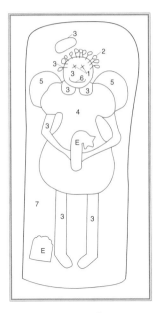

PLATE 10   *Spice Angel*

(1) Cross

(2) French Knot

(3) Tent

(4) Framed Scotch

(5) Alternating Mosaic

(6) Backstitch

(7) Hungarian Ground

(E) Embellishments

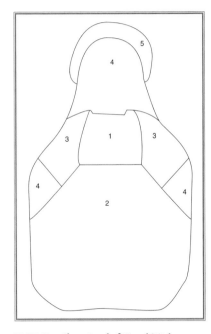

PLATE 11   *Clara, Angel of Missed Stitches*

(1) Old Florentine

(2) Chottie's Plaid

(3) Hungarian

(4) Tent

(5) Couching

PLATE 12   *Territorial T'ing*

(1) Tent
(2) Buttonhole
(3) Detached Weaving
(4) Brick
(5) Parisian Stripe
(6) Satin
(7) Padded Satin
(8) Byzantine
(9) Criss Cross Hungarian
(10) Woven Plait
(11) Web

(12) Gobelin and Cross combination
(13) Interlocking Gobelin
(14) Slanted Gobelin
(15) Couching
(16) Cross
(17) Lazy Roman II
(18) Alternating Continental
(19) Dotted Swiss
(20) Darning Pattern
(21) Outline/Stem
(E) Embellishments

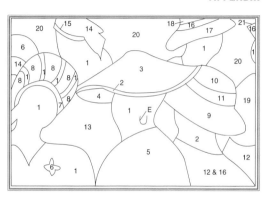

PLATE 13   *Far Horizons*

(1) Satin
(2) Pavillion Diamonds
(3) Double Parisian
(4) Tent
(5) French Knot (for accents)
(E) Embellishments

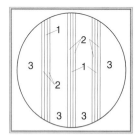

PLATE 14   *Christmas Ribbons*

(1) Couching
(2) Straight
(3) Lattice

PLATE 15   *Mardi Gras Mask*

(1) Tent
(2) Straight
(3) Woven Plait
(4) Satin
(5) Lazy Daisy
(6) Oblique Slav
(7) Padded Satin
(8) French Knot

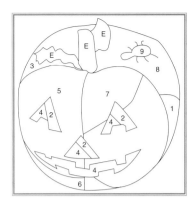

PLATE 16   *Halloween Pumpkin*

(1) Braided Cross
(2) Diagonal Mosaic
(3) Criss Cross Hungarian
(4) Tent
(5) Scotch
(6) Triangle
(7) Stem
(8) Moorish
(9) Spider Web
(E) Embellishments

PLATE 17   *Crystal Santa*

(1) Tent
(2) Interlocking Gobelin
(3) French Knot
(4) Buttonhole
(5) Hungarian
(6) Straight
(7) Turkey Work
(8) Oriental
(9) Rice
(10) Needleweaving
(11) Couching
(E) Embellishments

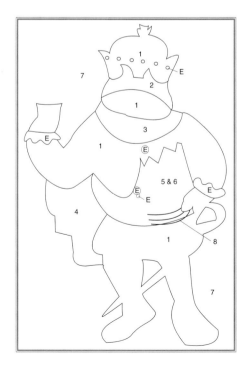

PLATE 18   *Tudor Frog Prince*

(1) Tent
(2) Smyrna Cross
(3) Slanted Gobelin
(4) Vertical Continental
(5) Couching
(6) Criss Cross Hungarian
(7) Spaced Cross Tramé, open version
(E) Embellishments

PLATE 19 *Hunt Scene*

(1) Encroaching Oblique
(2) Darning
(3) Tent
(4) Turkey Work
(5) Rhodes
(6) Interlocking Slanted Gobelin
(7) Encroaching Gobelin
(8) Greek
(9) Straight
(10) French Knot
(11) Satin
(12) Stem
(13) Smyrna Cross
(14) Couching

(15) Backstitch
(16) Cross
(17) Detached Buttonhole
(18) Chain

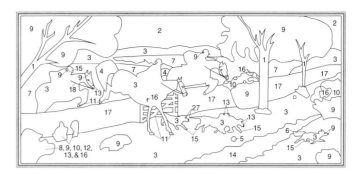

PLATE 20 *Sunflower Doll*

(1) Woven Plait
(2) Buttonhole
(3) Irregular Slanted Gobelin
(4) Cut Turkey Work
(5) Slanted Gobelin, 3 x 3
(6) Padded Gobelin
(7) Tent
(8) French Knot
(9) Knotted Stitch
(10) French Knot

(11) Split Gobelin
(12) Lazy Daisy
(13) Horizontal Hungarian
(14) Outline
(15) Giant Scotch
(16) Jacquard
(17) Diagonal Roumanian Leaf
(18) Smooth Spider Web
(19) Giant Brick

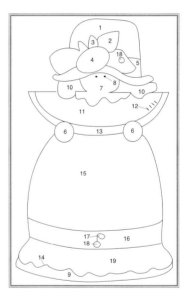

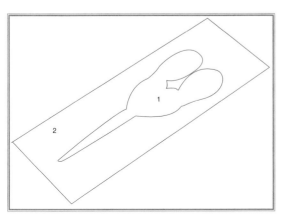

PLATE 21 *Scissors Box*

(1) Tent
(2) Straight

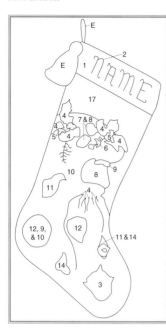

PLATE 22 *Santa and Critters*

(1) Brick
(2) Tent
(3) Diagonal Mosaic
(4) Stem
(5) Wound Cross
(6) Tied Scotch
(7) Smyrna
(8) French Knot
(9) Interlocking Straight Gobelin
(10) Chain
(11) Split Gobelin
(12) Interlocking Gobelin
(13) Brick (on the owl)
(14) Diagonal Leaf
(E) Embellishments

PLATE 23 *All Creatures*

(1) Raised Buttonhole on Raised Band
(2) Tent
(3) Double Straight Cross
(4) 1 x 1 Spaced Cross Tramé
(5) French
(6) Turkey Work
(7) Fly
(8) Split
(9) Colonial Knot
(10) Buttonhole
(11) Oblong Cross
(12) Straight
(13) Raised Cross
(14) Rhodes
(15) Bullion
(16) Needleweaving
(E) Embellishments

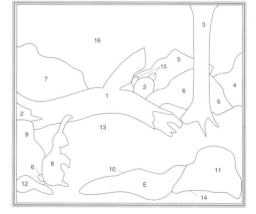

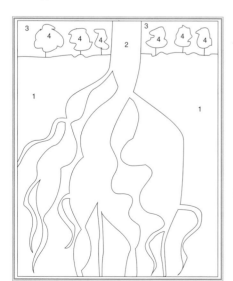

PLATE 24 *Cliff Hanger*

(1) Straight
(2) Wrapping of yarn around another
(3) Tent
(4) Interlocking Gobelin
(5) French Knot (in trees, for accent)

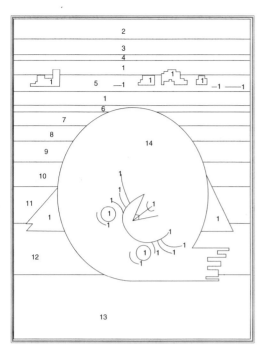

PLATE 25 *White Coat*

(1) Tent

(2) Ringed Daisies

(3) Star

(4) Smyrna Cross

(5) Darning

(6) Diamond Ray

(7) Wild Goose Chase

(8) F-106

(9) Jockey Cap

(10) Medieval Mosaic

(11) Hungarian Ground

(12) Bargello

(13) Swirl

(14) Interlocking Gobelin

PLATE 26 *Feathers and Lace*

(1) Tent

(2) Straight

(3) Encroaching Gobelin

(4) Detached Buttonhole

(5) Packed Stem

(6) Buttonhole

(7) Cross

(8) Padded Satin

(9) Split

(10) Satin

(11) Rhodes

(12) Stem

(E) Embellishments

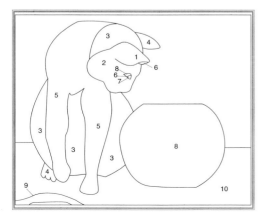

PLATE 27 *Cat and Fish Bowl*

(1) Double Parisian

(2) Double Brick

(3) Jacquard Palace Pattern variation

(4) Parisian Stripe

(5) Bargello

(6) Straight Gobelin

(7) Slanted Gobelin

(8) Couching

(9) Backstitch

(10) Satin

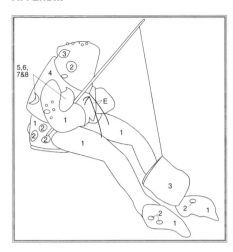

PLATE 28   *Mr. M. Fibian*

(1) Interlocking Gobelin
(2) Padded Satin
(3) Tent
(4) Alternating Continental
(5) Cross
(6) Mosaic
(7) French Knot
(8) Twisted Chain
(E) Embellishments

PLATE 29   *Bola Tie and Name Tag*

(1) Raised Buttonhole
(2) Upright Cross
(3) Tent
(4) Straight
(5) Reversed Mosaic
(6) Diagonal Roumanian
(7) Couching
(8) French Knot
(9) Running
(10) Mosaic Stripe
(11) Twisted Cord
(E) Embellishments

PLATE 30   *Colonial Quintet*

(1) Cashmere	(18) Byzantine Scotch
(2) Framed Mosaic	(19) Mosaic
(3) Waffle	(20) Arrowhead
(4) Star	(21) Hitched Cross
(5) Vertical Elongated Smyrna	(22) Oriental
(6) Scotch	(23) Half Framed Scotch
(7) Diagonal Scotch	(24) Diamond Ray
(8) Woven Scotch	(25) Leaf
(9) Knitting	(26) Alternating Oblong Cross
(10) Roman Cross	(27) Diagonal Beaty
(11) Raised Cross	(28) Dotted Scotch
(12) Web	(29) Tied Scotch
(13) Rounded Wheat Columns	(30) Padded Alternating Continental
(14) Nobuko	(31) Eyelet
(15) Continuous Woven Scotch	(32) Darning Pattern
(16) Beaty	(33) Milanese
(17) Woven Square	(34) Cross

PLATE 31 *Queen Elizabeth Tea Cozy*

(1) Tent
(2) Bullion Knot
(3) Reversed Mosaic
(4) Satin
(5) Buttonhole
(6) Detached Buttonhole
(7) Rhodes
(8) Rice
(9) Byzantine
(10) Chain
(11) Smyrna
(12) Bargello
(13) Eyelet
(14) Woven Ribbons
(15) Interlocking Gobelin
(E) Embellishments

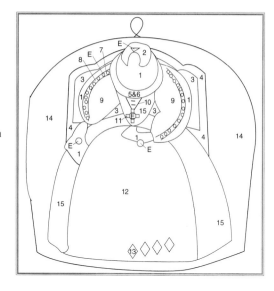

PLATE 32 *Easter Egg Diorama*

(1) Tent
(2) Diagonal Mosaic
(3) Satin
(4) Nobuko
(5) French Knot

PLATE 33 *Farmer's Delight*

(1) Tent
(2) Leaf variation
(3) Brick
(4) Double Straight Cross
(5) Woven Spider Web
(6) Ridged Spider Web
(7) Roumanian Couching
(8) Couching
(9) Roumanian Leaf
(10) Close Herringbone
(11) French Knot
(12) Fern
(13) Cretan
(14) Lazy Daisy
(15) Irregular Brick
(E) Embellishments

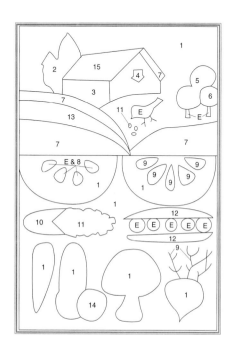

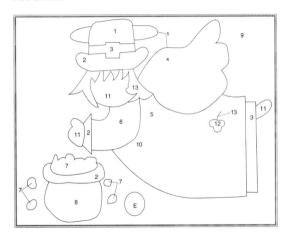

PLATE 34   *March Angel*

(1) Brick
(2) Straight Gobelin
(3) Slanted Gobelin
(4) Victorian Step
(5) Outline
(6) Scotch
(7) Rhodes

(8) Alternating Oblong Cross
(9) Darning
(10) Diagonal Scotch
(11) Tent
(12) Lazy Daisy
(13) Straight

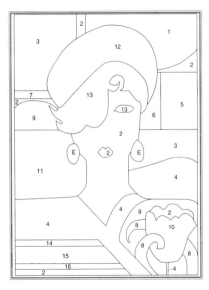

PLATE 35   *Lady with Red Flower*

(1) Running
(2) Tent
(3) Pattern Darning
(4) Satin
(5) Giant Framed Cashmere
(6) Continental, open version
(7) Smryna Cross
(8) Diagonal Scotch
(9) Alternating Tent

(10) French Knot
(11) Alternating Continental
(12) Web variation
(13) Interlocking Gobelin
(14) Greek
(15) Double
(16) Slanted Gobelin
(E) Embellishments

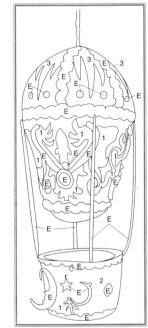

PLATE 36   *Hot-Air Balloon*

(1) Tent
(2) Roman III
(3) Leaf
(E) Embellishments

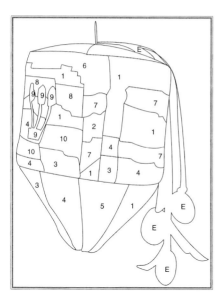

PLATE 37   *Dreidel*

(1) Mosaic

(2) Giant Knitting

(3) Diagonal Mosaic

(4) Smyrna Cross

(5) Gobelin

(6) Cashmere

(7) Brick

(8) Slanted Gobelin

(9) Tent

PLATE 38   *Gazebo*

(1) Pattern Darning

(2) Upright Cross (for dirt)

(3) Tent

(4) Satin

(5) Cashmere

(6) Spiral

(7) French Knot

(8) Looped Turkey Work

(9) Cut Turkey Work

(10) Bullion

(11) Woven Ribbons

(12) Ridged Spider Web

(13) Buttonhole

(14) Bargello

(15) Binding

(16) Checker Filling (not visible)

(17) Diagonal Drawn Filling (not visible)

(18) Hardanger Cut Work

(19) Loopstitch Bars

(20) Double Faggot Ground

(21) Coiling or Wrapping

(22) Free-form arrangement of leaves

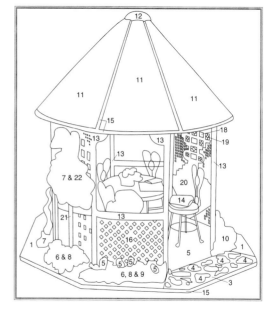

PLATE 39   *Cats and a Dog*

(1) Bargello

(2) Wrapped Backstitch

(3) French Knot

(4) Double

(5) Diagonal Cashmere

(6) Elongated Cashmere

(7) Scotch

(8) Rhodes

(9) Tent

(10) Jo-Jo

(11) Interlocking Gobelin

(12) Split Gobelin

(13) Wound Cross

(14) Criss Cross Hungarian

(15) Stem

(16) Rice

(17) Smyrna Cross

(18) Diagonal Mosaic

(19) Wrapped Chain

(20) Kalem

(21) Alternating Continental

(22) Woven Plait

(23) Cross

(24) Straight

(25) Nobuko

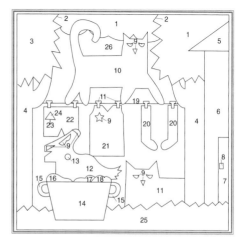

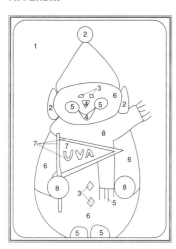

PLATE 40   *Collegiate Snowman*

(1) Four-way Bargello, open version
(2) Looped Turkey Work
(3) Smyrna Cross
(4) Cross
(5) Straight
(6) Pavillion
(7) Tent
(8) Knitting

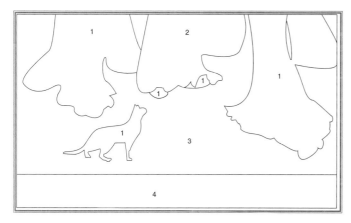

PLATE 41   *Cat and Feet*

(1) Tent
(2) Woven Plait
(3) Angelis
(4) Couching

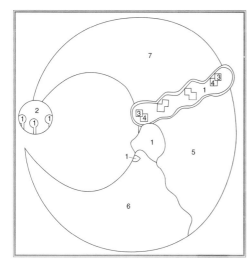

PLATE 42   *Crescent Santa*

(1) Tent
(2) Diagonal Mosaic
(3) Smyrna Cross
(4) Rhodes
(5) Bullion
(6) French Knot
(7) Jacquard

PLATE 43 *Scissors Case*

(1) Turkey Work
(2) Tent
(3) Giant Tied Oblong Cross
(4) French Knot

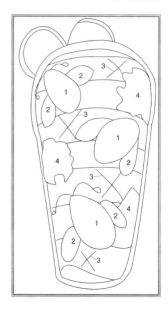

PLATE 44 *Mollie, the Calico Cat*

(1) Double Straight Cross
(2) Diagonal Mosaic
(3) Double Stitch
(4) Scotch
(5) Triple Leviathan
(6) Bargello
(7) Pavillion
(8) Leaf

(9) Cross
(10) Giant Tied Oblong Cross
(11) Windowpane
(12) Old Florentine
(13) Darning Pattern
(14) Straight Gobelin
(E) Embellishments

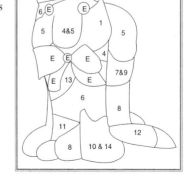

PLATE 45 *Jacket*

(1) Bargello
(2) Diamond Eyelet
(3) Byzantine
(4) Wild Goose Chase variation
(5) Tent
(6) Rhodes
(7) Scotch
(8) Darmstadt Pattern
(9) Triangle variation
(10) Diagonal Beaty

(11) Diamond Eyelet variation
(12) Ray
(13) Double Cross
(14) Couching
(15) Straight
(16) Milanese Pinwheel
(17) Horizontal Old Florentine
(18) Straight Gobelin
(19) Princess

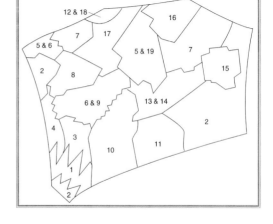

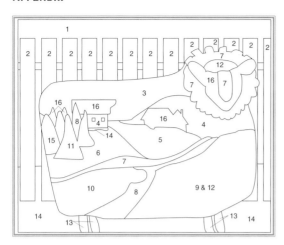

PLATE 46   *Winter Lambscape*

(1) Victorian Step   (9) Bargello
(2) Straight Gobelin   (10) Triangle
(3) Couching   (11) Long Upright Cross
(4) Slanted Gobelin   (12) French Knot
(5) F-106   (13) Paris
(6) Roman III   (14) Alternating Continental
(7) Satin   (15) Diamond Ray
(8) Upright Cross   (16) Tent

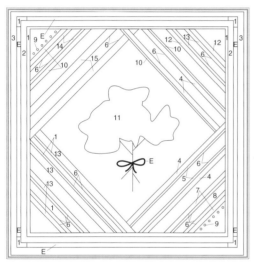

PLATE 47   *Columbines and Lace*

(1) Smyrna Cross   (9) French Knot
(2) Eyelet   (10) Straight
(3) Rhodes   (11) Tent
(4) Fern   (12) Cross
(5) Square   (13) Fly
(6) Backstitch   (14) Buttonhole
(7) Ray   (15) Algerian Eye
(8) Italian Cross   (E) Embellishments

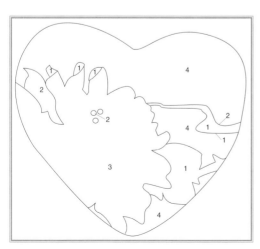

PLATE 48   *Rose Heart*

(1) Tent
(2) Smyrna Cross
(3) Diagonal Scotch
(4) Window Filling

PLATE 49   *Akiko*

(1) Tent
(2) Diagonal Flat
(3) Ringed Daisies (with #7)
(4) Encroaching Slanted Gobelin
(5) Ray variation

(6) Wrapped Chain
(7) Couching
(8) Satin
(9) Padded Satin
(10) Japanese Ribbon

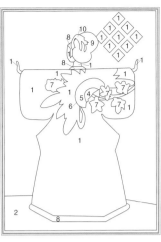

PLATE 50   *Southwestern Houses in the Desert*

(1) Irregular Jacquard
(2) Slanted Gobelin
(3) Interlocking Straight Gobelin
(4) Horizontal Double Brick
(5) Cashmere
(6) Diagonal Cashmere
(7) Brick
(8) Mosaic
(9) Smyrna Cross

(10) French Knot
(11) Diagonal Scotch
(12) Byzantine
(13) Staircase
(14) 3 x 2 Cross
(15) Divided Scotch
(16) Tent
(17) Straight Stitch
(E) Embellishments

PLATE 51   *Celtic Fantasy*

(1) Tied Cross
(2) Crescent
(3) Amadeus
(4) Chain
(5) Waffle
(6) Straight
(7) Outline
(8) Laid Filling
(9) Wheat

(10) Walneto
(11) Layered Double Cross
(12) Plaited Ray
(13) Double Straight Cross
(14) Crescent
(15) Couching
(16) Jessica
(17) French Knot on a Stalk
(E) Embellishments

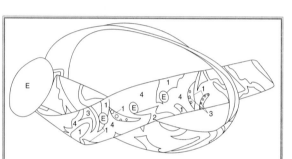

PLATE 52   *Edwardian Belt*

(1) Tent
(2) French Stitch
(3) Smyrna Cross
(4) Stem
(E) Embellishments

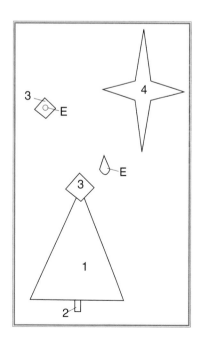

PLATE 53   *Forest of Lights*

(1) Amadeus
(2) Cross
(3) Windmill
(4) Diamond Ray
(E) Embellishments

PLATE 54 *Persian Fantasy*

(1) Tent
(2) Surface Embroidery
(3) Rice
(4) Framed Scotch
(5) Pavillion
(6) Greek
(7) Couching
(8) Smyrna
(9) Cashmere
(10) Wave
(11) Mosaic
(12) Hungarian Ground
(13) Old Florentine

(14) Leaf variation
(15) Four-Way Bargello
(16) Mosaic
(17) Hungarian
(18) Nobuko
(19) Bargello
(20) Straight
(21) Double Straight Cross
(22) Brick
(23) Double Hungarian variation
(24) Vertical Milanese variation
(E) Embellishments

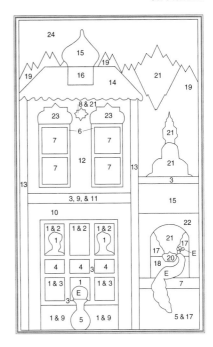

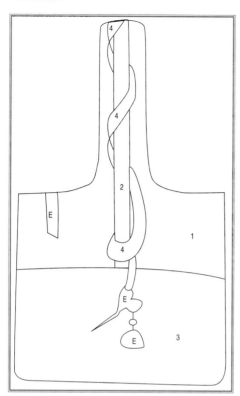

PHOTO 1   *Needlepointer's Tote Bag* (title page)

(1) Tent
(2) Willow
(3) Diagonal Beaty
(4) Giant Diagonal Mosaic
(E) Embellishments

PHOTO 2   *Candle Tunic* (page xix)

(1) Cross
(2) Double Brick
(3) Lazy Daisy

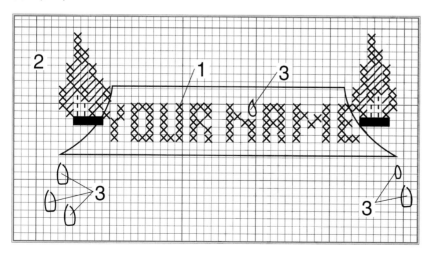

PHOTO 3 *Shop Till You Drop and I Shall Wear Purple* (page 1)

(1) Interlocking Gobelin
(2) Satin
(3) Chain
(4) Tent
(5) Colonial Knot
(6) Mosaic
(7) Slanted Gobelin

(8) Bullion Knot
(9) Detached Buttonhole
(10) Padded Satin
(11) Kalem
(12) Woven Plait, open version
(13) Greek
(E) Embellishments

PHOTO 4 *Akiko* (close-up) (page 2)

(1) Tent
(4) Encroaching Slanted Gobelin
(5) Ray variation
(6) Wrapped Chain

(7) Couching
(8) Satin
(9) Padded Satin
(10) Japanese Ribbon

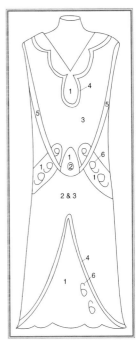

PHOTO 5 *Ball Gown* (page 62)

(1) Tent
(2) French Knot
(3) Kennan
(4) Chain
(5) Wrapped Chain
(6) Couching

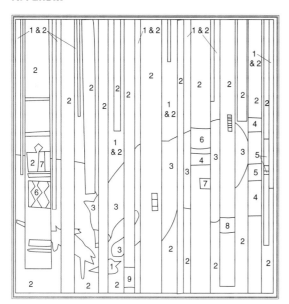

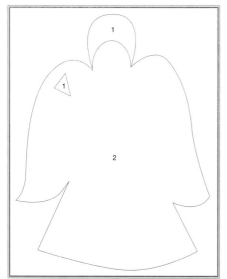

PHOTO 6   *Bear in Birches* (page 63)

(1) Tent
(2) Straight
(3) Split
(4) Mosaic
(5) Scotch
(6) Pavillion
(7) Rhodes
(8) Bargello
(9) Kalem

PHOTO 7   *Leaves* (page 64)

(1) Tent
(2) Scotch
(3) Mosaic
(4) Diagonal Scotch
(5) Chain
(6) Stem
(7) Satin
(E) Embellishments

PHOTO 8   *Angel Annalisa* (page 78)

(1) Tent, open version
(2) Tent

PHOTO 9 *Lily Band Pillow* (page 91)

(1) Tent
(2) Packed Stem
(3) Rhodes
(4) Encroaching Gobelin
(5) Backstitch
(6) Woven Plait
(E) Embellishments

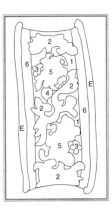

PHOTO 10 *Carousel Horse* (page 92)

(1) Bargello
(2) Diamond Leviathan
(3) Triangular Ray
(4) Satin
(5) Straight Gobelin
(6) Slanted Gobelin
(7) Tent
(8) French Knot
(9) Hungarian
(10) Windowpane
(11) Mosaic
(12) Double Straight Cross
(13) Pavillion Diamonds
(14) Backstitch

PHOTO 11 *Eyeglass Case* (page 112)

(1) Scotch Checker
(2) Alternating Oblong Cross
(3) Slanted Gobelin
(4) Diagonal Cashmere
(5) Mosaic Checker
(6) Lazy Daisy
(E) Embellishments

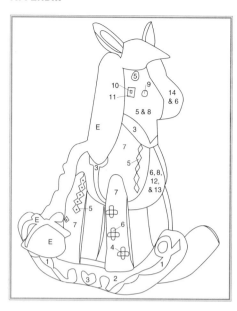

PHOTO 12   *Horace, Rocking Horse* (page 133)

(1) Packed Stem

(2) Mosaic

(3) Encroaching Gobelin

(4) Smyrna Cross

(5) Tent

(6) Cross

(7) Diagonal Brick

(8) Couching

(9) Ridged Spider Web

(10) Scotch

(11) Straight Gobelin

(12) Fern

(13) Darning

(14) Eyelet

(E) Embellishments

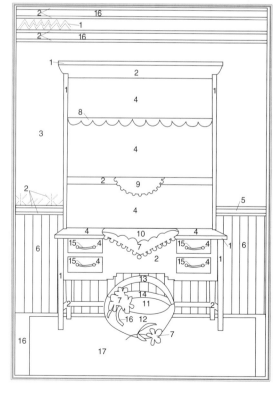

PHOTO 13   *Country Hutch* (page 134)

(1) Padded Satin

(2) Tent

(3) Darning

(4) Outline

(5) Greek

(6) Stem

(7) Lazy Daisy

(8) Buttonhole

(9) Detached Buttonhole

(10) Trellis

(11) Chain

(12) Packed Stem

(13) Couching

(14) Straight

(15) Bullion Knot

(16) Straight Gobelin

(17) Turkey Work

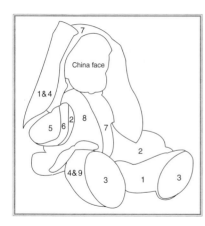

PHOTO 14   *T. S. Nicholas* (page 136)

(1) Tent
(2) Slanted Gobelin
(3) Squared Eyelet
(4) Slanted Gobelin
(5) Milanese
(6) Knitting
(7) Reversed Scotch
(8) Oriental
(9) French Knot

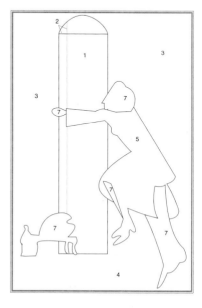

PHOTO 15   *Last Tango* (page 174)

(1) Jacquard, open version
(2) Tramé
(3) Darning
(4) Couching
(5) Hungarian Ground
(6) Mosaic Checker (skirt)
(7) Tent

PHOTO 16   *Crazy Quilt Vest* (page 375)

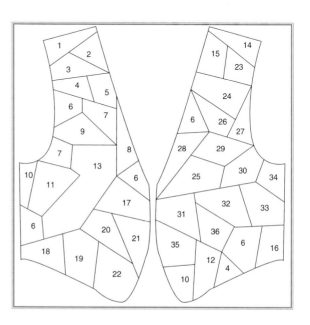

(1) Fern
(2) Irregular Jacquard
(3) Horizontal Cashmere
(4) Old Florentine
(5) Criss Cross Hungarian
(6) Tent
(7) Small Upright Cross
(8) Van Dyke
(9) Web
(10) Byzantine
(11) Brick Wall
(12) Milanese
(13) Rhodes
(14) Stem
(15) Scotch
(16) Web
(17) Upright Oriental
(18) Slanted Gobelin

(19) Gingham
(20) Plaited Gobelin
(21) Jacquard
(22) Triangle
(23) Byzantine #2
(24) Roumanian
(25) Eyelet Diamond
(26) Smyrna Cross
(27) Double Brick
(28) Diagonal Beaty
(29) Diagonal Cashmere
(30) Oriental
(31) Diagonal Upright Cross
(32) Horizontal Old Florentine
(33) Diagonal Greek
(34) Elongated Cashmere
(35) Van Dyke
(36) Scotch

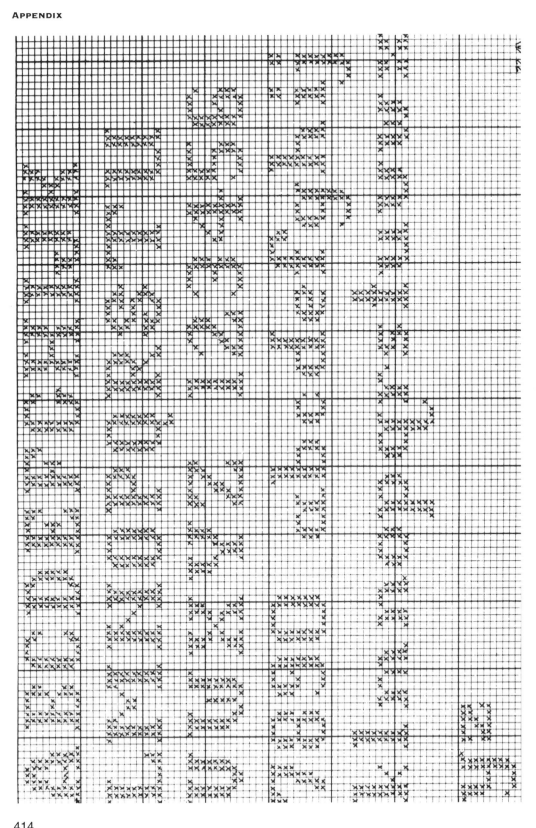

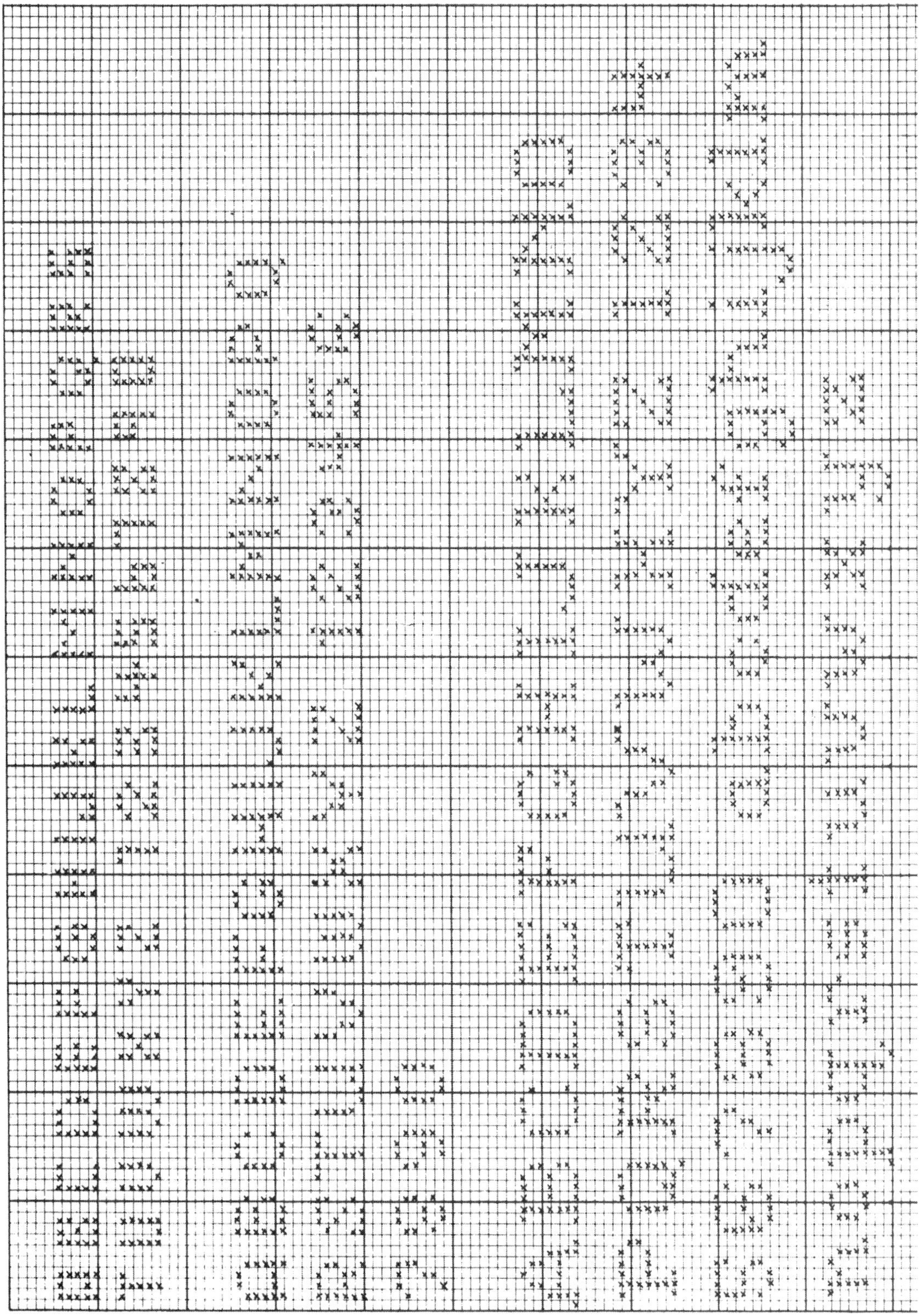

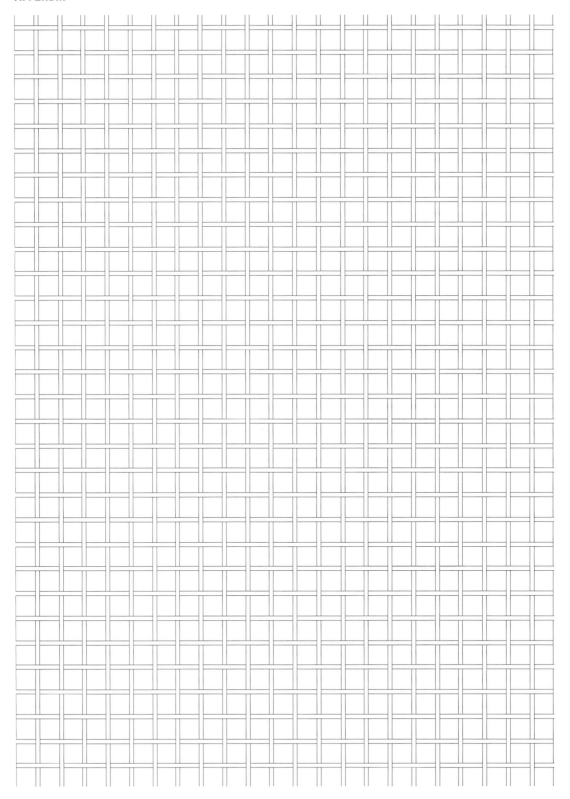

ALDERSON, CHOTTIE, *Stitchin' with Chottie: A Casebook of Needlepoint Stitches,* LadyBug Series 1. N.p., 1975.

————, *Stitchin' with Chottie: A Casebook of Needlepoint Projects and Techniques,* LadyBug Series 2. N.p., 1977.

————, *Stitchin' with Chottie: A Casebook of Needlepoint Gardening,* LadyBug Series 3. N.p., 1977.

————, *Stitchin' with Chottie: A Casebook of Composite Stitches,* LadyBug Series 4. N.p., 1978.

AMBUTER, CAROLYN, *Complete Book of Needlepoint.* New York: Thomas Y. Crowell Company, 1972.

————, *The Open Canvas.* New York: Workman Publishing, 1982.

BAKER, MURIEL; BARBARA EYRE; MARGARET WALL; and CHARLOTTE WESTERFIELD, *Needlepoint: Design Your Own.* New York: Charles Scribner's Sons, 1974.

BEINECKE, MARY ANN, *Basic Needlery Stitches on Mesh Fabrics.* New York: Dover Publications, Inc., 1973.

BLACKBURN, REV. ROBERT E., JR., *Father B's Book of Stitches.* N.p., 1994.

BOWLER, VIVIEN, *44 String and Nail Art Projects.* New York: Crown Publishers, Inc., 1974.

BRIDGEMAN, HARRIET, and ELIZABETH DRURY, EDS., *Needlework, an Illustrated History.* New York: Paddington Press, 1978.

BROWN, PAULINE, *The Encyclopedia of Embroidery Techniques.* New York: Penguin Group, 1994.

BUCHER, JO, *Complete Guide to Creative Needlepoint.* Des Moines, Iowa: Meredith Corporation, 1973.

BURCHETTE, DOROTHY, *Needlework Blocking and Finishing.* New York: Charles Scribner's Sons, 1974.

CARTER, SARA, *Handbook of Brazilian Stitches.* N.p., 1978.

CHRISTENSEN, JO IPPOLITO, *Trapunto: Decorative Quilting.* New York: Sterling Publishing Co., Inc., 1972.

————, *Appliqué & Reverse Appliqué.* New York: Sterling Publishing Co., Inc., 1974.

————, *Teach Yourself Needlepoint.* Englewood Cliffs, N.J.: Prentice-Hall, Inc., 1978.

————, *Needlepoint: The Third Dimension.* Englewood Cliffs, N.J.: Prentice-Hall, Inc., 1979.

————, *The Needlepoint Scraps Book.* Englewood Cliffs, N.J.: Prentice-Hall, Inc., 1982.

————, and SONIE SHAPIRO ASHNER, *Bargello Stitchery.* New York: Sterling Publishing Co., Inc., 1972.

————, *Cross Stitchery.* New York: Sterling Publishing Co., Inc., 1972.

————, *Needlepoint Simplified.* New York: Sterling Publishing Co., Inc., 1972.

CLARK, MARY, and VEE WEDOW, *The Bosa Nova Rose and Friends.* N.p., n.d.

CORNELL, PENNY, *The Liberated Canvas.* Cape Town, South Africa: Triple T Publishing, c.c., 1995.

DONNELLY, BARBARA H., *The Crewel Needlepoint World.* New York: Gullers International, Inc., 1973.

DRAKE, DORIS, *Needlework Designs.* Thomasville, Ga., 1967.

————, *Needlework Designs II.* Thomasville, Ga., 1967.

DYER, ANNE, and VALERIE DUTHOIT, *Canvas Work from the Start.* London: G. Bell and Sons, 1972.

EATON, JAN, *The Complete Stitch Encyclopedia.* London: Quarto Publishing Ltd., 1986.

FISCHER, PAULINE, and ANABEL LASKER, *Bargello Magic.* New York: Holt and Winston, 1975.

GOLDGERG, RHODA OCHSER, *The New Dictionary of Needlepoint and Canvas Stitches.* New York: Crown Trade Paperbacks, 1994.

GOSTELOW, MARY, *A World of Embroidery.* New York: Charles Scribner's Sons, 1975.

GRIER, ROSEY, *Needlepoint for Men.* New York: Walker and Company, 1973.

GUILD, VERA, P., *Good Housekeeping New Complete Book of Needlecraft.* New York: Hearst Corp., 1971.

————, *A Coats Book of Embroidery.* London: David and Charles, 1978.

HALL, NANCY, and JEAN RILEY, *Bargello Borders.* Franklin, Mich.: Needlemania, Inc., 1974.

HANLEY, HOPE, *Needlepoint.* New York: Charles Scribner's Sons, 1966.

————, *New Methods in Needlepoint.* New York: Charles Scribner's Sons, 1964.

HART, BRENDA, *Favorite Stitches.* N.p., 1994.

HILTON, JEAN, *Needlepoint Stitches.* Peoria, Ill., 1988.

—————, *Stimulating Stitches.* Peoria, Ill., 1992.

HIRST, ROY, and BARBARA HIRST, *Raised Embroidery.* Putney, London: Merehurst Ltd., 1993.

HOWREN, SUZANNE, and BETH ROBERTSON, *Stitches for Effect.* Alexandria, Va.: SHEAR Creations, 1996.

—————, *More Stitches for Effect.* Alexandria, Va.: SHEAR Creations, 1997.

HYMAN, DAVIE, *The Diagonal Basket Weave.* Chesterland, Ohio: Davie Hyman Designs, 1973.

IREYS, KATHARINE, *The Encyclopedia of Canvas Embroidery Stitch Patterns.* New York: Thomas Y. Crowell Company, 1972.

—————, *Finishing and Mounting Your Needlepoint Pieces.* New York: Thomas Y. Crowell Company, 1972.

JOSEPH, MARJORY L., *Essentials of Textiles.* New York: Holt, Rinehart and Winston, 1980.

KAESTNER, DOROTHY, *Four Way Bargello.* New York: Charles Scribner's Sons, 1974.

KATZENBERG, GLORIA, *Needlepoint and Pattern.* New York: Macmillan Publishing Co., Inc., 1974.

KENYON, CAROL, and LYNNE MALPELI, *Custom Designs for Creative Needlepoint.* West Bloomfield, Mich.: 1973.

LAMBERT, PATRICIA; BARBARA STAEPELAERE; and MARY G. FRY, *Color and Fiber.* West Chester, Pa.: Schiffer Publishing Ltd., 1986.

LAMPTON, SUSAN SEDLACEK, ED., *Needlepoint.* Menlo Park, Calif.: Lane Books, 1973.

LANTZ, SHERLEE, *A Pageant of Pattern for Needlepoint Canvas.* New York: Atheneum, 1973.

LONG, EDITH, and SARA SCHLINTZ, *To the Point About Needlepoint.* New York: Cornerstone Library, 1974

LYLE, DOROTHY S., *Modern Textiles.* New York: John Wiley and Sons, 1982.

McCall's Needlework Treasury. New York: Random House, 1964.

MARTIN, MARY, *Mary Martin's Needlepoint.* New York: Galahad Books, 1969.

MESSENT, JAN, *The Embroiderer's Workbook.* New York: St. Martin's Press, 1988.

MONTANO, JUDITH BAKER, *Elegant Stitches.* Lafayette, Calif.: C and T Publishing, 1995.

————, *The Art of Silk Ribbon Embroidery*. Lafayette, Calif.: C and T Publishing, 1995.

NICHOLAS, JANE, *Stumpwork Embroidery*. Burra Creek, Australia: Sally Milner Publishing Pty. Ltd., 1995.

PERRONE, LISBETH, *Needlepoint Workbook*. New York: Random House, 1973.

————, *The New World of Needlepoint*. New York: Random House, 1972.

RHODES, MARY, *Ideas for Canvas Work*. Newton, Mass.: Charles T. Branford Company, 1971.

RITTER, MARNIE, *Marnie Ritter's Canvas Patterns*. N.p., 1992.

————, *Marnie Ritter's Canvas Patterns Book Two*. N.p., 1994.

RODGERS, SANDY, *Needlework Tips for the Novice and Expert*. Medina, Ohio: Yarn Cellar Publishing Company, 1995.

ROME, CAROL CHENEY, *A New Look at Bargello*. New York: Crown Publishers, Inc., 1973.

————, and GEORGIA FRENCH DEVLIN, *A New Look at Needlepoint*. New York: Crown Publishers, Inc., 1973.

SCOBEY, JOAN, *Do-It-All Yourself Needlepoint*. New York: Essandess Special Edition, 1971.

————, *Needlepoint from Start to Finish*. New York: Lancer Books, 1972.

SEGAL, HARRIET N., "Fibers, Threads, and Yarns: An Introduction." Yardley, Pa.: n.d.

————, "Yarns on the Market: A Master Guide." Yardley, Pa.: n.d.

SIDNEY, SYLVIA, *Sylvia Sidney Needlepoint Book*. New York: Galahad Books, 1968.

SLATER, ELAINE, *The New York Times Book of Needlepoint*. New York: Quadrangle/New York Times Book Co., 1973.

SMITH, BETTY F., and IRA BLOCK, *Textiles in Perspective*. Englewood Cliffs, N.J.: Prentice-Hall, 1982.

SNOOK, BARBARA, *The Craft of Florentine Embroidery*. New York: Charles Scribner's Sons, 1971.

————, *Needlework Stitches*. New York: Crown Publishers, 1975.

STRITE-KURZ, ANN, "An Analysis of Diaper Patterns and Their Specific Use in Canvas Embroidery." 1995.

THOMAS, MARY, *Mary Thomas's Dictionary of Embroidery Stitches*. New York: Gramercy Publishing Company, 1935.

TORTORA, PHYLLIS G., *Understanding Textiles*. New York: Macmillan Publishing Company, 1982.

————, and ROBERT S. MERKEL, *Fairchilds Dictionary of Textiles.* New York: Fairchilds Publications, 1996.

WILLIAMS, ELSA S., *Bargello.* New York: Van Nostrand Reinhold Company, 1967.

————, *Creative Canvas Work.* New York: Van Nostrand Reinhold Company, N.d.

WILSON, ERICA, *Embroidery Book.* New York: Charles Scribner's Sons, 1973.

ZIMMERMAN, JANE, *An Encyclopedia of 375 Needlepoint Stitch Variations.* N.p., 1973.

GENERAL INDEX

STITCH INDEX

427